Ashok K. Banker is acknowledged as the pioneer of English-language genre fiction, English-language television, and series fiction in India. Best known for his internationally acclaimed and bestselling Ramayana Series, he is the author of over eighty books that have sold over three million copies in thirty-two languages and seventy-two countries. His hugely popular debut picture book *I Am Brown* (Lerner/Lantana) is a Bank Street Prize winner, a Book Trust Great Book, *Guardian* Children's Book of the Month, a Teach Early Years Award Finalist, UKLA Book Awards Longlist, and Derby Children's Book Award Longlist. It has been translated into multiple languages and published worldwide. His other recent books include: *My Father Drank My Lover and Other Stories* (Pan Macmillan); *The Haunted Centre: Secret School Mysteries*, Book 3 (Scholastic); *The Burnt Empire Trilogy* (Simon & Schuster); *A Kiss After Dying* (Penguin); and *Brown Girls Rule* (Beaming Books), among others.

ASHOKA

Prince of the Mauryas

The Complete Trilogy

ASHOK K. BANKER

SPEAKING TIGER

SPEAKING TIGER BOOKS LLP
125A, Ground Floor, Shahpur Jat, near Asiad Village,
New Delhi 110049

Books 1 and 2 first published as *Ashoka: Lion of Maurya* and
Ashoka: Satrap of Taxila by Westland in 2015 and 2017 respectively
Book 3 first published by Speaking Tiger Books 2023

This edition published in India by
Speaking Tiger Books in paperback in 2023

ISBN: 978-93-5447-613-6
eISBN: 978-93-5447-615-0

10 9 8 7 6 5 4 3 2 1

Typeset in Garamond Premier Pro by SÜRYA, New Delhi
Printed at Chaman Enterprises, New Delhi

Contents

Book One

1

She rose from the left bank of the Ganga like a gigantic lioness guarding her pride. Her high walls towered above the Uttarapatha, the great Northern Road that connected the capital of the Maurya Empire to its northernmost satrapy, Takshashila. From the dusty road below, a winding line of visitors craned their necks to peer at the greatest city in the known world. The fortified palisade spanned a length of fourteen kilometres and a width of two and a half kilometres, occupying an area of two thousand two hundred hectares: ten times the size of Vidisha, forty times the size of Takshashila. Capital of the Mauryan empire, home to a hundred thousand souls, pride of the subcontinent of Jambudwipa. There were many great cities but only one Patliputra.

The formidable outer wall, towering almost five metres above the awestruck travellers, was constructed from the wood of the oldest sal forests, timber so dense and indestructible that carpenters called it ironwood. In truth, it was more durable than iron, because the damp sub-soil of the Ganga's bank corroded any metal within weeks, while the fortifications of Patliputra could withstand floods, sieges, fire, invasions, elephant rams, and still stand tall for the next two thousand years.

Inside this intimidating outer wall was a second defensive wall of the same height and thickness. Both walls had slots through which defenders could fire arrows, plunge spears, or thrust swords. A few artfully concealed sally ports provided egress during a siege. Ramparts provided platforms for defenders to make a stand.

Between these two formidable walls, the ground appeared to be bare earth, but beneath the yard-high piled soil was a floor of timber planks concealing an underground tunnel bristling with the stuff of nightmares: horrific flesh-rending, bone-shattering defensive traps and contrivances. Pity the enemies who succeeding in climbing over or under the first wall would think they had breached the fortress, only to die horrible deaths without ever setting foot in the city.

City? This was no city! Takshashila, Vidisha, Ujjain, Champa, Chamunda, those were cities. Patliputra was a metropolis. A great sprawling fortress of humanity teeming with as much life as the river that ran beside her. In her winding streets and high-stacked houses, the business of life was waged on a war footing: art, trade, commerce, politics, sex, music, suffering, poverty, wealth and sewage battled constantly for her citizens' attention. Smoke from a thousand cookfires rose sleepily into the misty autumn morning, carrying the aromas of cuisines from across Jambudwipa and the world. The stores in the great bazaar sold everything from ornate amphoras filled with sweet Greek wine to delicately lacquered fans from the far east. Poets from Lesbos entwined openly in the streets, their golden hair and fair-skinned nudity a familiar sight in this confluence of races, religions, nationalities and dialects. Scholars argued philosophy, politics, medicine, astronomy and the odds on favourite for that day's wrestling bout. Fortunes exchanged hands daily in the coin of the realm: beautifully minted and milled disks stamped with the lion sigil and battered profile of the late Chandragupta Maurya, founder of the Maurya Empire, or, occasionally, the hook-nosed likeness of his son Bindusara, the reigning Emperor. There was an apocryphal saying that there was more gold to be found in a Patliputra merchant's arse-crack than in the vaults of any other city. Above the vast fields reserved for visitors, the gaily coloured banners and sigils of hundreds of noble houses from around the world waved in the morning breeze from the river. Prostitutes of all hues, shapes and sexes emerged bleary-eyed from the luxurious pavilions of the richer visitors, making their way back to the far less glamorous slums of the lower east side.

Momentarily dazzled by this rich pageantry of colour, smell and sound, the leader of the Lichchavi assassins paused at the gates. A merchant impatient to get off the road grumbled aloud until she motioned to him to go around; he glared at her from the seat of his mule as he trundled by, passing a lewd comment pertaining to her sex and her profession. Kaavala ignored him. As a woman warrior, she had heard worse insults, usually from male warriors who resented the superiority of women in combat. The merchant assumed she was a dancer because she was dressed as one. Good. It told her that her disguise was effective.

She admired the battlements and fortifications of the Maurya capital while the endless line of visitors streamed past her, noting as many details as possible while playing the part of an innocent country girl come to the big city for the first time. Part of her mission was to observe and gather information, and first impressions were invaluable. She noted the dimensions of the walls, the number of sentries, their placement, and a hundred other details that would be of great use when planning a siege or assault on the city.

Her survey completed, she rejoined the throng entering the city gates, shuffling forward a step or two at a time until it was her turn to be examined by the gatewatch.

'Name, Tribe, Age, Occupation and Purpose of Visit?' The muscular guard towered above her by at least half a dozen handsbreadth. Back home in the Confederacy, Kaavala was considered tall for a woman, and as tall as most Confederate men. This lout was a big one. Through discreetly lowered lashes, she gave him a quick appraisal, noting how and where she would strike if he were a target. She was confident she could take him down. He looked tough and seasoned but then so was she. She had dropped bigger.

'Kaavala of Kaavala tribe, twenty-six, wandering dancer, passing through.'

He looked her over quickly, searched her with impersonal efficiency, and let her through. She walked through the vaulting wooden gates, surprised at how easy it had been. Could she have smuggled in her blades after all? She thought not. They had let her in this easily because she was unarmed and seemingly harmless. Even her taut, sinewy body and muscular thighs were in keeping with her claim of being a dancer. Had they found a single blade or any other object of suspicion upon her person, she would have been on her way to Palace of Pain by now.

The presence of red-liveried guards reduced as she passed through the gloomy passageway between the walls. She noted the lack of illumination, no doubt designed to keep prospective intruders literally in the dark. She emerged from the gloom into bright gaudy daylight, and was assaulted by noise levels that rivalled a screaming brawl at the most boisterous Confederacy public house. She slowed to a stroll, taking it all in, playing the part of a wide-eyed visitor dazzled by the sights of the big city but she was really looking for her accomplices.

The plan called for them to travel the Uttarapatha and enter the city in small units or groups, posing as individuals, couples, families visiting Patliputra for purposes of trade or entertainment: Dancers, jugglers, bards, honey merchants, timber agents, elephant mahouts, all relatively low-key professions that were unlikely to arouse the suspicions of the Kings Guard.

She wandered the bustling streets for several hours, disgusted and more than a little envious of the sheer mass of humanity thronging the markets, shops, vending carts and places of business. She glanced down at a merchant's money box as he concluded a deal and spotted the coinage of every major kingdom she could recognize and then some. How much money changed hands here each day? A king's ransom, or enough to ransom several kings. No wonder Lichchavi, the central city of the Confederacy, had all but fallen off the trade map. Ever since the Confederacy had refused to join the Maurya Empire and initiated its campaign of armed resistance, fewer and fewer travellers visited it each year. Everyone was here in Patliputra, spending their money! Her own father, a merchant from a long line of merchants, had been one of the fiercest supporters of the Confederacy, but of late even he had begun to suggest that perhaps a compromise of some sort could be reached, if only to boost trade.

The truth was, the Lichchavi Confederacy was dying economically. They needed Maurya trade and goods to survive. Pride had cost them. But Kaalava was no economist or politician. She was an assassin, and she was here on orders from the Confederacy. Now that she was actually here in Patliputra, breathing its prosperous air, she wondered how assassinating the leader of the world's largest Empire would benefit her nation. Wouldn't it bring the might and power of Maurya down on the Confederacy with crushing speed? Thus far, they had been permitted to survive only because Patliputra considered them too insignificant. Once she and her band of trusty knives completed this mission, that would change instantly. But she had done this often enough to know that the whole point of assassination was to change the status quo, shake up the political balance. She assumed that the Confederacy expected Emperor Bindusara's murder to benefit Lichchavi substantially. That was evident from the price they were paying her to accomplish her task.

Over the course of the next several days, Kaavala made contact with all but two of her accomplices. There were a considerable number, almost three hundred in all, which probably made this an incursion rather than an assassination. But the assassination was the main task. The others were only there to provide a foot-in-the-door for the larger Lichchavi force that would enter Patliputra once it was plunged into chaos and anarchy. Her team's task was to assassinate Bindusara and keep the doors open for the others to follow afterwards. She focused on the minutiae of her plan and set about preparing to execute it. Despite her distaste at the ostentatious spending, consumption, wealth and decadence on display all around, she focused on the job at hand.

She was very good at what she did, and this was the most historic assassination ever planned. She liked the idea of being well paid and famous for committing the boldest assassination ever attempted.

Bring these Maurya greedy rich fat fools down? That was a bonus. Her team assembled in segments as per the plan, dividing up their mission into stages and teams handling different aspects. They searched discretely for the two missing members but after several days, she made the decision to proceed without them. She guessed they had found trouble on the road here or it had found them. Either way, two assassins less would make no difference. Or so she thought at the time.

She was wrong.

2

Ashoka stepped out into the akhada and the crowd roared with laughter.

The akhada had a capacity of five hundred but there were almost twice that many packed in today. Unlike the more ostentatious arena of the Upper City, this Lower City fighting ground was a glorified pit in the ground with stone steps that served as seats. Here, there was no one from the imperial family to preside over the duels, no imperial guards to keep crowds in check, no rules and nobody to enforce any rules. Only fistfuls and bagfuls of coin to be gambled, fortunes won and lost on fights, unrestrained combat between anyone who dared to enter the pits, no restrictions on weapons, fighting styles or the mayhem inflicted. Fight to the death, show mercy, or maim your opponent, the choice was yours. Listen to the crowd, pander to them, or not give a damn. All power lay in the hands of the fighter who won. Losers lost more than a fight: limbs, eyes, organs, lives, it was all part of the entertainment. The crowd lapped it all up, ate and drank and even fornicated while enjoying the entertainment. Fights were common in the stands: gamblers losing their temper along with their fortunes, winners losing their stash along with their lives.

Into this savage, brutal pit of barbarism, Ashoka stepped. The laughter that greeted him came as no surprise. He knew how he must look to these raucous viewers. One corpulent watcher wealthy enough to have personal bodyguards yelled a lewd invitation down, and the crowd roared again. This young stripling of a boy? Fight in the pits? He was a visual joke to them.

And here were his opponents, stepping out into the pit. Two hulking powerfully muscled grown men, each at least a head taller than Ashoka. They flexed their muscles, rolling their massive shoulders, stretching out their arms, squatting on thighs the size of sal saplings. Either one of them looked like he could pick up Ashoka in one hand and break him like a dry stick. Both together? It was absurd to even contemplate. No wonder the crowd was going wild, betting in a frenzy, eager to make back some of the coin lost on the last bout where one odds-on favourite had beaten another in a close finish, but both fighters had ended up dead, nullifying the odds and leaving only the pit keepers richer. These people wanted blood, but more than that, they wanted blood money, and they smelled it in this fight. The odds were good and the chances of a big payout considerable.

Ashoka did some stretching of his own, limbering up. This drew some more laughter from the crowd and lewd suggestions from his corpulent admirer that his slender body would be of more use on his lap than in the pit. Someone threw down a half-eaten leg of mutton, shouting to Ashoka he needed to eat that and the rest of the goat before he fought! Finally, the catcalling and laughter died down as the pit keepers waved the flags that indicated the start of the fight.

The pit was a rectangular clearing fifteen yards in length by five yards in width, with smooth straight walls that rose five yards straight up, then tapered to sloping terraced levels of rough stone. The ground of the pit was loamy Ganga mud, stamped down by elephants each day but still soft and damp enough to cushion fighters from falls and throws. There were fresh stains and patches, mostly blood but also other bodily fluids and substances from the two dead fighters who had been dragged out only moments before Ashoka entered the pit. One patch looked wet enough to slip on, he noted. Best avoided. There were a variety of weapons arrayed on the pit walls, hanging from or racked upon rusty nails. Ashoka had scanned them already and had chosen his weapons of choice.

He took them down now.

The matched pair of curved daggers felt well balanced. He hefted them, twirling each one in turn to accustom his fingers to the feel. Their blades were about eight inches long, curving sharply. He held them backhanded with the points aimed outwards, and worked his way through a few kathas.

His opponents had armed themselves meanwhile. The bearded

one with the wild hair had chosen a mace that looked as heavy as an elephant's foot and was stained with blood, gristle, bone fragments and hair from the many victims it had claimed in the pits. He hefted it with both hands, his massive shoulder and back muscles rippling like snakes under his skin. The other man, the one with the drooping oiled moustaches and the neatly groomed hair, had selected a spear for one hand, and a stabbing sword for the other. He worked both together, spinning around in place, arms whirling as he controlled the unequal lengths with impressive skill. The crowd shouted its approval. 'Crack the boy's bones open and scoop out that tasty young marrow!' someone shouted, and the majority of the audience slapped their thighs in applause.

The two fighters stepped towards Ashoka.

Ashoka stepped away from the wall, holding his daggers in the casual same backhanded stance, knees bent, legs taut and ready.

There was more at stake here than his life. He had challenged these two strangers to this fight in the pits for a reason that had nothing to do with gambling or providing an afternoon's entertainment to this rabble.

He had overheard the men, whom he believed to be Confederacy assassins, in a public house near the pits, talking about their plans. He liked to spend time in the public houses for just this reason: you never knew what you might hear. That conversation had led him to pick a quarrel by deliberately spilling his wine into the strangers' laps—the stains were still there on their crotches—and when they rose to their feet with outrage, he had challenged them to face him in the pits. They had agreed without a second thought, and that was how they had ended up here and now.

Ashoka had fought in the pits only a few times before. It was something he did incognito, neither the sceptical pit keepers nor the other fighters ever realizing who he really was. That was the whole point: to fight real fights, experience the thrill and danger of battle, with no guru yelling cautions or opponents who hesitated to hurt you because you were a prince of Mauryavansh, son of the Emperor himself. His wins on those earlier occasions had convinced the pit keepers to allow him in, that and the fact that they could earn a substantial profit because every one was almost certain to bet heavily against him. But he had never faced two opponents at once before, and both trained assassins. Pit fighters were mostly tough battered gladiators, young brutish men who drank too much, had lost most of their teeth and were covered with scars. These two Lichchavis were younger, fresher, better fed and trained, and masters of the art of killing.

It promised to be quite a challenge!

Ashoka took another step forward, raising his hands to point each of his daggers at his opponents. He held the pose for a moment, making his challenge and threat clear. The Lichchavis grinned at each other, wiggling their eyebrows to say, This Boy! He thinks he can challenge us and live! The crowd laughed and slapped their thighs again, enjoying the boy fighter's spunk in the face of certain death. A few gamblers put down more coin, this time on the boy fighter, on the off chance that the attitude reflected some real fighting spirit.

The assassins moved in perfect concert, habituated to fighting together. They placed themselves near the walls on the longer sides of the pit, moving steadily towards Ashoka, effectively pushing him back towards the short wall at his end. Their strategy was clear: Push him to the wall, strike and finish him. They expected to end this within moments. And from the gleam in their eyes, they intended to kill him before he had chance to draw breath enough to scream.

The crowd was eating, drinking, laughing, waiting for this obviously one-sided fight to be over so they could see some real duels. Most of them were already bored, feeling there was nothing to be seen here. Only the pit bosses were watching with the sharpness born of a lifetime of watching fighters beat the odds.

Ashoka backed away, pretending to play into the Lichchavis's strategy, till he felt his back bump the wall behind him. He even let his arms droop by his sides, as if giving up in the face of such impossible odds. Then, without any indication or warning, he made his move.

He leaped up a yard in the air, kicked the wall at his back with both feet, one foot about a foot higher than the other, shoving himself upward and towards his two opponents. He somersaulted through the air, passing over their heads—and more importantly, over their weapons. The Lichchavi with the mace tried to raise it but the weapon was too heavy and too cumbersome to lift higher than his shoulders. The one with the spear had an advantage and took it, raising his spear with deadly speed, seeking to impale Ashoka on the point, like a bug on a needle.

Ashoka was already tilting to the right, the result of kicking himself out with feet raised at different heights, spinning himself diagonally while somersaulting over their heads. This brought his right hand low enough to reach the bearded one's neck with his dagger. A single stab into the thick neck, the curved blade passing through one side and popping out the other, blood and gristle spattering freely. He left the blade imbedded: it would no longer be required.

The moustached one's spear point shot towards Ashoka's belly at the same instant, missing it by an inch because of the unexpected diagonal spin on his somersault. Ashoka used the force expended by the stabbing of the other man's throat to spin himself further, turning his back to the rising spear, turning all the way round, grabbing it with his free right hand, yanking it out of the moustached Lichchavi's grasp because of the sheer momentum of his somersault.

He landed on his feet, the spear in his right hand, the other dagger still in his left, behind the two assassins and facing away from them. He was moving the instant he landed, spinning around like the dervish bedouin fighters he had seen fighting in these same pits from time to time. The Lichchavi with the mace had dropped the heavy weapon, both hands grasping at the dagger stuck in his neck. Blood flew from his stuck throat, and from his open mouth, his eyes bulging as he tried to pull the dagger free and hesitated. Ashoka knew what was going through his assassin's mind at that moment: The dagger was the only thing helping keep his wounds partially closed. If he pulled the dagger out, his ruined throat would spew out all his heart's blood, ensuring death within moments. He fell heavily to his knees, choking, coughing up blood, trying to solve the unsolvable dilemma.

His companion had been knocked off balance by the spear thrust and the taking of that spear by Ashoka. He had lost his footing momentarily, spun in place to regain it, and was attacking already, the sword slashing through the air towards Ashoka. His movements were lithe for such a large man, his coordination perfect, his technique flawless. And predictable.

Ashoka danced under the slashing sword, feeling the blade slice the air—and a hair or two from his head—above him. He slid across the soft soil on his heels, slashing the dagger backhanded once, twice, thrice, then ripping upwards once.

He rolled away, landing back by the wall where he had been moments ago, leaping up to his feet.

The Lichchavi fighter stood still for a moment, facing away from where Ashoka was now. His sword completed its slashing arc and slowed to a stop.

He looked down at his torso, at the four crisscrossing cuts Ashoka had dealt him with the dagger's edge. As he stared down, the four cuts split open his belly, releasing the wet bilious mass of his guts and internal organs. Blood poured out copiously from the gaping wound: Ashoka's fourth and final thrust had been upwards beneath the rib cage, the long probing point of the dagger seeking and finding the man's heart and puncturing it.

The assassin fell forward, dead before he reached the ground.

Ashoka knelt down over the other fighter, who was still grasping at the dagger in his throat with both hands, trying to stem the outrush of his life's blood and failing. His bulging eyes and gasping bloody emissions showed how close he was to his own death.

He looked up in astonishment at the young almost hairless face of Ashoka. He looked like he wanted to ask Ashoka a number of important, pressing questions. They were the same questions every man asked when he realized he was dying: How? Why? Is it true?

Ashoka said a single word to him: 'Lichchavi.'

The man's eyes reacted.

That was all Ashoka needed to know. He had already heard the crucial details of the assassination plot itself. All he had needed to confirm was the identity of the assassins. He had that now. The man was indeed a Lichchavi Confederacy citizen or he would not have reacted as he just had.

Ashoka pulled the dagger from the man's throat. It tore more coming out than it had ruined going in. The assassin collapsed in a puddle of pumping blood and gasping death, then lay still.

Ashoka rose to his feet, raising the bloodied daggers above his head. He turned around, showing himself to the crowd. They were dead silent, as they had been for the past several seconds. The entire fight had lasted less than ten breaths for Ashoka. To some of the watchers, it must have seemed like much less. Many were still gaping, staring, frowning, bug-eyed, unable to figure out how it could have ended so quickly, or produced this unexpected outcome.

Ashoka dropped both daggers to the ground, and walked away, into the dark tunnels that led away from the pits. His work here was done for today.

3

The Emperor's palace sprawled high above the city, looking down its terraced nose at the rabble and babble. The tallest structure in Patliputra, it rested with imperial languor on its elevated platforms, built from the same 'ironwood' as the city walls. Its ornately carved towers, turrets and ramparts gazed with disinterest upon the people whose taxes paid for its construction. The closer one came to the palace itself, the less one saw of it. By the time you stood immediately below it, all that was visible at eye level was a thicket of wooden pillars, each carved from a single sal trunk.

Somewhere within this forest of pillars was C garrison, a wooden building hidden within the foundations of the imperial palace. This structure was ingeniously designed to blend in with the forest of pillars, and was a small fortress in its own right, with its own defensive walls, barracks, fresh food and water. Any intruder or assassin attempting to invade the imperial palace would have to contend with its eight hundred and eighty residents, the Chandikas. The odds that even a small army of invaders would make it past them were far greater than eight hundred and eighty to one.

Above the forest of ironwood pilings rose a succession of terraced levels that artfully concealed the royal apartments from the ground below. There was no natural elevation here. The hill on which the palace stood had been created by bringing in thousands of elephant cartloads of soil, then building an elaborate and intricate structure above it. To reach the uppermost levels, one had to climb up through a maze of staircases and passages, all manned with sentries in recessed guard stands at irregular intervals. Staircases ended in mid-air without warning, passages in cul de sacs, or narrowed abruptly to allow only a single person to pass through at a time. Even if you knew the correct way, you would eventually emerge into a large open courtyard surrounded by verandahs manned constantly by armed archers and spear throwers. And if by some extraordinary feat, you found your way into the royal apartments themselves, you would still have to contend with the Chandikas.

The Chandikas were democratically chosen from all the five hundred tribes that had merged together to form the Mauryavansh Empire, chosen by a double-blind system that ensured that even those making the final selection could not be certain which of their shortlisted choices would be promoted to the cadre. Once assigned to the Chandikas, a warrior had only one purpose in her life: To serve and protect the Emperor. Like most other Maurya traditions, it was the brainchild of Kautilya, guru to the first Emperor Chandragupta Maurya, co-founder of the empire, and the world's greatest military and political mind.

The practice had begun during the reign of Chandragupta Maurya, when the Mauryavansh empire had still been in the throes of bloody insurrection and strife. Five hundred warring tribes made for a deadly alliance. Assassination attempts were as routine as breakfast. The Prime Minister, as Kautilya had been at the time, had wanted female soldiers for the royal guard because almost all the tribes were patriarchal and chauvinist in the extreme. Women were not considered worthy of inclusion in power decisions, leave alone privy to plans and schemes. Who better to recruit to defend against the crude assassination attempts of those barbaric rustic tribes than their own women? Weathered and seasoned by the abuse of their own men, disenfranchised from the line of succession, relegated to serving, cleaning, cooking, child-bearing and sex-providing, the women leaped eagerly at the opportunity, any opportunity to further their fortunes. The first recruits had been raw and untrained, many had died, incurring greater violence as retaliation for stepping out of the domestic circle, by their own uncles, fathers, brothers, sons—. But very quickly, they had hardened like Deccan clay into formidable warriors, incorruptible, unyielding, and willing to go to suicidal lengths to protect their liege. In time, the assassination attempts had dwindled as even the most boorish tribesmen lost their stomach for killing—and more often, being killed by—women. Today, three quarters of a century later, the women's guard was a feared and hated force in the empire. There were women soldiers in the entire Maurya army, serving in all capacities and at all levels of command. But of all Maurya military cadre, male or female, the Chandikas were the most reviled and dreaded, the famed 'worst of the worst'. It was a reputation they had worked hard to earn and they owned it with pride, refusing to mingle with any other military cadre and, rumour had it, turning only to one another for lovers and spouses.

The outrage caused by the formation of this all-female force, especially to the chauvinistic, patriarchal, and extremely powerful brahmin caucus had been foreseen (like most everything else) by Kautilya who introduced an Oath for the cadre that forbade them from marrying, bearing children, or retaining any family property, name or affiliation. In essence, when a woman was appointed to the Chandikas, she lost all rights, except the right to serve the Emperor until her death. The Chandikas accepted this too with pride and grace. The prestige and honour of being a Chandika far outweighed the outrage of jealous priests. By creating a women-only cadre fiercely loyal only to one another and their liege, Kautilya had ensured that the brutal political game-playing of the brahmin priests and kshatriya chiefs would not affect the Emperor's and his family's personal safety. This lack of control infuriated the brahmins as well as the chiefs, for whom the right to plot assassinations and coups was an essential strategic weapon. The Chandikas had not only served their first master, Chandragupta Maurya, with great distinction, on his command, they had exceeded their range of duties to defend the city itself against a brutal coup attempt. Since his son Bindusara's accession, they had not had as much cause to display their considerable skills, but the lack of exercise had not blunted their edge. The Chandikas operated like a tribe unto themselves, using gruelling, time-honoured tribal methods to keep their members sharply honed and deserving of their reputation.

One such method was the Blooding, the ritual ceremony being conducted this morning in C Garrison. Six hundred and sixty Chandikas crowded the ramparts which overlooked the rectangular central courtyard of the hidden fortress. As per protocol set down by Kautilya over half a century ago, the Chandikas worked in four equal shifts of six hours each day. At any given time, there were two hundred and twenty on duty, posted at various points throughout the palace. Due to the rigour with which they had to discharge their duties and the need for absolute alertness, peak physical fitness and efficiency, the master statesman had decreed that four short shifts of six hours would ensure that each Chandika on duty would remain fresh and strong. Naturally, all Chandikas remained in a constant state of standby, ready to serve at a moment's notice. But the long hours of downtime left the women with a considerable amount of free time and they used it to train, strengthen and improve themselves constantly.

The Blooding was one of the most effective if brutal ways they accomplished these goals.

Like the deafening cacophony of the marketplace which Kaalava had walked through, the silence within C Garrison was deafening too, relieved only by a snick-snick sound that recurred at irregular intervals.

Six hundred and sixty lean angular faces watched with falcon eyes from the ramparts as two women danced in the courtyard below.

The two women swivelled, swirled, pirouetted and somersaulted, all the while wielding gleaming black weapons the length of a sword but with bone-knife blades sharp and thin enough to separate individual layers of gristle and muscle from bone in a single move. Both were specimens of Chandika training, bodies lean muscled, supple and impressively strong. Trained and groomed since early childhood for the cadre, they were finely honed instruments of warcraft, each a master warrior. To the unfamiliar eye, one woman appeared much bigger, taller and stronger than the other. It looked like an unequal match. This was deceptive. Chandikas trained to fight men, who were taller, stronger, faster and bigger. Part of that training to fight men came from pitting smaller-built Chandikas against bigger women, especially during trials like the Blooding. The smaller woman was the one undergoing the trial, the larger one the veteran randomly selected as her opponent.

The large woman moved with exceptional grace, belying her bulk by flipping through a series of sideways somersaults that carried her around at an unpredictable angle to bring her to her opponent's left flank, all the while slashing and slicing with the two lethal blades. The ebony blades blurred and whickered as they sought flesh, but the flesh they sought to separate from its owner was always a hairs breadth out of their arcs. The smaller woman whirled and somersaulted as well, incredibly managing to find a rhythm and pattern that was congruent with her opponent's moves. The result was a deadly but breathtakingly beautiful dance, the snick snick of the flashing blades and the thumps of bare feet landing on oakwood floors the only sounds.

The dance would have continued until one or the other drew blood—hence the name of the trial—but before that consummation could be achieved, the sound of two palms being brought together produced a trio of sharp explosions of sound. Three claps, indicating Cease!

Completing their in-progress somersaults, both opponents crouched low on the wooden floor of the courtyard, points of their black swords lowered in the submissive katha.

The rest of the six hundred and sixty women watching them turned their gaze to look at the person who had clapped and interrupted the trial. Though no irritation showed in their eyes, they were all disappointed at the intrusion. The Blooding was a sacred ritual to Chandikas and this particular trial was a special occasion. The smaller woman of the two fighters was none other than Chaand, the granddaughter of the original Chandika herself, the founder of the cadre, whose extraordinary bravery and sacrifice in the performance of her duties to Chandragupta Maurya almost fifty years ago had earned the cadre its name. It was only the second time in half a century that a Chandika had taken part in the ritual and every one of those watching had been eager to see if the third generation lived up to her name. Everyone sought out the source of the interruption, irritated but curious to know what crisis was responsible.

A small figure stood in the courtyard, beside the doorway through which it had entered the garrison. The figure wore a threadbare burlap robe with a hood. From the looks of the garment and the dirt-caked limbs and face, the person resembled one of the hundreds of mendicants that begged for coins in the city streets, often resorting to pickpocketing, filching and petty burglary to survive. But looks were usually deceptive and every one of the Chandikas knew that this was no ordinary beggar. On the contrary, this was one of their own masters, part of the imperial family whom they were oathbound to serve.

Ashoka threw back his hood, showing his grimy face to the garrison. There were fresh spatters of blood on his neck and hands and feet too. It was obvious they were not his blood. He glanced apologetically at Chaand and her opponent. His gaze held Chaand's a moment longer than was necessary and what passed between them was more intimate than a polite apology.

He raised his face to the watching Chandikas. 'Apologies, I have urgent news. There are assassins in Patliputra. And they intend to try to kill my father tonight.'

4

Rani Noor Khorasan was entertaining herself when Orzala came to see her. Today's entertainment featured two of her favourite dancers, both Khorasani of course. Noor's fierce loyalty to fellow Khorasani had less to do with their being superior entertainers—which they decidedly were not—than with her distrust of all non-Khorasani. A life spent surviving repeated invasions, genocide and the brutal deaths of close family members were the causes of that distrust, but it was also a matter of personal identity. Noor Khorasan defined herself by being proudly Khorasani. It was who she was. If she gave that up and accepted the cosmopolitanism of Patliputra society, she would lose her very identity. What would differentiate her from the dozens of other women who pranced in revealing outfits at every opportunity, hoping to catch the Emperor's eye and be made another queen in his palace? Or the aristocratic women who prided themselves on being 'Mauryavansh' rather than of any specific tribe or culture? What did it even mean to be Mauryavansh. She was queen of the Maurya Empire—a queen, surely, if not the queen—and she was fiercely Khorasani as well. To Noor Khorasan, not only were the two qualities not mutually exclusive, it was wrong to deny one's tribe. If you could be disloyal to your own tribe, then why not your empire? To Noor, being a Queen of Mauryavansh went arm in arm with being Khorasani. Indeed, she felt that it was because she was Khorasani that she had become Queen. After all, the Khorasani legions were among the fiercest warriors in Jambudwipa. By taking a Khorasani queen, Emperor Bindusara had acquired their undying support as well. Politics meant defining yourself and using what you were to get ahead, not denying it.

Orzala paused to give her queen time to notice her presence. Noor Khorasan was engrossed in the entertainment. The two men performing in the artfully illuminated chamber were quite eye-catching, even Orzala had to admit. Their sculpted naked bodies were perfectly defined, every muscle and tendon standing out under the sheen of oil they had massaged onto one another. They were past the initial dialogue and coy, flirtatious banter, as well as the slow stripping of garments and massaging of each other's bodies. Now they were about to engage in the next stage of the performance: the mutual exchange of pleasure. As Orzala stood just behind her queen's shoulder, watching, one of the two men, a handsome square-jawed brute with a body any god would die for, peeled off the last remaining garment covering his companion's groin, revealing a muscular vein-lined penis. With a sly smile up at the other man, he lowered his head to capture the member in his open mouth and began to pleasure him with convincing enthusiasm.

Noor Khorasan sighed softly at the sight. Orzala felt herself aroused as well. She had been with both of the men, separately as well as together, on more than one occasion, and the sight of them engaged in mutual pleasure evoked her own lust. She wished she could stay and watch—or even join in the performance—but her news was urgent and her Queen needed to hear it at once.

She knelt down on the marble floor and leaned forward to reach her mistress's ear. 'My queen, we must speak.'

Noor Khorasan continued watching the two men for another long moment, giving no indication that she had heard anything. But she rose suddenly to her feet and left the theatrical chamber. Orzala followed her close on her heels.

The queen spun around in her bedchamber, turning to face Orzala.

'Well?'

Except for the touch of colour on her cheekbones, Orzala could not glimpse any other sign of Noor's arousal, but she knew her mistress was and would remain aroused after that titillating entertainment.

'I have received word from a Chandika, a Khorasani Chandika, that the second prince has unearthed a team of Confederate assassins in the city.'

The piercing Khorasani eyes narrowed, thin lips pursed, and a breath was expelled. Not a lustful sigh, but an angry exhalation.

'How?'

'That is not known to me as yet. Ashoka is in chambers with the Inner Circle as we speak. He interrupted the Blooding of Chaand to deliver the news.'

Queen Khorasan walked away, leaving the chamber.

Orzala followed her outside, to the sprawling balcony that skirted the entire Khorasani apartment, affording her a sweeping view of both the Upper and Lower Cities. Chandikas patrolling the upper ramparts of the palace took note of their presence and kept an eye on them, but they were too far away to hear any words they exchanged.

Noor Khorasan stared down at the rooftops of Patliputra. The Upper City was partially hidden by the terraced levels of the imperial palace, but Merchant Plaza and the extravagant mansions and town houses of the city's richest and most powerful could be seen. Beyond them, in successive neighbourhoods of diminishing prosperity, were the rest of Upper City and then all of Lower City, a vast sprawling metropolis of markets and sellers and buyers. Queen Khorasan stared down at the gaudy, colourful panorama as if she hoped to see the object of her dissatisfaction, even though Ashoka was several hundred feet below, in C Garrison, rather than out there. It was a Khorasani trait born of growing up in a land so flat and bare that one could always see one's enemies from a distance. Perhaps one might not be able to do anything about them, as in the case of the Greeks, but one could see them coming. From the flash of fury in Noor Khorasan's beautiful light eyes, Orzala knew that she wished she could see Ashoka right this instant, clearly enough to fly an arrow into his young heart.

'How much does he know?'

'Too much, I fear. He spoke of spotting two of the Lichchavi assassins in the audience at the fighting pits, and overhearing them speak of their plans. It would appear he challenged them to a fight and took them both on in the pits. When they lost—'

'Ashoka fought them in the pits?' Noor showed her disbelief.

'Apparently he does that often, as part of his training. It's the only way he can practice his martial arts with fighters who don't hold back because he's a prince.'

'So he could get killed that way, fighting some brute in the pits?' She looked thoughtful as she said it, as if mulling over the possibilities.

'My queen, Ashoka is a problem for another day. Right now, our entire plan is in danger of unravelling. He beat the information out of the two Lichchavi. He knows about the assassination plot in some detail. He and the Inner Circle are meeting now to devise a plan to prevent the assassination and apprehend the Confederacy assassins.'

'If that is all he knows, it is a rancid mouthful of meat to swallow, but it will not kill us. The question is, does he know who is behind the assassination plot?'

'As of now, he believes it is the Confederacy.'

Queen Khorasan looked at her servant's face. 'But he suspects more?'

'I do not believe so, mistress. If he did, he would have brought the matter directly to his father.'

Khorasan shook her head. 'Would he really? His father and Ashoka have never been on the best of terms. No, if he suspected who was really behind the plot, he would not have gone first to the Chandikas. He would have taken the news to his guru.'

'Kautilya.'

Khorasan made a moue of disgust, distorting her attractive features. 'The Old Brahmin would sniff out the truth if he knew.'

'Kautilya is still in his ashram in the deep woods, a full day's ride from Patliputra. Ashoka has no time to take the news to him. The plot calls for the assassination to be carried out tomorrow.'

Khorasan smiled at that. 'Is that what he believes? And as you said, he is here in the C Garrison, so he could not have carried word to Kautilya. Do you think he sent word?'

'It is impossible to read the wind when it blows away from us, but I do not believe he would trust such news to anyone else. Ashoka is a solitary boy. Nobody even knew he fought in the pits until today when he revealed it himself.'

'True. Even I didn't know of this unprincelike pastime. He is a strange boy, is he not, Orzala?'

'He is a cactus in a field of roses, compared to the other princes, my queen. None of Bindusara's other sons would do anything but drink or whore or feast unless compelled to by the Emperor. Ashoka is a rare creature.'

Khorasan tilted her chin up as she contemplated the distant hills. 'Perhaps it is time he became extinct.'

'Would that be wise, mistress? It may draw attention to you?'

'To me?' Khorasan's shapely mouth slitted in a cruel smile. 'Why would I have any reason to kill the second-prince-in-waiting? I have no sons of my own, hence no claim to the imperial throne.'

Orzala smiled, catching her meaning. 'On the other hand, there are other queens who would benefit from his demise. Most of all, the mothers of sons who are below him in line of succession. That is a brilliant move, my queen. Kill he whom you have no discernible motive to kill, and you will not be suspected.'

'Also, Sushim.'

Orzala's eyes widened as she considered this addition. 'Of course, because what good would it do to kill the second-in-waiting if the first prince still lives. Remove both at once, however—'

'This is simple enough,' Khorasan said, cutting her servant off, 'what is more important is the how and when of it. It must be done in such a manner as to seem natural, unplanned, perhaps even an accident.'

Orzala thought for a moment. 'Crown Prince Sushim has a great fondness for killing creatures from the safety of his chariot, surrounded by his attachment of Chandikas.'

Khorasan nodded once. 'A hunting accident, very neat. But the Chandikas?'

'An assassination attempt during a hunting expedition. Followed by a tragic accident. One will draw away the Chandikas, the other will occur during the brief time that the crown princes are out of their sight.'

'Interesting,' Khorasan said, 'we shall discuss this further. In the event the Lichchavi assassination plot fails completely.'

'That is yet to be seen, milady. The plan anticipates discovery and is layered. Even if the primary plot is uncovered, there are backup contingency plans. The game is not over yet. Some damage will be done. The only question is how much and to whom.'

'Yes,' Khorasan said. 'The game is long and our players many. We have many moves to make before our ambitions come to fruition.'

She turned and placed a hand on Orzala's waist, then lowered it to the servant's groin, cupping her sex. 'Right now, I would have you make up for interrupting my afternoon entertainment.'

Orzala gasped as her queen found the centre of her pleasure and massaged it forcefully. 'I live to serve you my lady. How shall I entertain you?'

'Those two dancers I was watching, you are acquainted with them?'

'Intimately.'

Noor Khorasan leaned close to her servant, nuzzling her ear with her lips as she whispered. 'I would watch them do to you what I intend to do to this empire.'

Orzala moaned softly. 'I live to serve.'

5

'Make way for the Emperor of Mauryavansh!'

The sound of the Chandikas's voices travelled through the hallways of the imperial palace. Moving with practised efficiency, the scouts tracked ahead to ensure that no potential threat awaited along the Emperor's route, while the tight formation of guards immediately surrounding his person stayed at full alert, weapons drawn and ready. The whole contingent moved at great speed, taking their cue from their liege. Bindusara himself retained the slender frame of his youth. Only his balding pate and lined face betrayed his age. The striking stain-like blemish on his fore scalp marked the distinctive birthmark that had earned him his name: Dotted Forehead, literally: Bindu-sara.

A brief pause as his guardians halted at the entrance to his destination: the private apartments of his mother, the Dowager Queen Apama. Bindusara waited impatiently till at last the signal was given and they were permitted to enter. He paid no heed to the lavish Grecian architecture and décor of his mother's apartments, every item imported all the way from her homeland, crafted by the most talented artists and artisans. It was like being in Greece itself, as she often told him, which he always interpreted as her way of saying that she wished he could be there, instead of here in this monsoon-plagued land. But to Bindusara, this was the only country he had ever known, and even if he believed his mother and accepted her claim of Grecian superiority in all things, he was still the Emperor of Mauryavansh, not Greece, and if a man's home was his palace, his palace was most certainly his home.

The flaxen hair of the woman in question gleamed in the brightly lit chamber as he swept in. Apama turned her statuesque body, clad immaculately in a flowing Greek gown, her hair pinned up and brooched in the Hellenic style, her pearls and gemstones gleaming from her hands and her neck. She leaned forward a fraction, permitting her son to show his affection with a trio of air kisses: this side, that side, this side again. Then she indicated the silk-cushioned lounging seats and seated herself with her customary grace. The chamber and she were a perfect match. Had she been a statue placed in the room, she could not have looked more perfectly in place. It was he who felt out of place as he always did, as if their positions were reversed and it was she who was the Empress and he the one with the décorative title that came with no real power.

The Chandikas took their positions as he sat, blending into the background, ramrod still but alert.

'I see you have more than usual,' she remarked. She meant the guards.

'There is a threat. An assassination plot. The palace is on alert. Three-fourths of the Chandikas have been called to duty.'

She arched an eyebrow, feigning interest. 'The assassins are still at large?'

'Not for long. They are being hunted down as we speak.'

She nodded as beautiful blonde serving women in togas brought in a succession of refreshments, offering each in turn to both mother and son. 'I have no doubt they will succeed.'

It was his turn to arch an eyebrow.

She smiled. 'I meant the Chandikas, of course.'

He didn't smile back. 'This is no crackpot plot. We have word of an entire company of assassins in the city with an elaborate plan to kill as many and spread as much chaos as possible.'

She sipped her beverage. 'That is unusual. You were right to seek out my advice. An attempt on that scale means powerful enemies. Do you know as yet who is behind the attempt?'

'Ashoka says the Lichchavi Confederacy.'

The first glimmer of interest sparked in Dowager Queen Apama's blue eyes. 'Ashoka. Your second eldest. How is that he has this information?'

'He discovered the plot. He killed two of the assassins himself, after overhearing them discussing their plot.'

'That is quite strange. Trained assassins on a major operation, discussing their plans for anyone to hear?'

'Ashoka is not anyone. He has a sharp ear and an even sharper mind. They probably thought they were speaking in private.'

'Even so, to speak about it at all...' She shook her head. 'I find it difficult to believe that such an elaborate plan was undone by two loose-lipped idiots. It seems too convenient somehow. You were right to bring this to me at once.'

Bindusara sighed with satisfaction. 'What do you think? Could the information be false? Was it deliberately leaked to confuse us?'

Apama set down her golden cup and thought deeply, staring at the artwork depicting a battle on the banks of the Axios. 'If it is, you will know soon enough. But Ashoka is blameless in this.'

'How so?'

'He brought the information to you. If there is no actual plot, it would reflect badly on him. So whoever is behind this, he can't be part of the conspiracy.'

'But you believe there is a conspiracy?'

'As Alexander once said to your grandfather Seleucus Nicator, "When there is a throne, there is always a conspiracy."'

'That was Greece. This is Jambudwipa.'

'Thrones are thrones. Ambition is ambition. The colour or race doesn't change basic human nature. Where there is wealth, there is greed. No, Bindusara, do not make the mistake of underestimating this threat. Whether or not the Chandikas catch the assassins is irrelevant. I am sure your Chandikas will extract every bit of information out of them. But that will only be the information they possess.'

Bindusara blinked. 'What do you mean?'

Apama adjusted her gown, smoothing out an invisible crease. 'It is a common strategy of war to give an assassin or spy information that you want to fall into the enemy's hands.'

Bindusara sat back. 'Misinformation.'

'The assassination plot could be a shrewd way to obfuscate the enemy's real plan.'

'Which would be...what?'

'That is what you must try to uncover. The plot behind the plot.'

Bindusara shook his head. 'Layers within layers. I hate this doublethink. I wish Kautilya had not retired to the forest. If he was here now, he would know the truth at once. His brilliant mind can analyze anything, no matter how complex or intricate.'

Apama was silent for a long moment. Only the smallest tightening of her lips betrayed her disapproval. 'You set too much store by that old priest. I never understood why. Your father made the same mistake.'

'That old priest?' Bindusara smiled. 'Mother, it was Kautilya's ambition and vision that drove father to build this empire. He conceived the administrative system. The sabha, the samiti, every major institution and system of governance was his brainchild. Even the methodology for building roads, bridges, levying taxes, managing states, trade, transport... Every brick that built this empire, this city, bears Kautilya's mark upon it. There would be no Mauryavansh without him. There would have been no Chandragupta Maurya. No Patliputra. We live in the house that Kautilya built.'

The Dowager Queen picked up a savoury that she had no intention of eating. Bindusara knew this because he knew that his mother never ate savouries. Even at her age, mother of a middle-aged son, she bore her years beautifully. She rode, swam, ran and exercised herself in Greek sports with Olympian enthusiasm. She set down the savoury and brushed away imaginary crumbs from her exquisite gown.

'It is time you knew another side of your legendary mentor. The great...Chanakya.' She used the regional name with derision, just as the Chandikas who reported the assassination plot to Bindusara earlier used the word Lichchavis.

'The year before you were born, there was an assassination attempt on your father's life. Much like this Confederacy plot you brought to me today. Unknown number of assassins, unknown forces backing them, unknown motives. The political situation was far more complex back then. The Empire was young, a still uneasy alliance of the five hundred tribes, held together as much by your father's sword as by clever deal-making and compromises.

It was a far cry from the relatively stable Mauryavansh Empire that you rule over today.'

And that difference is largely because of the genius and hard work of my guru Kautilya. He made this possible through his elaborate deal-making and negotiations. My father was a great man but his solution to almost every problem involved raising his sword, just as his approach to parenting involved raising his hand. Bindusara thought these things, but did not say them aloud. He was curious to hear what his mother had to say. He had come to seek her advice and wisdom after all.

'There were tasters who tasted every item that the imperial family consumed, to protect them against the threat of poison. But when tasters began dying every week, Kautilya told your father and us queens that tasters were not enough. With children in the palace, sooner or later, someone would fall prey to the poison. It was only a matter of time. He wanted to insure us against poison permanently.'

'How is that possible?' Bindusara asked, forgetting that Apama did not like to be interrupted while speaking.

'By taking poison ourselves. A tiny dose of it, consumed daily over a sufficiently long enough period of time, can build up resistance to a fatal dose. This is a method known to us Greeks of course, since ancient times. Chanakya's idea was sound enough in theory and so I consented to his plan as did your father.'

Again the use of that tribe name, Chanakya.

'About a year later, your birth mother was pregnant with you. Chanakya had insisted on her taking the poison throughout her pregnancy to protect both herself as well as her unborn child against any assassination attempt. She had reached her final month, the baby due any day. A time when she was most vulnerable.'

Bindusara waited out the theatrical pause.

'That was when your mother was poisoned by Chanakya himself.'

'What?' Bindusara came to the edge of his seat, staring at his mother in disbelief. 'Kautiyla poisoned her?'

'He administered the daily dose himself. A tiny fraction, just sufficient to build resistance, but not enough to cause any harm. Yet that day, he administered a fatal dose. It was his own hand that added the deadly poison. There were witnesses. Daiimaas. Maids. And myself.'

'He poisoned her in front of everyone? That makes no sense.'

'He was administering the daily dose. Nobody expected him to try to kill her by giving her a fatal quantity.'

'But why would he do that?'

'To kill the heir before he was born. To ensure that after Chandragupta's death, which was sure to be soon as your father's health was failing by then, there would be only one person capable of holding the reins of the Mauryavansh Empire. Chanakya himself.'

Bindusara rose to his feet and began pacing the room. 'Even so, that is impossible. Everyone would know he had poisoned my mother and killed the heir. He would have been found guilty of treason and executed by law! He would never have lived to enjoy the success of his plan—if it was his plan as you claim.'

Apama remained calm and unruffled. 'I claim nothing. These are indisputable facts I speak of to you.'

'Then why have I never heard this story till today? I am almost forty-seven years of age. Why am I hearing about this alleged assassination plot by Kautilya only now?'

'Because we all agreed to suppress the real story and fabricate a narrative that would not endanger the empire's stability. Mauryavansh was at a delicate point then. The brahmin caucus was far, far stronger then than it is now. The five hundred chiefs were still restless at having united to form this nebulous thing called an "empire" which they barely understood or desired. To them, it seemed as if Chandragupta had made himself Chief of Chiefs and roped them into following in his wake of glory as he taxed their resources to enrich and strengthen himself. Kautilya provided the crucial balance needed to make that alliance work. The chiefs were god-fearing men and women. They feared and respected brahmins just as much as they distrusted other kshatriyas. Kautilya's presence by your father's side ensured their continued support of the five hundred tribe alliance which was the foundation of the empire. To discredit or accuse Chanakya of treason and execute him would be considered sacrilege. The brahmin caucus would rise up and summon down the wrath of the gods upon us all. The only thing a kshatriya fears is a brahmin's curse. What curse might Chanakya himself unleash upon them if they tried to execute him? So we agreed to cover up the truth and tell a different story instead, the story you grew up hearing.'

'That my mother died in childbirth, and that Kautilya was retiring to the forest to work on his great work, the *Arthashastra*.' Bindusara paced energetically. 'I still don't understand it, even if I believe that Kautilya really intended to kill off my mother and me, what did he finally achieve by exposing himself in this manner? He is a genius, a mastermind of political manoeuvring. Why would he risk everything with such a foolish, transparent mistake?'

'Because he did not expect to be found out by me.'

Bindusara paused in his pacing to stare at Apama. 'By you? But you said there were other witnesses, maids, servants, daiimaas...'

'None of them mattered. All they saw was Chanakya putting the usual tiny dose into your mother's food. Mine was the only testimony that sealed his fate. I was the only witness that your father believed.'

'And you saw something different? You saw him putting this much larger fatal dose of poison in my mother's food?'

Apama raised her eyes to meet his heated gaze. 'Are you doubting my word?'

Bindusara looked away. 'Of course not, mother. I believe you. But how did Kautilya make such a mistake? How did he let you witness him putting in the larger dose? He's a brilliant mind. It wouldn't be like him to make such a clumsy error.'

Apama shook her head. 'He made no mistakes, no error. He poisoned not only your mother's food but mine as well, and the food of every queen that day. He intended to kill us all at the same time, leaving no wives, no heirs, and no future for Mauryavansh.'

'But...' Bindusara stared. 'Only my mother died that day. You survived, as did my father's other queens.'

'I survived because I saw him poisoning us and stopped the other queens before they could eat. I wish I could have saved your mother as well, but by the time I reached her, it was too late, she was already on the floor of her bedchamber, frothing at the mouth, bleeding from her nether regions, the daiimaas and servants in a state of panic.'

'What happened then? After you saw her lying there bleeding?'

Apama shrugged. 'Chanakya was called in as usual. He examined your mother and announced that it was too late to save her but you could still be rescued. He cut open your mother and drew you out, blue all over and barely breathing.' Apama touched her forehead. 'The stippling of poison on your head is proof of how close you came to death that day.'

Bindusara shook his head, still confused. 'That part is exactly as I heard it then. Kautilya cut open my mother and saved my life. If as you say it, he had poisoned my mother to kill her and me, why would he bother to save me then? Why not simply let me die with my mother?'

Apama shrugged. 'Games within games, plots within plots. I don't claim to understand every working of his twisted mind. All I know is what I have told you. Kautilya killed your mother and tried to kill me as well.'

Bindusara was still for a long moment. 'And then? After that?'

'As the next queen in line, I took you to my breast, raised you as my own son, and groomed you to be Chandragupta's heir, preparing you to be the next Emperor of Mauryavansh, which you ascended to within the next two decades.'

Bindusara shook his head slowly. 'I still don't understand. So Kautilya's plan failed. He was exposed and exiled.'

'Eventually, yes. It took almost twenty years to extricate him from Maurya politics, to relegate him to the forest where he lives now. Political change happens in stages over time, there is no "overnight" action as in war. Everything requires time, patience, planning.'

'And in all that time, before that day, and since, he has never acted against the Empire, against the throne, against this family? It seems incredible.'

Apama sighed. 'Betrayal always seems unbelievable. Especially when those closest to you turn against you.'

'But Kautilya? He built Mauryavansh! He made our family what it is today.'

'That he did,' Apama admitted reluctantly. 'And it's possible that the assassination attempt was a single moment of weakness, a lapse of reason in a long and otherwise illustrious career. As I said, my son, I cannot explain everything to you. I am no mastermind or genius. Merely a daughter of Greece. But I am also the daughter of Seleucus Nicator, the greatest ruler that the civilized world has seen since Alexander, and before. I know one thing: Once a person loyal to you betrays you, even if it is in a moment of weakness, you can never trust that person again. Never.'

Bindusara nodded. 'That I understand. It is the rest of it I find incredible to believe. '

Apama then did something she had not done in years. She reached out and touched Bindusara's shoulder in a tender gesture.

'Son, listen to me.'

Bindusara raised his eyes to her aquiline features.

'Chanakya is a master of the long game. He invented the art of plotting and counter-plotting moves that would play out and pay off over decades, even centuries! In the game, nothing is as it seems. At times the attacker poses as the victim, or as an ally, or as an enemy of an enemy, and so on over the years, until it becomes impossible to tell who is truly who and what their plan really was at the outset. Only the attackers themselves know. It is like viewing only one moment of a long campaign. At that moment, one army may be seeming to retreat, but in fact they may simply be withdrawing to move to a better position later. Who knows how long Chanakya was plotting against our family or what his real plan might have been? All that we know for sure is that he created the system of spasas, the spy network, and the assassin's guilds, and he set into motion a complicated web of espionage and counter-espionage that even the most brilliant mind could never unravel without knowing the secret code. My father is a master of military history and when he heard about Chanakya's failed attempt and exposure, he raised many of the same questions and doubts that you did today. But he concluded with one clear response.'

Bindusara waited for her to go on.

'He said, "Sometimes the best way to destroy your enemy is to pose as his friend."'

Apama looked at him. 'Do you follow, son?'

Bindusara nodded slowly. 'I do but he can't have meant it, could he?'

'Why not?' Apama spoke her final words with authority, determined to eliminate any vestige of doubt left in her son's mind. 'Is it not possible to believe that a genius like Chanakya could all along have played the part of being an ally and friend of your father, while in fact, all that time, he was secretly using your father to get what he wanted from, namely, a military leader strong enough to lead the five hundred tribes to victory against the oppressive Nanda Empire? And once he succeeded in that goal, and built the Mauryavansh Empire, Chanakya was merely biding his time until the day when he could eliminate your father and his entire family, and take over the reins of the Empire himself? Consider the weapon he used? Poison. Not a sword or an arrow or a spear. Poison! He is a brahmin after all. A priest cannot take up a weapon, or he would lose the respect of the world forever. But by resorting to poison, under the guise of administering a daily dose of the same poison himself to protect the queens, he could eliminate them without aggressive violence, weapons or an army. It took your father forty years and the military strength of five hundred tribes united to defeat the Nandas and replace their evil empire with his own Mauryavansh. Chanakya could not use any armies, weapons or military tactics. So he used the only means available to him: a slow long poisoning of your family intended to lead eventually to the extinction of our line. That way, he could remove us but retain the empire.'

Bindusara nodded slowly, believing at last, his doubts removed by Apama's dominating narrative. 'Yes. Yes, I see it now. He would have got away with it too. Blamed the overdose on one of the daiimaas, or maids, or a Chandika even... The thing that undid him, the only thing, was being seen by you, adding the second, much larger dose of poison.'

Bindusara clasped his mother's hands, the contrast between her ivory complexion and his ebony skin as stark as the difference in their features. But in his eyes was the love of a son for his mother, the woman who had raised him as her own as much any biological birth mother. 'Thank the gods you saw him then. Kautilya...' he swallowed, then corrected himself, 'Chanakya may have been forced to pretend to save me to avoid being proven guilty of the assassination, but it was really you who saved me that day. You are the reason I am alive today. Why this empire still stands, this dynasty still survives. It is all by your grace, Maa.'

6

Kaalava watched calmly as the Chandikas surrounded six of her colleagues at spear point and challenged them to throw down their weapons and surrender. The Lichchavis looked around the market square, seeking ways out. There were several but Kaalava knew at a glance that all of them would end in certain death. These weren't Mauryavansh army cadets, they were Chandikas and this was their home ground. She had no doubt that they had positioned other Chandikas to block off all escape routes before challenging her fellow Confederates. The magical speed with which the public had fled the square itself proved her suspicion: not even a single gawker in sight? That was impossible in a country where the grislier the mishap, the larger the crowd that gathered to view it. This was a well-planned and perfectly executed roundup. The Chandikas had been watching these six and had made their move precisely when and where they chose. Which meant that they were onto the Lichchavi conspiracy!

She watched as one of her colleagues, a tall, wiry woman named Shastaki who was as famous for having three husbands as for her trademark coup de grace involving the use of a needle sharp hairpin which she kept in her luxuriant hair, made her move. Shastaki drew the pin and used it to attack the Chandika nearest to her. Taking a cue from her defiance, the other five Lichchavi also acted, striking out with hands, weapons, feet, or whatever was at hand.

The fight lasted only a few minutes. It was short but brutal. The Chandikas responded without hesitation, delivering on their threat that resistance would result in execution. Kaalava watched as her colleagues were despatched with savage efficiency. She looked down from the verandah at the prone body of Shastaki lying on the cobblestones thirty feet below. Shastaki's hand was twisted inwards, still gripping the six-inch long pin which now pierced her own ear, her elbow broken with the brute force of the Chandika's retaliation. Her body spasmed and shuddered in its final death throes, blood seeping from her ear as she surrendered her life spirit.

Kaalava bared her teeth in impotent fury. Shastaki was not just a colleague, she was a friend, and among the best in the assassins guild. Her death was a blow to the conspiracy but Kaalava was relieved she had chosen to fight rather than surrender. Dead assassins could not be made to talk, and right now, all Kaalava could hope for was that Patliputra was not aware of the full extent of the Lichchavi plan.

She retreated into the apartment, leaving everything exactly as it was, wasting not a moment longer for any reason. She exited not through the front but through a rear window, climbing out onto a running ledge and sidling over until she could jump into a balcony in the next building. She heard and saw no signs of pursuit or a trap but did not let her guard down. The certainty with which they had rounded off those six had shaken her. It suggested a traitor amongst her number. She did not want to believe any Lichchavi could betray their own and confess their plan to the Mauryas, but what other explanation was there?

After jumping and climbing across several blocks, she found a terrace that had an overhang that would conceal her from the view of other terraces as well as from the ground below. If they came at her from the stairway, she could leap out to the next rooftop and escape that way. She had no desire to go down to street level. At every turn, she had glimpsed Chandikas out in full force in the streets, moving through the river of commerce and humanity like sharks through shoals of fish. She guessed the rest of her fellow assassins were being rounded up and killed at this very moment. They would be given a chance to surrender but their orders had been clear: No surrender, no retreat. They would all go down resisting, and if the Chandikas didn't finish them off on the spot, they would make sure they drove their blades or pins into their own hearts rather than let themselves fall into enemy hands.

Face it, the conspiracy is finished. The plan is moot. The entire operation is a washout.

Yet a part of her refused to give up.

So long as we breathe, we resist.

So long as we stand, we fight.

The Lichchavi Confederacy motto was intended for times like these, when all hope seemed lost, all avenues closed. She was still alive and free. She was here to do a job, she intended to do it. Better to die trying than to die giving in to fear of failure.

There was a contingency plan provided for such a situation and her orders called for her to follow it.

She hid out all day and the next, waiting for the hue and cry to die down. Finally, when she deemed enough time had passed, she decided to make her move.

7

Chaand met Ashoka in his apartment at night. He was expecting her. She came into his arms at once, hungry for his touch. He embraced and kissed her but when she began to disrobe, he stopped her.

'We need to speak first.'

'You are making a habit of interrupting me!'

He smiled ruefully. 'I ruined your Blooding, didn't I?'

She kissed him and slipped a hand down into his groin, cupping him. 'You ruined nothing. You saved the day. You're a hero to every Chandika, you know that. You did our jobs for us!'

'That's saying too much. I learned of a threat to my family. I brought it to you. What else would I have done?'

'If someone else had been in your place, they might have done other things with that information.'

Ashoka was eating fruit. He tossed a piece to her, she caught it with her mouth. He tossed a piece up and caught it as well. They grinned and ate together. 'What else would they have done? And who's the "someone else" you're talking about?'

She gestured at the walls, indicating the imperial palace all around. 'Your siblings, for one. You think they would have reported news of Confederacy assassins to us Chandikas?'

'What else would they have done? It's a threat to the family, your task is to protect the family. What other option is there?'

She leaned back on his bed, her slender muscled body stretched out sleekly, strong thighs flexing as she lifted her legs onto the bedding. 'There are always options.'

He thought about it for a moment, then resumed chewing the fruit. 'You mean they could have let the assassination attempt go on as planned. To eliminate rivals to the line of succession.'

'He's not just an ugly face,' she said, clapping her thigh. 'He's a sharp mind too.'

'That never even occurred to me. I don't care about the line of succession.'

'How can you not care? You're second prince-in-waiting.'

'I'm not waiting for anything. I have no intention of ever being Emperor.'

She sat up, staring at him. 'What else would you be?'

'Free. I don't want to spend my life tangled in court politics, yelling in the sabha to be heard, deciding which queen to sleep with next and which to impregnate, or not to impregnate, or which kingdom to go to war against when they don't pay their levies. All that is not for me. I want to be free, like the Vyag of Girvan. Free as a lion.'

'A lion of Maurya?' she teased, stretching out one bare foot to nudge his groin with her toes.

'Why not? I envy the lions. Or any Vyag. They live free, they don't have any politics. They don't send assassins to kill each other because they disagree on political theory. They don't beat and abuse and rape and kill and steal and discriminate. They just live.'

She looked at him intently. He was serious about this. She knew his love for animals and wilderness and dislike of cities and luxury. But she had never realized how entrapped he felt by his privilege and entitlement.

'Those years you and your mother were in the forest, living that life, it must have been a contrast to the big city, to living in a palace, being a prince of Mauryavansh.'

He sighed. 'They were the best years of my life. Everything after that seems like a bad dream.' He gestured at the opulent apartment. 'A very comfortable luxurious nightmare. But still a nightmare.'

She moved to the edge of the bed, lowering her voice. 'You need to be careful not to say such things where you can be heard, Ashoka. This is Patliputra. Even the corn has ears.'

He smiled at her joke. 'Why should I care? My mother knows how I feel. She's the only one that matters to me in this house.'

'And maybe your brother Tissa and his mother? And your sister Tapasvi?'

He shrugged. 'Well, just a few people who matter. But everyone else can go jump in the Ganga and drown for all I care.'

'Said the boy who just saved those very people from the deadliest assassination attempt in fifty years.'

Ashoka leaned forward. 'That's different, Chaand. I can't stand by and let people be murdered. Not my family or anyone else. That's just basic human nature.'

She smiled at him. 'So smart a warrior yet so naïve a politician. I can name four dozen of your siblings who lack that "basic human nature". As far as they are concerned, the Confederacy assassins could slaughter everyone else in this palace, so long as they remain alive to claim the throne.'

Ashoka sighed, getting up to look out of the vaulting window cut out of the stone wall. He gazed up at the evening sky outside, filled with the tiny silhouettes of a flock of krauncha heading back to their habitat before nightfall, their plaintive cries faintly audible. 'I don't understand that kind of thinking.'

She came up behind him, pressing her body against his, sliding her hand across his bare chest. 'I know you don't. That's why I love you and sleep with you, Ashoka. Many Chandika sleep with the imperial family members, and many enjoy it too. But I don't come to your bed just for pleasure or to seek favours. I come because I think you are a breed apart. Who knows. Maybe you really are a lion of Girvan. I've seen you fight in the pits. You have more Vyag blood in you than human!'

He caught her hand which was doing tantalizing things at his groin. 'There is something I have to tell you, though.'

'Yes, you said that earlier too when you interrupted me. This time I won't brook interruption. Say it quickly and be done with it. I have to be up again for training in a few hours and I intend to make the most of the time.'

He caught her hand, sighing at interrupting his own pleasure, and turned to face her. 'Chaand, there is something I must tell you first.'

She caught the seriousness of his tone and frowned. 'What is it, my young lion?'

He sighed again, a heavier sigh this time, weighted with the gravitas of someone who has had too much responsibility thrust upon his shoulders at too young an age. 'There is a spy in your Order.'

She stared at him. 'In the Chandikas? Impossible.'

He looked at her silently, neither arguing nor explaining.

She saw the truth in his eyes. 'Devi Chamunda protect us. Honestly?'

He nodded once, slowly, reluctantly.

'How can you be sure?'

'I passed on all the information I had overheard about the Confederacy assassins...but left out one detail.'

'What?'

He sighed again. 'The two men I heard in the public house. The ones I fought and killed in the pit. I heard them mention a contingency plan in case they were discovered and the conspiracy thwarted.'

'You told us this already. You said you didn't know any more about that contingency plan because they didn't discuss it further.'

'That was true because they didn't know anything about the contingency plan. All they knew was that there was one.'

'So you left nothing out?'

He looked out the window again. The sky had turned shades darker in the time they had been talking. The plaintive cries of the krauncha were silent now. Dusk had fallen, drawing down the curtain on another day. 'Just one minor detail. Nothing that would affect the Chandikas foiling the assassination or apprehending the Lichchavis. Just a minor point that was not relevant to your Order at that time.'

She looked at him. 'Ashoka, don't make me beg you. Tell me!'

He turned to look at her again, the faint dusky light behind him throwing his face into shadow, painting his already dusky features the colour of night. 'They didn't know the contingency plan but they mentioned the person who did know it. In the event of any emergency, they were to contact this person who would then tell them, how many ever of them were surviving at the time, how to proceed.'

'And?'

'And this person was someone here, in the imperial palace. In the imperial family.'

She stared at him, not shocked but visibly turning wheels in her head, thinking through the permutations and combinations of this revelation. 'That makes sense. As I said, any of your siblings would be happy to reduce the line of succession, moving himself higher up the line, maybe even to the very top. So they resorted to enlisting a little outside help. Contacted the Lichchavi Confederacy, probably promising to lift the embargo, provide them trade or economic alliances if they did this. The Confederacy is on the verge of starvation, people are killing each other over food over there, they would have jumped at the opportunity. Killing off most or all of the imperial family and being rewarded for it? It would be a dream offer! There's nothing surprising about that. What does that have to do with the Chandikas?'

Ashoka leaned back, raising his knee to rest his foot casually against the stone wall. 'I didn't tell the Chandikas this last part. About the person who hired the assassins being a member of my own family.'

Chaand frowned. 'So?'

'So then why was it that within an hour of my bringing the news to the Chandikas, one of your Order went to visit a member of the imperial family, and passed on every detail I had shared?'

Chaand's face faded away. The dusky light from the high

slitted windows cast diagonal bars of light into the chamber, dimly illuminating parts and concealing others. She stepped back into a shadowy patch between bars, her face now concealed from Ashoka. 'It could have been for a number of reasons. She could have been assigned to that member of the family.'

'It was not her shift and would not be her shift for another twelve hours. Yet she went, leaving her barracks and violating a direct order forbidding all Chandikas from speaking of the Lichchavi assassins to anyone, including the imperial family.'

'Even so, it does not mean she went to betray that confidence. She could have spoken of any other matter.'

Ashoka shook his head slowly, sadly. 'If only she had. But I have it on good authority that she did exactly what she was forbidden to do, and shared the entire story of the assassins with my family member. After which she went directly back to her barracks and continued with her duties, serving her next shift as normal.'

Chaand folded her arms across her chest, her body stiffening and distancing itself from him. 'How can you be so sure that was what she told your family member?'

'Because as you said yourself, even the corn has ears in Patliputra.'

She hissed, releasing a breath. 'Spasas! Of course. Your precious guru Kautilya left behind a network of spies in every walk of life throughout the empire. Maids, servants, daiimaas, eunuchs, anyone and everyone. But Kautilya is long gone from Patliputra. His network now reports to the Emperor. Not to you.'

'I was Kautilya's most loyal disciple. I still am, in a manner of speaking. He was the one responsible for bringing my mother and me to Patliputra, for instating her to her rightful position as a queen of Mauryavansh, for ensuring our safety and wellbeing during those difficult early years when everyone in this house was an enemy who wanted us both dead. He still has eyes and ears in here as well as elsewhere. He makes sure even now that I continue to receive information that is relevant to my and my mother's safety. This assassination falls squarely into that category.'

'Spies who spy upon spies.' Chaand shook her head, wondering. 'Impressive. So you know of a Chandika who is loyal to one of your family and reports matters that may be relevant to that person. How is that different from your old guru's spies who feed you scraps of information?'

'Because I don't pay Lichchavi assassins to come to Patliputra to wipe out my whole family, that's a big difference, wouldn't you say?'

She shrugged. 'All's fair in love and politics, as they say. Don't be so naïve, Ashoka. There are always plots and conspiracies afoot. Alliances between enemies and even plots against friends. When snakes assemble in a pit, they won't hesitate to bite each other. This is Patliputra. It's the biggest snake pit in the world.'

'Maybe I am naïve. But I'm no fool. This family member hired those assassins to wipe out as many of the imperial family as possible, kill them all if they could. That includes myself and my mother. Yes, and it includes Tissa, his mother, Tapasvi and her mother, because I do care about them too. Anyone who is part of a conspiracy to kill those I care about, and to kill me as well, is no friend of mine. And definitely not a lover who slept with me because she loves me.'

Chaand shrugged. 'Perhaps she does love you despite that. Perhaps she has no choice but to be politic to survive. And being politic means killing a few friends from time to time. Even lovers. It's nothing personal, Ashoka. We had some wonderful times together. You are a great lover and an extraordinary fighter. But you're a naïve, idealistic, people-loving, animal-loving fool when it comes to politics and ambition. You don't have the iron in you to take hard steps, to kill when killing's needed, even if it's a friend or family member...or mother.'

Ashoka sighed. 'A day when I am willing to kill my own mother to further myself politically is a day that will never dawn for me.'

'You would be surprised. Politics and ambition will make a person do anything.'

He nodded. 'I can see that.'

'You see nothing, Ashoka of Patliputra. You see only goodness and hope in all humanity. You don't see the ugliness and cruelty and pain that lies beneath it all. Nothing comes without pain and suffering.'

'Especially justice.'

Ashoka stepped forward, into the last gloam of dusk. His hands were bare, but Chaand knew that his hands were themselves weapons. She had come prepared. She drew the shortblade she kept concealed in her lower garments.

'I'm sorry, my love, but you were doomed anyway. Even if you survived this assassination attempt, you won't survive this family. You are too sweet, too good hearted, too much a lion to survive for long in this den of jackals and hyenas. I am doing you a favour by killing—'

He moved so swiftly, she was still speaking when he grasped her arm and shoulder, twisted hard and pressed her own blade into her chest, penetrating between the ribs and into the heart, stopping her life almost instantly.

'—you,' she said, the light already gone from her eyes.

She collapsed in his arms, like a lover's body turned boneless in the paroxysm of ecstasy. He caught her and lowered her to the bed. He remained bent over her for a moment longer, kissed her forehead, bidding her farewell, then rose and left the chamber without looking back. He left only a single tear on her upraised face, proof of his first love.

8

'Father.'

Bindusara looked up, annoyed, ready to reprimand whichever of his sons had the audacity to barge into his chambers unannounced. He had no time or patience to deal with the petulant demands of one of his brood. Whatever princely problems they had, they could take it up with their mothers who would then take it to Dowager Queen Apama in turn. As head of the 'house', she would decide how to handle the problem, or even if it was worth handling. He raised his voice, prepared to whiplash whichever upstart one of his hundred sons had dared to intrude on his private time.

'How many times—' he began in a thundering tone.

When he saw Ashoka standing with half a dozen Chandikas, he trailed off.

'What is this? Why are you all here?'

Jugni, a senior Chandika and one of the old guard, stepped forward. 'My Emperor. There is need for discretion and caution. Send away your personal servants and maids so we may speak freely.'

Bindusara knew Jugni well enough to understand that it must be an emergency of the highest order. He gave the necessary order brusquely, clearing his apartments of the entire contingent of some thirty servants who served him at all hours, day and night.

He glanced at the Chandikas posted to protect him, standing at their usual stations.

'I assume you don't mean to send away your own Order.'

'Your Chandikas may remain on duty. The traitor in our ranks has been found and dealt with already by Ashoka.'

Bindusara was taken aback. 'A traitor in your ranks? You mean a Chandika was involved with this Confederacy assassination plot?'

'Not with the plot itself, but with those who ordered the assassination. This was a conspiracy, your Excellency, one involving members of your own imperial family.'

Bindusara sat back and regarded her intently. 'That is a treasonous accusation, Jugni. Punishable with death if found to be false.'

'I am aware, your Excellency. I would not make the allegation if it were not true. But Ashoka has brought us ironclad proof of this fact. I myself, along with these senior leaders of our Order, was privy a very revealing conversation he had with one of our own only a short while ago. After discussing the implications, we deemed it best to bring the matter directly to you for further consideration.'

Bindusara looked at Jugni, then at Ashoka, and leaned back in his seat. 'Make it brief. I am addressing the sabha shortly in an emergency session to discuss the Confederacy assassination plot and its political implications.'

'This information may be of value to you in that session, Excellency. We believe that someone within the imperial is directly responsible for the assassination plot and is aiding and abetting the surviving assassins. We also believe that even as we speak, these assassins are either within the precincts of the imperial palace itself or intend to enter here this very day.'

Bindusara stared at the head of the Chandikas, his eyes and face betraying no reaction. 'These are treasonous allegations, as I have already pointed out. Present your evidence substantiating the claims or face apprehension and immediate execution.'

Jugni nodded once, sharply, her eyes cutting to Ashoka.

He stepped forward. 'Father, one of the Chandikas shared my bed. I got her to confess her loyalty to the Lichchavi Confederation. She admitted that one of us was responsible for the assassination plot and that more assassins remain at large.'

Bindusara regarded Ashoka for a long moment. 'I assume you have this Chandika in custody now?'

'She attacked me. I killed her to defend myself.'

Bindusara continued to stare at Ashoka, as if watching the attempt and its outcome in his son's eyes. 'So the only person who can corroborate your story is dead and we have no way to confirm or deny its veracity?'

Jugni spoke up. 'I heard the entire exchange myself, Excellency. As did Niava, Kashiti and Sumanya.'

The other three senior Chandikas nodded in agreement. Kashiti spoke for all three. 'We did, Excellency. There is not even a shadow of doubt. Someone from the imperial family masterminded and controlled the Confederacy plot.'

'Who?'

All five were silent.

Bindusara looked at Ashoka. 'You said you extracted a confession from your Chandika lover. What was the name she confessed?'

'She gave no name, father. Only an admission that it was so.'

Bindusara breathed in slowly and released the breath, his smooth handsome features unaltered. 'So you claim there is a traitor in our own house. Do you know how large our family is, Ashoka?'

'Yes, father. A hundred queen mothers, a hundred and eighty-seven princes and princesses, three hundred and sixteen close relatives of the queen mothers. In sum, six hundred and four members, not counting daiimaas, maids, and other servants and Chandikas.'

Bindusara frowned. 'Six hundred and three, not four.'

Ashoka hesitated.

Bindusara caught the hesitation and narrowed his eyes. 'Six hundred and four—including me? You would count your own Emperor as a suspect?'

'I was merely offering the complete count, father. I made no such allegation.'

'They are one and the same thing. Including me in the count is an allegation. A treasonous one! I have executed my own sons for far less!'

He had indeed. Only a few maasas earlier, Bindusara had sentenced three of his sons to summary execution for being overheard criticizing their father's favouring of Sushim and Ashoka over them. All the royal heirs were required to watch the execution performed in the imperial courtyard within the palace compound. Ashoka still remembered Jash, Murugu and Favri, each begging for mercy before the executioner's sword fell, severing their heads from their necks.

Ashoka looked his father in the eye without betraying either fear or intimidation. 'It was not meant as such, father.'

Jugni spoke cautiously. 'Your Excellency, it would be impossible to discuss such a matter without seeming to speak treasonous thoughts. Yet it is not our thoughts or intentions that are treasonous, merely the facts as they appear before us. Ashoka is only stating these facts.'

Bindusara kept his eyes on Ashoka a moment longer, as if waiting for his son to look down first. Ashoka continued looking at his father, not with insolence or arrogance but with his direct, uninflected gaze. Both pairs of eyes gleamed with burnished copper heat, the similarity between their features ending there.

Ashoka had inherited his father's eyes and his ability to appear deathly calm even in the face of a life-threat. But where the father was strikingly handsome, even regal in his aspect, the son merely looked intense and dangerous. Nobody would have called Ashoka handsome but he exuded a sense of danger when entering any place that made even men twice his size glance sharply at him. His lack of good looks and his hawkish, piercing gaze could easily be mistaken for a threatening stare but in fact it was simply Ashoka's natural facial expression when thinking deeply or being serious. He couldn't have softened it unless he smiled, which would have been gratuitous in these circumstances.

Finally, Bindusara turned his piercing gaze back to Jugni. 'And is it your intention now to drag all six hundred and four imperial family members to the Pain Palace and interrogate them? Including Ashoka himself and me?'

Jugni looked uncomfortable. 'Excellency, we have no such intention. All we seek is permission to search the imperial palace thoroughly for the assassins and apprehend them before they can make their move.'

Ashoka spoke in the same direct tone, seemingly unaffected by his father having taken umbrage a moment earlier. 'We know every single one of the imperial family members and their approved staff. It will be a simple enough matter to root out the strangers amidst them.'

'So you say. Does it occur to you that if someone in this house is in league with the assassins, they might simply conceal these killers. They are probably providing them sanctuary even now as we speak.'

Ashoka shrugged. 'If they're here, we'll find them.'

'How? By tearing apart the palace? By rousting every nursing queen mother or sleeping babe and ripping open every concealed space that may hide an assassin?'

'If need be, yes. We are prepared to do whatever it takes to find these killers and end this threat.'

Bindusara sat back. 'I see.'

Jugni glanced from Ashoka to his father, assessing whether the father-son exchange was over. 'We must act quickly, Excellency. Before the assassins strike. This is a snake in our nursery, and we must root it out before it fastens its fangs onto unsuspecting throats. Will you grant us leave to act?'

Bindusara rose to his feet, striding slowly to the far end of the chamber, hands clasped behind his back. Jugni glanced at the other Chandikas: all four of them exchanged a look of concern. This audience was not going as they had expected. The brief discussion they had held after Ashoka's encounter with Chaand and before they had come to the imperial suite had not anticipated the Emperor challenging them! Already shaken by the discovery of a traitor in their own ranks, the Chandikas were visibly disturbed by this turn of events.

'This Chandika, the one who was in cohorts with the Confederacy...' Bindusara trailed off, his back still to them as he gazed out of the enormous bow-shaped window that looked out at the distant snow-capped mountains

'Excellency?' Jugni's voice reflected her uncertainty. Why was the Emperor wasting valuable time rehashing the same points when was so much to be done? Assassins in the palace! Hidden amongst the imperial family!

'How do you know she was the only one?'

Jugni and the other Chandikas opened their mouths silently, though no words came out.

'She was the only one.' Ashoka spoke matter-of-factly.

Bindusara turned to face them, his eyes finding his son and pinning him in place. 'I did not ask you. I asked the Chandikas. If their Order housed an enemy capable of colluding with the enemy, how do I know there aren't more like her? How do I know that the entire Chandika Order is not corrupted from within?'

One of the women gasped audibly. Jugni fell to her knees. 'Excellency! What happened with this one traitor is unthinkable to us. We exist to serve the imperial family. To protect it with our lives. It is our sole purpose of living, our dharma. This traitor committed blasphemy against our Order, an unforgivable crime. I assure you, such a corruption cannot happen to a single other Chandika. It is hard to believe it happened at all.'

'And yet, it did happen.' Bindusara stepped forward, hands still clasped behind his back, looking down at Jugni kneeling before him. 'And if it can happen once, it can happen twice, or a hundredfold. Presumably you did not know of this traitor's true allegiance until only an hour or two earlier? Who's to say that even now you remain unaware of a hundred other such traitors? What if your entire Order is corrupted from within, sold body and soul and sword to the Confederacy.'

'Excellency!' The other three Chandikas fell to their knees, all but prostrating themselves. Their faces expressed their extreme dismay at their liege's accusations. Ashoka could see how much pain each word his father spoke was causing them. He clenched his fists, feeling their pain, sharing their shame. He had been deceived by Chaand too, had shared his bed and his heart with an ally of their worst enemies, an ally of assassins hellbent on killing his mother, siblings, himself.

'Why is it so difficult to see?' Bindusara paced before them, his voice and face growing harder, more convinced of the argument he was proposing. 'The traitor was in your Order. You yourself acknowledge that fact. Why not others like her? My father used to tell me that the Chandikas serve as a single being. All act for one, one acts for all. The betrayal of this single Chandika represents the betrayal of all Chandikas. How can an Order that has betrayed its sworn duty be trusted any longer?'

The four Chandikas remained bowed, faces revealing their anguish. None of them dared interrupt their emperor while he was in the throes of his monologue. Ashoka's fists tightened: was this the way an Emperor dealt with a crisis? By turning on his own protectors? Precious time was being wasted here while they bickered. Even now, the assassins could be preparing to strike—or striking this very moment. He thought of his mother and siblings, helpless and trusting if an intruder should appear in their chambers, striking at them from behind without warning, and he felt his stomach coil with impatience.

'You expect me to give you permission to run amok through the private chambers of my family? For all I know that might be the very plan you had from the very outset! A shrewd way to gain access to the most vulnerable members of the dynasty. Simple enough then to strike at unarmed queen mothers and their children, to eliminate them all in a single bloody sweep, all under the aegis of authority, with my own sanction! Do you take me for a fool, expecting me to sanction such access?'

Ashoka could stand it no longer. He stepped forward, forcing himself to keep his voice free of the impatience he felt. 'The Chandikas are not our enemy. If they wanted to attack us, they would have done so already. They had no need to give us this notice, to ask your permission.' He pointed at the four kneeling women. 'Assassins would not prostrate themselves and endure abuse silently.'

'Abuse?' Bindusara's eyes flashed hotly. 'Watch yourself, son of Shubhadrangi!'

'Yes, abuse,' Ashoka said, standing up to his father. 'The Chandikas have devoted their lives to protecting us. They are our first, last and best line of defence in such a crisis. We need them to root out these assassins right now. We are wasting time standing here and arguing about moot points!'

'Arguing?' Bindusara tilted his head accusingly. 'You go too far, boy. I am the Emperor of Mauryavansh, I do not argue. I pronounce. How dare you question my pronouncements?'

'You have already gone too far, father. You have no right to make such accusations against your most loyal servants.'

Bindusara reared back, incredulous. 'I have no right? Upstart boy! You have no right to speak to your Emperor thus!'

Ashoka kept his voice level, his hands by his sides. 'Father, stop this. We need to go find the assassins before they act. Mother could be in danger!'

'Silence!' Bindusara's tone had risen several levels. His colour had risen as well. 'I will not brook such impudence. Not from my son or from anyone else!'

There was a scream outside the imperial chambers. At once the four Chandikas were on their feet, hands at the hilts of their swords. Ashoka reached for his own weapon. A commotion outside as drapes parted, someone gasped, and then a woman came into the room, hands covered with blood, on the verge of panic. The Chandikas stationed on guard outside accompanied her, swords drawn, holding her bloody hands.

'Excellency! Assassins! In the First Queen's chambers!'

Ashoka was moving as soon as the woman finished. He shot out of his father's apartments and past the startled Chandikas and the blood-spattered woman. She looked vaguely familiar. But then, it may have been her Khorasani features. From her attire and manner she was probably one of Queen Mother Khorasan's inner-chamber maids. He raced out of the Emperor's palace and across the courtyard and the imperial gardens that separated it from the Queens' Palace. Dark blue-clad figures kept pace with him, swords drawn. The four senior Chandikas, relieved to be in action again but anxious that they might already be too late. Ashoka felt his own stomach clench and churn as he sprinted around a group of elderly daiimaas and their little wards, his youngest brothers and sisters. The young princes and princesses stared in awe at their elder brother and the Chandikas, running with bared weapons in the imperial palace.

Marbled floors, perfumed corridors, smoky incense, diaphanous drapes billowing... He sprinted through the Queens Palace to the detached apartments of the First Queen, luxuriantly appointed on the outside, but with a sense of the desolation and sparseness of the Khorasani steppes. There were Chandikas and Khorasani women warriors everywhere, all milling about, hostile eyes and blades in hand. Everyone turned to stare as he entered, both the Khorasani and Chandikas starting to protest at the sight of a man, then drawing back when they recognized the second prince-in-waiting. He heard raised voices behind him and saw the Khorasanis say something harshly in their brash tongue to the Chandikas behind him. He didn't stop to see what that was about, just barrelled on into the inner chambers.

He came to a halt in the First Queen's bedchamber.

Queen Noor Khorasan was sitting on a diwan, her gaze directed inwards. The floor and furnishings were spattered with blood, a lot of it. He looked down at the three bodies, trying to make sense of what he was seeing. His mind reeled, his stomach lurched, his sword hand rose and then fell, unable to decide whether to be prepared to fight or to stand down. Confusion roared in his ears.

'Traitors.'

His stepmother spoke the single word like an abuse, spitting it at the bodies sprawled on the floor. She looked up at Ashoka, her light blue-grey eyes glinting with hatred. 'All traitors, every last one of them.'

Ashoka stared down at the bodies, then up at his stepmother. Nothing made sense anymore. He lowered his sword, unable to understand the world. Everything was upside down, the sky on the floor, the ocean in the clouds, the mountains on the edge of the world, slipping sideways.

'I...' He was trying to say that he didn't understand. But the words wouldn't come out. Language had left him momentarily.

The commotion outside rose to a fever pitch. There was shouting now, and a struggle, and the sounds of swords and blades clanging but not actually fighting. The drapes billowed and

Jugni and the other seniors forced their way in. Behind them, he glimpsed the other Chandikas struggling with the Khorasani warriors, both groups aggressively shoving and arguing, on the verge of cutting and stabbing.

The Chandikas stared down at the three dead bodies, uncomprehending. He saw his own confusion reflected in their faces. He tried to find something to say but the words still wouldn't come out.

'How...?' Jugni started, then stopped. She fell to her knees, lifting up the prone corpses, turning them over to see their faces, each of the three in turn. 'These are not our Order! They are not Chandikas!'

'They wear your uniforms. They came under the guise of being posted to my apartments. They tried to kill me. It was lucky for me that my maid and I are both Khorasani warriors, veterans of a hundred battles each. We put them down like the prairie dogs they are.' Khorasan rose and went over to the bodies, kicking them as if she would kill them again if she could.

Jugni stared at Ashoka's stepmother. 'But Queen Khorasan...'

Khorasan raised her eyes to Jugni's face. 'You and your Order were behind this all. The assassination plot. The Confederacy assassins. You brought these women into our home, to kill us all. You told them to start with the First Queen and work their way downwards through the imperial family. You wanted to wipe out the entire Mauryavansh dynasty in a single day!'

A muttering of voices and parting of bodies and Emperor Bindusara entered. He took in the scene—Khorasan angrily hurling accusations, Jugni and her fellow Chandikas staring in bewilderment, the three bloody bodies dressed in Chandika blue-black uniforms on the floor—and a look came over his face. Ashoka had seen that look before. He knew what it meant. It was the look of vindication. His father liked to be proven right. And he almost always was, with rare exceptions. He was proven right today, and he was pleased.

He looked at Ashoka, and his handsome face curled in a vindictive smile.

9

Apama's heart brightened as the camp came into view. The sight of Greek colours and faces always made her feel relieved. Not like coming home, exactly, but close enough. Even though Patliputra was home and had been for the past half century, she still thought of herself as Greek, she felt Greek, she thought Greek. Patliputra was home only in the sense that she lived there. Her real home was here, amongst her people, wherever they might be in large enough numbers.

The carriage slowed to a halt. Her personal guard checked that everything was in order, exchanged a few pleasantries with the guards on duty. Apama smiled at the sound of her native language being spoken freely and openly. That was a sound she didn't hear often enough in Patliputra. Another of the many reasons why Patliputra wasn't really home. Home was a place where people spoke your language.

The curtains of her palanquin parted and a familiar face looked in. Wizened with age, blonde hair turned grey and thin, limbs reedy and bent but that smile still as warm and maternal.

'Helena!' Apama reached for and embraced the old woman warmly. 'Aphrodite watch over you! I thought you said you would never travel to this wretched land again.'

The woman shrugged as she helped Apama dismount from the palanquin. 'I go where duty takes me. And if he can endure this wretched country, so can I.'

'Even the monsoons?'

Helena made a face. 'I can take Aegyean storms, Lydian gales, even Olympian whirlwinds. But Zeus spare me from another monsoon season. I came on condition that your father would be leaving within the fortnight, long before the sky bursts open and tries yet again to wash this mud-brown land clean again and fails!'

Apama laughed as they walked the carpeted runway to the largest tent in the camp, arms hooked together. 'He couldn't do a thing without you, and he knows it. If he travels on his own, he can barely remember where he left his sword!'

'But he never forgets where he left his daughter.' The gravelly voice of her father drifted out from the interior of the tent as he turned to greet her. He bent his tall frame to kiss her on both cheeks in the Greek fashion, his breath warm and redolent of good wine. 'It has been too long, my child. Your old father misses you every day, most of all when Mercury rises in the twilight sky each evening.'

'Father, you are most welcome to visit me anytime.' She smiled coyly at him, repeating the familiar joke. 'Just remember to bring your army with you and take over Jambudwipa when you do!'

He laughed as if hearing the joke for the first time. 'I would bring down all the gods from Olympus to rescue you from that swamp of Lethe you live in. But you know the terms of the pact as well as I do.'

'You signed that pact with my husband, Chandragupta Maurya, who has been in his grave these thirty years.'

Seleucus Nicator flashed a smile, not laughing this time. 'Yes but his son is still alive, and he has an army even larger and more powerful than his father. Besides, that pact was written not by your husband, who could barely sign his name legibly, but by his priest, Kautilya. And that old brahmin knew how to draft a contract better than the shrewdest philosophers in Athens. Even my presence here is a violation of the terms. If I were to be found here, Mauryavansh would have the right to claim all my territories and holdings.'

Apama waved away his comments, accepting the glass of warm mulled wine that Helena handed her gracefully. She sank into a comfortable seat, as did her father, while Helena tended the brazier to keep the tent warm against the infringing cold of the autumn evening. 'That has never stopped you before. You know as well as I do that it will never come to that.'

'Perhaps not in the past thirty years. But Mauryavansh is stretching its wings. Your stepson's ambitions are growing. He is on a spree. It wouldn't do for him to turn his attention to my satrapies.'

'Your satrapies are too far away for him to think about, leave alone manage. To even get to them, he would have to have a stronger foothold in Takshashila and he can barely manage to keep his footing there right now.' She sipped the wine, relishing the sweet tang of berries. 'No, his attention is turned to the South and the East at present. The Southern kingdoms trouble him greatly. And Kalinga.'

Seleucus Nicator snorted. 'He has never known how to handle a republic. Anything that smells of socialist people's unions confuses him. Fool that he is. He should have finished what his father started: invaded and crushed them before they could grow to this strength.'

She arched an eyebrow. 'And you would have let him? I thought your trade ties with Kalinga were stronger than ever now. I hear that two Greek ships land in their ports every moon-month. Laden with Greek foods, wines and philosophers. And they return home with the same weight in Kalingan spices, silks and artists.'

Seleucus toasted her. 'Your grasp of politics is as astute as ever. You need only look at the map of Jambudwipa to understand the importance of Kalinga. It is a gateway to the subcontinent. And my fastest source of replenishment. It takes a land contingent thrice the time to travel back home and return than it takes Greek ships to cover the same journey via Kalinga.'

'Bassein would be better though, would it not? It is on the West Coast, and that would be a straighter line to sail for Greek ships than having to go all the way round the horn of the subcontinent.'

Seleucus Nicator nodded, drinking deeply. 'It would. And someday we shall have that port as well. But until then Kalinga serves our purpose. You know what my old friend Alexander always said: Do what you can with what you have where you are.'

'You do a great deal with what you have, father, far more than even Bindusara suspects. If he was aware of a fraction of your activities and involvement in his country, he would forget the Southern kingdoms and Kalinga both and dedicate the might of the Mauryavansh army to pushing you back beyond the Himalayas, and far beyond.'

Her father laughed, his pale blonde beard bristling. 'He would want to crush me like an eel between ships! But that will not happen because he will not find out about my activities here nor will he suspect my involvement.'

She nodded. 'He has other matters more pressing to engage him right now. There was an assassination attempt.'

Helena offered them roasted chestnuts. Seleucus Nicator cracked open one and crunched it with the enthusiasm of a man one fourth his age. 'Alexander used to say the true worth of an emperor is measured by the number of attempts on his life.'

'Except this was not an attempt on his life. It was something more than that.'

He looked at her, interested. 'Tell me.'

'The Lichchavi Confederacy sent an entire company of

assassins, undercover, to infiltrate Patliputra palace and slaughter the entire imperial family.'

His face darkened. 'Including you?'

She shrugged. 'They never got far. Bindusara's second eldest learned of the plot and rounded up the assassins. All but three who managed to slip into the First Queen's apartments and tried to kill her.'

'Interesting. Did they succeed? Those three?'

'They were killed by the First Queen and her maid, both Khorasani warriors. But here's the thing, father. They were in Chandika uniforms. And Ashoka also exposed another Chandika who was apparently a spy for the Confederacy.'

Seleucus Nicator leaned forward, blue eyes glinting in the flickering light from the brazier. 'You don't say. I thought those Chandikas swore allegiance for life.'

'They do.' She corrected herself. 'They did. Bindusara believed they were all responsible for the lapses of those four who were caught and had the entire Order disbanded.'

'Disbanded?' Seleucus asked. 'You mean—?'

She nodded. 'They face a trial tomorrow. If found guilty, they face exile or worse. First Queen Khorasan wanted them executed on the spot, but because of the Order's decades of service and the fact that it had been founded by his father, Bindusara chose to grant them a fair trial before the sabha.'

Seleucus Nicator nodded thoughtfully. 'So the most powerful inner city guard in Patliputra is removed, just like that.' He snapped his fingers. 'Big changes in your city. What else is new?'

She paused while Helena refilled her goblet. She smiled at the old lady, who nodded affectionately. Taking a sip of the wine, Apama turned back to her father. 'I finally told him about the old priest killing his mother.'

Seleucus Nicator's face slipped into a sly look. 'As we had agreed. Well done. He believed you?'

'Not easily at first. But by the time I finished, he was convinced.'

'So now he believes that Kautilya was responsible for poisoning his mother to death, and almost killing him as well.'

'Yes.'

The old Greek smiled. 'Well done. If only he knew that it was we who poisoned his mother and tried to kill him as well. And that it was the old brahmin who saved him by cutting him out of her womb in the nick of time, barely breathing, and nursed him back to health.'

'Or that Chanakya was shrewd enough to poison me with the same poison I used on Bindusara's mother.' Apama's eyes glittered fiercely. 'Causing me to lose my own son prematurely.'

Seleucus placed his hand on her thigh in a gesture that was anything but fatherly. 'Our son. Had he been born he would have been Emperor today, not Bindusara, and all this would have been Greek territory under my rule.'

She nodded, her throat working as she recalled. 'I almost lost my life—'

'But you didn't.' He squeezed her thigh. 'You survived. And raised Bindusara as your own. Despite Chanakya's objections. He couldn't expose your attempt to commit murder without admitting to his own role in killing your child, Chandragupta's legitimate first-born son, had all gone as we had planned. So he kept his mouth shut and let you become surrogate mother to Bindusara, who grew up regarding you as his own mother.'

'And now, he thinks that it was all Chanakya's doing, and he hates Chanakya now.'

'Good.' Seleucus took his daughter's free hand in his own, caressing it slowly, rubbing his long elegant fingers over her slender, shaped fingernails. 'That is important. Because Chanakya is the only one who could see through to the end of our plan, and understand our long game.'

She nodded. 'Bindusara won't be consulting Chanakya again about anything, you can be sure of that. He hates him bitterly now.'

Seleucus looked pleased. 'Then the way is clear for us to move ahead.'

She looked at him. 'Takshashila?'

He nodded. 'Takshashila. I am headed there directly. I have started building our presence there for some years as you know. Now, I will foment rebellion among the Pashtuns. They are headstrong tribes, fond of drinking and feuding. It doesn't take much of a reason to get them to take up arms.' He gestured at the wooden chests piled in the corner of the large tent. 'And with some Grecian coin to finance it, a full-blown revolution can be easily arranged.'

'So you are finally moving ahead on the plan as we have discussed before. Trouble in Takshashila will draw Bindusara away from Patliputra.'

'Exactly. Then, when the time is right, we push into Mauryavansh territories from Kalinga as well. Forcing him to fight incursions on two fronts.' He picked up a sheathed sword and used it to tap the map laid out on a table nearby. 'It's a classic crab claw tactic, and it will be especially effective because of the geography of the region. But in both cases, he will be lulled into believing they are only local uprisings.'

'And when he's engaged with both fronts, his attention divided, you will invade Patliputra.'

Seleucus closed his fist around Apama's hand. 'And burn it to the ground, that shithole of a city, erase everything that Chandragupta Maurya built in his lifetime.'

'You will have to contend with the Mauryavansh army first. That is no small challenge. Bindusara may not be the military genius his father was, but he is no novice either. He has learned from the greatest mastermind of any age after all, and Chanakya's strategies foresee every eventuality, every outcome for a hundred years or more. He will have left detailed plans on how to confront and overcome a crab pincer of the sort your propose.'

He shrugged. 'Theory is no substitute for on-the-ground experience. I have used this tactic before a dozen times, and seen my mentor Alexander use it twice as many times. Bindusara may have the book on how to counter every possible strategy but the reality will not play out exactly as he will anticipate. Timing is everything. I will lull him into believing the Takshashila problem is resolved before re-opening that front. His forces will be on their way back when I attack—or on their way to Takshashila again perhaps, I will decide that when the time comes. The point is, child of my body, I know Mauryavansh strategy because I have studied it for the better part of my life. Bindusara has never faced a threat of this magnitude by an enemy like myself. Two fronts several thousand miles apart and his capital city invaded? His army will be spread into a front thousands of miles wide. He won't know where to fight us and how. While he's busy keeping out the Takshashilans and Kalingans, we'll take his empire piece by piece and swallow it whole. Even the largest army is no use when spread too far too thin.'

Apama stood and walked over to the table, looking over the carefully drawn map. 'It is a simple yet deadly strategy. I am sure you will execute it with the ferocity of a Stygian lion bearing down on sheep in a valley. Bindusara stands no chance.'

'Still, a good general leaves nothing to chance. I will fight the battle from without. I need you to fight the battle within.'

Apama smiled, pleased at being included as an equal in his estimation. 'The enemy within the gates. I will play my part. I have already begun by fomenting doubt in his mind about his precious brahmin's intentions. Even now he must be asking himself how much of Chanakya's rules and strategies were devised with secret agendas. In time he will question every manual of warcraft and statecraft from battle strategy to sewage disposal, he will end up so confused about how to administer his empire that he will have no heart to withstand your ferocious assault. He may even decide not to put Chanakya's counter strategies in to action when you use the crab pincer.'

'That would be a great help.' Seleucus rose and walked slowly to join Apama by the table. He set his wine goblet down on the map, leaving his hands free. 'Doubting and questioning Chanakya is a big step. That brahmin's strategies and ideas were the work of genius. Even our great Aristotle would admire his brilliance. By dismantling Bindusara's trust in those ideas and strategies, you have struck a deep wound at the core of the Mauryavansh empire. He will not even know how deep the damage is until it is much too late. Or he may be too confused by his emotions to even realize his mistake at all. You have done well, Apama. I am proud of you.'

Apama beamed. 'You taught me well, father. I am only the sword in your hand. Use me as you will.'

He showed his teeth, smiling at her in a manner that was predatory more than paternal. He placed a hand on her waist, still slender and firm despite her years and her failed attempt at childbearing in her younger age. 'I will use you in every way possible. A soldier uses everything and everyone to achieve victory. There will be a great deal of bloodshed in this campaign, and much of it will be shed by family killing family. The wolf within us is always the greater danger than the wolf without. My Greek legions will hurt the Mauryavansh army in the battlefield, but the enemy still outnumbers us three to one. We have to use strategy more than military might to ensure victory.'

She placed her palm upon him, slipping it into the open collar of his blouse, rubbing it against his firm chest. White hairs rippled beneath her touch but despite his age, the flesh beneath was muscle and sinew, a soldier's body. 'Tell me what you would have me do next, I will carry out your every command. Bindusara trusts me implicitly, I can manipulate him like a puppet on a string.'

He shook his head slowly. 'No. You must not overplay your hand. You have dealt Bindusara a body blow by sowing distrust against his mentor and advisor Chanakya. Do not push your luck by over-exploiting that relationship.' As he spoke he rubbed his hand across her rear, stroking her with unfatherly caresses.

'Then what would you have me do?'

'This assassination plot has given me an idea. If used correctly, such a move can tip the balance at the crucial time, distracting Bindusara just when he should be putting all his energy into the battlefield.'

'You wish me to have him killed?'

'No. The risk is too great. If found out, you will endanger yourself. I cannot afford to lose you. You must remain loyal to Bindusara outwardly. Remember that Chanakya's spies are all around you. Never say or do anything that could be construed as contrary to the Emperor's well-being. Continue playing the part of a concerned mother looking out for her son. But within that role, seek out others who have agendas. Foment rivalry within the imperial family. Pit queen against queen. Prince against prince. Breed paranoia, distrust, hatred. Encourage enmities. If they kill one another, it will create uncertainty, fear, confusion. Foment dissent, rage, fear. The more our enemy is disturbed within his own house, the less able he is to withstand our assaults from without.'

'I understand, father. I will do as you say. It will not be difficult. Every queen mother is constantly seeking ways to move her own son up the ladder of succession. Every son is looking for ways to bring his elder brothers down so he may rise.'

His hands began moving more aggressively. 'And watch any of them that bears watching. Especially the princes in waiting.'

'I watch them closely. Sushim is no danger. Ashoka on the other hand...he is a hard one to understand. The boy is part-general, part-spy, part-soldier. Whatever Chanakya taught him in the forest, he taught him well. The oddest thing is that he seems to have no ambition. He acts as if he does not care if he ever becomes emperor.'

'Watch him the closest. Those are the ones that can be real threats.'

'I will, father.' She then sighed softly. 'When do you leave for Takshashila?'

'I break camp tomorrow at dawn.'

'Then we do not have much time. Let us make the most of it.'

'I fully intend to.' He crushed her in his grip.

10

'Maa.'

Shubhadrangi turned at the sound of her son's voice. She was walking with Queen Mother Tissyanka and her daughter Tissya in the imperial gardens. Many of the queen mothers and imperial siblings were also in the gardens. Ever since the morning's shocking events, nobody wanted to stay in their apartments. There were still rumours circulating about the possibility of assassins still being in the palace complex—nobody was quite sure whom to trust or not, and it seemed safer to stay out in public where one could see and be seen, rather than in an enclosed apartment where your own guards could try to assassinate you.

'Ashoka!' His mother embraced him at once, hugging him tightly. He hugged her back, neither caring about the jealous looks from the other queen mothers preening about in all their finery. Most of the other queens couldn't get their sons or daughters to talk civilly to them, leave alone treat them with affection. The fact that showing affection openly was considered a sign of weakness may have had something to do with it. Ashoka was a rare exception.

He held his mother at arm's length and looked at her with genuine concern. 'I'm sorry I could not come sooner. I sent a message with Radhagupta...'

'He warned me...us.' She gestured to include Tissyanka who smiled in greeting. 'But I was so worried when I heard. Is it true about the Chandikas? I can't believe it!'

Ashoka glanced around, only now aware of the keenly watching eyes. He took his mother's elbow, leading her aside behind a large flowering tree. He sat her down on the stone bench beneath the tree, mostly hidden from their audience of non-admirers. 'I can't say much here, too many...' He gestured, and she nodded at once, understanding. 'But yes, the Chandikas have been taken off duty with immediate effect. By imperial order.'

She raised a hand to her mouth in a shocked reaction. 'I can't believe it. Surely not all of them could be involved?'

Ashoka glanced around again, saw no one close enough to hear them and spoke cautiously. 'As far as I know, only one of them was actually involved. Chaand.'

His mother nodded. 'Radhagupta told me about that. It's terrible what happened to you. But you couldn't have known.'

He sighed in frustration. 'I feel like I should have, mother. She and I...we became very close.'

'Son, I understand. And I can only imagine how painful it must be for you right now. But it's obvious in retrospect that she got close to you because she was working for the enemy.'

He nodded. 'I know that. But that's the point, maa. She was

working for the enemy, that was it. There was no evidence that any of the other Chandikas were involved.'

Shubhadrangi stared. 'But the Chandikas who attacked Khorasan? The assassins?'

Ashoka grimaced. 'Assassins? I examined the bodies of the attackers. One was surely an assassin. She had the physical condition of a warrior, the scars and the concealed weapons, even a leaf of a poisonous shrub in a layer of her vastra. But the other two? I would bet my right hand they were daiimaas.'

'You mean wet nurses? How could you possibly know that? Maybe they were Lichchavi Confederacy assassins disguised as daiimaas to infiltrate the palace.'

'That would have made sense. But it was the other way around. They were daiimaas who had been killed then dressed as Chandikas to make them pass off as Lichchavi Confederacy assassins.'

She frowned, absorbing that for a moment. 'But how could you be so sure?'

He looked down in embarrassment. 'They were...nursing. You know what I mean...' He gestured in the general direction of his chest, glancing away. 'There were milk stains on the insides of their garments. And their breasts were full of...milk. Their physical condition was soft and they clearly hadn't seen a day of hard exercise in their lives. Nor did they have any sword or bow callouses, scars, fighting injuries, not even any sign of rigorous training. They were daiimaas all right. I hardly think the Lichchavi Confederacy sends wet nurses in their condition to execute daring assassinations in the heart of Patliputra. Besides, they were supposed to be Chandikas who were secretly working for the Confederacy. In that physical condition? Impossible! But even if you believe that soft, flabby, nursing mothers could somehow be Confederacy assassins posing as crack Chandika imperial guards, how do you explain the fact that not a single Chandika had ever seen either of these two before in their lives?'

Shubhadrangi's hand covered her mouth, astonished. 'So you mean to say that... They weren't assassins at all? But then why did they attack Queen Khorasan in her chambers?'

Two queens strolled by, greeting Ashoka and Shubhadrangi with nearly mocking cheerfulness. Ashoka waited till they had passed out of hearing range. Then he looked around again before replying. 'I don't think they attacked her at all. I think they were killed and then passed off as assassins. Radhagupta says one of his sources among the daiimaas reported that one of the queens had asked for two new daiimaas to interview for the job.'

'But that couldn't have been Noor. She doesn't have any children so why would she need to interview daaiimaas?'

'All the more reason for her to escape suspicion. Also, the two daiimaas had obviously been killed first and only then put into the Chandika uniforms. They were both killed by stabbing but their Chandika uniforms were not ripped in the places they should have been. The blades somehow passed through the garments without cutting them and only penetrated their flesh! And there was almost no blood where they were found, even though the wounds were enough to spill enough to fill a bucket. Which meant they were killed elsewhere, stripped of their real clothes, put into the Chandika uniforms and then posed in Queen Mother Khorasan's chambers.'

'So you mean Noor Khorasan herself—?'

'And her personal servant Orzala, yes. It had to have been the two of them. They were the only two in the chamber with the dead women.'

'But you said that one of the women was an assassin?'

'Yes, she must have been the surviving Confederacy assassin still at large. She must have come into the palace to seek further instructions. And since she was found in Queen Khorasan's chambers and because of the other inconsistencies... Well, you get my drift.'

Queen Shubhadrangi was silent. The implications were obvious. Ashoka was saying that Queen Khorasan was the member of the imperial family who had masterminded the assassination plot, and when it was on the verge of failing, she had silenced the last surviving assassin to conceal her own involvement. 'But why blame the Chandikas? This will ruin their reputation. What possible reason could Queen Noor Khorasan have for discrediting them?'

Ashoka shrugged. 'I don't understand the politics of it. That's why I came to you. I thought maybe you might make sense of it.'

'I could try but you need to take this to someone who understands the larger implications.'

Ashoka nodded. 'I intend to make a trip to see Guruji. I want to leave tonight itself. That's why I came to see you.'

'Be careful, Ashoka. Who knows what other implications there are to this situation? Be careful whom you speak to and what you say.'

'I know that. The only person I actually regret speaking to is father. When I learned about Chaand's betrayal, I needed his permission to search the palace, so I took Jugni and the other senior Chandikas to see him. But we were already too late.' He slammed his fist against his open palm in frustration. 'If only Guru Kautilya were still here in Patliputra. He would have seen through the entire plot in an instant and told us how to anticipate every move.'

'But he's not here. And your father has too many things on his mind. He doesn't see things the way you or I do. Being emperor means looking at things very differently than citizens, or even a prince or a queen.'

'I get that. But it doesn't mean being unable to see things as others do. He's just too narrow-minded to see beyond the end of his nose, that's all. He was interrogating me and the Chandika seniors instead of letting us search the palace. If he had just given his permission when we asked, we might have—' He broke off, waiting until an entourage of several of the younger queens, dressed more for an imperial occasion than for a stroll in the gardens, had passed by, studiously ignoring their older sister-queen with the uncaring arrogance of youth. 'He is suspecting all the wrong people and taking all the wrong decisions.'

'But he was right to suspect the Chandikas, Ashoka. After all, Chaand was a traitor. You discovered that yourself.'

'Yes, but only Chaand. The rest of it was just a ruse, a clever trick to shift the blame for the plot to the Order, instead of the real people behind it.'

'Are you sure of that?'

'As sure as I am that this is a plum tree and that in a few weeks ripe juicy plums will be ready to pluck and eat from its boughs.'

She smiled at the comparison. 'Even so, he had a right to be suspicious based on the evidence.'

'The evidence was fabricated. I've told you how the two other women couldn't have been assassins or Chandikas. And the one who was an assassin was never a Chandika.'

'Your father must be aware of these facts. He would have had the bodies examined too.'

'By War Marshal Khorasan! Queen Noor's own mother. Whom do you think she would side with in this matter? The Emperor of Mauryavansh or her own daugther?'

'The Emperor, I would hope, since she is War Marshal and has pledged loyalty to the Empire. I am sure she will find the same details you found and draw the right conclusions. You will see, Ashoka. Everything will turn out right in the end. Your father will see the truth and do the right thing. Trust in him. Trust in justice.'

Ashoka looked at his mother, his frustration evident as he

tried to make her see what he saw. 'Justice? There is no justice in Patliputra. Justice itself is being put on trial.'

'What do you mean? Don't speak about your own country like that. I have taught you better than that. Besides, this is no time to make treasonous statements like that, son. You have to learn to be cautious and stay loyal to the family. Family is all we have when surrounded by our enemies.'

'Mother, I'm not just saying it. No just emperor would put innocents on trial and not question the ones most clearly to gain from such a plot.'

She looked at him curiously, her plain but pleasant features creasing in a frown. 'What innocents? What trial?'

'The Chandikas. They are being tried for treason in the sabha. The trial begins tomorrow and if found guilty, they face immediate execution.'

His mother stared at him in shock. This time, she had nothing to say.

Ashoka glanced around then rose from the bench. 'I must go now. I ride for Guru Kautilya's ashram at once. If I ride all evening and most of the night I should reach him in time to consult with him and return by tomorrow evening. I came to ask you to go to the trial tomorrow and attend it. Do what you can to prevent a final verdict being reached before I return. I will be back as soon as possible with Guru Kautilya. He will know what to do and say. He will set things right. He is the only one who truly understands justice and cares about Mauryavansh. Bye, mother, take care and stay safe. I will see you soon.'

He bent and kissed her on the forehead, then hurried away.

11

Kautilya woke from dreams of Vyag. Lions, specifically. The Sanskrit word Vyag referred to all great cats: lions, tigers, leopards, panthers. Local dialects had their own terms for each species but to most people they were all large, wild cats. The old guru knew better. Each had very different qualities and characteristics. Lions hunted and lived in prides; females caring for the cubs and keeping them away from the males, who lived mostly solitary lives from the time they were grown until they aged and had to once again find a female to support them. Most of the other cats were solitary creatures, but lions had a pack mentality and that made them unique. This was the chief reason he had chosen the Lion as the symbol and mascot of Mauryavansh. Back when he had mentored a young upstart rebel named Chandragupta, grooming him to overthrow the dreaded Nanda empire, they had needed a symbol, something around which people could rally, something representing heroism, strength, power, pride, and unity. Kautilya had had a dream of Chandragupta as a silver-haired emperor seated upon a throne in a chamber surrounded by animals of every species, all warring savagely with each other in a nightmarish bloodletting. But at the head of them all sat Chandragupta, older, scarred by war wounds but powerful and calm, surrounded by Lions. Several females stood, sat or prowled around him, protecting his perimeter, while a handful of cubs sat by his feet. There were no other male lions. Kautilya had interpreted this vision as a sign. Chandragupta would be a great emperor, with many queens who would bear him sons, and no rivals, but would rule over an empire fraught with warring factions. This vision had mirrored the reality of Jambudwipa at the time, with over five hundred warring tribe kingdoms, and he had known on waking that it was the perfect symbol of not just an emperor, but of a dynasty. That was the true significance of the Lion as a symbol: family. It was the only powerful jungle-dominating predator that lived as a family, working together to hunt, survive, breed, nurture.

Today, that Lion symbol marked every official item of Mauryavansh: coinage, signage, sculptures, art, declarations. The Mauryavansh empire and the dynasty founded by Chandragupta Maurya had brought peace and unity to the five hundred tribes, and apart from the inevitable local conflicts and feuds, the entire subcontinent had accepted, even welcomed the rule of the Lion.

Tonight's dream was a sequel to that one. It disturbed him.

He emerged from his hut to something less disturbing: the familiar faces of his protégés Ashoka and Radhagupta. Both were seated cross-legged, waiting patiently for their guru to rise. The clearing outside the hut was still dusky in the pre-dawn hour, the sky above the forest tinted with the promise of first light.

'Gurudev.' Both Ashoka and Radhagupta bent low to touch their guru's feet, touching the tips of the same fingers to their chests and then their foreheads, asking his blessings to strengthen their hearts and minds.

'Ayushmaanbhava, shishya.' He blessed them both, wishing them long life. He was pleased to see them. He had grown accustomed to his isolated hermetic life here in the depths of Girvan forest, but his ties to Patliputra were strong. Not a day went by when he did not miss the bustle and hustle of the big city. He breathed deeply and exhaled through creaking lungs, remembering those glory days when he had dominated politics from the side of the most powerful man in the known world. He missed Chandragupta, his booming laugh, his carefree attitude even in the face of the most venomous threat, his amazing ability to execute Kautilya's most complex plans with physical action breathtaking to witness.

He looked at the grandson of Chandragupta now, a young man neither as handsome nor as tall and imposing as his grandfather, almost ugly in fact, and short and slender, unimposing and unimpressive to look at, barely worth a second glance on a crowded Patliputra street. But there was something to Ashoka that recalled not just Chandragupta but other great warriors and rulers Kautilya had known in his ninety-six-year lifetime. A quality of stillness, both of body and mind, that one usually saw only in the most accomplished of sages. He had known brahmins who had spent lifetimes in ghor tapasya, deep forest deprivation and transcendental meditation, to acquire that level of calm readiness. Ashoka had been born with it. The daiimaas present at the prince's birth had been alarmed at the new born child's silence, fearing still birth or disability. It had taken three slaps on the chubby buttocks to get the infant wailing, not with shock, but with outrage. They had been relieved but Kautilya had noted how quickly the crying subsided and how quiet the babe was afterwards, even as the other infants within earshot had continued bawling in solidarity.

Ashoka stood before him with the same quietness of body and spirit, his palms joined in respectful greeting. Of all his more than one hundred siblings, he was the only one who made this arduous journey to Kautilya's ashram willingly and Kautilya felt pleased. Whatever other problems Mauryavansh faced, the lack of a suitable heir was not one of them. Not the prince-in-waiting, true, but a prince-in-waiting certainly. There was hope ahead for the empire and the dynasty and that hope was named Ashoka.

Kautilya's youngest disciples heard the sound of their guru's voice and rose sleepily from the straw pallets. Rubbing the sleep from their eyes, they came to greet their guru—prostrating themselves fully as befitted their novitiate status—and rising up to offer their assistance for his morning ablutions as usual.

'Gurudev, permit me.'

Ashoka stepped forward, taking the handle of the small copper pot from one of the young brahmins. The shishya looked surprised. A prince of Mauryavansh voluntarily offering to serve his guru? The young boy looked up at Ashoka, awe struck. Kautilya rubbed the disciple's bald head affectionately. 'Gauta, not everybody needs to be told to serve their guru, some do it out of love for service.' He gave the young novice's single hair braid a flick, then made his way through the narrow path through the forest to the river. Radhagupta came with them, following closely behind.

A soft dawn breeze made Kautilya shiver a little. Ashoka noticed but said nothing. That was another of the young man's many admirable traits. Unlike his sneering elder brother Sushim, who seemed to constantly bicker and comment on everything in sight, as if it were his life's calling to criticize everything and everyone. Ashoka reserved judgement and kept his opinions to himself, invaluable qualities for a future ruler.

The sky was lightening by the time Kautilya was done with his morning ablutions. Ashoka and Radhagupta joined him in the sandhyavandana. The three of them stood waist-deep in the river, chanted the auspicious mantras, as the jungle awakened around them. Birds called out, rising in gigantic flocks hundreds of thousands strong, large as clouds, wheeling one way then another. Predators growled and grumbled in the woods as their hunting hours came to an end and they slipped down to the river for a drink of water before retiring to sleep the day away in shady nooks. Leaf and grass eaters roamed freely, entire herds passing by. Even the crowds of Patliputra seemed puny by comparison to this dense animal thoroughfare.

They returned to the ashram and partook of refreshment. Ashoka ate the meagre fruit that was offered to him without complaint. Which other prince of Patliputra would eat such simple fare without complaint? Sushim was notorious for throwing tantrums unless served a veritable feast at every meal.

Kautilya sat on the freshly swept floor of the ashram's gurukul with his two best disciples.

Ashoka summed up the events of the past few days, detailing everything that had happened from the time he overheard the two Lichchavi Confederacy assassins talking in the public house up to the apprehension of the Chandikas on suspicion of conspiracy and treason. Radhagupta filled in what he knew, adding details that only the brahmin caucus was privy to in Patliputra. Due to the deeply ingrained bigotry of the caste system of Jambudwipa, the four castes or 'varnas' as they were known operated independently of each other, similar to the way guilds operated in western kingdoms. Unlike guilds, however, caste prejudice was deep-rooted, systemic and endemic. Only rarely did brahmins and kshatriyas ally together, leave alone befriend, love, or inter-marry. A preceptor or guru's bond with his kshatriya lord was an exception but even this bond was tested when a caste transgression occurred. Kautilya had lost count of the many times he had faced the wrath of the brahmin caucus of Patliputra back when he was guru to Chandragupta Maurya. His crime was mostly that he was seen to be favouring his Emperor—a kshatriya, as all rulers had to be warriors and killers as well as meat-eaters—rather than doing what was politic for the brahmins of the Empire. It had led to his growing unpopularity with his own varna, and his eventual ouster from the power circles of the caucus, the ambitious preceptors of the most powerful tribal chiefs among the five hundred who made up the sabha that governed polity and administration for the empire. That had been a big blow, leading eventually, inevitably to his forced retirement from Patliputra, and his setting up his ashram and gurukul here in the Girvan jungle.

It was only thanks to Radhagupta and Ashoka and a network of young supporters that he had been able to maintain his ties with the empire, continuing to draw surreptitiously on the vast secret network of spies he himself had recruited and installed decades earlier, to feed him valuable information on any goings on that had bearing on the fate and future of Mauryavansh. Still, no amount of information was of use if one did not have power, or the ability to influence those with power. After decades of being the force behind the emperor, policy maker and author of the rules and laws that governed the largest empire in the known world, it was hard for Kautilya to remove himself from the nexus of power and live a rustic life in this remote jungle, but he had no choice. Even now, with his two visitors looking to him for advice and guidance, he had no illusions.

He heard them out and when they were done, he sighed.

'What do you expect of me?'

Ashoka and Radhagupta exchanged a glance.

'Don't you see, the Chandikas are innocent. It's a plot to falsely blame them for the assassination plot, to deflect attention from the real culprit.'

Kautilya regarded Ashoka, seeing his mother's features in him more and more clearly each time he saw the young man. 'All true. Everything you have concluded is correct. The Lichchavi Confederacy assassination plot was masterminded by Queen Noor Khorasan, with her mother the War Marshal either privy to the plot or actively involved with it. It would be an easy enough matter for the War Marshal to meet with the Confederacy and negotiate such a plan, offering promises and rewards if successfully achieved, with no trace of suspicion ever leading back to the Queen herself. And no matter how the plot played out, those promises and rewards would never be forthcoming of course. The Confederacy died the day it was founded. Merely by banding together to resist the Mauryavansh Empire, instead of joining us when invited, they signed their own death warrant. They make the perfect scapegoat in such a plan. If they had succeeded, the War Marshal herself could petition the Sabha and Emperor for permission to invade Lichchavi and crush them for their insolence. Since they failed... well, if they had simply failed, that would have been even simpler. But because they failed so spectacularly, leaving a burning trail pointing back to Khorasan, something had to be done.'

'Then you agree that the posing of the daiimaas as Chandikas was deliberately done by Queen Khorasan to falsely shift blame to the Order?'

'Most assuredly so. It was a brilliant move. Because of your own testimony implicating a Chandika as a traitor, your father has every right to suspect all Chandikas now. In the interests of the dynasty's safety and the empire's security, he has done exactly what could be expected under the circumstances. Do not blame him for his actions. Blame those who masterminded this devilish plot.'

'Queen Noor Khorasan. Then we must expose her.'

Kautilya regarded his young protégé. 'That is the one thing you must not do. Already you have endangered yourself by thwarting the assassination plot and exposing the link to the enemy within. If you attempt to point the finger of blame at your stepmother, she will have no choice but to act against you. And mark my words, Ashoka, she will not hesitate to use violence.'

Ashoka gripped the hilt of his sword, laid out before him on the mud floor. 'Violence is a two-edged blade.'

'I have taught you warcraft. I have guided your training as a warrior. But I have also taught you there is a time to fight, and a time to think. This is a time to think, not fight.'

'What is there to think about? Queen Khorasan plotted to kill my father and my family. She must be exposed and brought to justice.'

'Do you think she doesn't know that? She has already been two steps ahead of you. Why do you think she blamed the Chandikas for the plot?'

Ashoka frowned, not understanding.

'Because of you, my prince. Had the word of the plot come from anyone else, she would not have taken it as seriously. But when you involved yourself, she had no choice. She knew you would not simply let the Chandikas handle the matter. They would have caught the assassins and stopped the plot, and that would have been all. But you exposed the Chandika traitor, and exposed the link to Khorasan herself. That was far more than she had bargained for. She had to take drastic measures to protect herself against you.'

'Against me? But—' Ashoka trailed off, his eyes drifting as he thought through the implications of the Acharya's words.

'If she had not acted proactively, if you and the senior Chandikas had convinced your father to grant permission to serve the imperial residences, you would have apprehended the surviving Lichchavi assassin. Perhaps even caught her alive. Tell me, did any of the other assassins talk under torture?'

Ashoka shook his head. 'Not one of them made it alive to the Torture Palace. Every last one of them had a leaf of a poison herb. They managed to eat the leaves before they could be stopped. All of them died bleeding from their...their orifices.'

Kautilya looked at Radhagupta. The young brahmin nodded. 'Sweetkiller leaf. Its action is instantaneous. The leaf only grows in the Lichchavi ranges. They came prepared.'

'So this last assassin was a threat to them, she had to die.'

'But the Chandikas? Why them?'

Kautilya looked at Ashoka. 'With the Chandikas gone, who remains to prevent another assassination attempt?'

Ashoka answered slowly. 'Nobody. The Order has protected the imperial family for half a century. But with them gone...'

'The Khorasans are thinking two moves ahead. Their every action is an endgame, not merely a counter-move. They will come for you next, Ashoka.'

'If they do then they will reveal themselves, Acharya.'

'They are too shrewd for that. They will find a way to attack you without being seen to attack you themselves. You must beware danger from unexpected places.'

'I expect danger any time all the time. It is how you trained me, gurudev.'

'Good, Ashoka. But you are a warrior. They are politicians. They are capable of things you cannot foresee or understand. Always be wary of the enemy who does not abide by the rules of war. They use terror itself as a tactic. Even now, their full plan is not yet revealed. You have only ripped open a small tear in the fabric of their planning. Their true ambition remains to be seen.'

'What other ambition could they have except to control the throne of Mauryavansh? You taught me that is the ultimate game of every political player.'

'It is. But how one controls the throne can differ. One can manipulate a kingdom from behind a veil, an empire from the queens' palace. There are many ways.'

'Queen Khorasan has no sons or daughters. She can never be Queen Mother.'

'That is why she resorts to such elaborate plots and ruses. There are three chief ways she can gain control of the reins of Mauryavansh.'

Ashoka thought about it. 'Through my father. That's one. She is already his most favoured queen.'

'And bedmate.' Radhagupta coloured as soon as he had made the suggestion. 'He spends more nights in her chambers than any other queen's. Including Queen Shubhadrangi's. Pardon my impudence, my prince.'

'No need to apologize, shishya. Ashoka is no infant. He is a full-blooded young man. He has taken lovers of his own. He knows well the intimacies between men and women, men and men, women and women, and the other sexes as well. For as we know, gender is not binary. You know your scriptures. The tale of Arjuna, the tale of Mohini, our literature is replete with intimate details of sexuality. Any kshatriya or brahmin seeking to rise in the ranks of power must be intimately familiar with the details of such relationships. Especially you, Ashoka, for unless you understand every knowable aspect of human nature, how will you rule yourself, leave alone a kingdom, or an empire?'

'I stand corrected, Acharya. My celibate vows make it embarrassing for me to speak openly about such matters.'

'Don't be embarrassed.' Kautilya paused. 'You must not take your vows to seriously. Find yourself a suitable partner, male or female or otherwise, as you wish. Inform yourself in the ways and wiles of sexual liaisons. It is vital to your progress as a thinker and advisor. I have groomed you to be preceptor of Mauryavansh someday, to act as Ashoka's advisor and mentor when I am gone. In order to do this, you must know of such matters.' The old sage's black pupils twinkled with a rare gleam of humour. 'And there's nothing like a good roll on a straw pallet to relieve you of your intellectual stresses!'

Radhagupta coloured even more deeply. The young brahmin bowed his shaven pate low, touching his guru's feet, his single braid of hair flopping forward, then flying back as he straightened up. He remained wordless, not trusting himself to voice any further comments on the matter. Ashoka smiled at his discomfiture.

'So Queen Khorasan has seduced my father well. But she would need more than that to control him surely?'

'You would be surprised, young Ashoka. You may not be celibate like Radhagupta here, but you are still a novice in the art of love and war. They are often two sides of the same bed. I have seen kingdoms raised and ruined by the manipulation of a mistress, battles influenced by the rise or fall of a penis, entire kingdoms lost for the lure of a yoni. Study your Vyasa. Sex was responsible for more political upheavals in the great Mahabharata epic than anything else. It was not very different in the Ramayana either. Whether a penis or a yoni, or both, the attraction of sexual fulfilment leads people to unexpected ends, and when those people happen to be kings and queens, the ends are often epic climaxes.'

Ashoka laughed, unable to help himself.

Kautilya joined in, laughing even louder, though more hoarsely and with some wheezing.

After a moment, hesitantly, Radhagupta joined in, tittering with the other two.

Later, after they had recovered from the bout of amusement, Ashoka picked up the lost thread of the discussion. 'One way Khorasan could control Mauryavansh is through sex then. You mentioned three ways. What are the other two ways, Gurudev?'

'The second is through a surrogate. Usually a son. Mothers of kings are often as powerful as kings themselves. Even more so at times.' Kautilya was silent, thinking of something. Ashoka wondered if he was thinking of Bindusara's own mother, Dowager Queen Apama—she was the one mother that came to his mind.

'But she does not have a son. And even if she bears a son now, it will be years before he can ascend the throne.'

Kautilya inclined his head in agreement. 'He need not be her own son. All she needs is a puppet prince. Someone who needs her support to stay on the throne, and who repays her support by yielding to her political choices.'

Ashoka shook his head, confused. 'I don't follow. Is that even possible...?' He stopped, remembering. 'Of course. Dowager Queen Apama. She is not my father's real mother. Yet he regards her as if she were his birth mother.'

'Precisely. Because she raised him as her own from the day he was born. By the time he was old enough to understand the fine distinction between a birth mother and an adoptive mother, he was already bonded to her. What conversations take place between them is known to no one, not even our spies.' Kautilya looked questioningly at Radhagupta. 'Unless our spies have succeeded at last in breaching that gap. Radhagupta?'

Radhagupta shook his head. 'Nay, Acharya. We have tried but each time the Greeks or the Chandikas caught our spies and sent them to the Torture Palace. We have been unable to insinuate a new asset into the Greek apartments since the last one. They are too alert and too suspicious of any non-Greeks.'

Kautilya accepted that calmly. 'To come back to my point about Khorasan. She needs a prince to manipulate, one who needs something from her in turn. There are not many candidates worthy of her consideration. You, of course, are the prime one.'

'I?' Ashoka looked astonished.

'You underestimate your own value. You are not only second prince-in-waiting, you are the only prince of Mauryavansh actually capable of ascending the throne and follow in your grandfather Chandragupta's steps.'

'You mean my father's steps?'

Kautilya merely looked at his protégé without answering.

Ashoka nodded, understanding. The guru had said what he meant. 'But Noor Khorasan would be wasting her time. I have no desire to ascend to the throne.'

'We do not always get what we desire, and what we desire is not always what comes to pass.'

Ashoka considered that for a moment. 'There are others who would be more interested in such an alliance. Sushim for certain. Vitashoka. Taranatha. Divyadan.'

'Almost any of the princes would leap at such an arrangement.' Radhagupta agreed.

'To my mind, there are only a handful that would serve her

purpose. Ashoka has named the prime candidates. Of them, he himself and Sushim are the best of the best. Noor Khorasan is no fool. She is seeking a surrogate who will stay the course.'

'Or at least until she bears her own son to replace him.' Ashoka shrugged. 'The way Dowager Queen Satyavati ruled Kurujangala through Vichitravirya and Chitrangada, and later through Pandu and then Dritarashtra.'

Kautilya's age-creased forehead wrinkled further. 'Khorasan has no Bhishma to act as Regent. Then again, she has Jezza Khorasan, her own mother, who is no Bhishma, but is a vicious and capable War Marshal. Yes, what you say is true, Ashoka. In such a scenario she may even prefer a less likely candidate such as your brother Tissa.'

'Tissa!' Ashoka smiled at the thought of his sensitive younger sibling having any dealings with the likes of Noor Khorasan. 'She would eat him alive.'

'And that would suit her purpose well. With a Tissa, she would never need worry about his power growing too great for her to manage. And he would always be under her thumb. Some of your other brothers—Vitashoka, Divyadan, Taranatha, for instance—have many major failings, some too major to make them competent monarchs. They would turn upon her within weeks of ascending the throne, leaving her back where she started, perhaps even worse off. Vitashoka's temper and his outspoken bigotry would alienate most of the sabha chiefs. Divyadan's excessive fondness for gambling and wine make him a less than ideal choice. Taranatha's hedonistic excesses outdo even the historic orgies of Phillip of Macedonia, father of Alexander.'

Both Radhagupta and Ashoka nodded. Despite almost never having seen the young princes in question, Acharya Kautilya's assessments were picture perfect. A master of analysis, he collated all the news and information received from his pupils through the spies still loyal to the founder of their guild, and sifted the gold from the grain, using it to deadly effect at such moments. Ashoka wondered once again, for the thousandth time, what it must have been to have known Kautilya in his prime, a younger more virile and physically robust man, dominating the affairs and administration of the empire. Still, he counted himself fortunate to know him at all. It was an advantage all his siblings lacked. He would pit a single old Kautilya against a dozen Queen Noor Khorasans any time.

'It will be Sushim or Ashoka, those are my predictions.'

'What of the third means?'

Kautilya sighed and looked up at the bright morning sky now visible above the clearing. The brahmacharyas of the ashram had completed their chores and one by one had gathered round to hear the discussion between their guru and the two glamorous visitors from Patliputra. Ashoka wondered what they made of the more 'adult' parts of the discussion and recalled that to a master of knowledge like Acharya Kautilya, knowledge was never anything to be ashamed of possessing. Knowledge is neither adult nor juvenile, merely knowledge.

It was a long time before the Acharya continued. 'The third method Khorasan would use to seize control of Mauryvansh is the most direct method of all. By simply taking over, in a military coup.'

Ashoka nodded. This had already occurred to him during the discussion. 'She would announce herself as Empress? But would the sabha chiefs accept her as head of Mauryavansh?'

'No. Never. As a Khorasani, she can never be bipartisan. The appeal of Chandragupta Maurya, and the chief reason I picked him as my candidate to overthrow the Nandas and create a new empire, was his lack of association with any one tribe or gotra. He was a Maurya and the Maurya clan itself had been wiped out by Emperor Dhana Nanda during their pogrom of elimination. To support Chandragupta was to support Chandragupta himself, not a clan or tribe with multiple alliances, enemies and entanglements. That was why he was perfect to rule as the first Emperor of Jambudwipa. Bindusara was equally acceptable though his association with the Ajivika made some chiefs uncomfortable and his close bond with Dowager Queen Apama makes some Greek-haters furious, Khorasan herself included. Noor Khorasan, or any other Khorasani, would never be accepted as the Empress of Mauryavansh. The five hundred chiefs would roar with fury. The sabha would dissolve and the empire fragment before such a thing could come to pass.'

Ashoka and Radhagupta both frowned. 'Then how would she rule after a coup?'

'She would not. Not over Mauryavansh as it exists today. She knows that. The Empire would fragment and the sabha dissolve. Without a ruler strong enough to hold it together, that is inevitable. Khorasan would seek military allies, anyone strong enough to join her in carving up the body of Mauryvansh, taking a choice portion for herself, leaving the rest to her allies. They would be like dogs tearing apart the body of the empire, each chewing their own haunch of bleeding flesh.'

'Who would ally with her?'

'There are many powerful armies resistant to Mauryavansh even now. None individually strong enough to stand up to our might alone, but allied with Khorasan, and backed by a single giant power, they would suffice to create an alternate power structure. The map of Jambudwipa would be redrawn, creating new states, new borders, a new empire.'

'This giant power. Whom do you mean, Acharya?'

'There is only one military force strong enough to challenge Mauryavansh. Allied with Khorasan and those few dozen chiefs disgruntled enough to throw in their lot, it would not match up to the empire your grandfather and I created, but it would still be a formidable political power.'

'The Cholas. The Chalukyas. Ujjain. Takshashila. Kalinga. The Lichchavi Confederacy.' Ashoka reeled off several names of several other smaller states that continued to resist the empire in overtly aggressive or less overt ways. 'But none of them is a giant power.'

'Nowhere near. There is only one giant in the subcontinent apart from Mauryavansh. Your grandfather and I successfully kept it at bay, though I always advised him to push all the way north and crush it completely, chase its dregs like a beaten cur with its tail between its legs, all the way back home to Macedonia. But your father was in a generous mood. He had already built the greatest empire in the known world, larger even than the one that Alexander had ambitiously sought to create through conquest. And his big heart was further softened when he fell in love with the daughter of the leader of that giant enemy force.'

Ashoka and Radhagupta exchanged a glance. Both knew whom their guru was speaking of. Seleucus Nicator, father of Apama, satrap of the armies of Alexander that had been left behind to administer the territories conquered by the late Macedonian emperor. The satrap had since become an emperor in his own right; though he retained the token title of satrap, his territories were known as the Seleucid Empire now.

'But the Khorasanis hate the Greeks.'

'Politics makes enemies friends, if only for a while.'

Ashoka absorbed this. Khorasan, Seleucus Nicator...He groaned. 'My head hurts. I wish she would only pick up a sword and attack openly. All this subterfuge is so complicated and confusing.'

Kautilya looked sombre. 'The sword will come soon enough. But it will not be held in her hand. Nor will it come at you openly.

But nevertheless it will come soon, when you least expect it, and from the most unexpected direction. Watch your back, Ashoka. And watch every side as well.'

12

Ashoka and Radhagupta rode back in silence to Patliputra. The sun was still low in the morning sky, but to Ashoka it felt like the day was already ending. A dusky quiet lay over the jungle pathway as their mounts trotted leisurely, picking their way through the wooded path. Kautilya had categorically rejected Ashoka's suggestion that he return with them to the city to argue on behalf of the Chandikas. 'There is nothing to be gained from arguing the inarguable.' Ashoka was deeply disappointed. He blamed himself in part for the plight of the Chandikas. It was he who had gone to them when he first heard the Confederacy assassins in the public house, he was the one who had exposed the traitor in their ranks, and he who insisted they go to his father to seek permission to search the imperial family apartments. Aside from the pain of having to kill his own lover, Chaand, even if it was in self-defence, he now faced the guilt of knowing that he had played a hand in precipitating this crisis.

Radhagupta sensed the tone of his thoughts. 'Acharya was right. You are blameless in this matter. You did what was right. It is not your fault that Queen Khorasan framed the Chandikas for the assassination plot. It was masterfully done. You are lucky that you did not get caught up in her web of lies and deceit too. Do not berate yourself for things you could not have anticipated or prevented.'

Ashoka manoeuvred his mare around an overhanging branch, ducking low to slip beneath the clawing fingers of the bough. 'But we could still do something. The sabha session starts at noon. If Acharya had agreed to return with us to Patliputra.'

'Ashoka, gurudev may not have wished to explain himself in detail about his refusal to come to sabha, but I can tell you that he was right to do so.'

Ashoka glanced back at the young priest. 'How could he be right when he is the only one who could persuade the sabha chiefs to show clemency to the Chandikas? Without him, I stand no chance of swaying them. I have asked my mother to do what she can to delay the verdict until we return, but it will not matter now. Without Acharya to speak, nobody will listen to her or to me. Father will make his usual thundering speech, War Marshal Khorasan will lie about the evidence to cover up her daughter's plot, and the sabha chiefs will vote with their swords. The Chandikas are certain to be exiled. Guruji could have prevented that! Only he can do that!'

'Not anymore. You are thinking of Acharya Kautilya of yore. The legendary architect of Mauryavansh, the brightest light of his age. That light has long since dimmed. The sabha chiefs would shout him down deafeningly if he stood before them now. Your father would be enraged, and with good reason. The age of the brahmin is past. It is the age of kshatriyas now. The time of the sword and the warrior. Reason, logic, common sense, dharma, none of these count for much anymore. Only violence speaks, and when it opens its fanged jaws, Vishnu preserve us from destruction.'

Ashoka guided his horse carefully down a stony sloping stretch, the loose pebbles skittering underfoot. 'I don't accept that. He is still Kautilya! The greatest mind of all time. His time can never be past. The sabha will see that. Father will see that. They must. The Chandikas have to be saved. They do not deserve to be punished for crimes they never committed. It is injustice.'

'There is always injustice, Ashoka. That is why we crave justice so deeply. Because there is darkness, we desire light. Injustice is the norm, it is dharma that is the exception. That is why evil proliferates and good men are so few in number. You are a good man, Ashoka. A good son and a loyal subject of Mauryavansh. But you cannot fight everyone alone. This crisis is beyond your ability to resolve. The fate of the Chandikas is no longer your responsibility or concern. Leave it be as Acharya said. Watch out for your own safety. You have made powerful enemies in the family now. You are within their ken. Like hawks from an eerie, they watch you now, marking your every move. Do not yield to your impulses. It will make you predictable and vulnerable. Stay aloof, resolute, mask your true emotions and intentions. Keep them wondering what you mean to do next, lead them to believe one thing, then do another instead. Show affection to your enemy and neglect your friend, so they will mistake one for the other.'

Ashoka snorted. 'I know how the game is played. I hate the game.'

'You are a prince of Mauryavansh, you have no choice, you were born into this game. It ends only when you end.'

Ashoka knew better than to argue the point.

They rode in silence for the next few miles. The path wound through the forest, passing close by other ashrams including the famous Kulapati Shaunaka ashrama where the sage Ugrasarava Sauti had narrated his guru's epic poem Mahabharata once in another age. The ashrama still flourished, each successive Maharishi taking pride in maintaining the tradition of Kulapati—literally, 'teacher of ten thousand minds'. Ashoka mused on the irony that an ashrama whose founder had died some thousand years earlier still enjoyed such great popularity while his own guru lived his last years in obscurity in a tiny five-hut ashram less than thirty miles away. The injustice of it infuriated him. He could not understand how people could fail to recognize the value of things that mattered, while giving importance to so many irrelevant and pointless pursuits. Wine? It was good to make one feel relaxed sometimes, but the way his siblings guzzled it down, often to such excess that they spent their waking minutes vomiting out the night's consumption, was disgusting. Sex? It was a pleasurable pastime, but the way the imperials went at it, one would think it was a necessity rather than a pleasurable indulgence. Food? Now there was a necessity, but people ate such vile things, and to such excess that it sickened him just to be in their presence. One could only eat so much. Anything more was just more shit for the gardens! In fact, no matter how lavish the feast or precious the delicacy, it was all going to turn to the same shit eventually. He enjoyed his food, especially after a hard day, or a good morning's training, or fighting, but he couldn't fathom the obsession some of his queen mothers and siblings had with procuring the rarest sweetmeats and delicacies and making a huge ceremony out of their consumption.

To sum up, he didn't understand his family. All they seemed to care about were what to wear, what to eat and drink, whom to fornicate with, and how they could outdo one another. But when it came to things that really mattered, like the plight of the poor who often went hungry at night, or those too maimed or crippled to work for a living, or injustices like the one facing the Chandikas, nobody seemed to care. A ruler should care. They should know what was important and what was not. They should root out injustice and stand for something. Not merely spend their lives in a stupor of intoxicated ecstasy and excess.

He was still fuming and seething when the sound of approaching hooves distracted him. Radhagupta had already stopped and was staring intently, trying to see the approaching riders. Ashoka reined in his mare and placed his palm flat on the trunk of a walnut tree. 'Soldiers, from Patliputra.'

'How could you possibly know that from a tree?'

'Three riders, coming fast, strong fresh horses. They can't be brahmins riding to one of the forest ashramas. So I assume they're soldiers sent to fetch us for some reason.'

He waited, letting the mare chew on some dewy grass. The riders came in sight a few moments later, reining in as they caught sight of Ashoka and Radhagupta.

Ashoka recognized one of the men from his riding stance when he was a hundred yards away. Dwadesh, his training partner. As they came close enough to show their faces, he recognized the other two as well, also from his morning training sessions in the yards. They were young boys, novices in training.

They drew up before him, saluting smartly. 'Prince Ashoka. Your brother has sent for you.'

'You will have to be a little more specific. I have a lot of brothers.'

Dwadesh grinned, glancing at his companions. 'First Prince Sushim.'

'I'm on my way back to the palace. I'll see him there.' Ashoka took up his reins.

Dwadesh held up his hand. 'Prince Sushim has already left the palace, he's on his way.'

'On his way where?' This conversation was irritating Ashoka. He had just been fuming about his brothers and their excesses. Sushim was the worst of them. First in every respect: debauchery, excess, addiction, wastefulness, assholery. The last thing he wanted to hear about was his spoiled arrogant brother's travel plans.

'To Girvan. To hunt.'

That was typical of Sushim. When he wasn't fornicating, feasting, hosting dog fights and other animal or human-abusive blood sports, he was off to the jungle, returning home with wagonloads of slaughtered beasts.

'So?'

'He has asked for you to join him.'

Ashoka snorted. 'I have no time to waste hunting with Sushim. He can slaughter deer and rabbits on his own. I am headed back to Patliputra. Now, if you could move from my path, my companion and I will continue on our way. The sabha session begins at noon and I have things to do before that.'

Dwadesh glanced at his companions, then at Radhagupta. 'Yuvraj,' he said, using the proper Sanskrit title for a prince—literally 'young king'. 'It is not a request, it is an order.'

Ashoka stared at the young soldier. 'An order? Since when do I take orders from my own brother? When he's emperor he can order the whole empire, but until then, he has no authority over me.'

Dwadesh nodded, showing that he agreed with Ashoka but also apologizing for arguing the point further. 'The order comes not from Yuvraj Sushim but from the Samrat.' He used the formal Sanskrit term for Emperor, once again underlining that he was conveying official orders. 'Samrat Bindusara himself instructed War Marshal Khorasan to send out a party to escort you to the site of Yuvraj Sushim's hunting expedition.'

'War Marshal Khorasan? Is it a hunting expedition or a war party?'

'Since the Chandikas are no longer on duty, the security of the imperial family is now the War Marshal's responsibility.'

'That is as per protocol,' Radhagupta said. 'You should abide by the imperial order.'

Ashoka felt like laughing but the laughter would have been a bitter outburst. 'An imperial order to attend a hunting expedition? The War Marshal sending out an escort to ensure he went along? Is that protocol too, Radhagupta?'

The young brahmin offered no reaction. 'The imperial family

did face a major crisis yesterday. The Emperor is only doing what he must to ensure their safety.'

Ashoka read between the lines of Radhagupta's noncommittal response. The brahmin had been trained in politics by the inventor of diplomacy himself. He was advising Ashoka not to express himself too freely in criticism of his father or imperial protocol. Ashoka understood the wisdom in that but he felt frustrated by this unexpected development. 'I need to attend the sabha session. I was the one who discovered the Confederacy assassins and the Chandika spy, I am a key witness in the trial. My attendance there is more important than accompanying my brother on one of his—' He paused. He had been about to say slaughter fests. He amended that now. '—hunting expeditions.'

Dwadesh nodded as if he had anticipated this argument. 'The War Marshal said to inform you that the trial today would be a closed session. Only essential persons are to attend. You are not on the list of attendees.'

Ashoka stared blankly at the soldier, reminding himself that he was only the bearer of the news, not the issuer. 'That makes no sense at all. I have to be there! I was a first-hand witness. I saw things, I heard things—I killed three conspirators myself. They need to hear from me before taking any decision.'

Dwadesh spread his hands. 'Yuvraj... Ashoka. We have trained together, played together. You are the only prince we,' he inclined his head to indicate his companions, 'consider a true friend. Everyone admires you hugely for the way you dealt with the assassination plot. We all feel for the Chandikas and what they're going through. But this is beyond you now. The Emperor, War Marshal, sabha chiefs, they have their own ideas on how to deal with the situation and they aren't going to listen to you or anyone else.'

'I can make them listen.' Ashoka tempered his tone, appealing to Dwadesh's friendly overture. 'You know me well enough to know that I am a friend of the common soldier. The Chandikas were only doing their job. They should not be punished for it. The traitor in their Order was an exception, she is dead now. The rest of them are blameless.'

'Ashoka,' Dwadesh said. 'My friend and I, we split off from the main party and rode ahead, just so we could warn you. The main escort party is only a few more minutes behind us, they will be here at any time. They are heavily armed and have orders to escort you to the hunting site, using whatever force necessary. You can't fight them. You can't challenge an imperial order. You can't battle your way alone into other sabha session. War Marshal Khorasan has ten thousand soldiers guarding the city and the palace right now, with another forty thousand on call in the city barracks. This is not the time to challenge the power of Patliputra. Come with us, we will take you straight to the hunting site, we'll get there ahead of the main escort if we move right now. You can avoid any conflict or unpleasantness.'

Dwadesh ended his long appeal by holding out an open hand to Ashoka. It was a gesture of friendship and support, of respect and affection. Ashoka looked at the young soldier's face and then at his companions, finally at Radhagupta.

Radhagupta inclined his bald head, concurring.

Ashoka took Dwadesh's hand and pressed it in acceptance and thanks. Dwadesh's eyes flashed a relieved smile. His companions relaxed and sighed as well. That response showed Ashoka how close he had come to risking everything. Without another word of protest, he turned the head of his horse and jerked his head to indicate that the soldier should lead the way.

There is a time to fight, and a time to think. This is a time to think, not fight.

13

Queen Shubhadrangi and Queen Tissyanka were greeted by a number of sharp looks when they walked into the sabha hall together. A small flurry ensued among the Khorasani guards that were stationed at the doorways and throughout the large chamber. Tissyanka reached out, took hold of her sister queen's hand, and squeezed it tightly. Shubhadrangi smiled back at her. She was grateful for Tissyanka's company. This was one occasion where she did not wish to be alone. She had a feeling she was going to be isolated enough as it was. The imperial palace had been buzzing all morning with word on the sabha session. There had been closed-door meetings amongst several groups of sabha chiefs all night and all this morning as well. There hadn't been such excitement around a sabha session in years. Something big was coming and the sinking feeling in her belly told her it was not going to be a very good something.

'Queen Shubhadrangi, Queen Tissyanka.'

The words were curtly spoken in a Khorasani accent. Even before she turned around, Shubhadrangi knew the speaker from the tone itself. However adamant the Khorasani guards may be, they dared not address a queen curtly. She turned to see, as expected, the weathered face of War Marshal Jezza Khorasan.

'This is a closed session of the sabha. You are not permitted to attend. I will have you escorted out at once.' She turned away and gestured to two Khorasani guards who hurried forward, spears held in the resting position, points aimed upwards.

'Most certainly not,' Queen Tissyanka said, equally curt. 'We are fully authorized to be here.'

'Yes we are,' Shubhadrangi added, her heart thudding.

War Marshal Khorasan looked at each one of them in turn,

taking her time. 'Queens are not permitted to attend this session. Even if you were, the queens gallery is up there.' She raised the hilt of her baton to indicate the upper galleries, the gesture serving to also remind them that the baton was a sign of her right to enforce the law by any means necessary. Shubhadrangi had seen her beating one of her own soldiers who had dozed off on duty once; it had not been a pretty sight. 'You have no place here in the main sabha hall.'

'Where else are sabha chiefs supposed to sit during the session?' Shubhadrangi heard herself ask, pleased at the calmness of her own voice despite her thudding heart.

Jezza Khorasan blinked once. 'Sabha chiefs?'

'Yes.' Tissyanka's voice was a little more breathy than normal, but still calm. 'We are here representing our respective kingdoms. I am here as sabha chief of Tissar.'

'And I as sabha chief of Sapramelu.'

The War Marshal looked at each of them in turn. Her leathery features betrayed no emotion, but her small grey eyes were focused now, whereas earlier they had been roving the hall, more concerned with her duties managing the security than with two trespassing queens. She was taking them seriously now, that's for certain. 'I see.' Her tone suggested that she didn't see at all, and what she saw, she didn't like. She turned her gaze to Tissyanka. 'Queen Tissyanka, your father is Chief of the Tissar nation.'

'And in his absence, I am the next in line of succession. He is unable to attend due to a pressing situation in our home kingdom. I am here in his stead. The Tissar seat is right over there, in the third row—'

'Yes, I am aware of the seating allocations. Queen Shubhadrangi, is your father also unable to attend this session?'

'My father is dead.' She was looking at Khorasan's face when she said it and saw no reaction. The War Marshal was well aware that she was an orphan; it was her job as War Marshal to know the heads and line of succession of every single one of the five hundred kingdoms. *She's deliberately taunting you by pretending you don't matter enough for her to remember your family. Don't rise to the bait.* 'My aunt serves as queen of the kingdom, and yes, she is unable to attend this session, which leaves me as the highest ranking member of the Sapremalu Tribe and Kingdom to attend—'

War Marshal Khorasan turned away before Shubhadrangi could finish speaking. Without another word, she walked away, the two guards going with her. Shubhadrangi and Tissyanka watched as the tall gaunt woman moved through the crowds of sabha chiefs milling about the vast hall.

Tissyanka made a face. 'Well, that's over.'

'Let's take our places. The session is about to start.'

They moved through the crowd together, hearing snatches of conversation on all sides as they sought out their respective seats. They were several rows and seats apart, unfortunately, but because of the circular arrangement of the seating, Shubhadrangi was pleased to see that she could turn her head and see her friend anytime she wished. She turned to squeeze Tissyanka's hand one last time before they parted. Most of the sabha chiefs were male, perhaps a 3:1 ratio, which was typical, since many of the newer tribal kingdoms favoured patriarchal rule over the traditional matriarchy of the subcontinent. These men were almost always large, hairy, bearded, smelly and rude, even arrogant. She was jostled hard several times and once felt a probing hand seeking to find a suitable place to pinch her from behind—she had been prepared for such behaviour and caught the offending fingers, twisting them back hard enough to feel a knuckle crack. The owner of the fingers swore behind her and then cursed again as he backed into another, taller man, the top of his head connecting with the other chief's jaw. She smiled as the two men exchanged abuses in their respective dialects, not bothering to look back at either one. She took her seat without further disturbance and sighed. It had been a very long time since she had attended a sabha session as a delegate. She liked the responsibility and power she felt but wished she was doing so under less gruelling circumstances.

'Attention! Attention! The Emperor is in the sabha!'

The criers called out the alert in high speech Sanskrit, repeating it in the Sanskrit-derivative common speech Pali and Prakrit dialects. The bustle of the sabha hall quietened as the chiefs turned to watch the Imperial convoy enter from the guarded entrance that led directly to the Emperor's Box. The Box itself was a canopied hexagonal wooden podium overlooking the sabha hall. Half a dozen Khorasani guards took up positions at the six points, armed with bows and arrows, each with an arrow already in hand, ready to loose at the sign of any aggression. Three additional guards guarded the Emperor's sides and rear, armed with drawn swords. War Marshal Khorasan herself stood directly below the podium on the sabha floor, her piercing grey eyes sweeping the hall in search of any suspicious movement or behaviour. The galleries above the hall, usually reserved for queens and wives of chiefs, were empty of spectators, but Shubhadrangi glimpsed the black and red uniforms of Khorasani guards positioned there, pointing throwing spears down at the five hundred chiefs. Was such intense scrutiny really necessary? Surely Bindusara was not expecting one of the chiefs to attack him right here in the hall!

'Are you afraid of us now?' This was shouted by a bearded giant of a man. She couldn't tell which tribe he was from but it was one of the western kingdoms, judging from the way he wore his anga vastra and dhoti, and the caste marks on his forehead. 'Do you think we are the enemy?'

Bindusara ignored the chief as he took his seat on the throne, adjusting his posture to suit his comfort. 'In the past few days, we have been betrayed. The security of Patliputra was compromised by those we trusted the most. The assassination plot had deep connections in the imperial palace itself. War Marshal Khorasan's security measures are intended to protect us from any further attack.' Without looking at the western chief who was still standing in place, awaiting an answer to his challenge, Bindusara continued in a hard tone. 'Anyone who challenges us at this time of crisis, is against us. All threats to Mauryavansh will be dealt with swiftly and conclusively. We were betrayed once. It will not be permitted to happen again. Either stand with us, or die opposing us. The choice is yours.'

He let the words sink in.

After a brief hesitation, the challenger took his seat again. But Shubhadrangi saw War Marshal Khorasan looking pointedly at one of her lieutenants standing near his row and signing to in some kind of code, giving her subordinate an instruction. The Khorasani lieutenant nodded once, acknowledging the order, and positioned herself in such a manner that the offending heckler would have to pass her in order to exit the hall after the session. Shubhadrangi guessed that the chief in question would have to answer some stern questions about his loyalty to the empire before he was allowed to leave the imperial grounds that day.

She exchanged a glance with Tissyanka who shook her head slightly while fluttering her eyelashes, a reaction which Shubhadrangi knew meant 'what is happening?'. She was wondering the same thing herself.

'The events of the past days have made us aware of the shortcomings in our security arrangements. The Lichchavi assassination attempt was a bold, brash attempt to challenge the supremacy of Mauryavansh. The Confederacy of Lichchavi Tribes were foolish not to have joined the Empire during the time of consolidation. Now, they have dared to attack our sovereignty openly. This leaves us with no alternative. This kind of behaviour cannot be tolerated or permitted to occur again. An example must be made of them and quickly. Our first order of business is to launch a war campaign to end all resistance in the Confederate tribes and integrate their lands into the Mauryavansh Empire. War Marshal Khorasan shall lead the 9th Akshohini herself in this campaign. It will be a short, sharp deployment. She estimates that it will take no more than one masa to crush all resistance in the Confederacy and assert our sovereignty over their territories.'

Shubhadrangi glanced around covertly, examining the faces and reactions of the chiefs within easy sight of her position. As she swivelled her gaze, she sensed a pair of eyes watching her and cut back just in time to see the War Marshal watching her. The Khorasani general's grey eyes bored with a disturbing intensity into Shubhadrangi's face for a moment before passing on. Shubhadrangi felt her skin crawl with unease. She restricted her observances to whatever she could see just by moving her eyes around, keeping her posture and head as still as possible. Every single other chief she saw was doing the same, she noted. She wondered how many were as unwilling to be scrutinized as intently by Jezza Khorasan, and had adjusted their behaviour accordingly.

'Let us put the battle campaign for acquisition of Confederacy Territories to a vote now. On the matter of Mauryavansh ending resistance from Lichchavi Confederacy rebels and using military action to integrate the Confederacy tribes into the Empire, how say you?'

The ensuing thump startled Shubhadrangi even though she knew that voting was always done by slapping one's hand down on the table once. The combined echo of five hundred chiefs slamming down their meat palms on their tables made a deafening sound, like a sal tree trunk cracking in a river. She moved her hand belatedly, miming the action of voting in favour and hoping that her slowness hadn't been noted. She had reservations about the methods Khorasan would use against innocent civilians in the Confederacy tribes who might not have anything to do with the assassination plot or the conspiracy, but on the overall question of how to deal with the threat, she was completely in agreement with Bindusara. Those assassins had sought to infiltrate her house, to kill her family. She had no qualms about voting to do what was needed to prevent them from launching any further attempts.

'Those in dissent?'

Bindusara waited. Shubhadrangi did not want to turn her head to examine the rows behind her, but from what she could see, not a single hand was raised to challenge the vote.

'Unanimously passed: The campaign is approved and War Marshal Khorasan is authorized to proceed as she sees fit. Mauryavansh anticipates your success, Chief Khorasan.'

Remaining exactly where she was, the War Marshal replied. 'I shall bring you the heads of those who plotted against us and the territories of the Confederacy, within the allotted time.' She did not pause her scrutiny of the sabha hall as she spoke these words. She might as well have been saying thank you and good day to someone in passing on a city street.

Bindusara continued. 'Our next order of business concerns the Order of the Chandikas. As you all know by now, the Order was created in my father's time to protect the Emperor and the imperial family against any threat. It served him well and continued to serve its function for some time after his passing. But as recent events have shown, that long tradition has been irreparably damaged by the betrayal of its members and their treasonous actions against our imperial safety. These were not dissident tribes seeking to attack us, they were the very persons we trusted with our own security turning against us. When a dog bites the hand that feeds him, no matter how long and loyal that dog's service, he must be put down at once. There is no forgiving or condoning such treason and betrayal. The Chandikas must be dealt with swiftly and decisively. They must be given the same punishment that any treasonous traitor would expect. No special treatment or excuses can be made for their unconscionable actions. The verdict I propose for them is mass execution, said sentence to be carried out at once, in full view of the public as an example of how Mauryavansh deals with traitors and assassins.'

'Your Excellency!'

Shubhadrangi's hearts stopped as the voice rang out. It was her own voice, speaking loudly and plaintively. She felt every pair of eyes in the sabha turn to look at her incredulously. She knew that the War Marshal was staring at her too. And that more than one of the bows and spears of the Khorasani guards were now trained upon her chest, ready to loose at the slightest hint of any sign of aggression. She was careful to keep her tone neutral, her voice level. She knew she had to speak out, but she had no wish to earn an arrow or a spear through her heart as a penalty for saying the wrong thing or using the wrong tone of voice.

Bindusara lowered his gaze to focus on her. She saw his eyes flicker as he saw her for the first time amidst the sea of five hundred faces. She knew from that flicker that he was not pleased by her presence but did not want to let his irritation show to the rest of the sabha. She kept her features composed and her voice calm. 'What of the trial of the Chandikas?'

The instant she had spoken, she wished she could rephrase the question. She had tried to be as brief as possible, knowing that the more she spoke, the more it would be construed as a challenge. But what came out sounded too terse to her own ears. She had voiced it evenly, intending it to merely be a question rather than an argument. But hearing it echo in the sabha hall, she understood that there was no question that was not an argument. The very act of asking it made it a challenge. Inwardly she cringed, but there was nothing she could do about it now. The question was out there.

Bindusara took a moment to draw in a deep breath, glancing down at his table as if referring to some scroll or other object that was of pressing importance. There was no such object or scroll but she understood that he was using the pause to give himself the opportunity to control the rebuke he would have given anyone else.

'A trial would be superfluous in the face of such overwhelming evidence. War Marshal Khorasan has investigated all the facts of the matter, examined all witnesses and suspects, and her conclusions are inarguable. The Chandikas committed treason, conspired against the Empire and plotted to assassinate one or more members of the imperial family. Even if there had been any doubt of their guilt, which is not the case, as Emperor I possess the authority to issue a summary command to execute any such behaviour without waiting for the sabha's ratification. This was not a political decision. It is a simple matter of self-defence. They threatened my family, they pose a continuing threat to my family, and as such, I have the right to end that threat immediately in the interests of self-preservation.'

He paused and looked at her sharply. 'And since it is you, Second Queen Shubhadrangi, who poses the question to me, perhaps I might remind you that you yourself are part of that same family, and as such, facing the same threat from these assassins.'

Shubhadrangi hesitated. Bindusara had already composed his face again to his patented wooden face, revealing no further emotion. She knew that her question had been stoutly answered and that his response was beyond any further argument. She sensed Tissyanka watching her with an expression of concern, openly worried for her now. She knew she should shut up and be still and not draw attention to herself again.

But Ashoka had told her to delay the proceedings until he arrived, or for as long as she possibly could. It was important to him. Very important. He would probably be back at any moment. Perhaps he was making his way up through the imperial complex even now, and would be entering the sabha hall any instant. He had come to her asking for her help in this matter and she had agreed to give it. She had not expected there to be no trial or for the sabha session to be little more than a ratification of decisions already made by Bindusara. And by War Marshal Khorasan, this had her mark all over it. A trial would have allowed for the sabha chiefs to raise any questions they had about the evidence or the witnesses. That was the normal process of justice, as laid down by Acharya Kautilya's Artha Shastra laws. She had not expected there to be no trial at all, no due process, merely a sentencing by the Emperor. It would not be possible for her to prolong this much longer. But she could not simply sit quiet after asking just one question. She had to say something, do something to delay this proceeding until Ashoka came.

'Your Excellency, it is as a member of the imperial family that I speak. As you know, it was my son Ashoka who uncovered the assassination plot and the conspiracy, and drew the attention of the Chandikas to it. He even killed two of the Confederacy assassins himself. And later, when he discovered that one of the Chandikas was involved in the conspiracy, he was quick to summarily execute her on the spot as well.'

Bindusara was glaring at her. Not just looking, or staring. He was making his displeasure plain for all to see. 'The Second Prince served the Empire well. Now, if you have finished singing his praises, we shall proceed with the business of the sabha.'

'Pardon my asking, Your Excellency, but is it not the business of the sabha to inquire for ourselves into the details of this conspiracy?'

'Details?' Bindusara's forehead creased with a matting of irritation.

'The Chandikas are an old and venerated Order, trusted by your father and yourself for over half a century. They live to serve the imperial family and the Empire. How were they corrupted and why? Surely understanding the causes behind their betrayal can only help us prepare ourselves against such lapses in years to come. It is for the purpose of educating ourselves that I ask these questions. That is my only intention.'

'To educate yourself.' Bindusara's tone was sceptical and impatient. 'If you wish, you may consult with War Marshal Khorasan at her convenience and educate yourself on all the trivial details of the matter. For now, the Sabha has important business to conclude and cannot indulge your petty curiosities.'

His tone said everything his words left out, casting the implication that she was asking these things only because she was, of course, a woman.

She knew better than to be irritated by that chauvinism; but she did take it as a sign of his impatience with her speaking out of turn yet again. It was his way of saying, 'Shut up now, or I will stop treating you as my wife and start treating you as I would any other chief here'. The reference to seeing War Marshal Khorasan was a veiled threat, and she knew it but she was desperate now. None of this was going as she'd expected. She'd known it would not be easy to keep the session going till Ashoka came, but she had not been expecting to expose herself to a charge of treason just for asking a question or three.

She tried frantically to think of something else to say that would not sound offensive, challenging or threatening to his male ego. She could not. Her mind was a blank. Already she was aware that several sabha chiefs were staring at her, some leering as they watched what they probably thought was a domestic quarrel being enacted in public. She could almost imagine the boorish thoughts that were going through their thick skulls: 'Emperor of Mauryavansh but he can't rule his wife outside the bed chamber.' She didn't care about that. Men were men, to hell with them. She cared about doing what Ashoka had asked her to do. But there were no more questions left to ask, no more ploys left that would delay the sabha session any further.

Bindusara was about to continue when a female voice spoke up unexpectedly, interrupting him yet again.

'Who will take their place?'

Shubhadrangi's eyes cut to where Tissyanka was seated, at the Tissar table. Her sister queen had come to her rescue. She could hug Tissyanka! Suddenly, the attention that had been focused on her had shifted across the hall to the Tissar table. Shubhadrangi was instantly forgotten. There was good reason for that. While Shubhadrangi came from a small, almost-non-existent tribe with no real power, influence, wealth or military strength, just a few handful of families scattered across Jambudwipa, Tissar was a nation of some importance. A substantial treasury with a steady, even good income from taxes and trade earnings, and a sizeable military force. Wealth and power, the two things that mattered to anyone in this hall, were always more interesting than domestic differences.

Tissyanka's question was a good one too, better than anything Shubhadrangi would have thought of. She was still thinking like Ashoka, looking to delay or derail the sentencing of the Chandikas. Tissyanka had taken an altogether different tack. By asking who would replace the Chandikas she had moved past the topic of the trial, avoided questioning the Emperor on his lack of due process, and simply posed a relevant question that showed respect for his judgement and enquired what he had planned next.

Bindusara turned to look at Tissyanka, the criss-cross matting on his forehead easing. 'The Khorasani guard are the best qualified for the task. I have decided to appoint them as the imperial guard with immediate effect.' He gestured, indicating the Khorasani guards already posted around the sabha hall. 'They shall act as personal bodyguards to the imperial family as well as protect the Imperial Capital, to ensure that any further attempts against Mauryavansh are quashed before they become a threat, rather than attempting to deal with them after they arise.' He continued to address Tissyanka but his next words were clearly intended for Shubhadrangi. 'We must ensure that our enemies never dare to even think of Patliputra as a nesting ground. And the way to do that is to make the city inhospitable to all such enemies. Better to crush the serpent's eggs in the nest rather than wait for the cobra to rear up and strike.'

This last was a quote from Acharya Kautilya himself, and Shubhadrangi understood that it was intended to drive home the point that both the long-retired guru, nor his young protégé, her and Bindusara's son, were ineffectual in preventing this crisis from befalling them, while he, Bindusara, would not let that happen in future.

Tissyanka said nothing further. Shubhadrangi did not expect her to do so. She had done more than she could have expected. She had spoken out and helped delay the session another few moments, as well as diverting the sabha and Emperor's attention away from Shubhadrangi.

'Enough talk. It is time to end this menace once and for all. I pronounce judgement upon the treacherous Chandika Order. For their crime of treason, conspiracy and betrayal of their oaths, they are sentenced to mass execution, said sentence to be carried out at once. I now ask that the sabha move to the Viewing Gallery, to observe and bear witness to the carrying out of this same sentence. This Sabha session concludes now. Thank you each and every one for your attendance and your support. Mauryavansh stands on the backs of we five hundred kingdoms. Divided, we were strong nations. United, we are the world's greatest Empire. Mauryavansh!'

With one voice came the response, roared aloud by five hundred throats. 'MAURYAVANSH!'

Shubhadrangi felt a pair of eyes boring into her. She turned to see Jezza Khorasan staring directly at her. The War Marshal met her gaze and held it a moment, just long enough to make it clear that she was sending a message to Shubhadrangi. I see you now.

14

'Ashoka!'

Sushim had a way of saying a name that made it sound like an obscenity. Not just his name, any name. Ashoka had even heard him address his Mother Queens in the same tone. But not our father; him, he speaks to with a completely different tone, like pouring honey. One of Acharya Kautilya's many lessons in politics had centred on the different types of rulers and their personality types. One of them he had termed the Prince of Postures. That was Sushim, described to perfection. He knew how to posture for different occasions and audiences.

Right now, he was posturing for a gaggle of young beautiful nubiles and rakish clingers. Ashoka supposed it was his usual entourage of aristocratic hangers on from the richest and most powerful families of Patliputra. He recognized none of them because he never attended any aristocratic functions or social gatherings. Avoided them, in fact. He recognized their type from their appearance, their attire and their attitude, but not the individual houses from which each spoiled brat had ensued. To Sushim, this was his usual gang. He was enjoying strutting about the camp, acting like he was Emperor of Mauryavansh lording it over his court. Sushim was gifted with a striking resemblance to their father and he made the most of it, mimicking Bindusara's physical mannerisms, attire, his expressions, tone of voice, even his phrases. Age differences apart, he could almost pass for Bindusara in the dark. And he probably used that to the hilt, especially when it came to his nightly activities. Sushim and Ashoka, standing side by side, were as unlikely to be mistaken for brothers as Bindusara and Ashoka were for father and son. This fact had never troubled Ashoka before but now, as every young man and woman in the clearing looked at him and several whispered to each other, he found himself gritting his teeth and wishing he had never been born into this family at all. The spoiled young lords and ladies made no pretence of their disapproval of his dishevelled, road-dusty appearance, his rough clothes, or his even rougher looks. But he knew that it was the lack of resemblance to the imperial profile and features that made them preen and bristle the most.

He was sure before this hunt was over, he would hear more than one insensitive comment about whether his mother had slept with the right Bindusara on the night he was conceived, the implication being that perhaps the rumours were true and he was in fact conceived by his legendary guru Kautilya himself. Ashoka had grown a thick skin to such insults, because they weren't actually insults: it was commonplace for the royal preceptor to act as a surrogate to father children upon the queens of his king. It was untrue in Ashoka's case, and in the case of all his siblings. Bindusara had many shortfalls as a parent; being able to father children had never been one of them. But he knew that reacting to such rumours and assumptions would only stoke them further. As his guru had taught him, people reacted most violently to insults which contained some element of truth. If he over-reacted to the ceaseless comments about his lack of resemblance to his father, he would only give the gossip mills more grain to grind into flour.

'Brother.' He spoke the single word in place of a name. Sushim was his brother, he could not deny that, much as he wished it were not true. But the act of saying his name felt unclean, knowing all that he did about Sushim's appetites and offences.

Sushim spread his arms wide in a parody of a warm greeting. Ashoka allowed the taller, broader boy to pretend to embrace him in a show of brotherly affection. He smelled the familiar wine breath and other substances Sushim had abused in the past several hours.

'My brother, saviour of Mauryavansh!' Sushim clapped him hard on his shoulder blades, the blow intended to throw Ashoka off-balance and cause him to stumble. Ashoka was prepared for it, standing with his legs wide enough apart and his body turned at an angle. Sushim's hand struck Ashoka's shoulder blade, making him wince and wring his hand, while Ashoka didn't budge an inch. Sushim recovered quickly and reeled off his litany with his usual mocking flourish. 'The... man of the hour. Slayer of assassins. Exposer of conspiracies. Destroyer of the Confederacy. Champion of Patliputra!'

Ashoka leaned into him, speaking just loud enough to be heard by Sushim but not anyone else. 'I can't stay, brother. I have pressing business elsewhere.'

'Now the hunt will truly be entertaining!' Sushim continued aloud. 'Ashoka is the finest tracker and hunter in the empire.' Tilting his head, he said for Ashoka's ears: 'Father said you are not to be seen in Patliputra till he sends for you. The Khorasani guard will bar you if you try to enter the city.'

Ashoka didn't waste time arguing this point, or asking what he had done to merit being banned from his own home—especially since he was supposedly the saviour of Mauryavansh, champion of Patliputra, etc., etc. He had anticipated Sushim's argument. 'Not the city, brother. Elsewhere.'

Sushim looked at him curiously, his handsome face creasing at the forehead in a matted pattern that resembled their father's mannerism. 'What business?'

Ashoka winked. 'The female kind.'

Sushim's eyes widened and eyebrows shot up. 'Really? Who is she? Is she from one of the Five Hundred Houses? Have I had her yet?' He waved himself down. 'If she's from the Five Hundred and is worth having, I've probably had her already. Or even if she's not worth having.'

Ashoka forced himself to keep the smile on his face, instead of punching his brother in the nose as he longed to do. 'You don't know her. She's not from the Five Hundred or from any of the high Houses. She's from the country.'

At the mention of the non-metropolitan world, Sushim's face twisted in an expression of disgust. 'A commoner? How can you stand to even touch such vermin? Really, brother. You are a prince of Patliputra. You have standards. There is a protocol. If not yourself, at least think about the family's reputation.'

Ashoka shrugged. 'The heart wants what the heart wants. She's quite a tasty morsel.' He forced himself to wink again, playing the part up.

Sushim looked less disgusted, even thoughtful, but shook his head. 'Even if she was from the highest Houses, it wouldn't matter. You are to stay with me, by my side, until father sends for us both. His orders were very precise. He even stationed the Khorasani guard to watch over us on the expedition.'

Sushim gestured across the clearing. Ashoka had already noted the unusually strong presence of soldiers. He now noted that they were all Khorasani, and there appeared to be enough of them to crush a minor uprising.

He also saw that a sizeable number were watching him intently, hands on the hilts of their weapons, ready to draw. That was wrong. If their purpose was to protect the princes, they ought to be watching everyone else. The way they were focused on him, watching his every move, suggested that they regarded him as a potential threat. He glanced back and saw that his horse had been taken in hand by the Khorasani soldiers and the three young soldiers and Radhagupta were standing off to one side, virtually ignored. There was clearly some agenda here but he knew better than to over react. The assassination plot had disturbed the delicate equilibrium of palace politics and it was natural enough for every person involved in the attempt to be kept under close watch for a while. Acharya Kautilya had explained the logic to him: The best way for an assassin or traitor to get close to his target is to pretend to be a hero. A champion can go where a mere stranger can never hope to penetrate. Killing off one's own associates and pretending to expose a conspiracy plot was often the opening gambit to a more complex series of moves, ending with an assassination, a coup, or a number of similar objectives.

Sushim sipped his wine, watching Ashoka as he took stock of the situation. 'You see how it is, Ashoka.' He grinned, taking a lighter tone. 'Don't be grim, brother. We will have a feast and a grand hunt and you can go find your tasty morsel and fuck her afterward.' He gestured grandly. 'You can have your pick of this litter for now. Any of these vixen will spread their legs for the Second Prince, Champion of Mauryavansh, Saviour of Patliputra...'

Ashoka tuned him out. He had heard enough of Sushim's chauvinistic misogynistic gibberish before to fill in the blanks. He came to terms with the central message: He was under scrutiny for a few days, until the situation in Patliputra was stabilized and any loose threads remaining had been unravelled and followed back to their source. The sabha session was probably over by now anyway, as it was well past noon. It infuriated him to think of the fate of the Chandikas. Exiled? Disgraced? Some senior leaders sent to the Torture Palace, executed even? He wanted to be there in the sabha hall right now, to do what he could to prevent such injustice. But he had no choice. Attempting to fight a hundred Khorasani and race back to Patliputra to face several thousand more was pointless. He would only incriminate himself with his actions, making everyone assume that he was guilty by association, or worse. That would not help the Chandikas. It might even hurt them further.

He squared his shoulders, drawing a deep breath and releasing it slowly. Whatever happened to the Chandikas was out of his hand now. He would have to play along with this charade, spending the days hunting and pretending to feast with his brother and these empty-headed High House brats until the storm passed. It would pass. Acharya Kautilya had taught him that. No matter how tempestuous or destructive, a storm always passed. It was the way of things.

15

'Rani Shubhadrangi.'

She turned to see the familiar face of Radhagupta, the young pupil of Acharya Kautilya, and a friend of Ashoka.

'Radhagupta. How good to see you.'

Her warmth was sincere. The young brahmin was a valuable link to the old Acharya and one person she always knew she could trust in the brahmin caucus. He was also a very likeable young man, erudite, well read in the classics, intelligent enough to discuss or debate points of philosophy or science, and a man she could spend time with openly without the other queens gossiping.

He glanced around quickly. 'Could we speak in private? I have news of Ashoka.'

'Of course.' They were in the corridor outside the sabha hall. The chiefs were still milling about, the mood sombre and guarded. They were to proceed to the viewing gallery in a few moments to witness the carrying out of the sentences, but she knew from experience they had enough time to step out and have a quick private exchange.

She led him away from the crowded corridor, waving to catch Tissyanka's eye. The other queen left the person she was talking with and followed them quickly. They passed through an antechamber which led to several doors. Shubhadrangi spotted bright blue afternoon sky and led them through a door which opened onto a balcony. The balcony overlooked the rear of the imperial complex, looking down onto a sheer drop of several hundred feet, with walkways patrolled by sentries. Only days ago, those would have been Chandikas on those walkways; now they were all Khorasani guards. The closest walkway was over ten yards below the balcony and the nearest other balconies were several yards to either side. This was about as private as it was possible to get in this part of the palace complex.

'How is he?' The question was out of her mouth the moment she turned back to Radhagupta.

'He is well, and in no immediate danger.'

She frowned. 'Why would he be in any danger? He went to meet with Acharya Kautilya.'

'He was detained by imperial soldiers on the way back. We both were. I was permitted to leave because I insisted I had to return to perform important religious duties here in the palace. He is still in Girvan.'

'At the Acharya's ashram?' She looked puzzled.

'No, he is in another part of Girvan. With Yuvraj Sushim's hunting party. The soldiers were despatched to escort Ashoka there to join Sushim on his hunting expedition. He is not permitted to enter the city until recalled by the Emperor.' Tissyanka arrived during this explanation, catching most of it.

'I see.' Shubhadrangi did see, quite clearly in fact. She looked at Tissyanka. 'It was a cleverly thought out plan. Detain Ashoka. Avoid a trial. Push the sentencing through without giving anyone a chance to object. And now.' She shook her head in despair. 'This execution. It's unbearable. Barbaric.'

Tissyanka came forward and gave Shubhadrangi a hug. She spoke just softly enough to be heard by her friend. 'Careful, Shubha. There are ears everywhere now. Khorasani ears.'

Shubhadrangi hugged her friend back and nodded gratefully. She had needed that reminder. She had always been too sensitive to accept the kind of casual brutality that was taken for granted by most queens. The thought of innocent Chandikas being executed merely to serve political expediency made her want to vomit in disgust. But she knew that expressing such feelings openly could cost her and Ashoka dearly.

She looked at Radhagupta. 'What of his talk with Acharya Kautilya? Ashoka went to ask him to come to Patliputra to intervene in the matter of the Chandikas.'

Radhagupta's smooth young face softened with compassion. 'Acharya felt it would not be wise for him to visit Patliputra. He advised Ashoka against protesting or speaking out as well. What is to happen will happen regardless. There is no point endangering ourselves by taking a stand. It is more important to survive and look to the future.'

Shubhadrangi nodded. 'The Acharya is wise as ever. He speaks truth. Even I felt Ashoka was venturing out on a limb in this matter. But his heart was in the right place. Those women are innocent and what is happening to them is monstrous—' She stopped herself. 'But as you said, what is to happen will happen regardless. Is there any advice for me? Anything I should do to help Ashoka's situation?'

Radhagupta shook his head slowly. 'The Emperor is already distrustful of his involvement in the assassination plot.'

'His involvement? All he did was expose the plot and help save us all from the attack. Why should our husband distrust his own son for doing what any good son would do?'

'It is standard protocol. The person exposing or intervening in a crime or assassination attempt is always assumed to have some involvement—until he is proved to be innocent. Which Ashoka certainly will be proved to be. Do not trouble yourself overly with this, my Queen.'

Tissyanka spoke up. 'You have to admit, he and you—and I as well—have been openly questioning Bindusara's actions and decisions. That may not have been the wisest thing to do.'

Radhagupta looked concerned. 'Did either of you say anything at the sabha session today? I came to advise you against speaking at all. It could be taken amiss.'

'We both spoke out during the session, to try and delay the trial. Except, there was no trial, merely a sentencing.'

Radhagupta clicked his tongue in that way brahmins had of expressing dismay. 'I would that you had not done that, my Queens. This is not a wise time to express one's opinions in open sabha. It is apt to attract the wrong kind of attention.'

'And the right kind too.'

Shubhadrangi looked quizzically at Tissyanka.

Tissyanka moved closer, speaking softly even though there was no one in sight or hearing distance. No one visible, Shubhadrangi corrected herself. Who knew where and how Khorasan's spies might be listening?

'I was approached by two munshis. That was who I was speaking to when you called me here. They wished to set up a meeting in private with you and me, both, after the viewing.'

'Munshis? I don't understand. Which munshis do you mean?' Munshi meant an accountant, though the term referred broadly to the associates-secretaries-assistants-interns-and-general-dogsbody types who hung around the sabha chiefs. Some of these men and women merely served as glorified servants, carrying scrolls, seals, sceptres, or even fetching food and running errands for their chiefs, but many were educated political experts, well versed with all aspects of Mauryavansh law, well connected to the political ups and downs of the empire—mainly through networking with their counterparts—and a few of them were bright, dangerous sparks who did all the real work while their chiefs merely pressed their seals and took credit when it was done. Shubhadrangi could not think of any reason why any munshi would want to meet with her and Tissyanka. Munshis met with other munshis, not with queens.

'They were general munshis, available to all chiefs for any clerical work for the sabha or otherwise. Not attached to any particular nation or chief. In this case, they were only acting as intermediaries for the persons who actually requested the meeting.'

'And who might they be?'

'I don't know. The munshis wouldn't say.'

Radhagupta nodded, approving. 'That is wise. As general munshis, they are free agents, serving no one nation. They are the ideal persons to use to convey such a request, although...' Radhagupta squinted, thinking through all the implications. '... if they were questioned sternly they would probably give up the names of the chiefs who engaged them for this errand. So the only way to ensure absolute secrecy would be to send a blind invitation.'

'A blind invitation?'

'Where even the person conveying the invitation does not know who sent him or her.'

Shubhadrangi sighed. 'All this political doublethink gives me a headache. Are you saying that these munshis approached Rani Tissyanka without knowing who sent them? Wouldn't they know who asked them to approach her?'

'Not if they were given the instruction in writing, left at their writing station. It is common for chiefs who do not have a munshi present, or who have sent their munshis on other errands, to engage the services of a general munshi. All the chiefs—or their munshis—need do is leave a request in writing at the writing station of a general munshi and he would carry out the request without being aware of the person who made the request. By using two separate general munshis, the person sending the request may simply be ensuring that it was delivered.'

Shubhadrangi shook her head. 'So this person is very secretive. How are we to meet this person then?'

'Persons. They will contact me again and specify a time and place. They wish you and me both to attend, Shubha.'

Shubhadrangi looked at Radhagupta. 'Would you join us? I am not accustomed to secret meetings with unknown persons. Whatever the political motivation, it would be good to have your knowledge and insight to guide us.'

Radhagupta bowed, showing Shubhadrangi his shaven head and single waist-long braid of oiled hair. 'I live to serve, Rani. It would be my pleasure.'

A disturbance from the outer chambers drew their attention.

'Shubhadrangi, the viewing must be starting. We should

proceed to the viewing gallery before we are missed and they come looking for us.'

'Indeed. We have gotten ourselves in enough trouble already today. Let's go.'

Radhagupta nodded. 'I shall see you directly tonight, my queens. Be cautious henceforth about what you say and whom you say it to. There are ears everywhere.'

Shubhadrangi and Tissyanka walked quickly through the ante chamber. She didn't see which way Radhagupta went but when she turned the corner and glanced back he was gone. She was glad for his news. She had been anxiously waiting for Ashoka, expecting him to turn up and perhaps have an argument with his father over the Chandikas. Ashoka and Bindusara had never had a close father-son relationship. For that matter, Bindusara was not close to any of his children. His perpetual reserve kept him aloof from everyone except those he was favouring at that moment. At present, that meant Noor Khorasan and her family. But there had been a time when Shubhadrangi and he had been close, very close. And intimate too. She wished she could get close to him again, catch him in a moment when he was more relaxed, less reserved, not the Emperor of Mauryavansh, but simply Bindu, the man who had fallen in love with her once, had made passionate gentle love to her, creating the wonderful person that was their son Ashoka. She was sure that Bindu would see reason, would understand that there was another way to look at the world, not as a forest of assassins seeking to exterminate you, but as a habitat filled with wild wonderful beings all seeking to co-exist.

She followed Tissyanka out the last door and then they were in the long verandah that went around the inner palace, surrounding and overlooking the central courtyard. This was the viewing gallery. There were hundreds of other people already gathered along the gallery, all the five hundred sabha chiefs, their spouses, munshis, other aristocrats and nobles from the Higher Houses, and who knew who else. Everyone loved an execution and this was one to beat all others. The high and mighty Chandikas themselves, defenders of Mauryavansh, confidants, protectors, and some said lovers, of the late great Chandragupta Maurya himself, now brought down low, to the very floor of the courtyard, where they would be severed from their mortal selves. The ultimate sacrifice for their Emperor.

She thought she saw expressions of gleeful anticipation on many faces. *These ghoulish people! What was she doing amidst them? Why was she even here? She did not belong with them, did not condone such barbaric injustice. Yet she was compelled to attend this brutal event. Because she was a queen of Mauryavansh.*

No, she corrected herself again silently.

Not because I am a queen of Mauryavansh.

Because I am a mother.

Mother of Ashoka. And the best way to protect my son is to pretend to be one of these people. Even though I'm not.

The torrent of voices rose to fever pitch, some actually gasping, whistling, cheering, and clapping their thighs, as the Chandikas were led out into the courtyard below, their dark uniforms soaked with blood and other fluids from the abuse they must have suffered all night long. Several looked as if they were nursing grave injuries, barely able to stay upright. But they walked proudly, keeping their chins high, their eyes level, their faces calm. They showed no shame, no dishonour, no emotion except proud acceptance. They had done nothing wrong but if they were to die they would face it like the warriors they were, stoic to the very end.

Shubhadrangi choked back tears as the Khorasani guards linked up the Chandikas in rows against the courtyard walls, while Khorasani bowmen raised their longbows armed with vicious sickle-moon-headed arrows designed to do maximum damage. They aimed at the throats of the bound Chandikas. They loosed.

The Chandikas sprouted arrows from their throats, blood gushed in great spurts and streams, pooling in the stones of the courtyard. Chandikas fell, their feet thrashing in death throes. War Marshal Jezza Khorasan herself appeared, carrying a great curved sword, walking along the courtyard wall, slashing at the prone bodies, delivering the final death blows, ensuring that none survived.

The executions went on for what seemed like an eternity. There were many, many Chandikas. The courtyard was awash when it was over, the stones glistening in the late afternoon sun with what, to Shubhadrangi, resembled a river of blood.

Innocent blood.

16

Something's wrong.

He had sensed it since that morning. The Khorasani soldiers were behaving differently. Nothing so obvious that it was easily noticeable. Minor things, such as the morning patrolling of the perimeter of the camp, which they had performed every day at dawn but this morning there had been no patrol, instead, the guards had remained by the fireplace, hunched in their blankets. The weather had taken a cold turn and mornings were particularly biting. Ashoka had remained in his tent, but by placing his palm to the ground, he could listen to the vibrations of feet and horses and know who was going where and why. Sushim and the rest of his spoiled, rich brat friends were all asleep by this hour, passed out from their night-long feasting, carousing, fornication. Ashoka could hear his brother's snores from the next tent, loud enough to rouse the jungle. The only people awake and about at this hour were the Khorasanis and for some reason, they had not sent out their usual perimeter patrol.

A short while later, he understood why. A single rider approached the camp, dismounting half a mile away and walking his horse upto the east side guard campfire, fifty yards away from the main campfire. The visitor then spoke with the guards at the east side post for several minutes. Ashoka had slipped out of his tent at the sound of the approaching rider and was up in a tree, looking down at the guard post when he arrived. The visitor was also a Khorasani guard, but not one of those Ashoka had seen in the camp. He heard the conversation between the new arrival and the other guards at the east post, then the visitor turned around and left the way he had arrived, heading east by north. This time, he waited only till he was a quarter mile out before mounting his horse and riding away. A short while later, Ashoka felt the vibrations of other horses bearing riders, several dozen of them, passing north and east of the camp, heading deeper into the forest.

He waited in the tree for another hour before he was rewarded with another unusual occurrence.

The Khorasani lieutenant in charge of the camp's security gathered his captains together: three women and two men. He then proceeded to give them all detailed instructions. Ashoka had to leave the tree and creep closer to hear what he was saying. It was worth the effort. The plan outlined by the Khorasani lieutenant was an interesting one. Ashoka admired the simplicity of the plan and the details such as the location and timing. He sensed War Marshal Khorasan's experienced mind behind the entire scheme. She had anticipated all contingencies and planned for them. The plan was foolproof, and there would be no escaping it alive.

The only part he wasn't able to overhear—mainly because no names were ever spoken—was the target of this plan. Someone was going to be killed, he understood that much clearly. But who and why? The why might not seem to matter right now but it could be crucial in helping determine the who. And the who definitely did matter.

He had a feeling it was likely to be himself.

It made perfect sense. Eliminate the one person who had foiled the earlier assassination attempt. Eliminate the possibility of that person interfering with future assassination attempts. Ashoka had no illusions about his importance in the larger scheme of things. To the preening daughters of the High Houses, he was the Second Prince-in-Waiting, only two steps away from the throne of Mauryavansh, the most coveted seat in the entire world. But so long as his father and Sushim lived, he was just one of a hundred sons. If they meant to kill him, it was not because of his place in the line of succession. It was because he wouldn't play their political games. Any other one of those hundred sons—well, almost any—would be easily approachable and open to a plan that involved power broking and deal making. After talking to Acharya Kautilya and ruminating on the known facts for the past several days, he was certain that the real goal of the Lichchavi Confederacy assassins had not been to assassinate anyone. The Lichchavi assassination plot had been designed to fail! That was why the two assassins had been bragging openly about the plan in a public house, within earshot of a dozen other patrons. That was why the last assassin had been eliminated, and the Chandika spy exposed. It had all been part of a larger plot. The real intention was to do away with the Chandika Order itself!

By wiping out the most powerful independent military force in the imperial city, the conspirators had left the imperial palace open to a takeover. Their plan had succeeded brilliantly. If the Lichchavi assassins had actually killed any of the imperial family, that would have been acceptable too—there were plenty of them to kill after all. But to have massacred the entire family would have been a political disaster. The one hundred queens were all from the hundred most powerful kingdoms in the empire. Kill enough of them and their families and nations would rise up in fury. Instead, by leaving the queens alive and eliminating the Chandikas, the palace itself was now available for immediate occupancy. Khorasani guards now controlled the entire imperial palace and the capital city. Even a military coup could not have yielded such a result without a great deal of bloodshed and opposition. This way the only blood shed had been that of the innocent Chandikas, who were the only ones who could have opposed the Khorasani in their end-game: killing the Emperor himself.

Now, the Chandikas were gone. The Khorasani owned the city and the palace. And the path was clear for them to kili Bindusara whenever they pleased—or to work out an arrangement which ensured total control over the things that truly mattered to them: the wealth, trade, and military power of the vast Mauryavansh empire. In time Bindusara would be killed, Ashoka was certain of that, because he was ultimately a Maurya and as such, he was Emperor only because the five hundred tribes had united to support him. Khorasan, on the other hand, did not care about the empire, Chandragupta's legacy, or the Artha Shastra laws of Acharya Kautilya that had transformed the subcontinent from a lawless land of warring tribes into a united conglomerate of integrated nations. Khorasan wanted wealth, power, control. So long as Bindusara fed these appetites, he would live and even rule, if only as a tool of the Khorasans. The moment he allowed his ego to stand in their way, foolishly believing that he was the Emperor and therefore could do as he wished, they would get rid of him. It was only a matter of time.

And to replace him, the logical choice was right here, snoring a dozen feet away from where Ashoka now lay again in his tent, fast asleep after yet another night in a long succession of nights spent indulging his most wanton, shameless appetites. It was a good pairing. Sushim didn't care about laws, the people, the empire or the throne. All he cared about was Sushim and his needs, his wants, his must-haves, his desires. So long as he got what he wanted when he wanted it, he would let them do as they pleased. An endless supply of warm bodies and cold wine and he would happily be their puppet emperor.

Which left only Ashoka as a hindrance. A thorn. An obstacle. The Ganesha in their path. The last hurdle. Kill him and their path would be open.

And they meant to do it today. Here, in the Girvan, during today's hunt.

He rose, pretending to awaken for the first time, making a show of splashing water on his face at the silver bowl, calling for a chamber pot and fresh attire and food. He had heard enough of their plan to know they intended to commit the assassination while in the forest itself, on the hunt. His main activity these past days had been to live up to Sushim's sky-high praise of his putative talents as a tracker. Tracking meant going ahead of the main expedition, often disappearing alone into the woods for extended periods of time. It would be simple enough to attack him when he was isolated. To throw enough bodies at him from all directions, until one of their knives, or arrows, or swords, or spears struck its mark and he fell. He would be torn to shreds and his remains left for the others to discover, his death blamed on the lions of Girvan. That was the plan he had overheard, in brief.

He was ready for it.

17

The three cloaked figures arrived on horseback, taking the route specified. It was late and the Upper City was asleep but from the Lower City the sounds of revelry travelled on the night air. When the rich and privileged of Patliputra wanted to partake of less acceptable indulgences, they went down to the Lower City. It was hypocritical because without their patronage, none of those brothels, taverns, and questionable activities that passed for 'entertainment' would even exist. Yet by day, when in their stiff roles as 'higher' citizens, the upper castes and classes looked down on such establishments with disdain and disgust. Many of the same individuals who were revelling at this late hour in those dubious places of business would be condemning them maliciously on the morrow. It was the way the world worked: the rich abused and exploited. The poor took their money and endured. But it could not last forever. Justice would address the balance some day.

The three riders dismounted at the door of a non-descript house at the lowermost end of the Upper City, low enough that no self-respecting noble would reside there, yet expensive enough that no Lower City denizen could dream of affording it—even if caste, class, regional origins, and other social strictures so permitted. The house, like several others on this abutment facing one of the several bridges that connected Upper City to Lower City, was unoccupied at night, used mainly for storage by a guild of merchants. It appeared darkened and deserted at this hour. This in itself was not unusual: most Upper City mansions and estates were dark by this late hour. Even the sophisticated cosmopolitans conducted their private parties discretely in inner chambers, out of view.

The three figures went up the door of the house and knocked in a certain pattern as instructed. The door opened and they entered. The door shut behind them and a moment later, a peon appeared and led the horses to a stable beside the house. Barely a minute after they had arrived, there was no indication that anyone had even stopped at the deserted house on the empty street.

Shubhadrangi lifted up the hood of her cloak. Tissyanka and Radhagupta did the same.

They were in a large chamber with stacks of various goods piled against the walls. In the centre were a few seats and a table with some wine and refreshments. Three women stood around the table, waiting to greet the new arrivals.

'Rani Shubhadrangi, Rani Tissyanka, Purohit Radhagupta, we thank you for accepting our invitation. Forgive the furtive nature of our contact and of this encounter. These are dangerous times and it would be best to keep this meeting as brief as possible. I need not remind any of you of the importance of keeping anything we say here completely confidential. I do not exaggerate when I say that our lives could depend on it.'

Shubhadrangi acknowledged the speaker, a woman a little past middle age with more than a little grey in her hair and wrinkles on her handsome face. She did not immediately recognize the lady but there was something vaguely familiar about her which she could not place. Perhaps it would come to her in time. 'May we at least have the pleasure of knowing whom we are addressing?'

The speaker glanced at her companions, one of whom was a much younger woman, the third about midway between the other two in age. All three appeared well educated, cultured and sophisticated. They were clearly aristocrats, not Lower City women. But their faces were clear of the various unguents women of their class usually applied before stepping out in public, and they wore no visible jewellery or lavish accoutrements. All three were covered with dark robes similar to the ones Shubhadrangi and Tissyanka were wearing, but Shubhadrangi glimpsed fine but understated garments beneath the robes. They were women of means, certainly, but not anxious or vain enough to need to remind every passerby of the fact. Or perhaps they were just trying to stay lowkey.

'You may call us Vichitra, Suchitra and Anumitra,' said the first speaker. 'I will not insult you by pretending those are our real names but they will have to suffice for now.'

Shubhadrangi nodded. 'I suppose we have no choice... Vichitra.'

Vichitra offered an apologetic smile. 'Nor do we. Names can be...dangerous at such a time. They can always be...extracted.'

Shubhadrangi's throat tightened. The woman was referring to extraction of information by torture. The very thought of ranked queens of Mauryavansh being subjected to such barbaric treatment was nauseating but she took it in her stride. After watching the brutal mass execution of the Chandikas, she could believe anything. And after all, she knew the meaning of those awful screams and cries audible from the House of Torture. Still, surely Tissyanka and she were above such treatment. Weren't they? 'I see.'

Vichitra looked closely at Shubhadrangi. 'I do not mean to upset you, Rani Shubhadrangi. I'm only trying to be truthful.'

'With false names?' Tissyanka glanced around, her delicate features cast in a suspicious expression. 'Clandestine meetings? Covert communications? It would seem to be the opposite of truthfulness.'

The three strangers exchanged glances. 'You are right,' said the youngest one—Shubhadrangi already thought of her as Suchitra now. 'But these are necessary precautions as you will soon realize. These are dangerous—'

'Dangerous times,' Shubhadrangi said. 'You said that before. In that case, please get to the point.'

The third woman, the one who was not quite as young and pretty as Suchitra yet not at old and handsome as Vichitra—Shubhadrangi thought of her as Anumitra, chuckled softly. 'I told you ladies, she's no puppet to be manipulated with invisible strings. She has a head on her shoulders and a will to move mountains. Her son takes after her, after all, not after his father, and thank the gods for that.'

Vichitra nodded slowly, her lined face showing creases as deep as knife cuts. 'Rani Shubhadrangi, we will not waste your time or ours. Your son and you are at grave risk. Your speaking out at sabha...' She gestured to include Tissyanka. 'Both of you speaking out at sabha...exposed your loyalties and painted targets on your backs. There are forces in Patliputra that regard your outbursts as declarations of enmity. They want nothing less than your utter destruction now.'

Shubhadrangi felt her heart shrink but held herself erect and kept her voice steady. 'I think you exaggerate. Mauryavansh is still a republic. Every tribe has a right to speak at Sabha. Tissyanka and I merely voiced concerns. We never opposed or—'

Suchitra waved her arguments away impatiently. The youngest of the three, she was exceedingly pretty but there was a cold edge to her beauty that suggested hidden strengths. 'You are speaking as if this were still the age of Chandragupta. This is Bindusara's Mauryavansh. Or should I say, Khorasan's Mauryavansh. Everybody knows who really controls the reins of empire. It's that vixen with the golden yoni and razor-sharp ambition. She has Bindusara as firmly in her grasp as if she were holding his balls in her fist.'

Shubhadrangi was frankly shocked by the young woman's crude language. 'No one doubts that our husband is fond of Noor Khorasan for the moment. He has had similar obsessions with other women in the past. It is a phase. It will soon pass. He is still the Emperor first, husband second. However much he craves her company in his bed, he will never let that cloud his better judgement. I find it offensive to hear him spoken of that way—or even her for that matter.'

The three women stared at her for a moment, then looked at each other. Vichitra sighed. 'She is more asleep than we thought. Perhaps this was a mistake after all.'

Anumitra nodded slowly. 'She is not ready. She could jeopardize everything.'

Suchitra shook her head, her pretty face hardening in an expression of distaste. 'I was against this from the outset.'

Anumitra sighed. 'I thought—'

Shubhadrangi leaned forward, striking the table with the palm of her hand. 'Enough!'

Everyone reacted. Even Tissyanka started and looked at her.

'Stop talking about me as if I'm not here. You set up this clandestine meeting days ago. Tissyanka, Radhagupta and I followed your strange instructions and came here in the dead of night. We have listened to you insult our husband and our sister queen. You owe us an explanation and the courtesy of treating us with intelligence. I want to know right now, what is your intention and why are we here?'

Tissyanka added her voice. 'Tell us now or we walk out of here and report this to the imperial guard at once.'

Anumitra looked at Tissyanka and Shubhadrangi in turn, then focused on Tissyanka first. 'You can do that, Tissyanka, and you and your children will be in the Torture Palace within the hour.' She turned to Shubhadrangi. 'You want an explanation and courtesy? Let us lay it out for you plain and clear. The Khorasanis have control of the Emperor and are pursuing an endgame. They mean to end the republic and turn it into a despotic regime, with the Emperor acting as a sovereign ruler and striking down anyone who dares whisper a word against him. Zero tolerance of dissidence. Khorasan will use the imperial seat to settle old scores. The slaughter of the Chandikas was only a drop of blood in the river that is about to flood our empire. Mauryavansh will be torn apart by the violence that is about to break loose. If you thought the days of the Nanda Empire were horrifying, you should prepare to experience the worst violence that Jambudwipa has ever witnessed. It will be an ocean of blood.'

Shubhadrangi stared at her, stunned. 'Bindusara will never

let that happen. He is a hard man, but he is no despot or tyrant. There is a limit to how much his passion for Noor Khorasan will let him—'

Suchitra exclaimed in exasperation. 'Are you so asleep that you cannot even feel the fire burning away your limbs? Bindusara is only a means to an end. If Khorasan has her way, he will be dead within the year, perhaps two. And there will be only one true ruler in Mauryavansh, that will be Noor Khorasan.'

Tissyanka also exclaimed. 'Impossible. The sabha will never accept a Khorasani as Emperor.'

Anumitra answered calmly. 'There will be no sabha. The Patliputra of today is already crumbling into ruin as we speak. But you are right. Politically speaking, it would be a tactical mistake for her to attempt to take the throne. She will control it, while remaining the puppet master as we said earlier. She will replace Bindusara with Sushim, most likely. Though she has other potential candidates in mind. That is one of the advantages of having a large litter to choose from. She will make whomever she wishes the top dog, so long as he or she wags his head whenever the tail demands.'

'And your son Ashoka is the only one who stands a chance of stopping her,' Vichitra added. 'That is why we have summoned you here with such elaborate secrecy. We wish to propose a counter plan to prepare an alternate to Khorasan's megalomanic scheme. We wish to make your son Ashoka the next emperor of Mauryavansh.'

Shubhadrangi felt the blood drain from her head. She swallowed. Her right hand reached instinctively for and found Tissyanka's left hand, and squeezed it. Tissyanka squeezed it back, communicating her own astonishment and support. Radhagupta, who had remained silent all this while as the five women spoke, shifted where he stood and cleared his throat to attract their attention.

'My queen Shubhadrangi,' he said. 'I suggest we hear them out. Acharya Kautilya has foreseen this very situation and anticipated it. Everything these ladies have said tonight has been predicted by him and it would be wise to prepare for this coming calamity. I advise you to continue the discussion.'

Shubhadrangi pursed her lips and leaned back, releasing a deep breath. 'I am listening.'

18

Sushim was in an unusual mood today. After his usual bout of vomiting, abusing, thrashing the servants for serving him bad wine or bad food the night before—it was always the food or wine that he blamed, never his own excessive consumption—and defecating loudly and noisily enough to outdo an entire musical performance, Ashoka's elder brother emerged from his tent, blinking in the morning light.

'Brother!' he said, catching sight of Ashoka.

He came up to Ashoka and clapped a hand on his shoulder. 'I have been meaning to have words with you.'

Ashoka could think of several words he would like to have with Sushim. Wastrel. Brat. Misogynist. Glutton.... 'Let's speak after the hunt.'

But Sushim was still holding his shoulder. Despite his excesses, Sushim was no weakling. A large frame, a big appetite, a reasonable amount of exercise and even some training when he felt like it, and most of all, an abundance of that magical elixir—youth—had gifted him a strong body which he abused and with which he abused other bodies frequently. 'Now would be best.'

Ashoka glanced up at him, sensing a difference in Sushim's manner. His usual bravado was barely sufficient to cloak his true meanness. Ashoka had seen every side of him, and there weren't that many sides to see. There were drunk Sushim, angry Sushim, arrogant Sushim and selfish want-it-now Sushim, and all of these were variants on the same basic theme: I. Me. Mine.

'Speak, brother. What troubles you on this fine morning?'

Sushim kept his hand on Ashoka's shoulder and looked at him with a leering expression that was probably his way of pretending to be friendly and relaxed. 'Change is coming. A big change. Like a...' He stopped and groped, not used to trying to find words or phrases to express himself. Mostly, Sushim stuck to the names of things he wanted to eat, fuck or kill. Ashoka waited, not offering to help him out. '...storm,' Sushim managed. 'Change is like a big storm. Those not prepared are hurt. Badly. Best to be prepared.'

Ashoka resisted the urge to smile at his brother's clumsy attempt at diplomacy. 'Like hammering down the pegs of a tent?'

'Yes! Exactly!' Sushim frowned. 'No, not a tent. More like a...' He snapped his fingers. '...an attack. You have to prepare for an attack, otherwise...you know what happens.'

'What happens?'

Sushim laughed at Ashoka's failure to guess the correct answer. 'You get hurt! That's what happens. Everyone knows that.'

Sushim stepped forward, trying to walk casually, keeping his arm still around Ashoka's shoulder. Ashoka remained where he was, causing Sushim some difficulty in completing the intended action with the degree of casualness desired. He stopped, turned back, and nudged Ashoka's back. 'Walk with me, brother. This is important. Your future could depend on it.'

Ashoka walked with him, sidestepping around a tree trunk, forcing Sushim to pull his arm out of the way to avoid hitting it against the tree. They converged again on the other side of the tree, Ashoka walking just fast enough that Sushim had to step faster to keep up. They strolled through the camp, past a cookfire with several joints and haunches of meat continued to be slowly basted, turned by flabby-armed cooks who avoided looking at either of the two princes. Ashoka saw the cook closest to Sushim flinch as the First Prince raised his arm while passing by, but Sushim was only pushing back the fringe of hair off his own forehead. Sushim was not known for being kind to cooks—or any other servants. They went past the cooks without any altercation.

'You have skills, brother.' Sushim sounded almost critical, as if pointing out obvious faults that Ashoka couldn't help possessing. 'This would be good if you were just a warrior with ambitions. But as a prince...' He shook his head.

'A prince shouldn't know how to fight and defend himself?'

Sushim grinned. 'Why bother? We have people to do all that for us. We rule! They serve.'

Ashoka knew better than to get into a debate about the importance of a future emperor being able to rely on his own sword in moments of crisis. He pretended to listen without revealing anything of what he actually felt.

'When this storm comes...soon. It will come very soon. Like...a monsoon typhoon! Those who are protected will survive. Everyone else...'

'Will get hurt?' Ashoka offered.

Sushim glanced at him sharply, suspecting sarcasm. Ashoka kept his face free of any expression.

'This is a serious matter, brother,' Sushim said, reaching out and breaking off wildflowers from a bush. He crushed them in his fist and dusted off his palms as if cleansing them of dirt. 'I am speaking to you because as your elder brother, I feel responsible for you.'

Ashoka almost laughed out loud but restrained himself with an effort. Growing up, Sushim had been the palace bully, and one of the worst tormentors of his younger siblings. Ashoka was probably the only one he had not been able to bully successfully—at least not since Ashoka was able to stand and fight for himself. There were things Sushim had done to his own younger siblings that were anything but brotherly. The rape of several of his sisters, wet nurses and maids, the deaths of several servants, the brutal treatment of any number of small as well as large animals, including the horrifying abuse of an elephant that had caused Ashoka to threaten to kill Sushim on the spot and came close to getting Ashoka—Ashoka, not Sushim—exiled for assaulting the crown prince. It was safe to say that the only reason Sushim was still alive was because Ashoka's mother had made him promise that no matter what Sushim did, Ashoka would not harm him. 'We don't fight our own,' Shubhadrangi had said, refusing to accept any argument to the contrary, and, gritting his teeth, Ashoka had obeyed.

Sushim folded his hands behind his back in conscious or unconscious imitation of their father's usual walking stance. 'I can keep you safe from the storm. But in exchange you must do something for me as well. Nothing comes without cost in this life. You would know that if you attended the treasury sessions.'

Ashoka had had no idea that Sushim attended the treasury sessions, or any sessions for that matter. Of course, Sushim probably only attended them to know more about the empire's finances, one of the few aspects of governance that actually mattered to him. He doubted that the minutiae of political administration interested his brother. He only cared about the gold.

'Are you making me a proposition?'

Sushim grinned. 'See? I knew there was something in that thick skull. I'm offering you a way to change your life.' He glanced around quickly, in that furtive way he had, cutting his eyes to the left then to the right. 'To save your life.'

Ashoka already knew where this was going. He was trying to think of a response that wasn't insulting, but it was hard.

He didn't have to think for long.

The Khorasani guard nearest to them yelled and suddenly sprouted an arrow from his throat.

19

Violence exploded.

Arrows whickered past Ashoka and Sushim, flying every which way. Khorasani guards sprouted arrows and fell. Their captains and lieutenants sprang into action at once, yelling orders. Swords and spears appeared in fists, soldiers took cover behind trees, and those who had bows notched arrows and searched for targets.

Sushim stared at the Khorasani guard near them. The man had collapsed on the ground, and was drumming his feet in his death throes, as blood splattered onto a bush, staining the white wildflowers red. Sushim stared at the man as if he had never seen a man struck by an arrow before. He was oblivious to the arrows flying around him. If he didn't take cover, he would be sprouting a few himself.

'Sushim!' Ashoka gestured to the ground. 'Down!'

Sushim stared at Ashoka, then looked back at the dying guard. He heard the shouts of other Khorasanis as they were hit by arrows and looked around. He took in the chaos of the camp in a daze. 'But the attack is to happen later, on the hunt,' he said slowly, in an irritable tone. 'And who's shooting at our own guards?'

He broke off as an arrow punched into a tree, passing through the space where his face had been only a second ago before he turned around. The arrow stuck in the trunk and shivered. He reached out to pull it from the trunk, putting some effort into it.

'Who authorized the use of bowmen?' he said loudly, holding up the arrow. 'Only swords and knives were to be used—'

Ashoka slammed into Sushim's midriff, knocking his brother off his feet. They both fell on the ground, behind the tree from whose trunk Sushim had retrieved the arrow. 'Stay down!'

Sushim stared up at him with his familiar petulant look of outrage. 'Did you just push me on the ground?'

'Yes, because they're shooting at you!' Ashoka gripped the hand in which Sushim was holding the arrow. 'This was meant for you, Sushim!'

Sushim stared at the arrow then at Ashoka. 'That's impossible. The Khorasani were only to kill the rest of the party.' He paused. 'And you, if you didn't agree to join us. There was no talk of bowmen using arrows.'

Ashoka had never felt like hitting his brother more than he wanted to now. 'Sushim! The bowmen are not Khorasani! They're killing the Khorasani. They're aiming at us too.'

Sushim frowned as if about to object again, then heard a series of shouts and screams, followed by the clatter of swords and spears clashing. He grew very still and quiet, his eyes widening as he considered the implications. 'But...who?'

Ashoka snatched the arrow from Sushim's hand. 'Look at the arrow. The notches on the end. Those are Lichchavi markings.'

'The Confederacy? How dare they attack us!'

'They did just try to assassinate our entire family.'

'But that was—' Sushim trailed off, trying to think again. 'I don't understand.'

'There's nothing to understand. We're under attack. We have to get out of here. There are too many of them for us to fight.'

'The Khorasani—'

'—are dying! Look around you!'

Sushim raised his head cautiously, peering around the tree

trunk. The Khorasani soldiers were fighting hand to hand with at least thrice their number. The attackers were all dressed in green, the end of their turbancloth wrapped around their mouths then tied off behind their necks. There was no doubt about it. They were Lichchavis.

More Lichchavis poured in from all around, cutting down Khorasanis everywhere.

As Sushim and Ashoka watched, screams broke out from the tents and imperial pavilion which they had left only a short while earlier. Sushim's young aristocratic friends and playmates were being slaughtered in their tents. Ashoka saw Sushim staring at the tent and mistook his look for concern.

'We can't do anything to help them. There are too many Lichchavi and too few of us.'

'She was good in bed,' Sushim said wistfully, watching a young merchant's daughter cut down by a Lichchavi with a sword. He shrugged. 'But there are always others.'

Ashoka wished he had let Sushim remain standing long enough to be cut down by Lichchavi arrows. 'We have to get out of here!' He rose and began moving towards a ditch behind a row of bushes. An arrow whickered at him and he twisted his waist, avoiding it by an inch. He tracked it back to its source and saw the flash of green about fifty yards away. He also saw about a score of Lichchavi fighters coming at a run, swords drawn. The bowman stopped shooting to avoid hitting his own.

'Sushim. We have to go! Now!'

Sushim scrambled to his feet, dusting off his clothes. 'You can't talk to me like that. I'm the Prince-in-Waiting.'

'You'll be Dead-in-Forest if you don't move. Come on!'

Ashoka grabbed his brother's elbow and rushed him in the only direction left to them: deeper into the jungle. 'Run!'

The Lichchavi fighters were less than forty yards away now.

To Sushim's credit, he was stupid but not suicidal. He saw the line of green uniforms and drawn swords coming at him and sprinted after Ashoka. He had always been a good runner, one of his few strong points. His taller height gave him a long stride which he used to keep pace with Ashoka.

Ashoka glimpsed fighting to his left. The Khorasani were putting up a strong resistance, taking down as many Lichchavi fighters as they could before going down themselves. A Khorasani lieutenant screamed as she swung in an arc, slashing several Lichchavis, even as fighters dropped from a branch onto her back. The last he saw of her was as she fell to her knees, turning her sword upwards to stab the man on her back. The sword point went through his groin and punched out through his lower back. The Lichchavi screamed. There was fighting all across the clearing and in the trees surrounding it. Fire billowed from one of the tents as the Lichchavis used the campfire to set it ablaze. Even at a conservative estimate, he guessed the camp would be completely in Lichchavi hands within a few minutes. From what he could see, the Confederacy was slaughtering without taking any prisoners, and the Khorasani were forcing them to pay as dear a price as possible. The loudest screams came from the imperial pavilion where all the rich young brats were contained. They would die the easiest, too hungover or addled to even think of putting up any resistance. Their lives until now had consisted of drinking, eating, fornicating, and indulging their every desire, served and protected by guards and soldiers at all times. They would die now like the spoiled brats they were, squealing and protesting. He could hear them cursing and yelling caste and class insults at their killers.

To the right were the Lichchavi fighters, a handful of them racing ahead to try to head off Ashoka and Sushim. That was good. Their presence obstructed their own bowmen from shooting at the two princes.

Ashoka glanced back over his right shoulder. More Lichchavi fighters were coming, shouting and running with sheathed swords. From their calls to one another he learned everything he needed to know: their orders were to try to capture Sushim and him alive if possible, or kill them if not, but under no circumstances allow them to get away.

'Sushim, when I say so, do exactly what I tell you. We'll have only chance to get through this. No time for arguments. Do you follow?'

Sushim turned his head to glare at him. 'I should—'

Ashoka cut him off. 'You can't talk to them! Lichchavi don't care about ransoms or gold.'

Sushim glared at him as if to imply that everyone cared about gold but a clump of eucalyptus trees growing close together forced him to concentrate on not bashing out his brains.

Ashoka used the merciful lack of response to make his move. 'Now, Sushim!'

Ashoka turned sharply left, ran several hundred yards as if he was circling back around the camp to head in the direction of Patliputra—the very direction the Lichchavi would expect the two princes to go—then, when they were in a thicket of bramble bushes, he turned sharply right and ran straight ahead. Into the deep forest. Sushim stayed by his side, his breathing louder now but his footwork strong and quick. Had he been in better physical condition, with less wine and gluttony, he would easily have overtaken Ashoka. At least he managed to keep up.

The ruse worked. The Lichchavis, in their effort to cut them off, had gone right first, and when Ashoka had gone left again, they had tried once again to anticipate and cut him off. Because there were so many of them and they were all spread across a wide area, they needed to yell out each change of direction to one another, swinging in a long unwieldy line moving first one way then the other. This time, when he cut right and ran into the forest instead of in the direction of the horses and Patliputra, they were caught completely unawares. He saw the gap between Sushim and he and the Lichchavis widen to two hundred yards, then three hundred. By the time they began to correct their trajectory and call out to the others fallen behind, Sushim and he were deep in a thicket of sal trees, too dense to see more than a couple hundred yards. He knew they would track them and find their trail but for the moment, he had the advantage.

'Run!' he yelled, leading Sushim on a criss-cross pattern that zigzagged so many times in so many directions that he felt certain the Lichchavi would be forced to stop and argue about which way to go next. Besides, once they finally realized where he was going, they would have to pause and consider their options.

Sushim realized it long before they did. Ashoka saw him slowing, then come to a complete halt. He was winded and heaving but those were not the reasons he stopped.

'You...you're...' He pointed. 'Haunted?'

Ashoka nodded. 'We're going into the Haunted Forest.'

Sushim looked like he was going to vomit. The next instant, he did vomit. Ashoka took several steps away, staying upwind of the stench of regurgitated honey wine and roasted boar meat. Finally, Sushim wiped the back of his hand against his mouth, still struggling to catch his breath. 'Can't. Go. Haunted. Forest.'

'Yes, we can. It's our only chance. At least some of them won't dare enter. Those who do will be on edge. We'll have the advantage.'

Sushim hawked and spat, then peered down at his moist production. 'Ghosts of Kurukshetra.'

Ashoka smiled. 'Yes, Sushim, I know the stories. I heard them from the daiimaas when I was a boy, same as you did. But whom would you rather face right now? The so-called ghosts of soldiers who died in the Great War thousands of years ago? Or living and angry Lichchavi Confederacy soldiers trying to kill us with real weapons?'

Sushim didn't respond. He was still leaning against a tree, looking like a rich gambler who had just lost his entire fortune.

'Come on,' Ashoka said. 'We have to keep moving.'

He started at a loping stride, then realized that Sushim was not following and doubled back.

'Sushim.'

'This is not supposed to be happening. There was a plan.'

'Yes, but then the Lichchavi attacked the camp.'

'How could they? We killed all the Lichchavi assassins!' Sushim looked outraged, as if he had personally fought and killed the assassins.

Ashoka sighed. 'The assassination plot was probably the first step. They intended to follow it with a larger incursion. Those fighters who attacked the camp were wearing Confederacy green. They must have had a contingent of Lichchavi regulars waiting for word from Patliputra, so they could attack the city.'

Sushim stared at Ashoka as if he were the stupid one. 'Attack Patliputra? Are they insane? That's impossible.'

'So is trying to assassinate the entire imperial family. They had to have had a phase two for that plan. What good would it do them to assassinate us all without following through?' Ashoka glanced around, scanning the distant foliage for signs of movement, then the strips of morning sky visible through the slender gaps between trees. There was no indication of any pursuit yet but he knew the Lichchavi were less than half a mile behind. 'We need to keep moving.'

Sushim leaned against the tree trunk. 'Grand-mother Khorasan said it would all go exactly as planned. Invite all the sons and daughters of the nobles who had opposed or failed to support Khorasan in the sabha. Make sure you were present too. Keep everyone happily drunk and lull them into a stupor. Then, one morning, her soldiers would eliminate everyone and we would blame it all on the guests, saying they began attacking me and prove they were complicit with the Lichchavi in the assassination plot. It would all be over in one morning, I could return to Patliputra and she would use my testimony to justify moving against the Houses that had betrayed the Empire.'

You mean the Houses that you lied about betraying the Empire. Ashoka felt sick to his stomach even though he knew by now that he could hardly expect anything better from Sushim or Khorasan. *What about father? Was he aware of this too? How much did he know?*

'We should move. They will come after us. They won't stop until they catch us or kill us now.'

'We go into the Haunted Forest. What then?'

'We go through. I know a way. It leads to Acharya's ashram. It's forty or fifty miles from here, no more.'

'Chanakya's ashram?' Sushim looked doubtful. 'Will we be safe there?'

'Safer than we are standing around here talking all day.'

Sushim looked around, as if suddenly realizing where they were and what they were running from. He glanced in the direction they had come from as if expecting to see green uniforms appearing anytime. 'There's no other way?'

'No. This is the only way to survive this.' Ashoka started moving. 'Come on.'

He began jogging again, giving Sushim a chance to build up speed, before building up to a steady running pace. He was relieved to hear his brother's heavy breathing follow him. He increased the pace. He intended to put as much distance between them and their pursuers before they began tracking their trail.

They ran through the day, heading deeper and deeper into ancient woods, into the jungle known as the Haunted Forest.

20

He smelled death before he saw or heard it. It smelled like unwashed cat, but beneath the rank, animal odour was another smell, a familiar, almost comforting one. A smell that reminded him of his infancy, of a dog that had lived with them since before he was born, and who had given birth to a litter once when he was old enough to understand the idea of birth. He knew that smell. Lactation. This was a female with milk in her mammaries, a mother. But not like his old faithful dog who had died of some mystery ailment when he was nine years old, breathing her last in his lap while he held her and stroked her lovingly till the end. He had cried for old Asu, using the cloth she used to sleep on as a pillow to keep her scent close. Over time the scent had faded away, but he had never forgotten it.

This scent was not Asu, he knew that. This was no dog that would come to lick his hand when called. It was the deadliest of predators in Girvan. The queen of the Vyag herself. A mature lioness who had birthed young cubs recently. That made her the most dangerous animal possible. She would be hungry, eager to replenish the nutrients she had expended during childbirth, to rebuild her own strength so she could care for her newborn cubs. She would be lean, hungry, desperate. That was why she had not simply pounced on him and Sushim while they slept, but had crept up to where they lay, in a little gap between trees, resting out of sheer exhaustion after running all day. Sushim was fast asleep beside him, snoring loudly and musically, blissfully unaware of the deadly threat only a yard away. Ashoka was awake now and fully alert, but took care to keep his breathing in the same steady sleep pattern, his eyes closed and his muscles relaxed. One false move and it would all be over. Having spent his early years in the jungle, living amongst wild creatures with his mother in a simple thatched hut, he had deep and abiding respect for all living beings. This was as much their world as his. They were neighbours, not enemies. But right now, at this moment, he was prey to this hunter. His neighbour had come calling and she was looking for dinner, not friendship.

He remained motionless, waiting to see what she did.

After a moment, Sushim's snoring grew muffled, as if he had turned over onto his stomach suddenly. Then a dragging sound, like a heavy object was being pulled across the dirt floor of the forest.

Ashoka opened one eye slowly, careful to keep it half-lidded; predators could see light reflected off the eyes of other animals.

He saw a mangy lioness dragging Sushim, still fast asleep. His head and one shoulder were in the lioness's mouth, gripping by her powerful jaws and teeth.

Ashoka weighed his options.

The lioness was clearly weak from birthing but those powerful jaws still possessed strength enough to bite through Sushim's neck and tear his head loose from his body. If she bit down, Sushim was as good as dead. The lioness was shrewd. Like all lions, she preferred to expend as little energy as possible, and right now she looked like she had little to expend. Dragging away a sleeping prey to kill and consume elsewhere was a typical Vyag technique. While pack animals would attack and kill a prey animal then eat it wherever it lay, Vyag liked easy prey, and always took them back to share with the rest of the pride and eat at leisure. The lioness needed only one of them to satisfy her hunger: by dragging Sushim away, she was trying to avoid a fight with Ashoka. He didn't flatter himself that she was doing this out of fear of him, she was merely making a judgement call and it was a smart one. Sushim was the heavier sleeper of them both, and was still fast asleep even now.

Ashoka could still hear him snoring somnolently, his face buried inside the Vyag's massive jaws.

Ashoka realized he was being handed a golden opportunity.

He could shut his eye and let the Vyag take Sushim away and kill him.

That would make him First Prince. The next in the line of succession. Future Emperor of Mauryavansh.

But if that was all he cared about, he would have let Sushim die back there, pierced by Lichchavi arrows.

He had no desire to be First Prince or Emperor. The snake's nest of politics disgusted him. He had no desire to take his father's place, or to become his father.

He didn't think Sushim would make a better Emperor than Bindusara, but it was Sushim's legacy. His birthright. Sushim was a terrible person, never mind that he was his brother. But Ashoka couldn't just let him be dragged away to be eaten by a lion. He couldn't let a fellow human being be killed without doing something to stop it. It was not sympathy or caring. It was not brotherly love or kinship. It was simply empathy. The way he was born and the way he had been brought up: to care and respect all life equally, regardless of what that life may represent. If he killed any enemy, it was only in self-defence. He couldn't let Sushim just die like this.

But he didn't want to kill the Vyag either. He loved animals. She was only trying to survive in her natural habitat. They were the intruders here, Sushim and he. She was only doing what she had to do to live.

It was a dilemma. To kill an animal which he respected, loved, admired, in order to save a despicable excuse for a living being. Or to let his own brother die and gain a measure of privilege that he had earned through his own negligence and inaction.

Ashoka had been taught the precepts of karma and dharma,

like every other young child. He knew dharma demanded that he protect his brother and kill the lion. But karma was in conflict with dharma. He did not want to kill the lion.

He rose slowly to his feet, moving in slow unthreatening steps toward the darkness between the trees. He could track the lion now only by the dragging sounds but as he approached, he could glimpse the two large eyes shining in the darkness. The sound of dragging ceased and he heard a low rumbling within that great chest.

The lion had released Sushim and was staring at him, ready to defend its prey.

Ashoka crouched down, then sat on the forest floor, crossing his legs, and keeping his arms on his thighs. He kept his eyes averted downwards, knowing that to look an animal, any animal, directly in its eyes was to challenge it. He kept his voice low, unthreatening, but firm and without any fear. Not because he felt no fear, but because fear was irrelevant here and would only rouse the Vyag into attacking.

'I know you are hungry,' he said softly, his voice sounding alien amidst the sounds of the jungle at night. 'I know you must eat and he is easy prey. But he is my brother. I cannot let you take him. If you try to take him, I will have no choice but to stop you. Release him now. Leave him where he lies. Walk away. Go home to your cubs. Find other prey. Live your life. Raise your litter. Rule your pride. I have no quarrel with you. We are both children of this forest, we can live together without conflict. I do not wish you harm. Go in peace, my sister. Go now.' More firmly, in a stronger tone: 'Go!'

The Vyag stared silently. The large eyes gleamed in the darkness. There was some faint luminescence from the sky that filtered down through the trees. He could just make out the great face, the whiskers, the great head and massive jaw, the long fangs and bone-crushing teeth. She was assessing him, gauging his intentions. She sensed that he intended her no harm, otherwise she would be growling and snarling. The fact that she was staying quiet showed that she smelled his absence of malice. He began to think that maybe he would get away with this after all, that this standoff could be resolved without violence.

'Ashoka?' Sushim's voice was quavering, scared. He was awake and aware that he lay on the ground, a lion's jaws hovering over his face.

The Vyag roared at the sound of Sushim's voice and the scent of his fear. She bent her head to grasp Sushim's head in her jaws again, clinching him in a death grip.

The time for indecision had passed.

Ashoka's body moved without requiring permission from his mind. A child of the jungle, trained from birth to be at one with the earth, he knew instinctively that the wrong move would cause the lion to crush his brother's head in an instant. There was only a fraction of a second to do exactly what was required and no second chances.

He threw the stone he had clasped in his fist while watching the Vyag draw Sushim away.

The instant the stone left his hand, he was moving, leaping, hitting the ground and running—away from the lion and his brother.

He sprinted in an arc that led around the place where the Vyag had Sushim pinned.

The stone he had flung struck the Vyag on its large snout, one of the most sensitive and vulnerable parts of its anatomy. The Vyag let out a squeal of pain that Ashoka heard as he sprinted around, concentrating all his attention on dodging tree trunks and overhanging branches. He could no longer see her but he was counting on her immediate reaction to be to loose her grip on Sushim and roar to express her outrage. A moment later, he heard her roar in pain and fury. He was already parallel to the spot where the Vyag and Sushim lay and turned inwards now, arcing back towards her, coming up on her from behind. If there were other Vyag in the darkness behind her, he would stand no chance. Female Vyag usually hunted in tandem but he sensed that this one was on her own. Her mangy condition, sallow ribs, heavy breathing, all indicated she had not fed since birthing. Had she been with one or more sister Vyag, that would not have been the case as the other female or females would have kept her fed till she could hunt for herself again. He was gambling his life on his observations. And Sushim's.

The Vyag heard him approaching. Distracted and outraged by the stone to her snout, she was still a Vyag, the queen of the jungle. She was swinging around even as he came running up from behind her. Her massive face turned to face him as he came at her, and her jaws were open wide, snarling, as she crouched and launched herself in a leap that would end only with him decapitated or disembowelled. His tactic had worked. He had succeeded in making her lose her hold on his brother and turn away from him. Sushim may or may not have the presence of mind and survival instinct to get up and run away, but at least he was no longer in immediate danger of having his skull crushed or neck severed by those razor fangs.

Ashoka leaped at the Vyag while running straight at her, twisting his body sideways as he jumped. She launched herself at him at the same time. Were they two Vyag colliding, he would have met her in mid-air, great jaws locking, paws with extruded claws ripping, and both would have rolled over in a flurry of dust, leaves, blood and saliva. But he was merely human, not Vyag, and he had no great jaws, razor-sharp fangs or claws capable of ripping open tough Vyag hides.

All he had was a dagger and his instincts and an indomitable desire to survive.

Mortal and Vyag flew at each other in the darkness of the jungle night.

The mortal's body spun, twisting around so he was flying upside down through the air, under the Vyag's body.

The Vyag flew overhead, her great jaws seeking his puny head and missing. Her deadly claws were out and sought his soft belly and vital organs.

Ashoka felt her claws skitter and scratch his chest and belly, scraping his ribs and sending stripes of fire ablaze, but he was thin and had angled his body so he passed between her claws, passing under her exposed belly. His dagger moved upwards, striking, piercing, ripping...and the force of his momentum and her own weight and motion did the rest.

Ashoka landed on top of Sushim, his brother's head striking his back, and rolled over, once, twice, thrice, before regaining his footing in a crouch, facing back the way he had come, dagger held out ready to strike again, eyes seeking out his antagonist.

The Vyag fell, tumbled, and rolled over twice before striking the trunk of her tree with her torso. Ashoka heard the thump and her squeal of pain and the soft wet sloshing sounds that told him she was done.

His keen sense of smell caught the unmistakeable odour of offal, blood, and assorted fluids and organs. He heard the sounds of distress from the Vyag, punctuated by her attempts to roar and growl to warn her enemy that she was not finished yet, she could still destroy him if he dared to come close.

Ashoka rose and walked forward, still crouched low, dagger dripping over his hand, wrist, forearm. The blood of the Vyag was thick and syrupy and hot, very hot.

Sushim was whimpering in a heap on the ground where the

Vyag had abandoned him. He cringed as Ashoka came close. 'Maa!' Ashoka walked past him and continued to where the Vyag lay against the tree trunk, her growls subsiding already as the life poured out of her through the great gaping hole in her belly. He heard her snuffling and her pain and his heart broke at the thought that he had caused such agony. Why did two children of the forest have to clash? Why did he have to kill her? He knew he would never know the answers to those and the other questions that came in the aftermath of taking another life.

He slowed, calming his breathing, trying to make himself as non-threatening as possible. He lowered the hand with the dagger and kept his voice low and unaggressive.

'Mother. I am not your enemy but I had to do what I did to save my brother. I mean you no harm or malice. Forgive me for what I did. It was only to survive.'

Those large eyes glistening in the darkness, the sounds of distress weaker and more plaintive now. She growled softly at her murderer, but had no strength to raise herself up to defend herself further from attack. She had been dealt a death blow and she knew it. In her already weakened condition, it was taking everything she had just to stay conscious.

Ashoka crouched down low before her, putting down the dagger.

He joined his palms in a namaskara to her.

'Forgive me, mother. I had no choice.'

She mewled then. A strangely disturbing sound that reverberated through his conscience, and pierced his soul. He felt tears well up in his eyes then, and held them back. What a world this was, where two beings who had no hatred for one another, had to fight to the death to ensure survival.

'I promise you this, on my own mother's oath, that I will care for your cubs as if they are my own blood. They will be loved and cared for and raised up to be strong and healthy and live full lives. I swear this as my name is Ashoka, son of Shubhadrangi and Bindusara.'

The Vyag raised her head then and roared once, a long mournful cry that echoed through the jungle.

Then she lay back and stared at him, her breathing coming in slow painful intervals.

She continued to stare at him, breathing painfully.

He understood what she was asking of him.

Ashoka wiped his eyes with the back of his hand.

He picked up the dagger.

He crawled forward, over the hot wet spillage of her life's blood and intestines.

He came close enough that she could have bitten his face off, or clawed his throat out, if she had desired. Even in her weakened state, it would take no more than a single snap.

But she lay still, watching him, waiting, beseeching.

He raised the dagger to her throat, felt the hot wet fur brush the back of his hand, smelled her most intimate death odours, the heat of her breath on his face like a blessing. He gripped the back of her head, the mane, with one hand, and used the dagger in the other hand, in a single decisive motion.

When he released that great head, the breathing had ceased, the great eyes were shut, the life had passed out of her proud body.

He crouched before her, kneeling to the queen of the jungle, and he wept his heart out for what he had done, what he had had to do.

21

'Yuvraj Ashoka! Yuvraj Sushim!'

Ashoka watched from a branch twenty-feet high as the soldier called out for the umpteenth time. There were other armed men and women in the woods, all searching for him and his brother. Except for Dwadesh who was still in his imperial colours, they were all dressed in a ragtag manner, displaying no affinity to either Mauryavansh, Khorasan, Lichchavi Confederacy, or any other nation or tribe. From what he could tell, they were of widely different tribes, regions, nations. Some appeared to be of mixed blood, local and foreign. Most were young, too young, yet seemed confident with a sword, or bow or whatever weapon he or she happened to be carrying. The weapons showed use, and the bearers experience belying their tender age. They had been in a battle recently, judging from their appearance, and from the cuts and bruises and injuries hastily bandaged. He had been watching and listening to them calling out for the past several minutes, trying to decide if they were seeking him out to kill him or for some other reason.

Sushim was sitting on the same branch, hugging the trunk of the tree as if it were his late mother and he would never let go. He had said very little since the encounter with the Vyag. Ashoka guessed he was still in shock at waking up in the middle of the night to find his head in the jaws of a lion. He had seen Ashoka slay the lion but had not expressed a word of gratitude. Ashoka had expected none but it was galling to have the entire incident ignored as if it had never occurred. It still hurt him to recall the death of the Vyag. He hated having had to kill that beautiful beast. The least Sushim could do is show some emotion, acknowledge the fact of her death. But then again, this was Sushim, who hadn't cried at the death of his own mother. Why would he care about the death of a Vyag who had tried to kill him. Brothers they were, but as unalike as the Vyag and mortal. More unalike, actually, since Ashoka found it easier to identify with the Vyag than with a privileged, entitled, spoiled brat of a young man like Sushim.

'Yuvraj! We are friends. We mean you no harm!'

Ashoka felt the ball of fur cradled in his anga vastra stirring.

The sound of the voices had woken up his little ward. Furball was an apt name for the time being, since the tiny Vyag cub was little more than a bundle of fur, teeth and claws. The last were still nascent but sharp enough to scratch. He felt the infant claws scraping at his chest as it tried to find purchase. He pressed his hand to the bundle wrapped in his upper garment, securely cradled by careful knotting, reassuring it that all was well. It mewled softly, too softly to be heard by anyone but Ashoka, and went back to sleep.

He felt for the poor cub. Its world had been turned upside down overnight. After mercifully ending the Vyag mother's pain, he had sought out her lair. By the time he reached, the scene was one of carnage. A pack of hyenas had attacked the cubs in the absence of the mother and killed all but one of the litter. Chasing them away had been an easy enough task—Ashoka only had to throw a stone or three and yell loudly and indignantly, and they had scattered, barking insolently as they retreated into the jungle, yellow eyes gleaming as they looked back. The lair was a mess of uneaten body parts and gore. What was left of the poor litter was barely enough to make out how many had been there before the hyenas attacked—either four or five cubs, he estimated. Huddled under the cover of a rock, crying and struggling for life, was the last survivor. A female cub, the runt of the litter from the looks of it. She had lost an entire leg to the hyenas, and the half-bitten fragment of bone jutting out from the wound had made him choke with sympathy. That shard of bone was causing her agony every time she attempted to step on it. He considered putting her out of her pain but when she tried to bite him, he thought perhaps she still had spirit enough left to fight on through the struggle that was life. He used his dagger to chop off the fragment of bone, leaving her with a cleanly severed leg, and three perfectly good ones. She howled and scratched and bit him but he repaid her with much stroking, a gentle voice and the comfort of his own warmth. Perhaps it was the fact that he carried the scent of her mother, or the fact that he was a warm body offering comfort and kindness. After a while she stopped struggling and fell unconscious, her tiny brain taxed beyond its limit by her experience. He held her close and kissed her gently on the top of her head. She smelled terrible. But then again, he was sure he must smell just as awful to her.

Sushim and he had spent the rest of the night in this tree, after he had forced Sushim to climb up. Ashoka needed some rest and he had no desire to be forced to fight a pack of hyenas who might well be bold enough to return to finish off their midnight snack.

Now, there were human hyenas calling out to them. And he had to decide if they could be trusted any more than the four-legged ones.

He came to a decision.

'Dwadesh.'

He spoke the single word just loud enough to be heard by the young man about thirty feet away. It was a test.

Dwadesh swung around at once, looking in the correct direction, behind and up. He spotted Ashoka standing on the branch of the tree and grinned.

'Ashoka! We have been searching for you since first light.'

'Who are your friends?'

Dwadesh looked at the other young men and women moving through the dense forest, still calling out Ashoka's and Sushim's names. None of them had heard Ashoka or realized that Dwadesh had spotted him yet.

'They are like me.'

Ashoka frowned. 'They look too young to be imperial soldiers.'

Dwadesh shook his head. 'Not soldiers. Not imperial. Just fighters.'

'Whom do you fight?'

Dwadesh shrugged and something came over his young face, an emotion Ashoka recognized well. 'It used to be anyone who is an enemy of the Empire. But that changed when our mothers were killed. Now we are fighters without a nation. Rebels without a cause.'

'Your mothers?'

'We are the bastard children of the Chandikas.'

Dwadesh did not explain further, merely said the words and waited for Ashoka to respond.

Ashoka nodded. The Chandikas were officially not permitted to have husbands and families. But many of them took lovers of different sexes, sometimes from within their own ranks, sometimes from outside. It was not officially permitted, but Mauryavansh employed a Don't See, Don't Know policy. There were also Chandikas who were, occasionally but not that rarely, sexually assaulted in the line of duty. When this happened, the Order took action, operating discretely and anonymously. The offending man, or men as was often the case, since a single Chandika was usually equivalent to at least two fighting men, would quietly just vanish one day, never to be seen again. Since his or their bodies were never recovered, it could not be termed murder, and without any proof of their death, it could not be termed retaliation. But everyone knew what it was and it usually discouraged other men from even looking at a Chandika with the wrong intention. Usually, but not always. Men could be stupid when it came to their gonads.

The bastard offspring of such illicit, forced or consensual relations could never be acknowledged by their mothers. They were usually taken in by the families of the Chandikas and raised as cousins or siblings. Some of them never came to know their true mothers, but a few did know and Ashoka had met some. He had been aware that Dwadesh himself was the bastard son of a Chandika but not which one. So it did not surprise him to know that the rest of the bastards banded together, especially in the wake of recent events.

'I see you're not wearing your imperial uniform anymore,' he said, still keeping his voice low.

Dwadesh had come closer to the tree which Ashoka and Sushim were occupying, his eyes watching Ashoka to ensure this was permissible. Ashoka nodded to let him know it was all right to approach.

'I was let go from the Imperial Army,' Dwadesh replied. He looked up at Ashoka. 'Some question about my parentage. It was never put into so many words but it was never a secret either.' He gestured at the forest. 'None of us can never find a place with the Empire, not officially.'

Ashoka nodded. That was Patliputra in action. Bias of every kind, institutionalized, was the cornerstone of empire. It was inevitable that once the Chandikas were decommissioned, anyone linked to them would also suffer a fall from grace.

'I don't trust these people! They could be sent to kill us. Don't believe anything he says!' Sushim's voice rang out plaintively, loud enough to startle away a hummingbird hovering nearby.

Ashoka ignored his brother. Dwadesh did the same.

'Why come looking for us?'

'The danger is over. We fought the Lichchavis and won.'

'You fought them? You mean...?'

Dwadesh's associates had heard Sushim's plaintive voice and

were closing in from all sides, approaching cautiously. Dwadesh made a series of gestures to communicate to them all was well and they relaxed, gathering the base of the tree.

'Our ragged bunch of outcasts, yes. Is that such a surprise? That we did what the Khorasani guard could not?'

'That is not what I meant, Dwadesh. The Khorasani were taken by surprise, arrogant and unprepared. They were busy slaughtering themselves, it was a perfect time for the Lichchavi to attack when they did. Besides, you are sons and daughters of Chandikas, the fiercest, finest warriors that ever walked the soil of Jambudwipa. I would wager you could face anything and win.'

The looks on the upturned faces showed their pleasure at his words. Ashoka smiled at them. 'Thank you for your service to the Empire.'

'We did not do this to serve the Empire,' said a young girl with close-set eyes and a scar across her throat that suggested someone had tried to kill her and failed.

'We are not servants of the empire. Any empire.' This came from a boy younger than Ashoka with short hair curled into ringlets on his dark scalp.

Dwadesh said quietly: 'We are free agents. We fought the Lichchavi because they were partly responsible for what happened to our mothers. And for you.'

'Me?'

Dwadesh nodded. 'You were a friend to our mothers. You stood up for them. Your mother stood up for them. Nobody else cared even to speak up once. You cared. We owe you a debt for trying, for caring.'

Sushim spoke up impatiently. 'If these ruffians are telling the truth, and the Lichchavi are gone, send word back to Patliputra, asking for an escort to accompany me back to the city. Go on, then. I will see that you are well rewarded.'

Dwadesh looked at Sushim as if he were an insect on the tree. 'We do not want your gold, Yuvraj Sushim.'

'Then what do you want?' Ashoka asked the question. He was still unable to fathom the true intention of this group. He had not forgotten his guru's warnings to be cautious.

Dwadesh looked around at his group. 'If word gets back to Patliputra, they will send reinforcements. But they will be Khorasani reinforcements. And you know what that means.'

Ashoka knew. 'Their orders will be to retrieve only Sushim alive.'

Sushim looked up at Ashoka then down at Dwadesh. 'I will tell them you are to be spared.'

Ashoka looked at Sushim, then at Dwadesh. His eyes met Dwadesh's eyes and they exchanged a look. In that moment, he knew he could trust the bastard, and that he could never trust his brother.

'How many are you bastards?' Ashoka asked. He used the word not as a pejorative, merely for want of a better collective term.

'A hundred and fifty maybe. Some of us were hurt in the clashes with the Lichchavi.'

'This is unacceptable! We have to get word to Patliputra! I have to get back. If you won't send word then...you do it. Escort me back this very minute!' Sushim's voice rose in pitch with each sentence. He released one hand from the tree trunk to gesture for emphasis and almost lost his grip and fell. He grasped the trunk again, hugging the tree. 'I command you as your First Prince!'

'I am not a servant of the Empire anymore, Yuvraj,' Dwadesh said casually. 'You are not my prince.'

Sushim looked startled. 'But you have to help us! You cannot leave us here! There may be more Lichchavi assassins. They could ambush me. Ashoka and I alone cannot fight them if they attack in force.'

Dwadesh shrugged indifferently. 'You can stay here in the forest or find your own way back to Patliputra. As you wish.'

'But...but...' Sushim spluttered but seemed unable to find words to sufficiently express his outrage.

'There is another way,' Ashoka said. He raised his voice, speaking loud enough for all the bastards to hear. They raised their young faces to him, male and female both, dark and darker skinned, eyes revealing souls older than their years. He found himself able to relate to these outcasts of Empire. They were not unlike himself. He had a place in the Empire, but did not want it. They neither wanted a place nor had one.

'Come back with us. I will see to it that you are not harmed.'

His words lingered in the silence. They exchanged glances with each other, expressing varying emotions but mainly one question. Dwadesh spoke it aloud.

'Why should we? This is not our fight. We are unwanted by Patliputra. Why should we fight to protect two princes of Mauryavansh?'

'Why did you come seeking me out? You could be a hundred miles away from here by now. You didn't have to.'

'And then what?'

Ashoka glanced at Sushim, who was looking at him with a combination of fear and confusion. Sushim understood that his authority meant nothing to these people but didn't like it. He was scared and angry but not foolish enough to think he could bully his way out of this situation. 'If you accompany us to Patliputra, First Prince Sushim and I will vouch for your role in saving us from the Lichchavi. He will personally guarantee that you are reinstated in the Imperial Army, every last one of you.'

Ashoka locked eyes with Sushim. 'What say, brother? Surely that is a small reward to repay these gracious fighters for aiding us in our moment of need?'

Sushim swallowed, both his saliva and his pride, and said in a desperate, over-eager tone: 'Yes, yes, of course! Escort us and I will endorse you myself! I will speak on your behalf to my father the Emperor.'

'Our father,' Ashoka corrected mildly. 'Yes, we shall both petition him together, Sushim. Because the lives of the First and Second Princes of Mauryavansh are worth that and much more.'

'Yes! Yes!' Sushim all but shouted.

Dwadesh exchanged a glance with his associates. They looked at each other and then up at Ashoka again.

'We have no desire to rejoin the Imperial Army,' Dwadesh said. 'But we would do this for you on one condition.'

'Anything!' Sushim cried. 'Name your price!'

'Our price is our dignity. We have no desire to serve the Imperial Army anymore. But it is true, we could use some coin, and some patronage. We ask only that we be instated not as regular army, but as a special order of the militia. Serving under you, Yuvraj Ashoka, as your personal guard. That is our condition, and you may either accept it or leave it, that is your imperial choice.'

Ashoka looked at Dwadesh and smiled. 'I accept.'

'Yes! Yes,' Sushim cried in relief. 'Now let me down from this wretched tree!'

22

Noor Khorasan watched with blazing eyes from the Queens balcony as the sabha session came to a conclusion. She watched Queen Shubhadrangi tearfully embrace her son Ashoka and wished she had a bow and arrow so she could drill both mother and son with a single shaft. Shubhadrangi's tears were tears of pride and relief.

Bindusara had just acknowledged and thanked his son personally before the entire sabha for his role in keeping his brother First Prince Sushim safe from the Lichchavi assassins in the jungle. There was also something about a lion attack mentioned, and how Ashoka had again intervened to save his brother. With these latest accomplishments, in addition to the earlier events in the city, and his role in exposing the Lichchavi Confederacy assassination plot as well as the complicity of the Chandikas, it now seemed that Ashoka had single-handedly managed to save the imperial family from grave threats, both external and internal, risking his own life and limb against assassins, traitors, and even wild beasts, to save his brother and heir apparent, and ensure the safety of his family. In recognition of their dual role in ending the Lichchavi threat, the Emperor had proposed sending both brothers to Takshashila, where a violent uprising was threatening the stability of the region. As First Prince, Sushim would be the Satrap of Takshashila, a great honour to be bestowed on one so young. But it was implicit that though he did not have the title, Ashoka nevertheless shared this honour with his brother, and would accompany him to his posting. Bindusara had made a speech extolling the virtues of brotherly service, quoting from the Ramayana and Mahabharata, and ended by implying that what Ashoka had done was what any brother ought to do if he followed dharma.

Noor Khorasan knew that Bindusara did not enjoy praising Ashoka or acknowledging his part in the recent events any more than she did, but as Emperor he understood the importance of appearances and political currency. Ashoka was a hero whether he was acknowledged as one or not. By acknowledging and rewarding him, Bindusara made himself seem bigger. More imperial, was the phrase he had used when they had discussed it yesterday. Noor had known when a cause was lost and had fumed and seethed but outwardly pretended to encourage his decision. She had even told him to give his blessings to Ashoka's unorthodox request to recognize the bunch of bastard ruffians he had brought home from the forest and grant them imperial status. Bindusara had been against the request, especially since Sushim, once safely home, had told his father that for all they knew those ruffians could well be in cahoots with the assassins themselves. But Noor Khorasan had seen an opportunity and had taken it.

'Send them with Ashoka to Takshashila, as their main guard.'

Bindusara had frowned. 'That would be highly unusual. They are barely children. Bastards and untrained. It would reflect badly on Sushim. Imagine a First Prince coming to take charge of his satrapy accompanied by a band of ruffians!'

'Then send a token imperial guard with them. But send them as well. Ashoka could have asked for much more. He could have asked for a Satrapy himself like Sushim did. This is the only thing he wants. Give it to him.'

Bindusara had looked at her. They were in her bedchamber, after sex, and his body still had a sheen of sweat on it. She was naked and languorous, reclining against silk cushions, enjoying the gentle breeze from the hand fans waved by the serving girls. In a moment, she would ask Orzala to wash her with cool scented water—and bring her to the peaks of pleasure that Bindusara was incapable of ever accomplishing.

'Very well,' he said, watching her shrewdly. She knew from his expression that he understood that she was asking him to do this for a reason. He did not ask the reason, which was wise of him. He knew her well enough to know not to do so. She smiled, lifting one bare leg and capturing his limp member between her toes. She began to work it back and forth slowly. 'An Emperor must be generous.'

He sighed, settling back against the cushions and enjoying the attention of her soft feet. 'An Emperor must conserve his resources.'

She watched him swell again to full hardness, working her toes and feet expertly. 'Sometimes, it is necessary to expend some resources in order to gain new ones.'

He groaned, totally in her control.

Now, she swept out of the queens' balcony of the sabha hall, ignoring the many sister queens who tried to catch her eye or smile to gain favour. She stormed out and along the corridors back to her apartments. Even though she had been the one to push Bindusara into acknowledging Ashoka's achievements, it still infuriated her to see that mongrel standing the sabha hall, beside the First Prince, as if he belonged there. And his mother? Oh, Noor wished she could use Shubhadrangi for target practice. That whole motherly act, lover of nature and little animals, made her sick. Obviously it was all an act. There was no room for motherly love, kindness and gentleness in this world. It was wolf eat wolf world. Anyone who knew anything knew that. Women who pretended to nurture their young and talked of things like honour and dharma, equality and love were deranged dangerous people. The kind of people who had no place in the world. They were the weak and the meek and they had to be destroyed, the way a pack of predators would destroy any creature that limped or had a weakness. Only the strong must survive, and that meant destroying the weak. She longed for the day when she would be able to see Shubhadrangi reduced to a mass of bleeding agony as she deserved.

She turned a corner and came face to face with the very object of her hatred.

Shubhadrangi and Ashoka paused, staring at Noor Khorasan.

Noor caught herself and composed her face to reflect a suitably neutral expression.

'Why, Queen Shubhadrangi,' she said aloud, assuming a smile. 'You must be so proud! My sincerest congratulations to you and your brave son, Ashoka. May you both enjoy your glory as long as it lasts!'

'Thank you, Queen Khorasan,' Shubhadrangi replied, bowing her head in acknowledgement. 'You are very gracious.'

Ashoka inclined his head slightly but did not bow or speak. His eyes bored into Noor's eyes as if he could see straight through to her soul and could read her innermost thoughts and feelings as clearly as if they were written out in Sanskrit on a child's board at an ashram gurukul.

She smiled again in parting and went on her way.

I will get you when you least expect it, she thought as she swept down the corridors. *I will show you what the world is really like, and on that day, you will bow and beg and kiss my feet and cry for my mercy.*

And I shall not give it.

EPILOGUE

'Bharata.'

The forest of gleaming cat eyes shone like a swarm of fireflies. It was the night before the first full moon of spring and the air was still cool, the leaves damp with dew, the forest deathly silent as every insect, leaf-eater, bird and animal showed respect to the Gathering of the Vyag. In the star-rich sky overhead, the children of Garuda drifted, watching with sharp interest, for when all the world is forest, every living creature is kin. If the Vyag had a problem, it was every creature's problem.

'Bharata,' said Whitest Whisker. An ancient lion who had been dam for so many litters, she was no less than Mother Goddess to the Vyag. She had seen a hundred mates come and go, a thousand cubs grow to maturity and wither, been matriarch to a hundred prides, survived sicknesses and stampedes, storms and avalanches, and had personally killed at least one mortal for every hundred Vyag present at the gathering.

There were six hundred thousand Vyag present.

For those Vyag who were poor at counting—which was most of them—it meant a kill score of some six thousand mortals.

'Bharata.'

When she spoke the word in the voice of the Vyag, it sounded not like a mortal spoken word. Mortal language, even at its most eloquent, was a clumsy attempt at communication. The Vyag conveyed more through a single growl and look, through scent and effusion, through context and day and time, than a mortal could convey through an entire scroll. That single name, growled thrice, sent ripples of awe and unease through the vast gathering. Even the monkeys perched on the high branches, noses twitching with the overwhelming stench of so many Vyag, shivered nervously at the scent released in response to that name. Who was this mortal who caused the Great Gathering of Vyag to twitch their whiskers?

'Bharata,' said the whitest whisker for the fourth time.

Combined with the ancient matriarch's scent, emissions, postures, tail twitches, whisker quivers, eyes, baring of teeth, and the context and setting, the fourfold repetition conveyed the entire history of the Vyag's ancient feud and truce with mortal kind.

Mostly, what it conveyed was that the truce had been broken. By a mortal of the same race as the one who had initiated the truce itself, a thousand generations earlier.

A Bharata.

The response of the gathering was instantaneous and momentous.

With the voice of a single great pride, the Vyag raised their heads to the full moon and roared out their fury. The sound of their rage filled the forest of Girvan for a hundred yojanas in every direction, sending terror into the heart of every living creature. Every creature, except mortals. They were the only ones who had no clue what was about to befall them. Even though it was upon them that this cataclysm would be unleashed.

Kautilya woke with a shudder, breath rattling in his sawdust-filled throat like the final gasp of a dying empire. For a long desperate moment, he struggled with the ghosts of the past, the fears of the future and the terrors of the present. At one point, he thought that this was the night. His wretched lungs would lose at last this ancient battle and he would die here, on his pallet, in his ashram in the deep jungle. Months, perhaps years later, his corpse would be found by some bandit or forager, withered to a dried husk, bones cracked by lion jaws, head smashed open and emptied of its edible contents—a stringy, unappetising mouthful or two to some passing Vyag.

Not just any Vyag.

A lion.

Symbol of Mauryavansh.

At this thought, his throat finally won the battle over his beleaguered brain. With a great effort, he succeeded in drawing breath into his tortured body. He focused on the intake and output of air until he felt well enough to trust his body to manage on its own. How could drawing breath pose such a challenge? He knew from his study of Ayurveda and anatomy that it was related to the brain which ultimately controlled all bodily functions and processes. That part of his brain that had mastery over the simple act of breathing had suffered some lapse. He wished that instead of the breathing part of his brain, some other part could have lapsed.

The part which controls memories.

Or better yet, the part which controls dreams.

Except he knew that what he had just viewed in his tortured

breath-deprived sleep had not been a dream. It had been a vision. A bizarre nightmare about Vyags of all kinds gathering in a forest to discuss the future of Mauryavansh. A bleak vision of a bleak future.

Rising unsteadily on bony limbs, he staggered slowly to the entrance of the hut and outside, to the tamped mud flat clearing before the hut. The familiar odour of freshly applied dried cow dung and cow urine lingered, discernible even above the jungle smells. With a start he realized that if his acolyte had already cleaned and disinfected the clearing, that meant the hour of bhor suvah was nigh. He looked up at the eastern sky. It was black as the hair on his head had once been, black as the jungle pressing in around him on all sides. He could not tell the hour, or even the watch, which was unusual for him. He had always known exactly what watch and hour it was, even when waking from the deepest sleep, and exactly where he was in relation to true north. It was the result of his own father's conditioning, from Kautilya's birth; his father, who had also been his first and only guru.

Be aware at all times, Kautilya, even when asleep.

Today, his father's conditioning had finally failed him. He was disoriented and confused, his brain still struggling, his breath still wheezing in his chest. He was in his own hut in his own ashram, but had someone burst in and told him that he was on the peak of Kailasa right now, he would not have been surprised.

Or in the depths of Naraka, he thought sourly. Then, in an uncharacteristic pique, he permitted himself to mentally voice a plaint: Mahadeva, you are the giver of all gifts, for that we are eternally grateful, but this gift of old age you can take and stuff it into a tree trunk, thank you. Declined with gratitude.

He sat and watched as the eastern sky began to lighten faintly by slow degrees. He ought to get moving, to perform his morning rituals, meditate, and prepare for another day of lessons to his acolytes, and the composition of his seemingly unending treatise. But for once, his limbs would not move, his brain could not bring itself to command them into action, and he just sat there and watched the crow-black sky turn the colour of a heron's wing.

The dream. It meant something. A dream of lions cannot be without significance. Who is the Bharata the old cat spoke of? It could not be Chandragupta Maurya, could it? He is long gone to the great cat-house in the sky. Then who? Surely not Bindusara. Since he turned Ajivika, he has foresworn violence personally. He only commands the commission of violence, he does not stain his own sword. Besides, he is more likely to be eaten alive by a pride of cubs than to kill a lion himself.

Who else then?

The sons of Bindusara?

Among their number, there was only one who could achieve such a feat.

Kautilya mused on the matter for a long time, till the sky turned bright blue and the sunlight found its way between the high trees into the clearing. Finally, he roused himself and strode back towards the hut. There was new purpose and strength in his movements. Perhaps strength was too strong a word: call it determination. He emerged from the hut moments later, carrying his staff, the one with the top meticulously carved in the shape of a lion's head by a gifted shudra artist. The end of the staff left clear indentations in the soft dung-coated floor of the clearing.

When his students came for the morning lesson, they found only these marks to indicate that he had gone.

The marks were headed in the direction of Patliputra, capital city of the Mauryavansh empire.

Ashoka woke as easily as any cat. No thrashing in sleep, no cold sweats, no calling out. He had learned from childhood that for a warrior, rest was a precious jewel: Steal it every chance you get. The more you get, the richer you are in health. So he slept in patches, a wink here, forty there, a few hundred some nights if he could afford it. But even in the deepest slumber in the cold dark watches of a winter night, he was ever just a blink away from wakefulness.

He blinked. And blinked again.

And saw nothing but fur.

He grinned in the darkness, moved his head a fraction, and was able to see the mud floor, walls and thatched roof of the ashram hut. The bundle of fur that had obscured his view continued to lay as it had, positioned in front of his face. As Ashoka raised himself to one elbow, the bundle stirred, raised its oversized head, and licked his face with a lavish slurping stroke. Ashoka grinned again and wiped the saliva off. It still smelled of the cow's milk he had fed the cub before bedding down beside only a few hours earlier.

'Glad to see you're feeling better,' he said, rising to his feet. The cub tried to emulate him, but her solitary hind leg shook and her flanks shivered. Ashoka watched, knowing better than to help. The cub whimpered as the injury on her remaining hind leg caused her pain, but she bravely completed the action and stood on her own three feet. Ashoka did not regret severing the pitiably injured leg at the topmost joint—it had been too far gone to save and had the wound festered, it would have killed the animal for sure. He had chosen to save the creature's life by cutting off the useless limb and tending for the beast until she was strong enough to hunt on her own.

As he went to the entrance of the hut, glancing out with his usual caution, he considered that decision. The cub would walk again, he was certain of that from the way she had already adapted to her new three-legged gait. But would she be able to hunt? How could she, when her mother had died too young to be able to teach her? Vyag usually taught their young to hunt from the age of three masas onwards—three moon-cycles being the time it took for a young cub to be able to crouch and stalk without tumbling over its own tail—but it took a cub another eight or nine masas more of constant imitation before she could actually hunt prey herself, under matriarchal supervision. He had seen the process first-hand twice in his young life, and it never ceased to inspire him. He had learned his own hunting skills by studying Vyag, supervised by his Guru, and that had made him identify intimately with these proud, beautiful creatures.

Even now, watching the three-legged cub shake off her pain and stand at a cautious angle to him, he admired her courage. She sensed him looking at her and yawned to feign disinterest, which he knew was the Vyag way. The moment he stepped out of the hut into the cool winter air, she pattered after him, afraid of being left behind.

He smiled and feigned disinterest too by taking long strides that must seem like enormous leaps to her, conceding to her condition by stepping with exaggerated slowness. He needed to challenge her just enough to help her fight her way back to full mobility. Molly coddling would be dangerous. He had known that she would be extra effort from the moment he had seen the smashed bloody mess that was her right hind leg, and her chances of surviving were nil without him, and slim even with his help. But he intended to do his best, which meant challenging her to do her best.

The act of sleeping head to head with him in the night was her way of showing she trusted and needed him, of saying, 'We are pack'. It had touched him more than he cared to admit and he slowed a tad when he heard her labouring to keep up even with his reduced pace.

You can't be a mother to a Vyag, Ashoka. This is a foolish enterprise, as Guruji would have said. Bonding with you this way will make it impossible for her to reintegrate with her own kind. And your life is no life for a three-legged Vyag cub!

But he had no choice. He couldn't bring himself to leave the injured cub lying there in its own blood and feces, mewling pitifully. He just couldn't.

Because he had just killed her mother.

'Come on then,' he said, moving just a little quicker, forcing the three-legged orphan to hop twice as fast. The earnestness with which it kept up was heartbreakingly admirable.

A moment later, they came upon the clearing where his fighters waited. Ashoka slowed, the cub reducing its brave pace with a whimper of relief. She smelled the horses and the men and snarled reflexively, cringing as she saw what must have looked like a small army to her. But she didn't turn tail and run. Instead, she moved closer to Ashoka and braced her fore paws in a fighting stance, growling at them. We are pack, the two-legged one and I, we stand together and fight together. Ashoka smiled at her show of loyalty. Barely a week and already she was ready to fight beside him. But then, that was Vyag loyalty. Humans on the other hand...

'The Yuvraj?' Ashoka asked, acknowledging his best man Dwadesh.

Dwadesh jerked his head in the direction of Patliputra. 'With the rest of our band, on the crossroads, waiting.' He emphasized the last word with a look.

Ashoka chuckled. He could imagine how well his brother the crown prince Yuvraj Sushim was taking the waiting. Ashoka had spent the last few days and nights at the ashram instead of at the royal palace in his official apartments. He had wanted to keep the injured cub away from the cruel pranks of his brother princes but he also preferred the simple rustic existence of the ashram routine to the debauched hedonism of the princes' palace.

He scooped up the little cub, turning it in a moment from

a growling predator to a surprised kitten. He swung up on his mount, carefully placing the cub on the leather saddle where its claws promptly dug in, anchoring it. A gentle stroke to reassure it, then he nodded at Dwadesh who turned the head of his own horse, leading the group through the woods back to the crossroads. They would join the main contingent and start the long journey to Takshashila, where Yuvraj Sushim was to negotiate the release of the city from the Pashtun rebels who had overrun it. Ashoka and his fighting band were the bodyguards to the prince and the only military, or militia, presence on the trip. The idea was that sending a large, official-looking Mauryan army presence would provoke further aggression from the rebels. Ashoka's scruffy-looking band was easily underestimated, though he knew that each one of them were worth ten of the average Mauryan soldiers.

As they rode, and the little cub stopped whining about this unorthodox means of Vyag transport, it occurred to Ashoka that he had finally found the name he had been seeking for his loyal band.

'Cubs,' he said aloud, testing the word.

'What's that?' Dwadesh asked, glancing back.

'We'll call ourselves Cubs from now on,' Ashoka said. He indicated the little three-legged creature dug into his saddle top. 'Even have our own mascot!'

Dwadesh grinned, glancing around at the others. They all nodded, grinning or grimacing in approval. 'Ashoka's Cubs,' Dwadesh said. 'I like the sound of that.'

The little Vyag purred unexpectedly. She was starting to enjoy the ride, especially after she had realized she was safe and that her newfound pack leader was right with her.

'She likes it too,' Ashoka said. 'Cubs it is then.'

War Marshal Khorasan watched from the cover of the high thicket as Prince Sushim and Prince Ashoka's expedition force wound its way through the valley below. The Khorasani guard ranged behind the War Marshal watched as well with their customary arrogant indifference. If they were ordered to attack the expedition now they would do so without question. Friend or foe, family or unknown, it was all the same to a Khorasani. Steel knew no blood kin, the blade had no friends. They would swoop down on the very princes they were assigned to protect, and kill, slaughter, torture, rape, or do whatever they were told to do to them, and at the end of watch, they would stand down, take their repast and retire and never dwell on the why or wherefore of what they had done. They were Khorasani, they did not waste time on thinking. Thinking was for poets and there were no Khorasani poets, not the kind that used words anyway. The song of steel was the only music they understood, and it consisted of a single lyric: Kill.

The War Marshal of Mauryavansh watched until the Takshashila expedition reached the end of the valley road and wound its way around the bluff, disappearing out of sight. Even now, they could easily be caught up with, easily ambushed, stalked or trapped. It was a long way to Takshashila and much could happen between here and there. No help would come from Magadha—they were the royal guard, dispatched to escort the expedition safely to the border.

Khorasan itched to do it, to fall upon the two princes and cut them open like bleating lambs. She had done it before, though not so blatantly. Each prince eliminated meant one less future rival to the throne. And these two, Sushim and Ashoka, were the two eldest, the first and second claimants by law. Sushim was crown prince and Ashoka was second in succession, although there was some debate about who was the older one. It did not matter that Ashoka made no claim to the throne and was apparently content to be his brother's protector and guardian, even riding alongside him on this Takshashila expedition like a common bodyguard. Khorasan did not believe such brotherly altruism nor trust it. All flesh craved power. Just as all steel craved blood. It was the natural order of things. Sushim she did not even count as a rival. The crown prince was a competent fighter if he stayed sober long enough to know the pointy end of a sword, but he was spoiled and weakened by self-indulgences. Eliminating him would be as easy as cutting a billy goat's throat.

Ashoka was another matter. For all that the boy made no claim to his inheritance, seemingly content to live out his youthful existence serving rather than ruling, he was a canny young man. A shrewd tactician. A promising fighter. A disciplined pupil of warcraft. And from what Khorasan had seen, a leader of men. His ragtag group of warriors, rough and only slightly experienced in battle, could be licked into fighting shape over time. Today was an example: the fighters had just returned with Ashoka from one skirmish, and here they were, already riding out to Takshashila to deal with a bigger challenge. Even she grudgingly acknowledged that such dedication was rare among the sons of Bindusara—or among the Mauryans in general. Khorasan had observed the young prince's dealings with the group as well as with individual warriors, some defiant, feeling their oats, others more vicious and looking to butt heads with any authority; Ashoka had dealt with them impressively well.

He had a flaw of course, a great big one that would eventually prove his undoing: he was soft metal, too easily given to forgiving and nurturing rather than setting right. The Khorasani believed that if a man or woman defied you, you put them down, otherwise the next chance they saw, they would do the same to you. The idea of forgiveness, or mercy, was alien to Khorasani culture. Ashoka's willingness to overlook transgressions was a weakness that would cost him someday. But even with these failings, he was still one to watch. If Khorasan had been the one giving the order, Ashoka and his ragtag group of warriors would already be a pile of steaming entrails strewn across the kings road down in the valley. A flare was best extinguished before it became a blaze.

But her orders were simple and clear: watch and report.

The princes would find a challenge up in Takshashila. They were unlikely to survive that. If they did survive, they would face a bigger threat later on. That was the plan. It was a good one. Her daughter Rani Khorasan was the political strategist and she, Senapati Khorasan, the tactician. The fist and the blade, each needing the other, both accepting their respective parts in this great game. Her age-lined face creased in a hard expression that was nothing like a smile and yet was as close to smiling as her war-seared face could ever affect. It was the expression of a wolf that has selected its prey but delays the kill until a better opportunity presents itself.

The War Marshal turned the head of her horse and began riding back towards Magadha. Her warriors needed no verbal orders or instructions to follow. The Khorasani way was to lead by action and example, not words.

She was looking forward to the day, not long now, when these tactics and strategies would be done and she could unleash her wolves upon all enemies, present or potential. That day was coming.

She would bide her time until then. And when it came, Prince Ashoka would be the first one to hear the song of her blade, the last thing he ever heard.

Book Two

1

The perfume of carnage hung over Takshashila.

Saffron, eucalyptus, and the scent of ripe apples mingled uncomfortably with the battlefield stench of rotting flesh and feces.

The city revealed itself in glimpses, like the punctured veil on a corpse. Smouldering fires and grey smoke made the ravaged city a cremation ground. The rebellion had torn through the city like a ravaging horde. Skeletons of half-burnt houses loomed. Corpses hung twisting in the wind, the eyes pecked out by carrion birds. Of human presence, there was no sign, only the occasional scurrying shadow too scared to reveal a human face.

Horses whickered. Stomachs churned. Someone retched: Sushim.

The crown prince proceeded to rid himself noisily of the venison and wine he had gorged on that morning, belched, then cuffed his servant soundly, blaming him for serving spoiled meat.

The meat had been anything but spoiled. Ashoka had tracked and brought down the stag himself just the day before, with a single arrow through the heart, his own losing a beat as those proud antlers fell to the ground. We live so we must eat, his mother always said. Sushim lived so he could feast.

He put his brother's gluttony out of his mind.

He wanted to be prepared for the ambush.

Anticipating violence, he had given over the Cub to the rear guard, who were hanging back on the outskirts of the city, at the

Uttarapatha, the great Northern Road that had brought them all the way from Patliputra to Takshashila. She had not wanted to leave him, had snarled and dug her nails into the saddle leather, but this was business meant for two-legged Cubs now. She waited now with the company for whom she had now been accepted as an official mascot, Ashoka's Cubs, ready to ride back to Magadha if Ashoka did not send word to them by the next sunrise.

They passed satrapy guardhouses: burnt banners, besmirched stone edicts, and corpses bearing the Maurya lion emblem.

A satrapy lieutenant materialized out of the fog, dangling from a pole. His squad dangled beyond him in a row, orderly even in death. Sushim made sounds of disgust as the stench reached him. Ashok caressed the roan's left ear and the mare sidestepped the butchery smartly, careful not to soil her hooves on the bug-swarmed pools of dried gore below each man: they had each had their bellies cut open by a spear point before being hanged.

At the crossroads, Ashok paused to examine the large oblong stone that marked the city's boundary.

It was a royal edict in Prakrit erected in the time of his grandfather Chandragupta Maurya, bearing the familiar mark of the first emperor of the Mauryavansh empire. The twinge of pride he always experienced when viewing the legacy of his ancestor was now tarnished. Something dark had been smeared across the carved edict. The stain looked damp. Ashok broke off a thin branch from an overhanging tree and rubbed the leafy end against the smear, confirming that the defacing was recently done, perhaps less than a day old. He sniffed sharply, the fecal stench unmistakable, and tossed the branch aside.

This wasn't mere vandalism. Someone was sending a message.

He coaxed his horse onwards, passing a satrapy post and barracks hut a few hundred yards ahead. The stench here was especially bad. He heard Sushim curse loudly behind him as his brother came upon the sight of Mauryans splayed out in grotesque poses. The other soldiers echoed their prince's dismay.

Ashoka concentrated on examining the scene of the war crimes. The absence of maggots and proliferation of flesh flies told him that the corpses had been here less than one masa, a lunar month. That jibed with the arrival of messengers who had brought the news of the uprising to Patliputra. Satisfied, he was about to turn back when something that was out of place caught his eye.

It was the body of a young Gandhari boy, too young to grow hair on his face. The position of the boy, the bound wrists and splayed ankles, also bound, indicated a different form of abuse. The large gaping wounds indicated the spear thrusts that had concluded the day's entertainment.

Somehow the abuse of that Gandhari boy irked him more than the fate of the Mauryan soldiers.

Ashoka was not concerned about the citizenry in general. Unlike the amatyas and Sushim making sounds of dismay behind him, he knew this looked worse than it was in reality. For one thing, there were far fewer corpses, human or otherwise, than there were houses here. Gandhari families were large, often as many as a dozen or more to a single small hut. They also hated to die inside doors and would have rather come out to fight than hide inside their domiciles.

Based on the number of houses and corresponding corpses, Ashok estimated that less than one-twentieth of the populace had fallen prey to this particular round of slaughter. Yet the corpses had been left untended and above ground for almost a full masa, more than one full moon cycle. Since Gandhari buried their dead, this suggested that the vast majority of the populace had survived and had fled at once when the uprising began. Ashok guessed they had done as their people had for seven hundred years—fled into the mountains where they would wait out the crisis. They would remain there until Patliputra sent troops to quell the rebellion, or the rebels killed each other off.

It meant the people did not support the rebellion. That was a very useful conclusion. It confirmed his own suspicions.

The Afghans of Gandahar were a hardy people. Since the great wanderer Afghana had settled in this rugged mountainous territory over seven hundred years ago, spreading his nation across the most travelled highway in the known world, his descendants had survived the incursions of many invaders and conquerors. Darius the Great, Xerxes I, Alexander the Great, Shapur I—despite the lofty titles and numerals appended to their names, all had bled dearly on the rocky slopes of these mountains. Each of these lofty conquerors, and others of their ilk, had sought to claim provenance over Gandahar, seeking to control the civilized world's greatest trade route where it was most vulnerable. Many had grasped at Gandahar, but like a lamb in a buzkashi tournament, the mountain nation had not stayed in any one ruler's grasp for long. That was why Ashoka was unconcerned about the people at large: the Afghans of Gandahar would bide their time, shepherding their goats and living frugally off the land until they deemed it safe to come back to their houses, to begin yet another cycle of rebuilding and resettling in their long and violent history. It would take more than a rebellion to break their spirit.

The only one who had come close to breaking that indomitable Afghan spirit was Seleucus Nicator, grand satrap of the late Great Alexander. Nicator's 'empire' overlapped contentiously with the Mauryan empire and his footprint was unmistakably left upon this insolent carnage. Little signs like the smearing of feces on the royal edicts, the public abuse of the civilian boy, the Mauryan satrapy banners wrapped around the private parts of denuded corpses, all these were messages meant to be seen and read by Patliputra, the seat of power of the Mauryan empire, the largest in the civilized world. The messages suggested something more than a simple bid for power. A rebellion overthrowing an oppressive empirical regime directed its fury against the empire's emblems and defenders. Not against mere boys or stone edicts. This was something else, but what? He ran a hand across his jaw, rubbing his palm against the grain of his bristling beard.

The boy bothered him more than he should have. Ashoka resisted the urge to dismount to cut the boy loose and lay him down, covering his glaring eye-sockets. (The eyes themselves had been long since pecked out by scavenger birds.) That boy had no role in either this rebellion or the Mauryan satrapy that governed this region. He was an innocent bystander made to suffer for no fault of his own. Nor was he the only one. Ashoka had seen other corpses similarly staged at every satrapy check post. Someone had issued orders to leave this breadcrumb trail of atrocities along their route into the capital city. Someone who thought nothing of expending young lives to send a message: Seleucus Nicator was here!

Sushim came up beside him, clearing his throat loudly. Between the retching, the complaints, and the throat clearing, apparently the crown prince now felt confident that his arrival had been sufficiently well announced.

'Take me to the palace. This stink is making me sick.' Sushim hawked and spat—the spatter landing squarely on the twisted, bleeding foot of the splayed boy.

Ashoka kept his voice quiet. 'The rebels will have taken the palace.' Stating the obvious was often a necessity when speaking with Sushim.

'So?' Sushim shrugged. 'It's still our father's palace. There will be food.' He cut his eyes sharply at the serving boy sitting on the mule beside him. 'Proper food. And wine. It's been a long journey and I'm bloody thirsty.'

Ashok nudged his horse onward. Facing the rebels seemed preferable to prolonging a conversation with his brother. And if Sushim was bloody thirsty, then Ashok was bloody angry. The plight of the boy, end of a long trail of tortured innocents, had sparked something within him; something he had thought had been burned out years ago. The rising rage he felt proved that it still endured. And right now, it was flaring phosphorescent, threatening to conflagrate. He urged the roan into a trot, trusting his men to keep pace. The Cubs knew when their leader was raring for a fight. Behind him, he heard the familiar sound of Sushim grumbling at having to ride a road littered with obstacles. The ambush he had been expecting had already come, he realized, but it had been an emotional attack, designed to get under his skin. His response, however, would be a physical one.

2

Without a word of warning to Sushim or the amatyas, he made his move.

Dropping to the stone floor, he crouched and wheeled in a dancer's pirouette, sweeping his feet.

His boot connected with the bare shin of the Pashtun standing before him. The man grunted and fell heavily on his side, striking his head on the lowest step of the throne dais with a wet crack. Ashoka seized the hilt of the long curved Pashtuni blade sticking out of the fallen man's waistband and used it to cut his throat. The Pashtun cried out and jugular blood spurted like a fountain.

Before the blood spatter could reach him, Ashoka had already rolled away, twisting, spinning on his heels to assume a squatting position. The other rebels were still reacting to the leader's fallen son, reaching for their weapons. The curved blade in Ashoka's hand flashed like heat lightning. He found his mark thrice in the lower bellies and groins of the men who had been standing behind the son, entrails spilling out wetly. The men bent over, clutching at their falling guts. With both their hands occupied with trying to gather up their spilling intestines, their weapons were forgotten. Ashoka took no chances: he had once turned his back on an old bastard who had crawled after him leaving a ten-yard trail of bloody intestines and stabbed him in the right calf. He slashed the blade across their throats in quick efficient movements, like a farmer harvesting ripe wheat. The sheaves fell. Ashoka continued spinning, enlarging his circle of attack, bringing down another two men by slashing at the hands with which they reaching for their weapons. Their hands scrambled across the hilts of their swords with spurting, severed fingers. He spun and slashed the blade again—across their faces, severing the first man's bearded cheek, florid nose, the lower half of one ear, then both the other man's eyes in a straight red line that left him squealing like a struck lamb.

The rest of the rebels were reacting now. They had been too confident in their strength of numbers, their easy victory, the drinking and feasting and rape and abuse, their leader's certainty of the way the game would play out. They had never expected this. Nobody had. Certainly not Sushim, whom was screaming the loudest, cursing his brother for disobeying their father's royal command!

Only the Cubs had known.

When they had not encountered any ambush on the way to the palace, they had understood, as Ashoka had, that the fix was in. And every last one of them knew that Ashoka hated the fix, hated the politicking and shady deals and compromises. Live or die, they were fighters one and all, and they would rather die fighting than brokering.

In glimpses he ascertained that they were holding their own.

Seasoned fighters all, they had been in situations before where they were weapon-less and outnumbered by well-armed enemies. They knew that surprise and first blood were their best chances of survival. Like Ashoka, they all attacked the nearest rebels with savage force, going straight for groins, eyes, smashing noses to bloody pulp, grabbing a fallen vase and slamming it into the side of a man's temple, using whatever was at hand to disorient the Pashtuns long enough to steal their weapons and reduce the advantage of superior numbers.

Ashoka reached the second step of the dais, jabbing the point of the blade into the side of a man's neck. The point emerged from the other side, below the man's ear, but the man snarled and still came at him. Ashoka turned the blade in the man's throat, using it to leverage him around in a running arc, then kicked him in the backside hard enough to send him sprawling into another two men who were coming at Ashoka from behind. The blade tore free of flesh and sinew and bone, rupturing the man's throat in a burst of gore, bathing them crimson. One of Ashoka's soldiers ran up and jabbed the point of a spear into the face of one of the fallen men, then into the heart of the other man. He looked up at Ashoka and nodded. Ashoka glanced around the throne room and saw fighting everywhere, his men chopping and hacking at rebels with savage precision. They knew the odds were against them. Their only chance lay in evening the numbers and fighting on as long as they could, to let Ashoka do what he had to do.

He saw the amatyas huddled in the centre of the chamber, eyes white and wide in their smooth brahmin faces, bald heads shiny with droplets of spattered blood and their own sweat. Sushim was in their midst, crouching on the ground, head lowered, hands covering his ears as he shook from side to side, in denial. A Pashtun came roaring at the cluster of amatyas and hacked at them with a giant axe. Two of them were cut nearly in half, screaming curses that were never in any Vedic scripture. The Pashtun chopped at them again and again, till the curses stopped and they lay intermingled in bloody death. Two of Ashoka's Cubs rammed spears into the man's sides from behind, rupturing his vitals. He turned without visible discomfort and roared as he swung the axe at them.

Ashoka assessed that Sushim was about as safe as he could be under the circumstances. He turned back to focus on his goal and leaped up another two steps.

A pair of red-eyed men who had been drinking from a giant jug when the list of demands was being recited were still holding the heavy vessel between them, each gripping one handle. They dropped it together. It bounced with a metallic clanging, wine splashing and flowing down the steps to wash against Ashoka's feet. But his feet had already left the ground. He threw himself forward in a standing jump, somersaulting feet-first into the lower chest of one of the red-eyed men. He felt and heard ribs crack like dry twigs and the body yield. But the man was either drunk out of his skull or insane. He grabbed Ashoka's feet and swung him around, using Ashoka's own forward momentum to send him sprawling. Ashoka tumbled roughly, striking his shoulder, banging his elbow, striking his cheekbone hard on the edge of a step, then slamming his collarbone almost hard enough to crack it. He lay stunned for only a fraction of a kshana—the bronze jug had bounced one more time and was now toppling over as it went down the steps—then rolled groggily as the gleam of steel came flying at him. The knife or throwing axe, or whatever it was, clanged behind his head, nicking his scalp and making it burn. Ignoring the burn and wetness, he took hold of the carved back of a heavy wooden seat meant for the satrap's wife, handstanding on the seat to throw his body up in the air, away from the descending arc of a rusty iron sword brought down by the second red-eyed man. Ashok went head over heels, landing in a crouch to keep his head low from flung missiles, and saw the sword draw sparks as it bit the stone floor in the place he had been a kshana earlier.

He turned his head and found himself looking at the bare thighs of two young scantily clad women. They swayed, gaping glaze-eyed in his general direction, not really seeing him: intoxicated on Afghani hemp. There was a sense of barely suppressed terror beneath the drugged dissonance. He grinned at them in an absurd attempt at reassurance, then threw himself sideways, cartwheeling out of the way of the rusty iron sword, a flung spear, several small tossed knives, glimpsing the mayhem in the throne room in brief slices, upside down, sideways, diagonally: blood-splattered amatyas screaming and holding out severed limbs, Sushim wailing like a tortured cat, Pashtun rebels clashing drunkenly with Ashoka's men, all now armed and bloodied. He saw one of his men fall under an onslaught of several rebels hacking at him from every side, slashing at their legs even as he went down. He saw two of his men standing back to back, one holding a spear, the other a curved blade, picking off a score of rebels assaulting them with a variety of weapons. He saw a cluster of rebels holding one of his men against a pillar, breaking off his arms, driving an axe into his groin, chopping him in half at the torso like a tree. The man was grinning through bloody eyes and teeth as he went down. As with all such battles, it was impossible to tell who was winning while you were in the thick of it. All that mattered was surviving—and taking down as many of the other side as you could before you went down too. Because, no matter how well you fought, sooner or later, you always went down. It was the only truth of war. The yoddha's reward: bloody death in the thick of battle.

His series of cartwheels had brought him to the far side of the throne dais steps, forcing his attackers to turn and rush towards him with weapons drawn. He was above them now and used that advantage. He leaped up and kicked hard at the foremost one, the heel of his boot taking the Pashtun under his chin, cracking the man's jaw and sending him flying back downwards, off his feet, to crash into the others. They all went down in a pile of tangled limbs and pierced flesh, their outheld weapons penetrating each other. There were several more Pashtuns coming from all directions, converging on the throne dais, roaring and yelling their native curses at Ashoka. The Cubs had understood his intention from the outset and now blocked the rebels, fighting them back to buy Ashoka more time. But there were too many rebels and too few Cubs. It was a matter of attrition and time.

There were other Pashtuns pouring into the chamber from all entrances, all except the one outside which the rest of the Cubs had been forced to wait. From the yells and sounds from that direction, Ashoka guessed that those Cubs were busy keeping other incoming rebels at bay, but even they could not hold their position for very long. It was now or never.

Ashoka turned and ran the last three stone steps up the dais. They were the largest and highest steps, narrowing as they ascended to create a space sufficient for the satrap's throne and one man to stand on each side. The Pashtun was standing before the throne now, blades in both hands, and there were three other men with him, two on the same level and one on the second-highest step.

This last one was already striking at Ashoka with the biggest wooden hammer he had ever seen. The man himself was short for a Pashtun, but built like a brick wall, and strong as one too, judging from the size and heft of the weapon. The hammerhead itself was twice as large as Ashoka's head, and the force with which the man swung it, he would smash Ashoka's skull like an egg if he connected. Ashoka swayed back, feeling his heels slip off the edge of the third-highest step, his back curving as he almost bent back double to avoid the deadly blow. He felt the wind of the hammer passing, and knew that even a whisper touch of that monster would crack bones with force enough to bring out the marrow. He had only a fraction of a kshana to counter and only one way to do it.

A straightening of his back as the hammerhead blew past, then a crouch and a springing hop. He leaped onto the hammer-man's shoulders. The man was still at the end of the hammer swing, both hands occupied with holding the heavy brute, and even to drop the hammer he would need a moment. Before that moment, Ashoka plunged the blade of his sword into the soft flesh between the raised tendons on the back of the man's neck, driving the blade downwards into the chest cavity and piercing the heart. The curved blade made the task harder than usual and Ashoka felt the tip of the blade snap off somewhere deep inside that barrel chest, probably caught between two ribs. He released the handle, leaving the blade embedded in the hammer-man's chest, and leaped again before the corpse could fall.

His second leap took him directly into the spears of the two guards positioned on the second-highest step, the last line of defence against their Pashtun chief. Ashoka had noted the spears and anticipated they would be thrust towards him. This was why he leaped head first at them.

He caught hold of the spears just below the blades, missing one slightly and feeling the edge slice open the bottom of his left palm in a deep wound. Using his forward momentum, he turned both spears back over the shoulders of the men who held them, to point at the rebel chief himself.

Seeing the danger, the Pashtun roared and slashed with the sword in his left hand, knocking both spears harmlessly aside.

Ashoka released the spears as he glimpsed the flash of the Pashtun's sword, and the sword's blade sliced the air barely a finger's width beneath his elbows—and his chin. He was still flying forward, and the Pashtun had another weapon in his right hand, a long-bladed short-axe. But he was still turning with the sword slash, and Ashoka was already past his defence and at his throat. The Pashtun saw the danger and tried to lunge out of the way, still roaring. All that mutton must have given him a goat's vigour!

Ashoka grasped hold of the only thing he could get hold of as he flew past the rebel chief, the man's beard. He clutched at the bristly thick beast, greasy with lard and juices, and yanked the Pashtun backwards and off his feet.

Both Ashoka and the rebel chief fell back onto the satrap's throne like a pair of tumbling fools in a court entertainment.

The satrap's throne was a strong enough seat to carry the weight of a man as large and heavy as the Pashtun. But it was not strong enough to withstand the force of both of them crashing down together. The seat tipped over, and with it went Ashoka and the Pashtun. Something struck Ashoka's head—a resounding wallop hard enough to make him see black for a moment and bite the inside of his cheek. The Pashtun's bearded mouth was near his right ear as they tumbled over, and the man's roaring was deafening. Ashoka had a kshana of lapse of consciousness, then blinked and found himself dangling several yards high in mid-air. He had gone over the rear end of the throne dais which dropped in a sheer fall to ensure no enemies could approach the satrap from behind. The blow to his head had come from the stone ledge behind the toppled seat. His legs flailed in the air, almost three yards above the floor of the throne room. He could have jumped without difficulty but then he would lose his chance at the rebel chief. Already, the Pashtun's men had seen him dangling and were approaching with raised weapons. A sword flashed between his boots, less than a foot beneath the heel. He was vulnerable in this position. And the only thing keeping him up was his grip on the Pashtun's greasy beard. Which was slipping gradually.

The Pashtun was bent backwards over the toppled satrap seat, roaring and flailing as he tried to strike at Ashoka over his head. The sword above and sword below both flashed together as if in concordance, and Ashoka had to pull his legs up and duck his head at the same time. One of the Pashtuns below was reaching for a spear fallen on the ground. If he threw that at Ashoka's exposed body, this would be over. Ashoka's men were all on the fore side of the dais while more and more Pashtun rebels were pouring in from the rear entrance. If he fell, he would be overwhelmed instantly. Even the fiercest Cub couldn't hope to fight his way out of a score of raging Pashtuns.

Ashoka reached up and grasped the rebel chief's beard with his other hand too. It was difficult, the beard was disgustingly greasy, but there was enough of it at least. His fingers struck the man's roaring mouth and had the Pashtun bit down hard enough at that instant, he could have taken a finger or two clean off. But he was too busy roaring and struggling to turn around. The chief's head was twisted backwards. Ashoka clenched tight, one hand above the other, and kicked his feet back till the soles of his boots found purchase on the rough stone back of the dais. Bracing himself, he bent his body forward like a bow, pulling on the Pashtun's beard with the two-fisted grip. He felt his arms and neck and shoulder muscles strain, his abdomen tightened like a drum, his vitals exposed to any sharpened blade from below, and he bellowed a cry of his own. It was the battle cry of the Cubs, but also that of his grandfather. A single word, shouted in a single expelled breath.

'MAURYAVANSH!'

He felt the Pashtun's powerful muscles resist with all their might—aiding him. And then, with a tearing of tendons, popping of joints and ripping of sinew, the chief's spine cracked at the neck and his head was separated from his torso. The roaring turned to a grisly whistling sound that expired momentarily to be replaced by sounds of flesh and muscle shredding. And still Ashoka continued to pull with all his might.

The screams and cries and shouts of the fighting men died away to a sonorous hum.

The stench of roasted mutton and fresh blood and guts and slaughter faded away.

The pain in his joints and head and collarbone and inside his mouth receded.

The world shrank to a single kshana within a kshana.

His entire being converged upon the point where his two-fisted grip was pulling with all the strength in his lean but muscular sixteen-year-old body, focusing all his power and force and weight on that tiny space where the Pashtun's already deceased body was resisting the force he was exerting.

Then, with a final tearing and crackling, the broken neck and throat tore apart, and Ashoka felt the Pashtun's head break free of the spine and body, and fall into his hands.

He fell with it, unbending his body to brace for the impact.

The rebels below had frozen at the moment that their leader had let out his death rattle, unnerved. In another kshana they would recover and resume fighting with renewed vigour to avenge their fallen chief.

But that moment was all Ashoka needed.

He landed with one boot apiece on the heads of two of the rebels more out of sheer luck as from intention, knocking the men out with the impact, and somersaulted forward, landing with both feet on the chest of a charging Pashtun who had just joined the fray and had not observed the death of his chief. The Pashtun flew back several yards, and Ashoka rolled over several times, coming to a crouching landing, one knee raised, the other knee bent, his hand already reaching for the nearest weapon—a straight shortword—while one hand still clutched the greasy beard attached to the head of the Pashtun chief.

Ashoka turned, fire in his eyes, sword in hand, and faced the throng of stunned rebels.

He raised the head of their chief as high as he could, showing them the dead face and dripping, ruined neck and dangling tendons and nerves and roughly torn skin. The Pashtun's mouth hung open, tongue lolling loosely, his eyes popped wide open from his final death throes, tears of blood running down each cheek, no longer capable of tearing at mutton haunches or giving orders or leading rebellions against the satrapy or the Mauryan empire.

Ashoka called out hoarsely but loudly.

'Join him in hell. Or throw down your weapons and live.'

There was a moment when he felt certain that they would fight. Pashtuns were driven by honour and loyalty and would have fought on. But these were bought men, easily seduced by promises of plunder and booty and easy ransom from the rich Mauryan empire. They had been seduced into this rebellion by the chief. And the chief was now dead. Killed by a stripling of a boy less than half his size—less than half the size of any of them. That earned him their respect, he hoped.

One of the men, the one who had picked up the spear and had been about to pierce him with it as he had dangled, pointed to Ashoka's bared chest, exposed by his ripped anga vastra which had torn open in the fight.

The man spoke a single word: 'Vyag.'

Lion.

He meant the lion's head tattoo on Ashoka's chest.

The others all peered at the tattoo, then at the head of their leader clutched in Ashoka's fist and repeated: 'Lion!'

'The Lion of Maurya!' someone else cried out and the cry was taken up and passed around the throne room.

The sounds of fighting died out, barring the pitiful moaning and screaming of those too badly injured to care about anything except ending the pain.

Ashoka heard more men behind him and turned in a full, slow circle, holding his enemy's head up high, allowing the shortsword to fall with a loud clang to the stone floor, letting all the rebels see their leader's ruined head clutched in the fist of the one they believed to be Chandragupta Maurya, his grandfather, reborn.

'The Lion of Maurya returns!' they cried. 'The Lion of Maurya!'

He strode forward, walking towards the crowd of armed bearded fierce-eyed men. Weapon-less, defenceless, he walked with only the severed head in his hand, the tattoo on his chest, and the stirring of legend in their superstitious minds.

That was how he took back Takshashila.

3

Acharya Kautilya acted his age as he climbed the last steps to the dais. He felt the fox eyes of the amatyas and mahamatyas watching him without appearing to watch him. They were assessing his condition: Radhagupta had been reporting back to him each day, with rising concern in his young excitable voice, of the rumours surrounding the Acharya's health, or lack of it.

'To hear the gossip,' the young acolyte had said indignantly, 'You are lying on a funeral pyre and all that remains is for someone to light it.'

Kautilya had almost smiled.

What Radhagupta did not know was that those rumours had been spread by Kautilya himself. There is nothing that makes your enemies happier than believing you are ailing, possibly near death. Happy enemies are careless enemies. And the longer they live under an assumption, the more rooted it becomes in their minds. He had used the tactic a thousand times before, spreading misinformation and creating misassumptions. At times, he had built an entire political network based on such misassumptions, only to bring it crashing down when the opportune time came. He had an end in mind in this instance too. When the Samrat's summons came, it was the moment Kautilya had been awaiting these past masas.

Now, he milked this climb to the royal dais for everything it was worth. He had studied the precise gait and posture of an elderly Ajivika monk and had adopted it for himself. It didn't matter that the monk was probably a decade or two younger than Kautilya's eight. It was the perception of age and weakness that counted. Kautilya climbed those steps with geriatric slowness as if it was the last physical act he was capable of accomplishing. He had considered stumbling as part of his act, but there was a point when pretending could well become reality. He was ninety-six years old after all and the dais was ten yards high on the edge of a hillock. Falling half a hundred yards was not in his plan.

A roar from the battlefield below distracted the happy watchers. Every bald head with a chotti turned to look out from the dais at the theatre of war. Even so, Kautilya continued to maintain his painfully awkward gait, underlining each turn of his right hip with the exact same grimace. He had learned a long time ago that the only way to deceive someone was to maintain the deception at all times.

'Allow me to assist, Guruji.'

A young hand was held out, offering support.

Kautilya looked up into the warm brown eyes of young Tissa. Among the youngest of the sons of Samrat Bindusara, he was too low in the line of succession to ever expect to ever become Raja, leave alone Maharaja or Emperor. That was the price of being one of over a hundred brothers.

Yet, unlike his other younger siblings, he did not act resentful. He was a kind, good-hearted young man with only one flaw: a tendency to care for animals more than humans. His mother, a follower of Mahavira, abjured meat, and her son followed her example. He was the best of Bindusara's sons, and the only one Kautilya would not suspect of moving against him. Even so, Kautilya climbed the last and highest step without accepting the proffered hand. Never take unless you are able to give back. He could give this young prince nothing, and so he could accept nothing, not even a helping hand.

'Ayushmaanbhava,' he said as he stood upon the dais before the young man.

Tissa, tall and gangly for his age, used the outstretched hand to touch the Acharya's feet before retreating to let him pass. He accepted the refusal of the offer of help as well as the blessing with a smile and a namaskara before running back to join his brothers. They were all too preoccupied with pointing out different formations and sights from the railing. The few who glanced to look at the newest arrival showed no sign of caring that it was Acharya Kautilya. It was a far cry from Kautilya's earlier career but he had come to accept the way of things now. Change, the only constant.

He paused a moment to catch his breath as well as observe the princes. Tissa was having difficulty finding a spot on the railing again—his brothers clearly felt that by leaving for his pointless attempt to greet the old brahmin, he had surrendered his right to a prime spot. Tissa reluctantly accepted and settled for huddling in the second row, standing on tiptoe to peer over his brothers' shoulders. That young man is not going to last long, Kautilya thought. Then Tissa and the other princes were all dismissed to a distant rear corner of his capacious mind. It was their father he was concerned with now.

The dais was as broad and wide as the sabha hall at Takshashila—wider and broader actually, since the one thousand carved pillars that held up the throne chamber were not absent here. There were twice a hundred persons here already, and yet the vast platform appeared spacious. That was because everyone was on the extremities, the better to get a view. Kautilya took several kshanas to catch his breath, perhaps twice as many as he needed, to give him time to spy the lay of the land. The queens were on the West side, all facing inward or toward one another in clusters and groups. The amatyas were on the East side, also mostly facing inward or toward each other, grouped according to their orders: Brahmins, Ajivikas, Buddhists, Jains. The Emperor, his generals and the War Council took the North railing. And the dasya servants, both male and female, the South. A full score of royal guards stood around, watching all points of the dais. At present, all of them were looking in Kautilya's direction. Their Khorasani features were unmistakable, their boredom typical.

Another pair of Khorasani eyes were also watching him: Rani Noor Khorasan. Even here in the naked raw light of the Deccan plains, she was a lioness in her den. Her slender frame curled in an attitude of queenly comfort, her beauty a rare diamond standing out even from the cluster of other feminine gems around her, her heart-shaped face, and penetrating grey eyes watching him as stealthily as a predator from the high branches. She needed but to raise one of those delicately cared-for fingers and the Khorasani guards would pick up Kautilya like a dried husk and toss him off the dais to certain death. He could see in her cat's eyes that she would like nothing more than to raise that finger and send him plunging to his doom.

Yama knew she had tried more than once to despatch him, in an impressive number of ways: poison, assassins, snakes, scorpions, death beetles, a bear trap, needles, building collapses, road accidents involving a variety of carts, wagons, horses, elephants, camels, and llamas, an impromptu riot in the marketplace... It was a long list of attempts in a lifetime of constant threat and even he could not be sure which of the many attempts were at her command or by his other enemies. What he did know for certain was that she would never be a friend, an ally, or anything resembling one; and when he did yield his aatma to Yama's burlap bag, she would celebrate the news. Of all his many enemies over a lifetime of making enemies, she was one of the worst and deadliest. Even now.

He met her eyes and acknowledged her hatred with the faintest of sala'ams and thin ghost of a smile. She returned it with a return sala'am, maintaining the illusion of courtly protocol. Then she turned her lovely features away to address her maids sharply.

The other queens present there paid him little heed after their first condescending glances; they were too preoccupied with gossiping amongst themselves. Only two of them acknowledged his presence respectfully: Rani Shubhadrangi and Rani Tissyanka. Kautilya met the eyes of his protégé Ashoka's mother, careful not to indicate in any way that they were better acquainted than the other queens present. Palace politics was a dangerous business. Shubhadrangi had already endured more than her rightful share of suffering owing to her caste and her son's claim to the throne. Why, for a time Kautilya had even resorted to disguising her as a maid in order to shield her true identity and origins from the other vicious hellcats. Even Samrat Bindusara had not known of her true identity at first, and once he learned of it, he seemed to approve of the arrangement well enough to want it to continue indefinitely. Bindusara hated conflict within his house and back then, Rani Khorasan and her father had been capable of resorting to any means, even open assaults on life and limb, to secure their place in the royal hierarchy. Kautilya had known what others had not, that Bindusara actually feared his father-in-law. It had taken nothing less than the carefully plotted assassination of Lord Khorasan, blamed conveniently on some of the others who had proved thorns in Kautilya's side, to remove that obstacle. But he knew that while Rani Khorasan was shaken to the core by her father's death, she would not stay mute for long. She had not withdrawn from the fray, merely changed her tactics to match Kautilya's shrewd manipulations. And now, although Rani Shubhadrangi enjoyed a place on the royal dais as befitted her status, it was only accepted because of Ashoka's publicly stated vow renouncing his claim to the throne. The son had sacrificed his own future to ensure his mother's, but some day even that would not matter. Eventually, Kautilya knew, the likes of Khorasan would have their vengeance. All he could do was prepare his pupil for that day.

But enough reminiscing about past intrigues. New challenges beckoned and he had spent long enough pretending to gather his breath after the long climb.

Kautilya drew himself up visibly, gathering up the strength he needed to endure what he knew must come next.

He shambled across the dais, continuing his performance.

Those on the dais were too preoccupied with peering over the railings to pay heed to his approach. Even Samrat Bindusara himself was facing Northwards, his entire attention on the view.

Kautilya guessed that the battle was about to begin.

This guess was confirmed as he approached the royal presence, gaining a glimpse of the theatre of war below.

The site where the battle was to be fought was one he himself had selected years ago. It had taken him the better part of a full masa of rough travel in uncomfortable chariots. He hated chariot travel because it always reminded him of wheat being threshed—with the people the grains of wheat and the breakneck rattling over bumpy ground the threshing. He had settled on this site for a number of strategic reasons but as he recalled, the other mahamatyas had argued bitterly against it because of the bare flatness of the terrain. They had recommended the cliffs and valleys of the Deccan hills instead, where the Emperor could position himself favourably high, viewing the battle in the valley below. Kautilya had countered by commissioning a design for a platform that would elevate the Emperor and his entourage safely above the field of war, and reiterated his reasons for that site.

Bindusara seemed to have taken Kautilya's advice in the end. Not that he would even mention it now: Kautilya had no doubt that in the intervening years, the Emperor had convinced himself that it was his, not Kautilya's idea. After all, he had done the same for almost every piece of advice he'd taken from Kautilya after their falling out and Kautilya's unceremonious departure from Patliputra.

Still, Kautilya took satisfaction in his choice of site.

In this particular location, the plains of the Deccan were as flat and bare as the top of Kautilya's own head. Unlike his bald head, the plains extended for what seemed like endless yojanas in every direction. At some point, they gave way to more diverse terrain, and eventually, the undulating volcanic ridges and hills and cliffs and valleys of the Deccan ranges. But right here, at the cusp where the Mauryan empire ended (for now) and the sixteen kingdoms began, it was all flatland as bare as a brahmin's shaven pate. Hence the need for this royal viewing platform. The battle itself had been held up for three ahoratras, the troops armed and armoured and ranked in lines, waiting restlessly in their respective akshohini, as the royal carpenters had toiled day and night to raise this veritable palace of an edifice. The wood had to be carted all the way from Patliputra by elephants, all twelve score tons of it.

Kautilya's mind, always given to computation, had estimated the total timber, the number of planks, nails, workmen, wastage, labour, cartage, during his geriatric climb up those many steps. To that figure he added what most amatyas would not: the cost of the three days delay to the battle, feeding the troops, animals, the support staff, the royal entourage.

The total sum was enough to feed a hundred villages for a year. And that had given his opponents in sabha their strongest argument against this site. But Kautilya had seen the look in Bindusara's eyes and known even then that the Emperor was convinced.

Bindusara hated to fight. And therefore he loved the idea of a site which required the Emperor to build a platform to seat his royal person. That way, it would not be considered weak of him not to venture into the fray and violence of actual combat. And that was precisely why he had eventually overridden the amatyas and insisted that this was where they would pitch the Lion flag.

His father Chandragupta Maurya would have laughed at the very thought of building such a platform, leave alone watching a battle from its lofty heights. When Chandragupta went to battle, all he needed were two things. 'My sword and my arse. The one to kill, the other to shit. Yama can have the rest.'

His son, Samrat Bindusara, apparently needed only one of those two things: His royal backside, presently seated upon a throne that was an exact wooden replica of the great Lion Throne in Patliputra. Even the lion-head armrests were perfectly carved, the blonde timber leaving the leonine heads not quite as fearsome as when they were carved from stone, but their somewhat more summery aspect aptly suited to the Emperor whose hands rested on their wooden manes. Bindusara, son of Chandragupta Maurya. The profile was regal enough. Straight aquiline nose, sharp features, well-shaped chin and jaw, strong clear black eyes, a handsome physique and good posture. If Kautilya asked a royal artist to sketch a great emperor, the result would be very like the man seated before him right now.

Appearances were deceptive.

Portraits lied.

Statues were idealized representations.

Features and physique did not reveal all.

And yet.

This was the emperor of the greatest empire in the known world.

The son and heir of Chandragupta Maurya himself.

Master of the Mauryan Empire, lord of all he surveyed.

All, except three pockets of resistance that stubbornly refused to join the empire.

Kalinga to the East of Patliputra, so close to the Empire's capital that their resistance was a constant affront.

Chola, to the South and East, who were allies and friends, but insisted on supporting the empire without actually joining it.

And the Sixteen Kingdoms of the Deccan and Southern plains.

It was against the Sixteen that Maurya would do battle today.

'Ah, Chanakya,' said the sonorous voice of the Emperor.

Bindusara glanced peripherally his way, remaining seated, his attention rapt on the view below the railing, keeping his profile to Kautilya.

Chanakya. Son of Chanak.

It was his name, that was true. But his village and clan name. It was akin to addressing Bindusara himself as Patali, because he was born in Patliputra. Or Empress Noor as Khorasani because she was born in Khorasan.

It served to remind him, yet again, that the Emperor showed him the least amount of respect possible, while still maintaining the code of court protocol and décorum, a code Kautilya himself had written.

Kautilya took no offence at the petty slight. His relationship with Bindusara had long since passed all pretence. Each hated the other, and both knew it. There were more important things to dwell on.

'Samrat Bindusara, I came as soon as I received your summons. How may I be of service?'

Bindusara remained seated on his facsimile throne, pretending to observe the battle preparations, issuing minor instructions to his assistants and generals who duly passed them on through an elaborate system of signals and messages to the troops below.

Those signals and messages, codified to prevent any enemy from knowing their true meaning, had also been created by Kautilya in Chandragupta's time and he knew that they were all irrelevant make-work communiques. He was only presenting the appearance of an Emperor in command, as always.

As Chandragupta used to say to Kautilya, slapping his shoulder roughly and not caring that a kshatriya did not touch a brahmin in such a manner, 'I don't know how emperors fight battles. I only know how to fight battles! I need to smell the enemy's fear, see his sweat pop, his horses shit themselves when they see us charging. I need to fight! You figure the strategy and the grand plans. I'll do the fighting.' And he had held out his sweaty blood-encrusted arm to Kautilya, who had shaken it dubiously, agreeing.

Now, he stood beside an Emperor who did not fight except on rare occasions, and used a team of amatyas, none of whom had ever seen battle or known what war was up close and personal, to decide how his vast army should be deployed strategically and used tactically, seated on a comfortable throne fifty yards above the field of battle.

'I have received news from Takshashila.'

It was the word Kautilya had expected to hear when summoned. Takshashila. Along with Ujjain and Kalinga, it was a word ever fraught with anger and a complicated mixed-potion of emotions. He had received word from Takshashila too, a good two days before Bindusara. The system of espionage that the Empire used had been set up by Kautilya himself. He had also set up a system of counter-espionage, spasas who spied on other spasas, but reported back only to Kautilya. Only Kautilya knew of their existence and only he received their missives. He had received word from them that the regular spasas were carrying news from Takshashila to Patliputra, and he had learned what that news was as well as the subtler undercurrents and related news that did not accompany it.

'Your pupil has done it again,' Bindusara said, still presenting his left profile to Kautilya, his eyes ostensibly directed at the field below, though even the amatyas to either side of the throne had reacted subtly to his change of tone. An emperor never shows more emotion than is required in a given situation: even when he loses control, he loses it only to the extent that it serves his purpose, not an iota more or less. Kautilya's own words, from his own teachings on the proper etiquette for a ruler. Bindusara's voice did not betray him, but his choice of words and posture spoke scrolls.

Chanakya. Word from Takshashila. Your pupil.

'Does the Samrat refer to his son, Prince Ashoka, or his other son, Prince Sushim?' After all, both were officially his pupils, as were all the princes, even though Sushim had stopped coming to Kautilya's gurukul within masas of being sent there, the other princes following suit not long after. Ashoka, and Ashoka alone, had continued to this day, still attending his guru's ashram every day he was able.

The slightest clenching of that perfect jaw. 'I speak of the former.'

'Indeed, Samrat, he has done it again. Once more, he has successfully quelled the rebellion in Takshashila and retaken control of the kingdom of Gandahar.'

Somewhere in the distance, to the East, a number of elephants raised their voices in a trumpeting chorus. All eyes turned in that direction, while Bindusara's remained steadfast on the field below.

'He has disobeyed a direct command. His disobedience has endangered the crown prince's life, caused the deaths of several amatyas, and negated all chance of reaching an equitable arrangement with the Pashtuns.'

'I see.' Kautilya allowed a moment to pass, as if he were absorbing his emperor's words and considering their meaning seriously. Instead of doing as you asked, and brokering a one-sided deal with untrustworthy allies who had just ravaged our own satrapy, slaughtered your queens and children there, and terrorized the people you are supposed to protect, he killed the bastard chief who led them and took back what was ours by force, as is our right. 'Would you like me to go to Takshashila and reprimand him?'

Now it was Bindusara's turn to be silent. He was calculating the benefits versus the costs of sending Kautilya to Gandahar. 'Yes. He must be reprimanded sternly. Sushim was the rightful satrap of Takshashila. Whatever decision had to be taken, it was Sushim's to take. Your pupil had no right to take matters into his own hand and exceed his authority. Such insubordination to the Empire cannot go unpunished. I must not be perceived as being partial towards him because he is related to me.'

When have you ever been partial towards him? You have always treated him like a serving boy, a valet, a common soldier, and at best, a bodyguard for your favourite son Sushim, to whom you are openly partial. The revolt in Takshashila happened only because of Sushim's incompetence and misrule. Sushim was rarely present in Takshashila, he was always traipsing with his companions, making merry and enjoying his princely pleasures. To reprimand Ashoka who quelled the rebellion and punish Sushim is a travesty of justice. Your father would never have been so foolish and pig-headed. But then again, you are not your father, are you? Not even a patch on his greatness, Chandragupta Maurya.

'Samrat, do you wish me to travel to Takshashila? I shall make arrangements to leave at once.' It would give him an opportunity to reach Ashoka and warn him personally.

The generals turned to Bindusara and indicated the latest signal from the army below. 'It is time, sire.'

Bindusara stood, his rising alerting all upon the dais. The chattering of the amatyas and the whispers of the queens died instantly. The guards stood to attention. All eyes and ears were on the Emperor.

He glanced once towards Kautilya, not meeting his eyes but simply looking in that general direction. His tone was stiff, his jaw tight.

'The battle is about to commence. We shall discuss this after our victory today.'

Kautilya bowed as was expected of him. Bindusara turned away without even acknowledging the gesture, and gave the signal for battle to commence.

4

Tissa ignored the smirks and sneers of his brothers. They thought he was a fool to waste his time on the old brahmin. Acharya Kautilya's time was past. Even his own mother said so, and she was not one of the spiteful ones; the others said much worse. In a family where over a hundred heirs vied for succession, with who knew how many more to come, every gesture, word or deed counted.

Tissa didn't care. They were the fools. With Sushim and a dozen others at the head of the line, none of them would ever have a chance at the throne. His mother, sisters and he were reconciled with the reality of their situation and were content with what they had: being a member of the most powerful royal dynasty in the civilized world, wasn't that enough? He had everything a young person could desire: Power and prestige and the freedom to do as he wished. Yet he wanted...less. The excesses of entitlement sickened him.

His brothers showed their scorn for him by preventing him from retaking his place at the railing. He didn't care. They were eager to view the battle. He hadn't even wanted to come; his favourite foal was ailing, and he hadn't wanted to leave her side. But with every sibling and mother expected to attend, he had been left no choice.

He didn't make an effort to push through the jostling elbows, instead seating himself on the cushioned seats and worrying about the sick foal. He imagined her as she had been when he had left her last night, laying on her side in the hay, swollen belly rising and falling heavily, body hot with fever. He had paid the stable boys a coin apiece to pay her special attention. They were to wipe her down every hour to keep the fever down and squeeze drops of water into her mouth to slake her thirst.

'Tissa, look!' one of his siblings shouted, forgetting that they were ignoring him. Everyone was pointing and chattering excitedly. Tissa rolled his eyes. They were acting like it was a naming day celebration. He saw the cause of their excitement: the Mauryavansh flag being waved from side to side slowly by father's flagmen, passing on the Emperor's order to commence battle.

Queen mothers and children covered their ears as the flagmen blew their conches next. Tissa saw his mother, Rani Tissyanka, actually shudder in response to the sheer volume of sound. Beside her, Rani Shubhadrangi leaned over and said something reassuring, touching her friend's arm. Rani Tissyanka opened her eyes reluctantly but looked as if she wanted to be anywhere but here at this moment. Tissa understood; he felt the same. He wished Ashoka was here. Like his mother, he needed a friend he could trust more than anything else right now. He could not have felt more alone right now than if he had been in the middle of the enemy army, rather than amongst his siblings and family.

Other conches sounded in response, hundreds of them, the sound moving successively down the field, growing farther and farther away until it seemed as if the ululating call was being echoed around the world. It was an awe-inspiring wall of sound, simultaneously rousing and fearful. Despite his hatred of violence and war, Tissa felt his skin prickling and a cold thrill shiver through his body. So this was war. His first battle; the first that most of his siblings were viewing too. Mother said it was because father was confident of a victory and had no fears of any turn of fortune. 'The outcome is a foregone conclusion,' she had said, repeating what the other queens were saying as well. 'And your father wishes you and your brothers to see what a thing is war, to prepare yourselves the better.'

What a thing is war. As if it were a literal living thing, a gigantic beast shambling out from its dark subterranean cavern, rarely glimpsed, forever feared.

The echoing of the conch trumpets died away at last.

It was replaced by the dull low drubbing of war drums.

Their gurus were standing at intervals among the princes, commenting constantly on the battle arrangements, reeling off figures that they were expected to memorize and recall later at gurukul. For Tissa and his siblings, this field trip was part of his education as a prince.

There were six thousand drummers, ten for each of the six hundred regiments of the Mauryan army. He had heard them practise in the field behind the royal stables, the constant beating as familiar as the smells of horse, elephant, and dog. Most were no older than he was, skinny little boys who marched up and down all day, drumming. He wondered how they felt now, those boys, no longer standing shoulder to shoulder with their companions in the practice field, each now uniformed in the Mauryan purple, standing in formations of ten at the head of a regiment of a thousand foot-soldiers, split into ten lines, each comprising a company of one hundred men. Six hundred times a thousand was six hundred thousand. That made six hundred thousand foot soldiers of the Mauryan army on the field below today. There were over a million enlisted in the empire's service. The other four hundred thousand were occupied across the length and breadth of the empire, including the capital Patliputra, ensuring that no enemy tried to take advantage of a battle to attack the Lion Throne.

As the drumming swelled, a pounding wall of thunder that Tissa felt in every bone of his body, a second sound rose: a flat metallic object striking against another hollow metal object. This was the ceremonial salute of the cavalry, striking their swords upon their breastplates. There were eighty mounted regiments on the field today: Eighty thousand cavalry, in full battle armour. Tissa's heart went out to those horses: what must they feel at this moment, in this mad cacophony of sound, bearing the weight of those men and their battle armour?

A third sound joined the first two: The striking of a wooden object against a metallic one. That was from the chariot regiments, the spearmen (who were also archers) banging the wooden shafts against the sides of the chariot wells. Again, Tissa thought not of the gleam of the polished chariots, inlaid with fine filigree patterns, or the oiled bare chests of the men aboard the chariots, standing proud as they awaited the order to charge; his thoughts were with the two horses that drew each half-chariot, and the teams of six that pulled each full chariot. Thirty times a thousand chariots on the field today, every nine half-chariots led by a lord in a full chariot. Each lord had two sarathis, one to control the six horse team, the second to hand him weapons as required. The half-chariots were each manned by two sarathis who took turns steering and fighting. That made a total of seventy-two thousand horses, and sixty-three thousand men in the chariot regiments. He prayed none of those horses would be badly injured or killed today; though he knew even as he prayed that it was an impossible request to make of any god. While animals had no varna in the caste system, these creatures served kshatriya masters; that made them kshatriya by default, warrior caste. Warriors went to war, and the only gods there were gods of war, and they had no mercy in their hearts for any living creature, be it gods, mortals, demons or beasts.

A fourth and final sound joined in the symphony: the shrill proud trumpeting of elephants. Nine thousand of the great beasts were on the field today, each with three men on his or her back, one to control, two to fight with spear, javelin, and short bow. Nine thousand more souls to pray for. Which god could he pray to for their safekeeping? Even the general of the Devas, the gods of the Bharatas, was half-elephant himself, Ganesa, the elephant-headed one.

The fourfold sound continued unabated for several moments, producing a deafening symphony. The music of war had silenced even the loudest of the gurus on the royal platform. They were themselves watching with rapt attention now, as mesmerized as their pupils. Tissa was still sitting sprawled on the cushion, the only one not pressing the railing. Even the old Acharya Kautilya was watching from behind father's Lion Throne. The air was dense with the excitement and anticipation of the moment. Tissa could not deny feeling something.

What a thing is war.

The full might and glory of the Mauryan army was on display here. Even without seeing the field itself, just staring at the backs of his brothers' heads, Tissa felt the power and magnificence of the event. Eighty-two thousand finely bred and trained animals and seven hundred and seventy thousand Mauryan warriors were gathered on that field fifty yards below his feet. Each and every one of them with only one intent and purpose: to destroy the enemies of the Empire.

The thundering symphony died abruptly.

The silence that followed was deafening.

The gurus began speaking again, but in hushed quieter tones. This brief interval of silence before the final command demonstrated discipline, the legendary synchronicity of the Mauryan army. The ability of such an enormous fighting force to act as one, obeying its leader's orders implicitly. Right now, not a soul was moving on the battlefield below, not even a horse twitching its tail or an elephant flapping its ears. (So said the brahmins!) Such was the discipline of Samrat Bindusara's great army.

Tissa was tempted to ask the nearest guru if Mauryan discipline was able to prevent a fly from buzzing near a horse's flanks, or a gnat from bothering an elephant's eyes. Because otherwise, horses would twitch their tails and elephants flap their ears. Not to mention the uncontrollable motions of nature. He guessed that it was typical royal propaganda, exaggerating the perfection of the Empire to instil pride in the princes and princesses. But he knew animals well enough to know it was horseshit—and elephant shit too.

Still, the silence was impressive, coming as it did immediately after that deafening clamour.

Tissa heard faint sounds in the distance. The gurus commented that that was the sound of the enemy forces, approaching from miles away; they were making their own war music. Tissa listened, turning his head this way and that to catch the sounds, a trick he'd learned from his dogs. He made out flute-like sounds, drumming, shouts, animal calls. The gurus informed them that the enemy consisted of The Sixteen: these were kingdoms that had united in common enmity against the Empire. Refusing to join with the five hundred other kingdoms that had accepted Mauryan rule since Chandragupta's time, The Sixteen, as they were unimaginatively dubbed, preferred to go to war rather than bow to the Lion Throne. The gurus reeled off the figures of the enemy ranks:

One hundred and seventeen thousand foot. Thirteen thousand mounted. Four thousand four hundred wheel. Eight hundred bigfoot.

Tissa was shocked. He might not have viewed a battle before in his eleven years, but as a prince of Maurya, he had studied enough battles to know that those were impossible odds. The Sixteen were outnumbered by almost one to six! He had never heard of any battle where any army had overcome such odds. He understood now why everyone had said that victory was a foregone conclusion. There was not a shred of doubt about it. At that very moment, a guru spoke his mind by saying that The Sixteen had been harrying the Empire for too long: Samrat Bindusara had decided that they could not go unpunished any longer. That was why he had brought the full force of the Mauryan Empire to bear on the field today, intending to intimidate the enemy by sheer size and power.

'Then why fight at all?'

As heads turned towards him, surprised eyes and faced glancing at him, Tissa resisted the urge to clap a hand to his mouth, embarrassed that he had spoken his thought aloud. But not embarrassed to have asked the question.

It was too late.

The nearest guru had heard and was answering him seriously.

'Because they are Mleccha. Uncivilized barbarians. They do not understand that their only hope for a better future lies in seceding to the greatness of Mauryan civilization. So they fight, even though their struggle is hopeless. As an angry ant bites at the foot of an elephant, not caring that the elephant can crush a thousand ants with a single stomp.'

Tissa wanted to argue the point. They were hardly elephants or ants. This was no accidental misstep into an anthill. These were mortal men choosing to disagree, fight, become sworn enemies, then raise armies and train animals and finally go to war against one another. Animals were too intelligent to waste their time on such madness. No animals that Tissa knew of did all this just to smash an anthill. He saw his mother and a few of the nearest queens looking around at him and he kept his thoughts to himself.

What a thing is war!

A new sound began. The sound of conches, again, but this time sounding a shorter, sharper call. It was followed by the war drums again, slower, more sedate, more menacing now.

Accompanying the drums came the sound of men lifting and dropping their feet in unison. Six hundred thousand pairs of sandaled feet, marching. Then the clip clopping of horses, the rumbling of well-oiled chariot wheels, and finally, the reverberating thump of elephants on the move. Tissa loved the sound of elephants walking in herd; it was as if he was hearing the heartbeat of nature itself. He shut his eyes, listening.

The commentary of the gurus reminded him that this was not nature he was hearing.

It was the sound of death marching.

Laying back lazily on the cushions, he opened one eye to peer around. Even from his prone position, he could see evidence that the battle formations were on the move.

Dust clouds rose from the plains around the platform, visible for miles on both the eastern and western sides of the platform. The Mauryan army was moving northwards. The gurus took a moment to explain the geographical layout of the kingdoms involved and the field of battle. Tissa sighed and shut his eyes, resigned to listening even though he knew all this by heart. The Sixteen were all situated on the South and East of Patliputra, the capital of the Mauryan Empire. The most powerful kingdoms in the South of the subcontinent were an alliance of three Tamizh states: Chera, Chola and Pandya. While not a part of the Mauryan Empire, all three were friendly allies to the Lion Throne and had no objection to Samrat Bindusara using their land as a staging point to launch his army's attack. This sent a message to The Sixteen beyond the actual battle itself; they would find no help from their Southern neighbours. To the far side of The Sixteen was the only other nation still hostile to Maurya: Kalinga. The Kalingans had not joined The Sixteen but would not join the Empire either. They were a different problem, one that would be dealt with at another time, the gurus added, hastily moving past the sensitive topic. Right now, today's battle was to teach The Sixteen a lesson: Nobody dares defy the Lion Throne.

'Yuvraj Tissa.'

Tissa looked up, startled.

A Khorasani guard stood over him, his large jaw and brow reminding Tissa of a wolfhound in the palace pen. The hound belonged to Sushim and was a gift from Rani Khorasan. Tissa wondered if Khorasani men and hounds were somehow related. That would explain the similarity of appearance and nature.

'Samrat Bindusara desires that you view the battle that you may learn from it.'

Tissa jerked his head around. He saw his father surrounded by a five-deep throng of amatyas and generals. How could he have seen Tissa through that crowd? Then he saw Rani Khorasan seated a little ways from his mother, both looking in his direction. Rani Khorasan smiled at him, reminding him as always of a leopardess preening. His mother cut her eyes towards the railing, her instructions clear. Tissa understood the message was in the Emperor's name but came from Rani Khorasan, endorsed by his own mother.

He stood up irritably and went to the railing. His brothers were too caught up to elbow him away. He slipped through easily and slammed his forearms on the wooden railing, leaning over it and looking out at...what? What was there to see anyway? All he could see were clouds of dust. He stood morosely, missing his foal, his dogs, his horses, and elephants and other companions, wanting to be back with them, away from this wretched family and this, this thing called War.

'Look, Tissa! The dust is clearing!' Fingers pointed.

The battlefield lay before the platform like a Kashmiri carpet.

The sky was the colour of a Greek vase.

The only clouds were clouds of dust raised by the two armies as they moved towards each other. A rising wind bore the dust clouds inland, westwards. Tissa felt the wind on his arms and upon his face as he stared at a sight that would haunt him the rest of his life.

The South Deccan plain was an endless ruddy carpet.

Closer to Tissa, but already many hundreds of yards away, the four akshohini of the Mauryan army were clearly distinguishable.

The foot soldiers made up enormous dark rectangular purple patches.

The armoured cavalry formed shiny gold squares.

The chariots moved in undulating shapes, sunlight catching the burnished sides of the chariots and the glint of the sarathi's weapons.

Ragged clusters of dark grey brought up the rear: the elephants.

As Tissa watched, new calls were trumpeted, the drumming changed rhythm and even at this distance, the sound of officers yelling orders and men shouting in response was audible. He heard and saw the purple rectangles of infantry move towards the waiting lines of the enemy. Seen from this vast perspective, the Maurya infantry appeared like a giant wave about to sweep over a small island.

The gurus reminded their pupils that the Maurya infantry alone was sufficient to overwhelm The Sixteen. They were now running towards the enemy lines at breakneck speed. Imagine what the enemy must be staring at right now, a fearful sight unmatched anywhere in the world: Six hundred thousand armed Mauryan warriors racing towards you with your death in their hands. No army can stand such a charge, they added proudly. Once the infantry were done breaking the enemy's resistance, the cavalry would sweep in to finish off the task. Finally, the chariot lords would roll in to take the surrender. There would be no need for the elephant regiments to be used at all today, they were present merely to demonstrate the formidable strength of Mauryavansh.

Tissa felt a wash of relief. The thought of those beautiful giants being hurt sickened him. It was bad enough that those lovely horses would be forced to endure such suffering. Thank you Ganesa for sparing some of your children from this thing called war!

As he watched, the two armies met in a resounding collision of men, shields, weapons, bones, flesh, wood, metal, steel, that produced a sound unlike anything he had heard before.

Even at this distance he could see the faint reddish mist that was the blood released by tens upon tens of thousands of bodies bursting apart on impact, brave men who had sacrificed their lives knowingly, demanding to be in the frontline that they may die for glory. What glory? Tissa wondered. Red glory? He saw the debris rise into the air with the blood mist, pieces of bodies and armour and splintered shields and who knew what else. The two armies met in a collision like a flesh-and-blood thunderclap. The red mist rose and hung in the air, then turned thicker and denser. The fighting had begun, the gurus announced almost gleefully. Soldiers were now fighting man to man at close quarters, barely enough room to move one's arms and legs, often standing braced against other fellow soldiers and even enemy soldiers, all swaying together in a vast dance of death. They would be stabbing, slashing, cutting, chopping...killing one another by any means, or getting killed. Many thousands would be trampled underfoot, their bodies broken and smashed in the melee. Limbs and organs would be intertwined as if upon a gigantic slaughterhouse floor, the ones at the bottom beaten into the dust till only fragments and chips of bones and teeth were left.

Tissa clasped the railing with both hands and vomited the contents of his belly over the side of the royal platform.

What a thing is war.

5

Cub was angry at his betrayal. She snarled at first when he picked her up and scratched him, a long wavy cut on the back of his wrist. A streak of red appeared to mark it. He laughed and held her to his chest, breathing in her familiar animal stench. She mewled then and rubbed her furry skull against the underside of his chest and he knew she loved him.

'Yes,' he said. 'We prevailed.'

She looked up at him with big green eyes and mewled again.

'No, you could not have helped fight them. They were too big and armed with steel.' He held her tiny paw, touching his fingertip to the ends of her claws. 'When these are big enough to slice open a man's belly with one strike, and these,' he touched her whiskered lips, pressing against the teeth within, 'long enough to tear out his throat, then you may join me. We shall fight together as partners in combat, you and I, fellow Cubs.'

She was silent, exhausted from the long journey and the stressful wait. Snuggled against his chest, breathing in his scent, listening to his heartbeat, his breathing, the vibrations of his chest as he talked, she gave herself over to sleep. He held her like that till her breathing grew regular and her little furry chest rose and fell steadily. Something about her peaceful surrender and complete sense of trust made him surrender to his own exhaustion and battle weariness and, with the Vyag cub nestled on his chest, he fell into a dark dreamless well without a bottom.

He was woken by Cub, snarling softly in the darkness that had engulfed the chamber.

He was standing even before his brain could fully awaken, Cub held securely in one hand, his sword in the other.

Then he saw Dwadesh and relaxed his guard.

Dwadesh was carrying a large banana leaf with a leg of roast meat left. He set it beside the spot where Ashoka had been resting. 'Takshashilan goat. They breed them for strength and vigour in carnal relations.' He made an obscene gesture near his crotch that left no doubt as to his meaning.

Ashoka yawned, putting his sword down and leaning back in the makeshift seat made up of garments piled together. Cub remained in his hand, no longer snarling but offering a paw with claws extruded in warning to Dwadesh. Come no closer to my Master... 'I have no need of aphrodisiacs, Dwadesh. You, on the other hand...'

Dwadesh scowled. He was several years older than Ashoka,

but still less than twenty years of age. 'Eat to keep your strength up.'

Ashoka squatted cross-legged on the pile of pelts and plucked out choice bits of meat from the roasted leg. He offered them to Cub who sniffed suspiciously, licked tentatively at the meat, smacked her lips and then tried to snatch the morsel from Ashoka's hands. He laughed and held it out of her reach for a second, teasing her before he gave her the morsel. She quickly worked her way through the leg, he sharing the occasional bite as well.

'How are the men?' Ashoka asked Dwadesh, who was standing by the slitted window, glancing out at the darkness.

'Ardhendhu died of his wounds a short while ago. Suvendra, some hours earlier.'

Ashoka nodded grimly. 'I should have been there.'

'They would still have died. Besides, the only person they both wanted and called out for in those last hours were their mothers.'

Ashoka shrugged. It was a universal truth, on battlefields and in sickhouses, that when soldiers were mortally wounded and out of their senses with pain, they called for their mothers. Even the older ones. 'And the injured?'

'They'll all live. Morale is good. Taking Takshashila was a boost. They'll be talking about this one for a long time.'

The meat finished; Cub wanted to gnaw on the bone. Ashoka gave it over to her. She began pawing it to make it roll one way then the other, leaping out of the way with exaggerated three-legged hops, snarling. He watched her as he talked to Dwadesh about various and sundry matters to do with the handover.

They were almost done when another man entered, bowing to Ashoka and gazing wide-eyed at his Master. Ashoka recalled the boy being one of the new recruits Dwadesh had picked up, on Ashoka's orders, to replenish their lost numbers for the expedition.

'My Lord, Yuvraj Ashoka,' the boy began nervously.

Ashoka interrupted him. 'What's your name, boy, and how old are you?'

Dwadesh replied, 'He's twelve,' at the same time as the boy said, 'Sundar.'

Ashoka preferred their recruits to be at least as old as himself. Or damn good fighters. There weren't many boys strong enough to lift a sword even at fourteen. The boy looked less than ten and barely capable of raising a heavy dagger. His nervousness didn't help.

'How many men have you killed until now, Sundar?' Ashoka asked him.

Sundar glanced at Dwadesh who ignored him. 'None, my Lord Yuvraj. But—'

It was Ashoka's turn to look at Dwadesh now.

Dwadesh shrugged. 'We needed bodies. Our numbers were down.'

Ashoka sighed and looked at the boy again, his large black eyes darting nervously from Dwadesh to Ashoka and back again. 'Sundar, just call me Ashoka. We in the Cubs don't stand on formality.'

Sundar gulped and nodded.

Dwadesh nudged the boy. 'You brought a message, boy?'

Sundar's eyes glazed over for a moment. Ashoka and Dwadesh exchanged a glance. Dwadesh shrugged again with a minimal movement.

'Yes, my Lord!' Sundar almost shouted as he remembered his purpose. The other Cubs nearby glanced around, amused. The boy looked aghast and corrected himself, dropping his voice to a conspiratorial whisper: 'There is a visitor to see you. From Patliputra.'

Ashoka's smile disappeared. 'Why didn't you say so in the first place? Send him in.'

Sundar shook his head. 'He would see you in private, my Lord Prince. I mean, Ashoka. He said to come to the gardens, in the statuary. I was to let no one else know that he was here or that he had a message from Patliputra.' Belatedly, Sundar glanced at Dwadesh, then turned crimson. 'I should not even have said this in front of you, Captain Dwadesh, but I forgot.'

'And he delivered these instructions especially to you?' Ashoka asked.

Sundar frowned. 'I think so, sire. Ashoka. I thought he was a local at first. He asked who was the newest recruit to the unit. I said I was. Then he gave me these instructions. I came straightaway.' He looked uncertain. 'Did I do right, my Lords?'

Dwadesh frowned. 'Odd way for a courier to deliver a missive.'

Ashoka put a hand on Dwadesh's shoulder. 'I'll see to him. Sundar, you did right to come straight to us. But in future, when given an instruction, follow it to the letter, do you understand?'

Dwadesh started as Ashoka began to walk away. 'You're not going to meet this stranger on your own, are you? It could be a trap. There are assassins everywhere.'

'Sure, there are,' Ashoka replied. 'I'm one too.' He gestured at the new recruit. 'Sundar, watch Cub for me. I think she's still hungry and could eat another haunch. Just be careful it's not yours!'

He left Sundar staring at Cub who eyed him suspiciously, tail twitching, as Ashoka walked away.

The statuary consisted of old half-broken effigies of Afghana and his family members. Someone, the rebels most likely, had taken weapons to them, and most were missing arms, elbows, heads, noses, ears, even a foot in one instance.

He strolled around the stone pathways lined with hedges on one side, flower beds on the other. The cloying sweetness of some flower in bloom made him nostalgic for his mother suddenly. He always associated the scent of flowers with her. Even when they had lived in the forest, back when he was just a little boy, waiting for his father to return to their jungle hut and take them to the palace, his mother had tended flowers in the clearing beside their thatched hut. Ashoka hadn't seen the point of taking so much effort to grow flowers when flowers could be had anywhere in the forest. 'Yes, but not these flowers, not right here,' his mother had said. 'And not grown by us.' Later, when Guru Kautilya, rather than his father, had come to fetch them to the palace, she had been sad to part with her beloved flowers. Guru Kautilya had told her she could have her own arboretum in her apartments in the palace, and it was true, but it had been a long time before Shubhadrangi and Ashoka were accepted into the royal family and given their own apartment. It was only during that long absence and the terrible indignities they had suffered that Ashoka had fully understood how necessary it had been to his mother's wellbeing to tend to the delicate buds and blossoms on a daily basis. Just as caring for and nurturing little creatures defined Ashoka himself. What we do defines us, it is the expression of our inner selves, Guru Kautilya had taught him.

'Yuvraj Ashoka.'

Ashoka checked his surroundings. Surviving in hostile conditions was so much a part of his nature that even while strolling through a garden, he had not failed to keep check on every possible approach or angle of attack.

The voice had spoken from behind the tall hedge to his right. The hedge was over a dozen feet tall, and perhaps a yard thick, too thick to see through. But if he could not see the speaker, neither could he be seen, which put them on equal footing.

'Show yourself,' he said.

'I bring a message from your Guru. It is a matter of life and death.'

'I should believe a hedge that speaks? Let me see your face.'

A brief pause, then the voice resumed. 'To reveal one's identity defeats the very purpose of being a spasa. All that matters is my message.'

A spasa? Ashoka was not surprised. It was to be expected that his Guru would send a spy to deliver a secret message. Kautilya had created the Order of Spasas back during the reign of the Nanda Empire, when Kautilya and his then-protégé, Ashoka's grandfather Chandragupta Maurya, had been condemned rebels wandering the country and attempting to foment civil rebellion. The whole point of the Spasas was that they were ordinary people working in ordinary professions, belonging to all varnas, tribes, races. Their effectiveness as spies lay in their identity remaining unknown, even to each other. How could anyone betray you, or even accuse you, if there was no way to tell who was a Spasa or not? Officially, the Order of Spasas had been disbanded by Kautilya himself once Chandragupta wrested power from the Nandas and established the Mauryan empire. Unofficially, as Ashoka knew, the Spasas had continued operating and feeding Kautilya vital information about the allies and enemies of Mauryavansh. And because the identities of the Spasas had been known only to Kautilya himself, there was no way to tell who was or was not one.

'Speak then,' Ashoka said, and began to climb the hedge as the voice resumed.

'Your Guru says to tell you that you are "among friends".'

Ashoka grimaced. As with most of Kautilya's code phrases, that meant the exact opposite of what it sounded like. Kautilya had a wicked sense of irony. 'Among friends' meant that Ashoka had a traitor in his immediate circle. He cursed silently as he continued to ascend the hedge, wondering who could be the traitor. Surely not one of his Cubs? It had to be one of Sushim's entourage. He was cautious not to cause the foliage to shake or make any sound that would alert the messenger.

'He also says that while the Elephant and Lion both respectfully avoid one another, if one endangers the other one's young, they will fight. In the event that they clash, the Lion would be best served by riding on the Elephant's back rather than attacking it face to face.'

Ashoka lay on top of the hedge now, manoeuvring carefully till he was able to look down the other side. He frowned, trying to decipher the second part of the message: The Lion meant his brother and himself, because the Lion was the sigil of House of Maurya. The Elephant meant brahmins, keepers of knowledge and wisdom. Surely not the priests who had accompanied Sushim? What could those poor bastards do to him? He would need to think on that one a while.

He crawled over the top of the hedge, ignoring the chopped ends of branches digging into various parts of his anatomy. Peering down, the view left much to be desired. All he could see was a lithe figure in a roughcloth robe with a cowl covering the head and face. From this angle, he couldn't even make out the height or age of the Spasa. All he could tell for sure was that it was a very athletic, slim physique. A boy's physique, or an exceptionally lean man's.

'The last part of the Guru's message is to remind you to surely say your prayers at sandhyavandana. When night befalls you, you must seek solace in your recitations and meditations. In particularly, meditate on the lesson of the Buddha, his inspiring life and great legacy, despite facing great odds both personal and public. That concludes the message.'

The Spasa was already moving. Ashoka launched himself over the top of the hedge, using gravity to somersault once. He landed on the balls of his feet—directly in the Spasa's path.

'Thanks for delivering the message,' Ashoka said.

The look of astonishment on the face beneath the cowled hood mirrored the surprise Ashoka himself felt.

'You betray our Code!' the young woman—girl, actually—hissed. 'Ungrateful brat!'

Ashoka shot out a hand to grasp her wrist before she could bolt. But the Spasa was quicker. She ducked under his hand and twisted deftly past him, racing away. He spun and gave chase.

She's fast, was his first thought as the Spasa leaped over a low hedge, rolled twice and turned sharply to sprint away from the garden. Ashoka gained on her in a straight run till she abruptly turned again and leaped over a wall. He followed her, landing on a gravelly road. Her feet barely stirred the loose gravel as she sprinted, suggesting someone much lighter than he. Ashoka sprinted after her, hearing the shirring sound of his heels kicking up gravel in his wake. He admired the Spasa's heart-shaped rear end outlined by the roughcloth robe as he gained on her again. She sensed his imminence without looking back over her shoulder—a sign of good training which made him respect her all the more—and turned with remarkable ease, dodging one way then another, sketching a roughly diagonal route through an apple grove. He saw that he would never catch her in a straight chase; what she lacked in power and speed, she made up for in agility and litheness. He grabbed the largest greenest apple he could spy as he ran, ripping it from its stalk. Aiming on the fly, he threw it as hard as he could, under-hand to avoid losing momentum or losing his balance, and saw it strike its target: the bunched nerves at the back of her left knee. The effect would be like hitting one's funny bone. She stumbled and tripped, stepping on a treefall apple and went sprawling. She was rising to her feet as he reached her but he was taking no chances and threw himself rather an apple this time, tackling her hard around the waist. They both went flying and tumbled over a small hummock and down the other side, ending up somehow entangled together, limbs and mouths and bums and faces all wrong end up and right end down. He smelled spices and the coarse odour of cow dung which probably came from the roughcloth and felt something soft and yielding beneath his palm. Definitely not an apple. Hmm.

'Get away from me,' she said, striking him across the nose with the heel of her hand. He turned just in time and took the blow on the side of his head, the impact making his ears ring like the aftermath of a temple bell sounding. She tried to maul and maim him with both hands and legs and he was forced to grab her wrists and pin her legs down, using his greater weight to prevent her from doing any real damage. Still she wriggled and wrestled.

'Stop,' he said, 'I will not harm you.'

She continued to struggle, her face contorting with fury. 'You should not see my face! Violation!'

'That's not a violation,' he said. 'What the rebels did to the people, that is a violation.'

She reduced her efforts, glaring up at him. He met her gaze until she subsided. He rolled off her lower body and watched her eyes as he released her wrists. Her eyes darted away but she did not run.

'You are not Takshashilan,' he said. Her colour was too dark, her features too eastern. Her accent, though she spoke Prakrit well enough, was also eastern. 'Chola perhaps? No. Kalingan. That's it. Kalingan.'

She looked into the distance at nothing, brown eyes smouldering.

'I need to know, did you bring that message directly from Guru Kautilya?'

She shot him a scornful glance. 'It's called an Order for a reason. We have a network.'

'So you were given the message to pass on by a fellow Spasa. How certain are you that it is genuinely from Kautilya?'

She stared at him insolently.

He nodded. 'Stupid question. You stake your life on the loyalty of your Order. Thing is, your Order is supposed to have been disbanded decades ago.'

'That's what you people are supposed to think.' She smirked.

Her arrogance irritated him. 'By "you people" you mean all non-Spasas, I suppose? Because to be a Spasa is to be a supreme being elevated above all other beings? Well, I have news for you, sister. I caught you and now I have seen your face.'

She lost her smirk. 'You must forget my face at once.'

'That's easier said than done. It's such a pretty face.' He couldn't help letting his eyes rove over her body. 'And everything else besides.'

The brown eyes flared again. 'You royals. You think you own everything. I'm not your property!'

Ashoka laughed. 'You're confusing me with my brother perhaps. He's the crown prince. Me, I'm just a fighter. A glorified bodyguard. Not very different from you actually. We both serve in the shadows.'

She stared at him as if he was delirious. 'You are Yuvraj Ashoka, heir to the throne of Mauryavansh, first in line of succession.'

He dusted off his garments, getting to his feet. 'See there's the confusion right there. I'm Yuvraj all right, but neither an heir nor in line to succeed. I abdicated my right to claim the throne for life. Now I only serve my brother and the Empire.'

She blinked. 'I heard the rumours about your great vow of sacrifice. Just a ploy to make your brothers drop their guard until the day you swoop in and snatch the crown for yourself.'

Ashoka shook his head sadly. 'Such cynicism in one so young. You Spasas really should learn to have a more open outlook. Not every prince is a turd. Not ever warrior wants to be a king. Besides, you obviously failed to catch the reason why I took that vow.'

She shrugged, feigning disinterest though he could see a flash of curiosity in her eyes. She was nice to look at, in a sharp, angular faced kind of way. And that softness beneath his hand that was not an apple... Hmm. 'They said you took the vow because your mother told you to do it.'

'Wrong!' he said, more sharply than he intended, making her look up in surprise. 'My mother didn't tell me to do anything. I chose to take that vow to reassure my father, brothers and step-mothers that I would not stand in the way of my brothers' claims or succession. I did it for my mother, it's true, to ensure her safety and wellbeing for as long as she lives. But it was entirely my choice and my doing.'

She looked away, an amused smile playing on her lips. She had a way of looking at you, a certain turn of the lips and twist of the cheek that gave off a sense of insouciance. Ashoka found that very...arousing.

'Easy to make vows when you are born into privilege. Royal by birth is still royal.'

He started to answer then broke off. 'Kalingan,' he said thoughtfully.

'So?'

'Your people don't believe in royalty.'

'We are a Republic. We believe all people are created equal.'

He nodded. 'Uh-huh.'

'What's that supposed to mean?'

'Some people are more equal than others, surely. You have a king. Raja Anantha Padmanabhan.'

'The Raja is an inherited title. The people call him that affectionately. He is no different from any commoner.'

'But how many commoners have an inherited title and are called "King" affectionately by everyone else?'

She glared at him.

He smiled at her.

'Thank you for the message,' he said. 'I have one for Guruji. Will you take it to him?'

She turned her face away. 'That's not how it works. As you well know.'

'How does it work then? I've never received or sent a message by the Spasa network. Educate me.'

'You have to contact the local agent,' she said. 'And they—'

A horse whinnied nearby.

Ashoka turned and saw Dwadesh bearing down on him, ducking low to avoid being blinded by the low hanging branches.

'I got word you were seen chasing or being chased by assassins,' Dwadesh said, drawing up short. The horse whickered, nostrils flaring as it smelled the apples all around.

'Not assassins,' Ashoka said, 'just a stranger I wanted to question.'

He turned to the Spasa—she was gone.

6

'War Marshall on the floor,' announced a sentry. With a single crack of heels, every sentry stationed at ten-feet intervals along the long hallway snapped to attention, presenting her weapon and staring directly ahead. Senapati Khorasan strode past without acknowledging a single soldier with even the slightest gesture or glance; Khorasani warriors were trained using a system based entirely on negative reinforcement. If she stopped by or looked at a sentry, it would imply that the soldier had committed some infraction. The penalty would be severe. There were no mild penalties or warnings among the Khorasani. A mistake was a failure, and failure endangered not just the individual soldier but her comrades as well, and brought shame to the Khorasani nation. The War Marshal had lopped off arms and heads for lapses of protocol.

These soldiers made no mistakes. They were the elite of the Khorasani military hierarchy. The worst of the worst, as their enemies called them. That was why they were here in the inner palace, the last line of defense. Their cadre was charged with protecting the royal family, as they had done since the days of Chandragupta Maurya.

It gave the War Marshal much satisfaction to see only Khorasani faces along the long corridors of the inner palace. Not that she would ever show this or any emotion to the rank and file.

Originally, it had been Kautilya who had asked for only female soldiers to be assigned to the royal guard. That was during the reign of Chandragupta Maurya, when the Mauryavansh empire had still been in the throes of bloody insurrection and strife. Five hundred warring tribes made for a deadly alliance. Assassination attempts were as routine as breakfast. The Prime Minister, as Kautilya had been at the time, had wanted female soldiers for the royal guard because almost all the tribes were patriarchal and chauvinist in the extreme. Women were not considered worthy of inclusion in power decisions, leave alone privy to plans and schemes. Who better to recruit to defend against the crude assassination attempts of those barbaric rustic tribes than their own women? Weathered and seasoned by the abuse of their own men, disenfranchised from the line of succession, relegated to serving, cleaning, cooking, child-bearing and sex-providing, the women leaped eagerly at the opportunity, any opportunity to further their fortunes. The first recruits had been raw and untrained, many had died, incurring greater violence as retaliation for stepping out of the domestic circle, by their own uncles, fathers, brothers, sons—but very quickly, they had hardened like

Deccan clay into formidable warriors, incorruptible, unyielding, and willing to go to suicidal lengths to protect their liege. In time, the assassination attempts had dwindled as even the most boorish tribesmen lost their stomach for killing—and more often, being killed by—women. Today, three quarters of a century later, the women's guard was a feared and hated force in the empire. And of their cadre, the Khorasani were the most reviled and dreaded, the famed 'worst of the worst'.

The War Marshal smiled secretly to herself as she turned yet another long corridor and approached her destination. Kautilya must be seething at the knowledge of an all-Khorasani cadre. During his time, he had always insisted on a mixed cadre, to avoid favouring any one particular clan, but after he had been asked to step down by Bindusara almost a decade ago, the War Marshal's daughter Rani Khorasan had used her influence to ensure that only Khorasani women soldiers were enlisted. The other cadres still existed, but were relegated to lesser duties, such as guarding the distant relatives of the royals, or posted in remote summer palaces, hunting lodges and satrapy posts.

She reached her destination and turned into the First Queen's apartments. She luxuriated in the knowledge that her daughter's chambers were more than thrice as spacious and well-appointed than the other queens'. What use was power if one did not use it to press down the less powerful?

The sentries were already at attention as she entered. Orzala stood, ready to greet her. Jezza Khorasan could not help casting an admiring glance at the young woman's person. Admiring, envious and covetous, all rolled into one. Khorasani tradition encouraged the taking of mistresses by powerful lords. Rani Khorasan could have kept an entire zenana if she desired, a queen's harem. But she chose to let only Orzala into her bed. Her mother could see why. The woman was a harem unto herself.

'War Marshall, well met.'

'Well met, Orzala.' Jezza took the liberty of taking one of those beautiful mango-shaped breasts in her palm and hefting it, the way she would a prospective male lover's genitals. 'You recall my invitation.' She leaned closer and whispered into a perfumed ear, taking the opportunity to nuzzle the earlobe with her lower lip. 'My bed is always open to you. As is the flower of my love.'

Orzala sighed—or feigned a sigh, for she was politic if nothing else—and placed her petal-soft hand full against Jezza's rough palm, kissing it softly. 'If desire were my only mistress, wild bulls could not keep me away. But Rani Noor will not spare me for even a night.'

Jezza suppressed an urge to disrobe the woman and lick her from head to toe right there and then. She sighed too, sincerely, for it had been too long since she had allowed herself a night of frolic, and stepped ahead. 'For a brief respite then. An afternoon delight perhaps.'

'Petition my mistress,' Orzala said in parting, her eyes smouldering with a lustfulness that made Jezza want to forget who she was and why she was here. 'I am ever your willing servant.'

Jezza passed on into the inner chamber, needing no further direction or guidance. Her meetings with her daughter were always private. Even Orzala did not attend them. She forced herself to suppress the images and sensations of longing that the brief encounter had evoked within her. She would have to do something about that this very evening. But for now, she had business to attend to with her daughter.

'The old fool is upto his tricks again.' Rani Noor Khorasan began without preamble. The queen was in her evening robes, richly embroidered silks décorated with patterns from the Far Eastern tribes. With her high cheekbones, deep-set eyes and strong jawline, the rich reds, golds and greens gave her the suggestion of Eastern ethnicity. Only her dusky complexion denied the possibility. War Marshall Jezza Khorasan knew better than anyone else that no Eastern seed had spawned this extraordinary young woman standing before her—she had known every male rod that penetrated her flower in the year before Noor's birth. Well, almost every. None had been Far Eastern. Yet, she sometimes marvelled at which particular joining of rod and flower, seed and furrow, had produced this unique specimen she had expelled onto the dusty canvas-covered floor of a ragged tent on the plains of her homeland, thirty-some years ago. Khorasani cared nothing for paternity; a mother was all that mattered. But in this one case, Jezza wished she had known which particular flower-fucker's seed had produced this result; she would have used him to produce more, and then whored him out to her sisters to seed their furrows as well!

'The old fool is a toothless fish,' Jezza replied, going over to the table and pouring herself a much-deserved flagon of queen's ale, a special blend brewed exclusively for Noor. She drank greedily, spilling some down her leather tunic and not caring a damn. The flagon was two-thirds drained when she set it down on the polished surface with a thump. 'He can lip-catch our flowers and suck on them if he derives pleasure from it, but he has no teeth to bite us where it hurts.' Jezza resumed her consumption of the ale till the flagon was completely empty.

'He's coming to see Bindu,' Noor said, with an expression that suggested she had a sour lemon in her mouth. 'I don't want him poisoning his mind. You know how susceptible he is, especially when he's all puffed up after a victory.'

Jezza snorted, a fine spray of ale droplets exuding from her nostrils. She sneezed, blew her nose on the nearest cloth available—a silken something that probably cost as much as a flock of sheep back in the old country—and grinned, showing her daughter her cracked and yellowed front teeth. 'Victory? That cowardly goat turd sat on a throne surrounded by a hundred spears high above the field, watching. Like it was a melee staged for his entertainment. If he had the balls of a king, he would have been there in the thick of it, fighting with his armies.'

Noor did not react to her mother's outburst. This was a familiar refrain. 'He's an emperor, mother, not a tribal chieftain defending his claim to the women's tent. He has to stay above mere brawling, leave the bloodletting to others. That's the difference between an emperor and a lesser liege.'

Jezza poured herself more ale. 'That's what you think, Noor. There's no difference. An emperor is nothing more than a chief, his problems multiplied hundredfold. Thousandfold. The longer he goes without showing his own strength, the bolder his enemies grow.'

'Like the Takshashilan rebels?'

Jezza paused, the flagon halfway to her lips. Noor was looking at her with a crease of annoyance on her beautiful forehead, a twist to her lips that indicated the first signs of anger. 'What about the Takshashilan rebels?'

'Their task was to eliminate the entire entourage, take no prisoners. They appear to have been somewhat less than successful in the enterprise.'

Jezza lowered the flagon, setting it down carefully on the already wet surface. 'Noor, every time you start talking like one of your fancy Ujjaini pundits, I know you're pissed. Why don't you just come out and say what's causing your ass to itch?'

'Since you don't like fancy talk, let me ask you in plain speak. Why the fuck did the Pashtuns not do their job? We paid them well enough.'

Jezza tilted her head in the Khorasani equivalent of a shrug. 'It seems the young Cub was more resourceful than we thought.

He managed to lop off the head of the Pashtun chief, in a palace filled with the Pashtun's fiercest fighters. Unarmed.' There was a grudging hint of admiration in the War Marshal's tone.

'He can't have strangled the whole tribe to death singlehandedly,' Noor said, her eyes flashing. 'Why didn't the others tear him to pieces? Did they just stand by and watch him choke the life out of their father?'

'Tear the head off,' Jezza corrected absently. 'Well, according to my spy, it seems they were overcome by some kind of a… supernatural misgiving.'

Noor stared at her, her beautiful face contorted. 'What?'

Jezza resisted the urge to chuckle at her daughter's reaction. Even she had found it hard to believe when she had first heard it, though the spasa who brought her the account had sworn it was true to the last detail. 'Seems like they thought he was the ghost of Chandragupta Maurya come back in another body. Rebirth. Karma. All that Vedic claptrap. "Lion of Maurya" is what they were calling him. Hailing him. It's like they made him a surrogate chief in their father's stead! Who could have predicted that turn of events? Not I.'

Noor paced her chamber furiously. Jezza watched and waited, sipping a little more ale but going slow now. The silk robes rustled.

Finally, Noor turned to her with a swirling of her silk robes. 'Kill them all.'

Jezza tilted her head back to look at her daughter. So beautiful and so deadly, what a combination. 'The Mauryan expedition to Takshashila?'

'Them too, I don't care. I mean the Pashtun rebels we paid to lead the coup. Kill them all. This talk of rebirth disgusts me. It must not be permitted to proliferate. Lion of Maurya indeed!'

'That may not be easy to accomplish. The rebellion has been successfully quelled. Ashoka is a hero to the local Afghan populace. They paraded him in the streets. He is satrap of the region now, under Sushim's seal of course. That means he is the local Mauryavansh law, operating under the Emperor's own authority. It might reflect badly on Bindusara if I—'

Noor cut her off. 'I'll handle Bindu, you end this Takshashilan fiasco. Before the brahmin pulls one of his tricks.'

'I wouldn't worry about Kautilya. Like I said—'

'I said, kill the Pashtun rebels and the Mauryavansh expedition to Takshashila. Kill some locals too, to leave a reminder of how unheroic their karmic prince really is. Leave Takshashila bleeding and in tears, on its knees.'

Jezza looked at her daughter. 'Noor...'

'War Marshal.' Steel could not have cut through that tone or that look. 'Heed your queen. My word is law. You have your orders. Leave at once. This time, I want no supernatural surprises. Or real ones.'

Jezza held Noor's gaze a fraction longer than anyone else would have dared, then put her heels together. 'Your word is law, my queen.'

On the way out, she did not stop to flirt with Orzala again.

7

It was with a very different aspect that the First Queen presented herself only a short while later, at the apartment of her mother-in-law, Dowager Queen Apama. The only queen's apartment larger and more luxurious than her own, its luxury was offset by its location, right next to the nursery and prince and princess apartments. The sound and smell of infants, children, and young people reached her even as she entered through the ostentatious Corinthian archway. Noor wrinkled her nose. What was the use of recreating the glory of Hellenic civilization when the stench of baby feces and the sounds of children squabbling tainted the air. She kept her perfumed silk kerchief pressed to her nose as she waited in the foyer.

'Daughter-in-law, what a pleasant surprise,' said the towering fair-skinned older woman with the flowing golden tresses. In a nation of brown and black and all shades between, Apama lost no opportunity to show off her genetic differences. The very sight of those straw locks made Noor want to tear them out by the roots and then stab Apama to death. Even a lifetime later, the associations of that hair and skin colour with the Greek invaders who had raped her homeland, slaughtered her tribe and publicly tortured and killed her father and brothers were as fresh and pulsating as they had been when she was eight years old. She had killed her first Greek at that tender age, while the man made the mistake of trying to rape her, and she had killed many Greeks in the years that followed, but once she married Bindusara and accepted his half-Greek parentage as her own family, she had no choice but to put aside the thirst for vengeance. Still, the thirst was banked not quenched, and would never be until every last Greek in this part of the world was reduced to meat in the dust.

'Mother Apama,' Noor said, her smiling face, air kisses, and genial embrace concealing her inner loathing artfully. 'You look younger and more beautiful each passing day.'

Apama smiled shrewdly as she led Noor into her chambers. The two women sat on pristine white seats, their feet placed on immaculate white fur. Even the walls, pillars, and statuary were white. Born and bred in a land where dust ruled everything, Noor Khorasan was stung by envy at the sheer audacity of such a décor scheme. But it also meant that if she spilled her Greek mother-in-law's blood here, it would make beautifully aesthetic stains. 'Looks can deceive, but Chronos counts our age in years, not beauty. You are losing your precious childbearing years, daughter. When will you grace our House with a Prince?'

Trust the old Greek witch to harp on that sore point. 'Soon, mother, soon. As you know, it is all written in the stars. The pundits say the time of my ripening will come upon me very shortly. The rest, as we know, is up to your son.'

Apama gestured to the crystal goblet being proffered to Noor. 'Juice of the pomegranate is good for fertility. Drink. As for Bindusara, he has sired a hundred sons on other queens—and twice that many daughters—so his virility is not in question.'

And my fertility is? You straw-haired sow! Noor smiled and sipped the blood-red juice, hating to admit that she enjoyed its taste. 'It is all upto the gods then, Apama, only what they will comes to pass. We mere mortals must perforce submit ourselves to their divine plan.'

'I shall continue to sacrifice bulls to Aphrodite till they are appeased.'

You do that, you fool, because of course the Vedic gods, who are Bindusara's gods officially, are highly impressed by the slaughter of bulls...not! Sacrifice your pale-skinned self too while you're at it, why don't you? Save me years of plotting and strategizing and waiting.

Both mother-in-law and daughter-in-law smiled sweetly at each other.

The juice consumed, the small talk dispensed with, Apama dismissed the servants—all Greek, of course, for this was the only part of the palace guarded and serviced only by Greeks and Greek-Indians. Noor was the only Khorasani even permitted to enter these apartments, and she had to leave her personal guard a hundred yards away, at the entrance, when she visited. This was sovereign Greek territory to all intents and purposes.

'Speak your mind, daughter,' Apama said, her bright blue eyes settling on Noor's face. 'What ails you?'

'Mother, I will not insult your intelligence.'

Apama's blue eyes danced. 'I trust not!'

'I know that your father, Bindusara's grandfather, is behind the rebellion in the North West.'

Apama did not react. She continued smiling, her cerulean gaze unwavering. Noor had only stated the obvious: there was obviously more.

'Somehow, Bindusara's imbecile son has managed to create chaos there.' Noor gave her own version of the events in Takshashila, painting Ashoka in the worst light possible, making him out to be the very incompetent that Sushim was. She did not so much as mention Sushim's name except in passing. She saw from Apama's expression that the Dowager Queen knew exactly what she was doing and what she was leading up to. Then why not simply stop me and say you understand, you old white-skin hag! But Apama said not a word until Noor was finished.

'And this as you know, reflects badly on Bindusara himself, and by implication, the House of Maurya. What will our enemies say if they know of the chaos in the North West?'

Apama's polite listening smile turned to a superior look. 'The North West has always been chaos. You should know, my dear, your people come from there, don't they?'

Noor resisted the urge to slap the older woman. 'We are residents of Mauryavansh now and have been for decades. The subcontinent is our only home.'

'As refugees, you mean. Immigrants. Guests.' Apama used the words that Noor had heard flung in her face a thousand times during her growing years, spoken with contempt and loathing. By saying those words sweetly and casually, Apama made the insults sting even more. 'The point I make, dear daughter-in-law, is that even if things are as you say they are in Takshashila, the North West has always been a troubled zone. As is the principality of

Ujjain and of course, our tiresome neighbour, Kalinga. Until a short while ago, the Sixteen Kingdoms were equally a source of annoyance, but they have now been quelled effectively by my son.'

Who watched from a high platform while my mother and her generals did all the quelling.

'So, what I am saying is that, peeving though the Takshashila situation may be to you, I am sure in time things will resolve themselves. These things have a way of working themselves out.'

Noor frowned. Was Apama saying what she thought she was saying? 'So you admit that your father Seleucus Nicator is instigating the unrest in the North West. With a view to intruding further into the subcontinent?'

'If my father were to make any aggressive move in the North West, he would only be doing what he was entrusted with doing since the passing of his lord Alexander several decades ago. The Greek agenda in Asia has never been in question. What is in question, however, is your intentions.'

'Mine?' Noor looked aghast. 'My only concern is for the House of Maurya.'

'Of course, but by that you mean your House of Maurya, do you not? Come off your high horse, Noor, I know that you paid the Pashtuns to stage the revolt in Takshashila. And I have no doubt you will put them up to provoking further hostilities in the region. The Takshashila rebellion has your scheming style stamped all over it.'

Noor suppressed the urge to lash out. It was difficult suppressing her lifelong hatred of the Greeks, but this woman was the only one who had true power over her. She could not afford to antagonize Apama directly. Seeing the warring emotions pass over her face, Apama pressed down on Noor's hand and laughed as she did so. 'Do not worry, daughter-in-law. I know there is no love in your heart for my people. But I also know that you are loyal to my son and the military strategies you plant in his head are quite brilliant. Even my father says so and he is a Greek Emperor, heir to the great Alexander of Macedon himself. That is why we let you go about your political gameplaying unchallenged.'

Noor's eyes widened, her nostrils flared. She knew that Apama knew almost everything she did, but to hear it admitted openly was another matter. She dared not say anything. Apama was not quite done, though Noor wasn't sure she wanted to hear everything the older woman had to say.

'Yes, quite brilliant at warcraft, my father says. But you have a weakness, Noor Khorasan. You allow yourself to get swept up in personal vendettas and petty feuds. This vendetta against Prince Ashoka is one such instance. Why do you waste time trying to thwart and eliminate the boy? Let him do as he does. He is loyal to his father's cause and serves the House of Maurya well.'

'Perhaps he is just loyal to his own cause and serves his own interests which for the present happen to be allied with those of Mauryavansh.'

Apama went on as if Rani Khorasan hadn't spoken. 'And if his claim to the throne concerns you, well, he has already sworn a vow publicly that he will never claim his place in the lineage.'

'And you believe him?'

Apama frowned. 'He has been disinherited and stripped of his princely status. That is why he does not even have an apartment in the princes' palace, only in the guardian's quarters! How can the five hundred chiefs support his candidacy even if he makes a bid? Besides, why does Ashoka or any other prince cause you such concern, Noor? You haven't even a child of your own, leave alone a son in line for succession. And even if you do eventually bear a son, he will be over a hundred numbers down the line.'

You assume that Bindusara's hundred other sons—and five hundred queens—will be alive to threaten my son's inheritance at that time. Fool!

Apama saw the unspoken malice in her daughter-in-law's eyes. Her tone softened somewhat, became conciliatory. 'Leave him be, Noor. Ashoka has dedicated his life to being his brother Sushim's keeper and he is a good one. Sushim is an incompetent nincompoop, and what happened in Takshashila would have indeed been a disaster had Sushim alone been in charge. But Ashoka was with him, and Ashoka did what he does so well—he cut through the Gordion knot with a single sword-stroke. I understand your irritation comes from the fact that the mere stripling of a boy outdid your clever geopolitical manoeuvring. But that is what makes Ashoka special. The lion attack, the assassination attempt, the Ujjaini assault on the whorehouse where Sushim was celebrating, now the quelling of the Pashtun rebellion in Takshashila...Ashoka has done some interesting work at a very young age. Yet he is but a servant. Let him do as he will. He does so in service to us.'

'And yet,' Noor said, 'he is still blood kin to Bindusara. First born son to the Emperor of Mauryavansh. If he were to stake his claim someday—'

'We will deal with that when the time comes. For now, he is an asset, not a threat.'

'We Khorasani believe it is wiser to kill the youngling serpent before it grows into a mighty dragon.'

Apama caught hold of Noor's forearm again, her grip iron hard this time. Her sculpted Grecian features were as hard as marble as she leaned closer. 'If and when he does, I will be the first to have his head cut off before he finishes speaking. But until then, I am telling you, let this foolish vendetta go. Your hatred of Ashoka comes from your jealousy of his mother, whom you cannot openly attack or harm, because it will be tracked back to you and that is the one thing Bindusara will never forgive you for. The same holds true for Takshashila. If you assassinate Ashoka there, Bindusara will know it was on your command.'

'Not if it is done by Greek hands,' Noor said quietly.

Apama leaned back, releasing her hold on Noor. 'So that is your game. Tactically brilliant. But as always, you fail to take into account the individual factor. I will never do as you propose. My father has already anticipated that you might make such a request and instructed me to refuse you without hesitation. He wants no part of this conspiracy in Takshashila. Whatever you do there, you do at your own risk. I will not speak of it to Bindusara but if he finds out, I will not protect you either. Do you understand?'

Noor smiled nonchalantly. 'He will never know—unless you tell him. In which case, I will know it was you who did.' She held Apama's gaze so the older woman knew that she meant it. 'And as for your father refusing, how could he have refused a request I have not yet made?'

Apama rose to her feet, indicating that the audience was ended. 'You are not the only strategic genius, Noor. Remember that we Greeks invented everything, from civilization to war. That is why in the end, we, and we alone will triumph. Accept that and you will prosper. Challenge it and you will go the way of all Greek enemies.'

Noor couldn't resist a parting shot. 'Alexander the Great made much the same claim. He invaded our land with the greatest army ever assembled. And yet, he never even made it across the Indus river!'

Apama's smile faltered and for an instant, Noor had the satisfaction of seeing the steel behind the diamond glitter of those blue eyes. 'Focus your efforts on bearing a son of your own, Rani Khorasan, instead of resenting other queens the existence of their sons. Go in peace and prosperity now. I bid you come again soon. My doors are always open to you.'

Noor turned and left the white apartments feeling frustrated but also oddly satisfied. At least she left a little bloodstain on those pristine white cushions. It would do until the time came when all that glorious arrogant white décor would be splashed from ceiling to floor with Greek blood. And that day would come, she would see to it.

8

That brahmin. That damned brahmin.

Bindusara kept the Acharya waiting for an almost unacceptable amount of time. He intended to take every possible opportunity to inflict injury upon the man, in every way legitimately available to him. Hours later, when Kautilya did not display any sign of impatience or take offense, Bindusara finally conceded. The Mauryavansh Empire was governed by protocols and courtesies, many of them instituted by the Acharya himself in earlier decades, and with the brahmin caucus more powerful than ever, the Emperor could not be seen to deliberately snub He Who Laid the Blueprints of Civilization, as Kautilya was referred to by every brahmin.

'Send him in,' Bindusara said.

As the stick-thin wizened old man walked in, his sunburnt complexion and red ochre garments gave him the appearance of a forest hermit rather the former prime minister of the Empire, Bindusara experienced a spontaneous surge of fury. Even the sight of the old brahmin awoke deep rage. Once again, as he had done for years, he fought to repress the urge to give vent to his fury and went through the motions of protocol.

Someday, brahmin, someday...but not today.

No sooner had Kautilya broached the matter he had come to discuss when they were interrupted. A servant whispered into Bindusara's ear and waited patiently while the Samrat composed a mental response, then conveyed it to her, speaking almost in a whisper himself.

When she had left, Bindusara turned back to his visitor. Without overtly apologizing or offering any facial expression, he asked the Acharya to continue. The implication was that the message had been too urgent to ignore. After all, had the Acharya himself not famously said that 'An Emperor's work is never done'? No apology necessary.

Throughout the discussion that followed, similar messages of presumed urgency contrived to interrupt their discussion. Each time, Bindusara dealt matter-of-factly with the intruder, neither displaying any irritation at the interruption, nor proffering any apology to his visitor.

The message he was sending was clear. His servants would never have dared to intrude on a private audience with the great Acharya Kautilya. The fact that they did so, and did so with such frequency, with no admonishment from the Samrat, left only one conclusion: that these were pressing matters of great import.

The truth was, they were the most trivial messages possible.

Most were amorous messages from a queen, one of his hundred odd wives, whom he had not visited in several masas and who had been cunningly sent gifts of flowers and jewels by him earlier. Under the impression that the Emperor was desirous of her attention, she had prepared herself for a night of erotic abandon and as the day progressed, she kept sending him poetic fragments indicating her increasing level of arousal. The later messages in this series were ribald enough to increase his own levels of arousal. It had been a while since he had visited her particular charms, he mused. The serving girl bringing the missives, the queen's own pleasure servant, was no less charming, and after her delicately whispered voice had warmed his ear, he found himself musing on thoughts better suited to the wine hour.

He had had no intention of visiting the queen in question tonight. But the dusky glances and perfumed beauty of the pleasure servant was making him have second thoughts. Perhaps the queen and her pleasure servant together...

He brought himself back to the present moment, knowing that his features or body language betrayed none of these lascivious thoughts. Outwardly, he remained the picture of disinterested but polite empirical dignity.

But he was in the company of a master of emotional disguise.

Kautilya was watching him with that unnerving lack of expression that the Acharya appeared to have perfected early in life. There was a statue of Kautilya in the palace foyer that strove to capture this exact stony quality. As a boy, Bindusara had always felt that if he gazed at the lifelike statue long enough, it would sooner or later change expression and display some emotion.

As he grew to manhood, he had come to know better.

Kautilya had been a presence in Bindusara's life ever since his birthing, and in all the years from that day to this one, he had never observed the Acharya giving vent to any strong emotion. Was the man incapable of emotion? Surely no mortal could be so perfectly in command of his senses? Then again, the stories of Kautilya's austerities and dedication to the ancient Vedic ways were legendary. In even the most rabidly casteist kshatriya families, he was acknowledged to be the worthiest successor to the great saptarishis and brahmarishis of yore, on par with the Vishwamitras and Vashishtas.

Bindusara refused to let himself be intimidated by this stony aspect. He was no longer a boy, in awe of the greatest mind the world had ever known. He Who Laid the Blueprints of Civilization. He was Samrat Bindusara now, master of the great Mauryan Empire, the greatest and largest civilization in the known world.

While Acharya Kautilya... What was he really?

He's just a tired old man, a celibate *man who has never known the pleasures of the flesh, wine, revelry, the blood-lust of battle, the sense of power one gets when riding an elephant's back and trampling enemy bodies underfoot, the intoxicating knowledge that to be emperor of the civilized world is to be as close to a god as any man can get. Just a brahmin who must sit by and watch as men like me—gods like me—indulge themselves in all the pleasures this world has to offer. We are the kings and masters of the world. What is he? A master of the Vedas?*

Just a damned brahmin.

Bindusara pretended to listen seriously to the Acharya's complicated explanation of the politics of the North Western satrapies of the Mauryan Empire. All the while, he was thinking of how much more of the Brahmin's time he could waste before Kautilya finally realized that Bindusara would never relent or yield.

Use all the erudition in your power, brahmin. You will not get what you so desperately seek. So go on, talk your head off. I'll hear you—and send you back disappointed.

Kautilya knew even before he walked in that Bindusara had no intention of giving him what he desired.

Outwardly, Bindusara displayed no inappropriate expression or indicated by any means, gesture or word, that he was anything less than completely attentive to Kautilya's lengthy and complex dissertation. But Kautilya knew how to read faces the way a hound could conjure up a complete image from droppings and dried urine. He knew that Bindusara was staying within the bounds of acceptable protocol, while pushing those limits sufficiently to test any brahmin's patience.

He knew also that Bindusara was only humouring him, using these pre-arranged interruptions by maids and servants delivering irrelevant messages to deliberately test his patience. There had been a time when even the late great Chandragupta Maurya would never have dared give Acharya Chanakya anything but his undivided attention. As for Chanakya himself, at the peak of his power and privilege, for servants to hustle in and out this way would have cost them their lives—not because of the rudeness of such interruptions but on account of the potential intelligence threat. The brahmin who had created the world's first spy network had to take his own security seriously.

But that was decades ago. This was a different time, and a different Samrat.

Nothing would give Bindusara more delight than to see Kautilya take offense, stalk out in a huff, lose his temper, deliver an outraged diatribe, or in any way act out the usual responses of any high-ranking minister or advisor treated in this cavalier manner. It was what Bindusara wanted, and would never get. Not because Kautilya was exercising control over his responses, but because he had none. At ninety-six, Kautilya had endured all that could be endured as a human being, and many things besides that most humans could not endure. He had survived the Nandas, Mahapadma Nanda foremost among them in his cruelty and demagoguery, followed closely by his eventual assassin and usurper, his own son Dhana Nanda. Like most tyrants, their cruelty had set an example to all under them, from their own family, to their servants to the citizenry itself. After a childhood and youth spent enduring all the Nanda dynasty and its minions had to offer by way of human cruelty, a little brusqueness by Bindusara was hardly worthy of Kautilya's response.

He was more concerned about Bindusara himself.

Never a good king, he had at least until a few years ago, been an able king. One capable of holding the seething reins of the Five Hundred Tribes and steering them in more or less the same direction: the direction in which the Mauryan Empire desired to go.

But as the Empire grew, so did his sense of self-worth and entitlement.

Now, it was clear to Kautilya that Bindusara had forgotten all the precepts and fundamentals of kingship that he himself had attempted to teach the son of Chandragupta during his crucial formative years. Those lessons gleaned from a lifetime of observing, studying and analyzing itihasa, both past as well as unfolding present events, which were popularly known as Chanakyaneeti, or the Wisdom of Chanakya. Kautilya, who preferred his richly deserved and earned title, did not correct brahmins who touched his feet in reverence and quoted verbatim from Chanakyaneeti. What did it matter if the teachers knew the learnings by rote, if the pupil forgot them when the time came to apply said learnings?

Reluctantly, after observing the decisions and pronouncements of Bindusara over the past few years, Kautilya had come to a conclusion:

Bindusara was not worthy to be a king, leave alone the ruler of the greatest empire in the civilized world.

It had taken Chandragupta Maurya the achievements of a lifetime to attain this chair that Bindusara sat on.

It was a mere accident of blood that had put Bindusara upon that chair.

Yet Kautilya respected the chair, and so he had no choice but to respect the man attached to the hindside that presently warmed that chair.

Aloud, he completed his analysis of the political situation in the North West, knowing full well that Bindusara's mind was occupied with visuals of sensual coitus rather than savage butchery. The way the Emperor's eyes followed the swaying hips of the 75th queen's maid each time she left the chamber were sufficient to reveal what really interested Bindusara at the present moment.

This private audience was a travesty. And yet, he had little choice but to play it through.

Despite Bindusara's arrogant pronouncement that they would discuss the Takshashila problem after the Battle, he had kept Kautilya waiting a full masa after the Battle of the Sixteen Kingdoms. It had taken three petitions through the most formal of channels before Bindusara had even consented to this audience.

Meanwhile, precious time was wasting away.

Kautilya's network of spasas had brought word from Takshashila that the Pashtuns had begun creating trouble again. Though the sons of the Pashtun rebel leader had surrendered their arms to Ashoka after his killing of their father, they in turn had been assassinated by their own tribesmen, ostensibly for failing to avenge their father's death. Kautilya did not need a scroll with a Greek seal to know that the force behind the resurgence of the rebellion was the same one that had instigated it in the first place. Seleucus Nicator would not be shut up so easily. If one Pashtun puppet failed him, he would raise another, and another, and so on, until he finally got what he truly desired: to destroy the Mauryan satrapy in the North West. He would not stop until Takshashila was his, and once he had Takshashila, he would get Ujjain, then Kalinga, and then he would be within kissing distance of Patliputra itself, this very chamber in which Kautilya now sat, attempting to talk sense into a distracted Emperor's clouded head.

To quell the threat of Seleucus Nicator, Ashoka needed the support of the Mauryan army, the more the better. With sufficient force backing him, he would be able to not only hunt down and root out every Greek puppet in the region, he would be able to march over the Hindu Kush ranges to knock at the back door of Nicator's own playing grounds, the contentious territories that he had laid claim to after his own master Alexander's departure, and which he now pompously referred to as the Seleucid Empire! Whether or not those territories were Seleucid's to claim, or if indeed Alexander himself had annexed them, was irrelevant. If Ashoka could get the backing of Mauryavansh's formidable armies, or even a third of that great military might, he could present Seleucus Nicator with the ultimatum that was so urgently required: Fight or Flee.

Kautilya was not a gambling man, but he was willing to make an exception and lay odds that whichever option Seleucus Nicator chose, it would be the end of him. If he fought, then he would be repeating history: Chandragupta Maurya had knocked Seleucus Nicator's Greek army off their horses and into the dust with a fifth of the might of the present Mauryan army. It was only Seleucus Nicator's plea for mercy and Chandragupta's lust for the Greek's blond-haired blue-eyed daughter Apama that had saved his skin back then. Ashoka would be swayed neither by pleas nor blondes: he would finish the job his grandfather had started and that would be the end of the so-called Seleucid Empire.

If he fled, then he would travel back Westwards to certain doom. Seleucus Nicator's betrayal and assassination of Perdicass, and the subsequent wars of the Dadiochi, as well as his enmity with the now-powerful Antigonus, would earn him the cold justice of Greek blades in his flesh rather than Mauryan ones. He had nowhere to go: which was why he was so dangerous and must be dealt with at once.

There was more at stake here than injured egos and dynastic politics. Kautilya had hoped that Bindusara would have the sense to realize that and put his personal feelings against Kautilya and Ashoka aside. But the attitude with which Bindusara was treating the discussion suggested otherwise.

As if acknowledging this fact, Bindusara now spread his

hands in a gesture of sincere perplexity. 'Fascinating, fascinating, Acharya. Good material for your treatise. How is that coming along, by the way? I hope to receive a copy when you are done with it eventually. What did you say you were titling it?'

'*Arthashastra*.'

Bindusara made a dismissive gesture as if to say, whatever. In a tone as patronizing as his body language, he went on. 'Fine, fine. But what does this dissertation on North West tribes and their history of strife have to do with Maurya?'

Careful now. He opens the door to entice you in, only to slam it shut on you. But still, I have no choice. I must attempt to ingress as far as he will let me.

'The current Satrap of Takshashila.'

Bindusara held up a hand. 'Stop. The Satrap of Takshashila is my son Sushim. Before you speak against him, remember whom you are speaking with.'

'Samrat, it is not my intention to judge Yuvraj Sushim—' though if I do, I find him severely lacking, 'merely to suggest ways in which the Takshashila problem can be resolved once and for all.'

Bindusara was showing Kautilya his profile, a fine regal one with an aquiline nose and a perfect chin. Perhaps too perfect. He said nothing, which Kautilya took to be an encouragement to continue.

'As I have explained in my summary of the past history of the region, the true instigator behind the most recent "revolt" and the real force in the North West is no Pashtun, it is that treacherous Greek Seleucus Nicator. I wish that I had been able to persuade Chandragupta to wipe out that entire bloodline when he had the opportunity. It is a cursed and treacherous line and the mercy shown to him back then is the root cause of the misery being caused even today.'

Bindusara rose to his feet, his posture stiff, his tone remote. 'You are speaking of the father of the Dowager Queen Apama, my nurse-mother, the one who raised me after my own mother died.' He shot Kautilya a look that flashed with rage, taking Kautilya unawares. 'It seems that you are determined to lay blame only at the feet of those beloved to me.'

Kautilya got to his feet too. There was no need to maintain the façade of old age. Sudden stand-ups were hard enough for him. Several joints cracked noisily. 'Samrat, I do not speak of Dowager Queen Apama at all. Only of Seleucus Nicator. The evidence of his instigation of the alleged "revolt" and the troop movements reported outside the Indus Pass make his intentions clear. He is preparing for a full-scale invasion and Takshashila is only the staging point for his ingress. I have information that—'

Another maid. Another whispered missive.

This time, Kautilya had to exercise extraordinary restraint to keep from lashing out at the maid, even though he knew it was hardly her fault. There was something in the manner in which she spoke to the Emperor, standing much too close to him, meeting his eyes with a coy, flirtatious invitation, smiling and whispering in a way that hinted at erotic encounters that tested the limits of his self-control. He had spent his life around princes and kings and emperors—from Mahapadma Nanda to Dhana Nanda, to Chandragupta Maurya and Bindusara and his sons—but never before had any liege entertained such flirtatious license in the presence of a Maha-amatya (even a former Maha-amatya) or been permitted to interrupt a conference of this importance. This was the security of the Empire they were discussing!

Finally, the distraction ended and the maid left with a swirl of her gossamer garments, her hips swaying with a certain extra bounce for the Samrat's benefit. The Samrat's face showed that he clearly appreciated the extra bounce. This irritated Kautilya even more and he made the fatal mistake of being the one to speak first, and to do so in a tone that, on later reflection, been considered to be authoritative.

'Samrat, it is my belief that unless we take certain steps, this will happen again, and the next time, the revolt may not be confined to Takshashila alone.'

Bindusara's eyes narrowed. He leaned forward, staring sharply at Kautilya. 'Are you threatening me, Acharya?'

Kautilya was caught off-guard, not by the absurdity of Bindusara's premise, but by its timing. 'Of course not, sire. I am but a servant of Mauryavansh. The empire's welfare is my only concern.' *A servant who created this thing we call Mauryavansh. The very concept was mine, the choice of Chandragupta Maurya as its first liege was mine. The seed that created you had not been formed in your father's testicles when I had decided that the Nanda dynasty must end and dharma return to the land of the Bharatas.*

Bindusara regarded him closely for a moment longer than was polite. With a display of anger that was quite obviously staged for Kautilya's benefit, he rose from his seat and walked away, crossing the large chamber to a wine server, gesturing at the girl. Unprepared for the suddenness of the order, she fumbled the pouring and Bindusara slapped her hard, sending her reeling to the floor. The finely crafted amphora and the mud cup both smashed to pieces, filling the chamber with the sweet odour of Greek wine. Kautilya knew the wine was a gift from Antiochus I Soter because there was a famous story attached to it. It had been carted several thousand miles, all the way from Greece and was worth a fortune. Bindusara had smashed the amphora and abused the serving girl only to display his anger at Kautilya. And yet, Kautilya had done nothing to provoke such a display.

There is something very wrong here. This has the reek of a pre-planned staging by someone expert in such matters.

Bindusara shouted an obscenity at the distraught serving girl, sending her scurrying away from the chamber. He stalked the floor in a fury that made no sense at all to Kautilya.

What did I say to warrant such a temper tantrum? But no sooner had he thought this when he realized, *Nay. It is not I who provoked him. He was seeking to provoke a fight, in order to justify... what? Not merely a smashing of priceless Greek wine. There is a larger game afoot here.*

'Samrat, if I have in any way offended you or caused offense inadvertently, I apologize profusely.' The words stuck in Kautilya's throat but he forced them out. He could not leave here empty-handed today. A decision must be made.

He consoled himself that at least Bindusara was able to control his behaviour in public at least, displaying such outbursts only in the privacy of his own chambers. Though even the rumour of such weakness could serve him ill when known by his enemies in the palace and sabha.

Still thinking of Mauryavansh, Kautilya? You truly are a servant of the Empire. But as you have just witnessed, this is how the Empire treats its servants now. Mauryavansh has come a long way since Chandragupta's time when you were the voice of Mauryavansh and not even a king dared raise his voice to you, for fear of being parted from his tongue.

Bindusara remained standing with his back to Kautilya. His voice was hot and strained. 'You should have remained in your mountain ashram, Chanakya. Writing your treatise which no one will ever read.'

Kautilya rose to his feet, his limbs creaking with age but still steady enough to bear his pride. 'I am a servant of Mauryavansh, Samrat. So long as the race of Bharata is under threat, I cannot stand by and simply watch. It is my dharma to do everything in my power to defend this nation and defeat its enemies.'

Bindusara produced a sound that Kautilya first mistook for a sob before identifying it as a snigger. 'Servant, my ass.' The casual obscenity shocked Kautilya more than the smashing of the Greek wine. He had never heard Bindusara mouth an abuse since he was but a boy with a hairless chin. 'You are the chief cause of all our distress, the architect of disaster. If left to you, I would be ashes in the Ganga now and your protégé would be on the Lion Throne. But you are mistaken. It is not I but your plans that will turn to dust now, Chanakya. All your political manipulation and manoeuvring will come to nothing. Because I have prepared the path for your removal and you have conveniently delivered yourself into my hands at the perfect moment.'

This is more than an attempt to insult or humiliate me. This is a coup.

Except that the removal of an old 'servant of the Empire' by the Emperor himself could hardly be termed a coup. Kautilya kept forgetting that this was no longer Chandragupta Maurya's Empire, it was Bindusara's. He was no longer the Architect of the Civilized World, but merely a retired maha-amatya, a former Chief Minister and Advisor to the Emperor. He understood in a flash what Bindusara meant when he said that Kautilya ought to have remained in his ashram. In that distant hermitage, far removed from the course of Mauryan geopolitics, Kautilya was irrelevant and obsolete. But here, in the very heart of the capital, taking sides on an immediate and deadly threat to the Empire, he was anything Bindusara perceived him to be: a conspirator, an assassin, a rival, a treasonous politician...

I have walked into the Lion's den and put my bald pate into his gaping jaws.

As if to confirm this fear, Bindusara turned back to Kautilya. 'Your usefulness to the Empire is at an end, Acharya. I commend you for your long years of service, but your advice is no longer required.'

Kautilya knew when he was being dismissed. He knew also that he ought to let this go. But he could not. Too much was at stake here for the kingdom, the empire, the political stability of the entire subcontinent.

'Samrat, what of the Takshashila problem?'

'The Takshashila problem is no longer your problem. You need not trouble yourself any further with concerns for our political stability.'

So then you do grasp the situation. After all, who was your teacher if not I myself. But why are you behaving in this manner with me? What is this new game?

'Samrat, if I have in any way offended you or caused offense inadvertently, I apologize profusely.' The words stuck in Kautilya's throat but he forced them out. He needed to understand the reason for Bindusara's hostility.

'Your very existence offends me,' Bindusara said with the tight face and clenched jaw of a man who is restraining himself from taking much more aggressive action. 'I no longer wish to see you or engage with you in future. If you have any needs to be met, you are free to ask the relevant palace authorities. They will take care of you.'

And with that insulting offer of charity and summary dismissal, Bindusara exited his own chamber, leaving Kautilya standing in utter bewilderment.

9

The chief cause of the Acharya's bewilderment was barely a stone's throw away in her apartment in the palace, standing naked beneath a waterfall of milk and honey.

Noor Khorasan was a beautiful woman, arguably the most

beautiful of Bindusara's queens, and she was well aware of it. But she was never more beautiful than at two particular times: When she was laughing. And when she was engaged in kwassui baz; her people's term for the aggressive hunt-and-conquer ritual of mating.

She was laughing now.

The instigator of her delight was standing beside her on the marble steps of the bath. Orzala, her maid and confidante, had just reported to her the entirety of Acharya Kautilya's dialogue with Samrat Bindusara, concluding with the Samrat's outburst and departure. Noor Khorasan had instantly burst into laughter. Her slender body, cup-sized breasts, delicate shoulders, and long graceful neck all shuddered now as she showed her delight at the news. Because she had not a gram of excess fat on her body, there was nothing to wobble or quiver. Every limb, every curve was taut and firm. Her laughter was a silent one, a shuddering that began from within and rippled upward and outwards through her chest, arms, throat, the runaway emotion released finally through her widespread arms. She embraced the slowly descending unguent flow of the milk and honey, relishing the bath and the minor triumph in a decades-long vendetta. Khorasani women learned from infancy to express their emotions soundlessly. In the vast open plains of Khorasan, sound travelled great distances especially at night, and a Khorasani always had enemies somewhere within hearing distance. So though Noor laughed, she did so silently in the Khorasani way. For despite being married to Samrat Bindusara for almost fifteen years, she was still and would always be, a Khorasani.

The bath done, Noor stood on the marble floor of her stately bathing chamber while Orzala, the maid, gently wiped her down. Orzala was the only individual in the world that Noor permitted to touch her person. Apart from the Samrat himself, of course.

Orzala knew this and her touch was intimate and sensual. Noor's lips parted as she sighed soundlessly. Her eyes remained open, another Khorasani survival trait. During kwassai baz, a Khorasani often expressed their passion by cutting their lover. Even though Orzala would never do so to her mistress, Noor could no sooner let her eyes roll shut than keep herself from experiencing the sensations caused by her trusted servant's artful touch. Soon touch gave way to tongue and pleasure verged on passion.

'Enough.'

Noor put a firm hand on Orzala's head.

Orzala stopped, smiling a sly familiar smile as she fetched Noor's gown.

Moments later, her nakedness draped in a diaphanous garment that covered her from head to foot while successfully failing to conceal any part of her anatomy, Noor sat on a silk upholstered diwan while Orzala did her hair in the manner she favoured. From time to time the Empress of Maurya smiled, basking in the knowledge of her triumph. It was Orzala who introduced a note of caution.

'The old brahmin will not take this lying down. He is a crafty fox.'

'But an old one. And what will he do? As of now, he doesn't even have access to the sabha. All his old connections are useless.'

'There are always the brahmins.'

'Those young ferrets? They would sooner tear his throat out than let him step back into his old domain. It took them a lifetime to push him out and if he had not gone willingly into retirement, they might not have let him leave on his feet. No, he is done here and he knows it. That is why he endured the humiliation of waiting like a supplicant, and the shame of being shouted at and dismissed in such a manner. In his prime, the great Kautilya would never have tolerated such behaviour even from his precious protégé Chandragupta Maurya.' A thought lit up her cat-green eyes. Noor snapped her fingers. 'Spread the word of his humiliation. Make sure everyone comes to know of how he has fallen in the Samrat's favour. Especially the brahmin caucus.'

Orzala smiled down as she worked on the long lustrous dark locks. 'It is done, Sultana. Ashniya is the most indiscreet maid in the palace. By now, even the beggars who queue up daily for the leftovers from the servants' kitchen will be talking about the Acharya's fall from grace.'

Noor smiled. 'She will lose her job for it.'

'No, Sultana, she will lose her head.' Orzala smiled impishly. 'After the last scandal, your father had issued a diktat that any royal servant found guilty of speaking of private matters would be executed summarily without trial.'

Noor arched her delicately shaped eyebrows. 'Ashniya knew this and still dared to defy the order?'

Orzala shrugged. 'She might have gotten the impression that it was the Samrat's wish. She may have been informed that Bindusara himself had asked her to go tell all the Masters of Duties to deny Acharya Kautilya access henceforth.'

Noor's rosy cheeks dimpled. 'And how might she have gotten this impression and information, I wonder? From a certain flower of our palace, perhaps?'

'A very fragrant and radiant flower, Sultana.' Orzala winked at Noor. 'One that flourishes even in the brutal cruelty of a Khorasani winter.'

Noor held up a hand thoughtfully, marking off each point as she spoke: 'So that is Kautilya cut off from Bindusara. Bindusara so angry with him that he will never entertain any advice given by Kautilya—and if he even hears that Kautilya has a point of view, he is likely to do the exact opposite. This will be known by everyone who matters by now, which means a further loss of face and power for Kautilya. And finally, any trace of our involvement in this is neatly erased once Ashniya is pulled up for violating my father's diktat and executed.'

'Which will probably happen shortly, if it has not happened already.' Orzala paused and turned away for a moment to pick up something that flashed metallic in her hands. Noor's eyes followed her as sharply as a baz-falcon its prey on the desert floor. Orzala turned back to her mistress with an oval of metal polished to a mirror finish. She noted the watchfulness in the empress's eyes but took no offense: as a Khorasani she understood mistrust. 'I have tried pulling every alternate strand away, instead of toward, your brow. It is impossible to flatter your perfection further, Sultana, but perhaps this may please you better than the usual style?'

Noor glanced at the mirror, wishing as every vain woman did, that one could actually see oneself clearly in its surface, instead of the malformed approximation that it reflected. She could make out enough to know that the variation in styling was just a touch different yet pleasing. Bindusara would never notice—men rarely noticed such things—but like all the things Orzala did for her, it made her feel better, and that was all that really mattered. 'We shall wear it in this fashion.'

As Orzala turned to put the mirror down again, Noor caught hold of her hand, stopping her. 'Orzala, your work today has pleased me.'

Orzala's face softened, as it rarely did, in a smile that eschewed her trademark sly sneer. She bowed low, addressing her mistress from below her eye level as befitted her station, and with her eyes cast downward in servility. 'I live to serve, Sultana.'

Noor grasped her servant's angular face in both hands and bent over it, applying her lips to Orzala's in a passionate kiss. As the kiss continued for several moments, both women's affection for one another disinhibiting their customary reserve, Noor's hand found its way to other, softer, less angular parts of Orzala's anatomy. Soon, she was rocking her knuckle against the most sensitive part of Orzala in a rhythmic motion.

This time, it was the servant's turn to part her lips wetly and moan with silent pleasure.

Their liaison was interrupted suddenly by a voice from the outer chamber.

'My queen?'

Orzala started at the sound of the Samrat's voice but Noor continued her knuckle-play without pausing.

The gossamer drapes parted to admit the familiar figure of the Samrat. Bindusara took in the scene: Noor pleasuring Orzala with one hand while caressing the maid's bared breast and erect nipple with the other. Without changing position or pausing, Noor raised her eyes to her husband, the predatory heat in her cat eyes conveying all that needed to be said without a single word spoken.

Bindusara needed no translation.

The Emperor reached down to take hold of his own garment, yanking it upwards and with one smooth action rid himself of his only accoutrement. Naked and visibly aroused, he approached the diwan where the two Khorasani women were entwined in mutual pleasure. He touched the back of Orzala's back and neck with a familiarity that spoke of previous intimacies and brushed his moustached lips against the curve of her neck and shoulder. Orzala shuddered and reached behind herself, seeking the imperial sceptre. As the heat of her damp hand closed upon its length, Bindusara closed his eyes momentarily, pressing himself closer to the maid's shapely rear. As his body pressed against hers from behind, Orzala moaned. Bindusara began to plant a line of wet kisses on her neck and upper back, grasping her sides and running his palms down to her wasp waist which he gripped tight, as if trying to make his fingers meet around her body. Noor saw his knuckles whiten with the intensity of his grip, and intensified her stroking.

Losing control of her senses, Orzala's hand slipped from Bindusara's damp length and the Samrat raised his waist long enough to allow his erection to slip between himself and the servant. Orzala's slender but strongly muscled thighs were shaped in a curve that left a gap between her inner thighs. The sceptre found the wet heat between her legs and the tip brushed against Noor's fingertips on the other side. Noor captured the imperial sceptre with her fingers, pressing it upwards against the entrance of Orzala's sheath. Slick and wet and aroused by her mistress's attentions, Orzala needed only part her legs slightly, and the sceptre slipped in, finding the heat of her core. Bindusara groaned, throwing his head back, eyes rolling up as he enjoyed the moment of initiation. With her other hand, Noor continued rubbing her knuckle against Orzala's bud, while she cupped the joining of sceptre and sheath, enhancing the sensation for both her maid and her husband.

Slowly, languorously at first, Bindusara began rocking back and forth on his haunches. Orzala, impaled on her master's organ from behind, grasped from the front by her mistress's double-handed grip, pleasured within and without by both, gave herself over to ecstasy. Her hot dark brown eyes remained slitted but capable of observing, even as the rest of her body surrendered.

Noor manipulated the body she knew so intimately. She alternated between flicking Orzala's bud with her finger and knuckling it roughly but rhythmically. Orzala began tossing her head right and left, her bound hair falling loose, cascading across her naked shoulders and back, thrashing Bindusara's face. The sensation of her hair on his flushed face, the scent of her attar, the knowledge that she was building to a climax, aroused him further, and he increased the rhythm and intensity of his strokes.

Noor gasped as she felt the force of his sceptre as it pounded the maid's sheath. Dropping one hand to the burning centre between her own legs, she began pleasuring herself, joining her lovers as she too began to build steadily to her own climax.

With a facial paroxysm that would have been called a scream if seen from afar, although not a sound escaped her gaping mouth, Orzala achieved her apogee and shuddered and shook violently. Her taut muscled body rippled as her breasts, twice the size of Noor's, shivered deliciously, her engorged nipples standing out an inch from the pink aureoles. She grasped her mistress's shoulders firmly as a man would at such a moment, bending over to allow the Samrat to penetrate her harder at her moment of climax.

Aroused by the slick ooze of her climax, Bindusara's own passion increased to a frenzy. He pounded hard against Orzala's delicately curved buttocks, slamming against them with every thrust, remaining inside her heat a moment longer each time as he sought the primordial male quest for total penetration, then rearing back with an animal expression on his face. A handsome man with more of an imperial nobility in his features than his illustrious father, at this moment he appeared less an Emperor of Maurya, but as a primal savage tearing into his chosen mate. He grunted loudly with each impact, the wet slapping of his body against Orzala's almost as loud as his own grunts.

Orzala herself made no sound, in the Khorasani way, but her grip on her mistress's head and shoulders was intense enough to crush the life out of Noor had she been so inclined. She was a powerful woman and her passion was as intense as befitted such a specimen. She shuddered one final time and dropped her head on Noor's face, kissing her mistress as she endured Bindusara's continuing pounding.

Noor sucked Orzala's tongue into her mouth, hard enough to make it difficult for the woman to breathe. She slipped the fingertips of one hand into Orzala's sheath, forcing it alongside the pounding sceptre. Orzala's head started to jerk upwards in shock but her captured tongue, still drawn deeply, painfully, into Noor's open mouth, prevented her from moving a fraction.

Bindusara felt his queen's fingers inside the same sheath he was ravaging and his arousal grew as well to fever pitch. He increased his pounding rhythm, gasping for breath now as the intensity of his passion tested his body's capacity. His body, once as tautly muscled and fit as Orzala's or Noor's, had lost some of its youthful power, some excess weight and old injuries capping his limits. But the pursuit of ecstasy was too powerful to ignore and he pushed himself to the limit, increasing his pace and force, pushing himself roughly into the crowded orifice.

Noor continued to pleasure herself at a faster rate, matching pace and passion with her two lovers. All three worked intensely towards a common peak now, like workmen labouring under a searing noonday sun. Sweat glistened and dripped from their naked intertwined bodies. Their faces, eyes, organs were swollen and inflamed with passion.

The absence of breath and the exquisite pain of having her sheath forced to take in both her master's sceptre and her mistress's probing fingers were pushing Orzala to another climax. The second time always took a great deal of effort and time for the young serving girl. Noor was well aware of it. She also knew the way to hasten and enhance that second climax for Orzala.

Glancing up at Bindusara's clenched face and tautly striving body, Noor knew instinctively that he too was approaching the climax of his passion. She released her hold on her own sex, foregoing the pleasure she was experiencing for a greater thrill. Reaching behind her maid's slender body, she found Orzala's parted buttocks with her already slick fingers and probed till she found the woman's smaller, much tighter, puckered hole. She slipped one finger easily into that opening, finding it already lubricated by the combined juices of both Bindusara and Orzala herself. Orzala's eyes, slitted till now, flew wide open as she stared into her mistress's face. Her tongue was still captured by Noor, and she could not say a word or move, even had she wanted to do either. But her reaction was unmistakable. Noor knew how sensitive Orzala's nether orifice became at such a time. Lacking the opportunity to apply her tongue to that delicate spot, she used her touch instead.

But none of the gentle rhythm that she had used on the maid's bud. With a savage, proprietary motion, Rani Khorasan plunged all four fingers into Orzala's behind with full force, causing a sensation of such pain and unspeakable pleasure that Orzala screamed silently into Noor's mouth, her body racked by enormous spasms. Noor released the tongue she had grasped, knowing that Orzala would tear it free if she did not let go, and as she watched the maid rear up like a mare in heat, she felt the onslaught of her own climax.

Bindusara felt both hands of his queen inside the woman he was ravaging, and the reaction of the woman, and the combined intensity of their pleasure precipitated his peak as well.

All three lovers exploded with a purging of fluids and a venting of heat that continued unabated for several kshanas.

When it was over, they all collapsed in a naked sweaty pile of bodies on the diwan. Their juices mingled and dribbled on the velvet cushions and onto the marbled floor.

Bindusara lay on the bottom, on his back, legs and arms sprawled, his dwindling sceptre oozing one final trickle; Orzala lay face-down upon his right arm, her abused nether eye gaping from her mistress's assault, her other orifice still spasming with the aftershocks of pleasure, dribbling fresh juices, and on Bindusara's other out flung arm, and draped across his lower body, Noor Khorasan lay face up, face glowing with contentment.

She was never as beautiful as she was at this moment.

10

'Shubhadrangi!'

Tissyanka entered her sister queen's apartment with a familiarity earned through long years of friendship. The young queen's face was flushed, her voice excited. She went through the outer rooms one by one, their elegant but unostentatious simplicity a stark contrast to the decadence of some of the other queens' domiciles. She glanced into the bathing chamber in passing even though she knew that Shubhadrangi always took her bath before dawn, after performing the ritual sandhyavandana.

She found her friend in the akasa chamber, tending to her indoor garden. Shubhadrangi was on her knees, working on a flowering plant of some sort. She had told Tissyanka the name of her plants more than once, but Tissyanka could never seem to remember them all. She paused at the entrance out of respect for her senior queen, admiring the single-minded dedication that Shubhadrangi applied to her work. Tissyanka loved flowers; as in, she loved holding them and inhaling their delicate perfume, but she couldn't imagine working with dirt and roots the way Shubhadrangi did.

'Shubhadrangi, you have to hear this.'

The older woman, though only by a few years, remained bowed over the plant she was working on. 'Just a kshana, Tissyanka. Almost done.'

Tissyanka strolled around the akasa chamber, open on three sides to the sky and elements, hemmed on all those three sides by a yard-wide trough of fresh water that contained fishes, some of them fat and curious enough to poke their mouths up from time to time as if checking to see the visitor. She was always tempted to lie on her stomach on the cool stone floor and dip her hands into the water as she had seen Shubhadrangi do, but the sight of the tendrils of plants and the touch of the fish, the schools of tadpoles swimming energetically around the water made it out of the question. One touch from any living or growing thing and she would run off screaming to bathe herself from head to foot in hot water. She couldn't help herself. It was the way she had been seen she was a little girl.

She had a deep dislike of dirt engendered in her by her noble birth. Her mother had always placed a great emphasis on cleanliness, and of course, on one's place in life. One did certain things, and other things one had other people do them for you. It was only after marriage and befriending Shubhadrangi that she had come to accept that even some nobility and royalty chose to spend their time on such pursuits. She had been shocked once to find out not long after that her own mother had taken to raising a rare exotic species of flower in a corner of their royal garden. Just a hobby, her mother had said sniffily when Tissyanka found out accidentally, something to while away the afternoons. Tissyanka knew that her father's death and the gaping hole it created in her mother's life had something to do with the new hobby but she still found it difficult to wrap her mind around the thought of that prissy aristocratic old lady doing what Shubhadrangi was doing now: running her bare hands through dirt. Then she had learned that Shubhadrangi had taken to growing her own produce back in the time when she was 'away', the euphemistic term they used for her long absence when she had been sent away for reasons Tissyanka still didn't understand fully, and she had suddenly seen the connection between her mother and Shubhadrangi. One, losing her life partner to death. The other, losing her life partner to palace politics.

It had made her understand Shubhadrangi better. Even like her better. It had melted the last barrier of formality between them, and from that day on, she had come to look on Shubhadrangi as something akin to an elder sister—or even, a surrogate mother.

Now, she liked Shubhadrangi dearly. She was the only queen Tissyanka trusted completely and confided in fully. In a palace of almost a hundred queens, she could honestly say that Shubhadrangi was her only real friend. That was why she had come herself to deliver this news, not wanting to leave it even to her maid, whom she trusted with more routine matters and errands, but not something of this personal and intimate nature.

Finally, her work done, Shubhadrangi rose to her feet and smiled warmly at Tissyanka. She brushed away an errant lock of hair with the back of one hand, smudging her forehead with dirt. 'There. That's done. I had to clean up those roots and trim the stems before re-planting it. Otherwise the graft simply wasn't taking properly and these eastern plants can be so stubborn in our soil.'

Tissyanka smiled vacantly. She had absolutely no idea what Shubhadrangi was saying except that it had something to do with roots and soil. 'You have dirt on your face.' She heard the slight hint of dismay in her tone but couldn't help it. There might be worms in that mud! Or other smaller, tiny, almost invisible... things.

Shubhadrangi lay down on the ground and immersed both her hands in the water upto her elbows, rubbing her palms together gently. She dabbed at her forehead with her wet fingers, turning to show Tissyanka. 'All clean now?'

Tissyanka indicated a spot on Shubhadrangi's left temple, almost in her hair. If it had been she, she would have wanted a full bath and a hair wash. Shubhadrangi simply splashed some water on the side of her head, not caring if she wet her hair or got any of those trailing plants on herself. Then she undid the end of her own upper garment and used it to wipe herself off. She rose to her feet again, beaming. 'Is that all right now, Tiss-Tiss?'

Tissyanka grinned shyly at the nickname. It was true: she did tend to go 'tiss' a lot, didn't she? As had her mother—until Tissyanka's father died. She wondered if such a change would come over to her someday, and what would cause it. Surely not Bindusara's death? Her mother and father had been...close. The only equivalent in the Maurya house was perhaps Noor and Bindusara. Certainly not herself or Shubhadrangi or any of the other queens. She knew she ought not to even think such a thing but the truth was she couldn't pretend to care half as much about her mostly absent husband the way her mother had cared for Tissyanka's father.

The two queens sat side by side on the stone bench facing the North view, which was Tissyanka's favourite. The clever design of the akasa chamber created the illusion that they were seated almost in mid-air overlooking a panoramic vista of rolling green hills, densely forested valleys, and a white-water cataract. It was breathtaking. Every other queen and prince wanted the western view, which was the city of Patliputra. When Tissyanka had first come to live in the palace, over a decade ago, she too had been impressed by that view. The grandeur and majesty of the empirical capital lying below the hill on which the emperor's palace stood, was an astonishing sight. Especially to many of the queens who came from the more rustic tribes, where no structure was much taller than a tall man's height, and the very idea of people living in stacks of stone chambers piled to such enormous heights was terrifying. Not to mention the larger-than-life-size stone lions on the corners of all official empire buildings: there were still first-time visitors who screamed in terror when they looked up and saw those stone lions lunging in mid-air, believing they were real. She was quite the opposite of those country bumpkins of course. To her, the great city had been a treasure trove of wonders. But she had come to associate this verdant Northern view with these intimate talks she shared with Shubhadrangi and that association made her love the view. They had spent so many wonderful days here, just talking, that it seemed almost as reassuring as her mother's chambers back home.

Except for the dirt. And the worms. And the fishes.

'So will you tell me what this great news is or do I have to push you into the water?' To underline her threat, Shubhadrangi raised her hands.

Tissyanka scooted back a few inches on the bench. 'You wouldn't dare!'

Shubhadrangi laughed, dropped her hands, and splashed her feet into the water. 'Just tell me then, will you! I am dying of curiosity now.'

Tissyanka laughed too. 'I'm such a scatterbrain. Well, Acharya was here to see Bindu.'

Shubhadrangi frowned, her smile fading. 'Acharya Kautilya came to see the Samrat today? Where is he now? I need to speak with him.'

'He left, Shubha. He had already left by the time I came to know. I'm sorry, if I had known...'

'You could have done nothing, if he'd already left. In any case, it's better that I don't speak to him within these inquisitive walls. Go on, then, what did he come to see Bindu about? No, wait. That much is obvious. He wanted to reiterate his petition for more military support for Ashoka in Takshashila and—'

Tissyanka shook her head. 'No, this was far beyond that. He said that the Greek fellow, the one who used to be Alexander's satrap, what was his name?'

'Seleucus Nicator?'

'That one. He's preparing to invade us.'

Shubhadrangi absorbed this for a moment. 'That makes sense. Seleucus Nicator has tried to invade earlier too, during

Chandragupta's time. After all, once Alexander died, there was nowhere else for him to go. It was either go back and fight his own people to get back the lost territories which they took as reparation for the cost of Alexander's campaign, or fight the other Greek satrap, Demetrius. And from what I know, Seleucus Nicator needs Demetrius's help to fight Ptolemy so unless the alliance between them has ended...No, even if the alliance is ended, Maurya remains the biggest prize for him. With the conquest of Maurya, Seleucus Nicator could go back to Greece a conquering hero, the hero that even Alexander never truly became, despite his great legend. It's a big temptation, worth violating the terms of the treaty Seleucus Nicator signed with our late father-in-law Chandragupta Maurya.'

Tissyanka shrugged. 'If you say so. You know this political crisscross is all Greek to me.'

Shubhadrangi thought for a moment. 'Did he say when this invasion is supposed to be launched? Is it a real incursion or just a plan? What are the points of ingress? What forces are being deployed?'

Tissyanka frowned and crossed her arms across her ample chest. 'Would you like me to do some gardening as well? Dig some mud up so you can re-plant it or something? You know I don't understand any of that.'

'Well, what else did you hear then apart from this supposed invasion?'

'That was the whole thing. Oh, and Bindusara refused to listen further to the Acharya and dismissed him very rudely, then walked out on him—to go have sex with one of his queens!'

Shubhadrangi stopped what she was doing and looked anxious. 'Really? That doesn't sound like Bindu. What is he thinking, behaving this way?'

Tissyanka unfolded her hands and leaned closer, her voice changing to a mischievous tone. 'Perhaps he was just...in the mood?'

Shubhadrangi looked at Tissyanka with prurient curiosity. 'Have you been playing with our husband this afternoon?'

Tissyanka slapped Shubhadrangi on the shoulder affectionately. 'Not me, silly. Whorasan.'

Shubhadrangi nodded, her smile slipping at the mention of Noor Khorasan; the nickname was self-explanatory. 'Of course. Who else. She does have a way of getting him all charged up.'

Tissyanka leaned close again. 'She lures him like the royal hunters lure innocent game, just before they chop their heads off. Remember the time he left the sabha in the middle of the session and we saw him doing her in the middle of the—'

Shubhadrangi looked up at her friend and sister queen. Tissyanka's sweet innocent face was never as animated as when she talked about Rani Khorasan or one of the more risque queens in the palace. She wondered if Tissyanka understood that the reason she found it so enjoyable to gossip about such activities was because she herself secretly longed to indulge in them, but would rather die of shame than admit it. She wouldn't be the one to make her sweet friend aware of her own secret longings; she liked Tissyanka too much to upset her. Besides, she felt just as envious of Khorasan herself. Perhaps she wouldn't want to be seen fornicating in sight of other people the way that shameless hussy did, or went at it in all the decadent shocking variations that rumour spoke of, but she would love to have more attention from Bindusara. She would love him to try at least to seduce her once in a while, or failing that, at least come to her bed. When was the last time he had visited her? Too long ago. And with that absence came an absence of favour too. The queen that shared the Emperor's bed also shared his thoughts, his dreams, his innermost desires. And in Mauryavansh Palace at present, the only queen who could claim that insight was Noor Khorasan. Whorasan she might be to the other queens, but to Bindusara she was lover, wife, confidante, and Empress of Maurya.

'What of War Marshall Khorasan?'

Tissyanka, interrupted in the middle of a juicy retelling of another of Noor Khorasan's more shocking escapades, stared at her friend. 'What of her? She's a scary one. Huge as a giant and as cruel as one.'

Shubhadrangi shook her head impatiently. Tissyanka was sweet and sincere, but she could be thick-headed. 'This news. Of the Samrat insulting the Acharya. How did the War Marshal react to it when she found out?'

'How would I—?' Tissyanka stopped and frowned. She had been about to say How would I know but of course she would know. She still had access to eyes and ears around the palace thanks to her wealth and position as the daughter of a powerful tribe, something Shubhadrangi could not claim. That was why Shubhadrangi depended on her for these little titbits of information. If not for Tissyanka sharing, Shubhadrangi would remain in the dark like so many other queens. 'I heard she has given the order for mobilization.'

Shubhadrangi's heart lurched. She caught hold of Tissyanka's hand and squeezed it tightly. 'Where?'

Tissyanka swallowed, nervous at the intensity of Shubhadrangi's tone. 'Takshashila, I think.'

Shubhadrangi released Tissyanka's hand and rose to her feet. She strode to and fro. Suddenly the simple pleasures of her akasa garden, the fish, the flowers, the plants, the view of the North forest, the afternoon sunshine, nothing held any attraction. The only thought that filled her mind was a single name, a single person: Ashoka.

Tissyanka watched her anxiously.

'I must go to Takshashila,' Shubhadrangi said at last. 'If the Acharya's mission has failed and War Marshall Khorasan is mobilizing the army, then it's imperative that I warn Ashoka at once. I must make arrangements to leave within the hour. I will need your help, Tissyanka.'

Tissyanka nodded vigorously then found her voice. 'Yes, of course, Subha. Anything.' She rose to her feet.

Shubhadrangi clasped Tissyanka's hands. 'Nobody must know that I have left Patliputra. I must travel incognito and my journey must be kept secret.'

'I will help you, sister. Tell me what I can do.' Tissyanka's voice was solemn now.

Shubhadrangi looked into Tissyanka's eyes. 'Thank you, Tiss. Whether he knows it or not, Ashoka is surrounded by enemies in Takshashila. With the Acharya shut out and Khorasan in control of the army, no Mauryan soldier will dare ally with my son against the might of Maurya.'

Tissyanka did not hesitate for a kshana. 'My private guard. They are loyal to a fault. I trust them with my children's lives. They are yours. Every last man. Take them.'

Shubhadrangi embraced Tissyanka warmly, her eyes filling. 'You are a true friend and sister queen, Tissyanka. Devi herself bless you and all your children.'

Tissyanka's eyes spilled tears with girlish innocence. 'Just do me one favour, Shubha. Please, for Devi's sake. Come back alive.'

Shubhadrangi smiled but said nothing. That was the one thing she could not promise.

11

Ashoka watched from behind the rock as Trishul stalked her prey. That was the name he had finally settled on, 'Cub' being too generic and besides, it would soon be inaccurate. Vyag cubs grew up quickly. Already Trishul was thrice the size she had been when she arrived in Takshashila and he was teaching her to hunt. Or rather, he was encouraging her to follow her natural instincts and hoping she would learn how on her own. To this end, he spent all his free time out in the hills above the city, letting her follow scents, sniff out prey and track them. She often began stalking prey, even attempting to ambush or chase them but today, for the first time, he thought she might actually catch something.

He stayed behind a boulder the height of his chest, crouching to avoid being seen by the prey. He was upwind and taking care to watch as silently and unobtrusively as possible. Proudly, he watched Trishul as she stalked the prey. He was especially proud of the grace with which she managed to move on three legs, somehow manoeuvring herself in a manner which appeared wholly natural. She ran surprisingly quickly too. But sharp turns were her weakness and once any prey knew it, she would be unable to keep up with its manoeuvring. Which was why it was crucial to catch and pin down the prey before it bolted and picked up speed. Trishul was a perfect name for her: the fabled three-pronged trident of Lord Shiva was an apt symbol for a three-legged hunter-warrior.

He watched as she approached the prey now, crouching low in the waving grass. She made her move, leaping from her higher vantage point onto the prey's back. The hare bolted with the famous reflexes of its kind and Trimurti missed its back, but she still landed with her right front paw firmly pinning down its bob-tail, slowing the frightened rodent's speed for a fraction of a second. That was enough: Trishul's left forepaw swiped with extruded claws at the creature. Ashoka saw blood spurt against the lush green grass and knew it was over for the hare. Even if it bolted now, it would leave a telltale trail that Trishul would have no difficulty tracking.

It never got that far. Ashoka saw another blur and then a big stain of red and it was all over.

He went close enough to see Trishul's head buried in the hare's steaming belly, eating the hot guts even as the last lifeblood pulsed from the body. He smiled and squatted down, letting her enjoy her treat, and her moment of triumph. There was a warm sensation in his chest and a constriction in his throat. He wondered if this was how a mother Vyag felt when she watched her cubs feed on their first kill. Perhaps. Not the father Vyag though: those bastards were indifferent to their offspring. Ashoka had learned from his guru as a young boy that male Vyag would often kill and eat the offspring of potential female mates, so that the females would mate with them in order to produce more progeny. That was a bastard move to beat all bastard moves. But then all fathers were bastards, at least from all Ashoka had seen in his short life.

Except that now he was a father too of sorts: Trishul's father. Which made him...what? A good bastard father?

Trishul finished eating her fill and trundled over to a shady patch nearby. She rolled over on her side in the grass, furiously rubbing her muzzle in the grass as if trying to scrub it clean. She rolled over fully onto her back and lay there, her belly swollen and distended from the big meal she had just eaten. Ashoka watched her and felt the sense of pride grow until it almost choked him. He went over and squatted down behind her. She opened her eyes and twisted her neck at an unnatural angle to stare up at him. The sunlight caught her light grey-green eyes and turned them to brilliant diamonds. He scratched the top of her head, then patted it, upside down. 'Your first kill, well done.'

She purred up at him as if understanding what he meant, though he knew she was only responding to his tone and his touch. Then for good measure, she licked the back of his hand, still upside down. She left a smear of hare's blood and her own copious saliva on his hand. Her tongue lolled out the side of her mouth and she let it lie like that, almost touching the grass. Her body was twisted around in a curved semi-circle, her tail sweeping the grass in slow, lazy arcs as she basked in her moment of glory and digested her meal.

He looked up at the distant mountains of the Afghan ranges, unable to stop himself saying what he said next.

'It was Sushim's stupid idea, to go Vyag-hunting. Once he gets it into his head to do something...' Ashoka shook his head. 'So naturally, I have to go along to make sure he doesn't end up being hunted himself. There we are, deep in the Girvan, with no sign nor track of any Vyag of any kind, Sushim already starting to grumble and talk about turning back, when of a sudden, out of nowhere, she appears. The biggest female Vyag I ever saw or heard of. She leaps straight at Sushim, whose horse rears, saving his life the first time. Sushim falls off, the horse collapses on its side, the Vyag is on the side of the horse trying to get at Sushim. The horse kicks out in terror, hitting the Vyag almost accidentally, and the Vyag retreats for a minute. That's when I come up and shove Sushim out of the way. The horse scrabbles back on its feet and gallops away—headed straight for the high Himalayas or whatever lies beyond, it's terrified out of its wits. The Vyag focusses on Sushim and gets ready to pounce. I move in, coming between her and Sushim, waving my arms and making a noise, forcing her to look at me. Now, at that moment all I'm armed with is a bow and arrow. I never thought I'd be hunting Vyag with a sword so had left mine with my men, to avoid it hitting trees or catching on bushes and disturbing the forest. The Vyag is so close and so ready to spring that I know that even if I loose an arrow as fast as Indra looses a vajra, it will likely only wound the Vyag and just make her madder. So I drop the bow and hold just the arrow in one hand. The Vyag jumps. All this happens in a split second or two.'

Trishul stared up at him with an inscrutable expression,

listening to his voice and watching his hand gestures. He knew she could not possibly understand anything he was saying, but somehow, just saying it to her and seeing her acknowledge him speaking and seeming to listen felt oddly right.

'I know that just the arrow won't be enough to kill the Vyag so I use it to block the Vyag's mouth instead. As the Vyag leaps at Sushim, I shove the arrow—into the Vyag's gaping mouth. The arrow goes right into the mouth, vertically, and I smell the heat and stench of the Vyag's breath as her forepaws strike my chest and knock me down, feeling like a small mountain fell on me. The Vyag lands partly on top of me. Not hard enough to crush me or crack my ribs but still hard enough to knock the wind out of me and to pin me down. I struggle to break free, and while I'm struggling I see that the arrow has lodged itself vertically in the lion's mouth, the tip penetrating the Vyag's upper palate,' Ashoka pointed to his own palate to show Trishul, 'and the lower end jammed in between the Vyag's lower teeth. The pain of the arrowhead penetrating is causing the Vyag tremendous irritation, but the arrow staff is holding the Vyag's mouth open, preventing it from shutting its jaws. The Vyag is flailing its head from side to side, slashing out with her paws, trying to get free of the thing keeping her mouth wide open. I see my chance and jump onto the Vyag's back, grabbing hold of her upper jaw and pulling it back upwards as hard as I could. The Vyag is already going crazy trying to get free of the arrow and all I have to do was pull hard at just the right place with just the right amount of pressure. I use all my strength, pulling hard until I feel the jaw yield. And then I hear a crack and feel the upper jaw give way, all the way. All of a sudden, the fight goes out of her and she collapses right there. She is in great pain obviously, from the broken upper jaw, and her mouth still gaping wide open. I see my chance and pull another arrow from the quiver at my back. I use this one to stab the Vyag between the ribs, in her heart. It takes me more than one or two tries, and each time the Vyag cries out furiously. But by the third or fourth stab, she is already weakening, and then I suddenly punch the arrow home, right into her heart. And that is the end of her.'

Trishul stared up at him, then her eyes cut away to look at something beyond his left shoulder. He glanced that way and saw a butterfly hovering over a bed of flowers. Trishul's golden-brown eyes tracked the butterfly as if considering it as an after-dinner snack.

'Sushim of course is furious with the Vyag for daring to attack him. He must have known he was that close to being eaten by it had I not intervened but he makes it out to be his kill. He makes me promise to tell everyone that he killed the Vyag, which I agree to because I only serve him so in a sense it was as if he killed it. When our soldiers catch up with us, he orders them to fan out and find any other Vyags in the area. They don't find other adult Vyag but they do chance upon the nest that your mother was protecting. I hear the squealing of the cubs and come running to see the whoresons hacking and stabbing at your brothers and sisters with spears. Cowardly swine-fuckers! You are the only one still alive, and only because the fool soldier who had tried to stab you missed and hacked through your rear leg instead. It hangs by barely a thread of sinew and you are screaming and bleeding terribly, but I can see the fight and the spirit in you. You look at me then as I come running up, and though you are probably only snarling at me, to me it feels like you are asking me for help from that monstrous savage. I shove the soldier aside and pick you up in my arms. I take you aside, telling the soldiers that they are to stop harming any more Vyag, there had been enough killing that day. But by then all your siblings are dead already. You are bleeding and squabbling pitifully, tearing my anga vastra to shreds.

I know that your half-severed leg cannot be saved so I do the next best thing, I put you down again and use a soldier's knife to cut it off completely. You howl and scratch me, but the pain makes you unconscious. I use the opportunity to tie the wound tightly and swaddle you in an old robe in a makeshift sling. I sling you on my back and carry you away from there. I take you to Guru Kautilya's gurukul, where I nurse you back to health.'

Trishul's large golden eyes were glazing over in that way she had when she was very sleepy. A moment later, she started to snore lightly.

'So that's how it happened,' Ashoka said. 'How I killed your mother. I'm so sorry about that, my sweet child, if I could do anything to take it back, I would. But I did it to save my brother's life, for I am sworn to protect him even at the cost of my own life. That is the vow I took as a Bharata and I stand by it to the end of my days. But by saving your life I hope to repay the debt to your mother and siblings in some small measure.'

He knelt now on the grass and lowered his face until he was able to press his lips to the underside of Trishul's jaw. He kissed her wet muddy bloody whiskery chin. 'Forgive me if you can, dear one. I meant you or your kin no harm. We live in a cruel world and the balance of nature demands that someday I must experience as much pain and loss as I caused you. It is what I believe and I know it will come to pass. I do not care about what destiny or karma hold in store. I will take what is my due, when it comes. But it is your loss that pains me, for I know what it means to have a mother that loves you dearly and to see her suffer. I know this well. If you can, find it in your furry heart to forgive me, dear one. It is all I ask.'

He raised his head and looked down at Trishul.

She was fast asleep, her jaws flecked with blood from her first kill, swollen stomach rising and falling steadily. The sun had moved on, leaving her entirely in the shade. While the sun was hot, the air was cool in the Afghan mountains and it was pleasant and peaceful here, away from the bustle and cacophony of Takshashila's markets and the incessant bickering and arguing of the court.

He sat there on the grass, watching her sleep. After a time, he lay down too and stretched out on the grass, in the shade, beside her. His arm passed over her and he let it rest lightly on her side, the sensation of her breathing and her soft fur soothing to his conscience. She lived. He had done that. She could hunt and eat and fend for herself now. He had done that too. The debt was not paid, not by a mile and a yard, but there was some compensation for the loss he had caused. Besides, he loved her dearly, and he knew she loved him too, and for now, that was all that mattered.

He woke an unknown time later, feeling the vibration in the ground.

Riders, several of them, approaching fast.

He was on his feet instantly, reaching for his bow. His sword was on his saddle, but he had a longknife strapped to his waist too. His horse was still tied to the tree by a long rope, allowing her to graze freely. She was alert too, her ears twitching as she sensed the approach of the riders.

Trishul was nowhere to be seen. From the angle of the sun, he knew at once that he had not been asleep long enough for morning to turn to noon but the sun was high and the shady patch in which they had fallen asleep was almost completely encroached by sunlight. He presumed she had gone off in search for water, or even shade. He whistled softly but saw no sign of her anywhere. The remains of the hare had disappeared, only a few scraps of bloody fur and smeary stains on the grass. Ashoka knew that the carcass would have been taken away by carrion birds by now, he had a vague recollection of hearing them cry out as they approached the spot, but Trishul was too young and naïve to comprehend the concept of others stealing her food and he had been too sleepy to care.

Now, the riders were on the far hill, just a valley away, and he positioned himself behind a tree, arrow notched and ready. He had taken a moment to retrieve his sword from his saddle and it was strapped around his waist now.

They came over the hill and he relaxed almost immediately.

Dwadesh was in the fore, riding his tan stallion. The men he led were Afghans, not Cubs, but that didn't worry Ashoka. They had integrated well with the locals and the mood of the people had been one of gratitude for quashing the Pashtun rebellion. The Pashtuns had made no friends among their own people, with their rape and pillage and wanton destruction. The fact that the Mauryavansh expedition had brought coin and trading items helped too. Sushim and the surviving brahmins had protested roundly when Ashoka gave it away to those affected by the rebellion; the coin had been intended for bargaining with the Pashtuns, not to donate as charity. He had ignored the protests and given it away as he pleased. He had told Sushim he needed all the friends he could get in Takshashila, even if that meant buying them. But in fact, he had given the money to the poor and needy, while using other means to rebuild alliances with the richer nobles and power players of the kingdom. He knew that several of the larger houses had to have supported the rebellion openly or tacitly and he had no intention of rewarding any of them for the treachery. That, coupled with the fact of his providing aid to the poorer victims didn't sit well with the high families. So right now, when he saw Dwadesh at the head of a band of locals, he presumed that this had something to do with that situation. Either the rich and powerful had complained about Ashoka's uneven distribution of wealth and favours or Sushim had found out through his nosy brahmins and yes-men. That still didn't explain why Dwadesh had ridden out with a bunch of Afghan mercenaries, but his lieutenant's presence and unharmed condition indicated he was accompanying them of his own free will.

Still, Ashoka kept an arrow ready, and his fingers on the drawstring.

Dwadesh drew up and dismounted, coming towards Ashoka with a smile on his face.

'Did you miss me already?' Ashoka asked. 'You didn't need to bring the whole city to find me. I would have been back shortly.'

Dwadesh grinned and spread his arms. 'Good news, master. Your father the emperor is in Takshashila. He came personally to congratulate you on your brilliant coup!'

Ashoka frowned. 'Samrat Bindusara—?'

Before he could finish the sentence, Dwadesh had his sword out and slashed at the bow, severing the wood a hand's breadth above Ashoka's left fist. The taut line crumpled and suddenly all he had was a stick and string in his hand. He dropped it and drew his sword back-handed, turning as he did. His other hand pulled the longknife from its sheath as he turned and he kept the tree trunk behind himself as he moved on Dwadesh.

But Dwadesh used his elbow to strike a hard sideways blow at Ashoka's temple. Ashoka turned into the blow, but the corner of his man's elbow caught his forehead and twisted his neck, destroying his swing. Dwadesh used the momentary advantage to slip into Ashoka's bodyline and suddenly Ashoka felt the point of a shortblade prick the underside of his chin. Blood ran down his throat and anga vastra, spattering on the grass below.

The Cub had been cornered by a hare.

Dwadesh had his sword pressed sideways to Ashoka's lower abdomen, pressing him back against the tree trunk. If Ashoka tried to break away, the sword would slash Ashoka's belly, disembowelling him. The shortblade at his throat prevented him from using his arms for a counter.

'Drop them both,' Dwadesh said pleasantly, still smiling at Ashoka.

Ashoka took a moment to glance over Dwadesh's shoulder.

The Afghan mercenaries had dismounted and drawn their swords. Some half dozen of them had shortbows and they were pointed at Ashoka. Even if he overcame Dwadesh and broke free, he would be riddled with arrows before he came within striking distance.

Even the Lion of Maurya could not fight such odds.

Ashoka opened his palms and let the sword and longknife drop. 'What are you doing, brother?' he asked.

Dwadesh gestured to the mercenaries. Two of them came up on either side of Ashoka and snatched up his fallen sword and longknife. Dwadesh continued to watch Ashoka with the same grin on his face. They tucked the weapons into their own waistbands without any change of expression, then stayed out of sword reach. Ashoka glanced over the group. They were hardened men, all with considerable fighting experience behind them, which meant they were too expensive to work for anyone but the wealthiest. The lack of emotion in their actions suggested that they were not politically motivated or cared a damn either way who lived or died, or why, so long as they were paid well.

'New friends?' Ashoka asked.

Dwadesh grinned at him. 'No friends of yours.'

Then he side-swiped Ashoka in the side of the head, hard, with the heel of his swordhilt, knocking him unconscious.

12

Rani Khorasan was watching from the viewing gallery of the courtyard when Rani Shubhadrangi was brought back to the palace, escorted by the Khorasani gate watch. They were Kh'uar, the coarsest crudest clan of the Khorasani, men and women mingled indistinguishably. They all wore their hair long and open, wore metal body piercings and henna tattoos of mythical creatures on every square inch of their bodies. They only had the most peripheral respect for mores and morals and were barely better than the ruffians and thugs they spent their days beating and exploiting. No Kh'uar would ever get the opportunity to serve in the prestigious cadres like the palace guard or expeditionary escorts. So to be able to arrest and escort an actual queen back to the palace was something of a celebration for them. They rode in with wide grins on their ink-and-metal encrusted faces, leering at the royal sentries in their shiny armour and velvet plush. Noor laughed at the sight of Shubhadrangi, proud and haughty as ever, surrounded by these ruffians. It was hard to say which was more humiliating for her, to be arrested and brought back to her own palace like a common criminal, or to be in such close proximity to these goons.

Khorasan called out as Shubhadrangi began to dismount.

'Wait.'

Shubhadrangi looked up, her attractive mature face creasing as she recognized Noor's voice. She looked up at her sister queen, seated on the gallery above.

'Noor. I should have known this was your doing.'

'What did you think you would achieve, Shubhadrangi? Sneaking out of the city with an armed company? Did you think to ride to Takshashila so you could aid and abet your son in his treasonous rebellion?'

Shubhadrangi looked startled. 'Ashoka has committed no treason. He was the one who quelled the rebellion! It was why Samrat Bindusara sent him to Takshashila.'

'The Emperor sent him to protect and watch over Crown Prince Sushim, who did indeed quell the rebellion. But new information has come to the Samrat's attention that confirms that it was Ashoka who was rousing the rabble against the Mauryavansh Empire. Even after Sushim pacified the unruly people of that violent region, Ashoka continued to foment rebellion. And now, he has taken a fatal step, challenging the might of the Empire itself in outright defiance.'

Shubhadrangi's hand flew to her chest. 'This is not true! Ashoka is the most loyal son. He would never do such a thing!'

'We have undeniable proof of his treachery. And now, we have proof of your complicity in this conspiracy as well.'

'Noor, you are misinformed. I was only taking extra forces to go and assist my son. We both serve the empire. Mauryavansh is everything to us!'

'The Emperor gave no permission for you to leave the palace, nor to take armed reinforcements to Takshashila. The fact that you do so surreptitiously, without informing anyone, proves your guilt.'

Several other queens and princes and princesses had appeared on the viewing gallery, around the courtyard. They were all watching the face-off between the queens with great interest. Shubhadrangi saw Tissyanka among them. Tissyanka stepped forward, about to address Rani Khorasan. From the high colour in her cheekbones and her indignant look, Shubhadrangi knew she would implicate herself. She made a firm gesture to Tissyanka, forbidding her from speaking. Tissyanka's face crumpled, but she obeyed Shubhadrangi's instruction and stepped back.

Shubhadrangi drew herself up, sitting on her horse with as

much dignity as a queen upon a throne. 'I am guilty of nothing except being a mother who cares for her son's welfare. I am guilty too, of being a wife who desires her husband's success. And I am guilty of being a loyal Mauryavanshi who is willing to risk life and limb to serve the Empire and fight its enemies. I have done nothing wrong or treasonous and neither has my son. But why am I even bantering words with you, Noor Khorasan? You are not the Emperor nor the Emperor's voice? It is to our husband Samrat Bindusara that I shall address myself. If he has any doubts, let him have words with me and I shall set his mind at rest. But in the meantime, I ask you to at least let the Tissyani company of soldiers ride for Takshashila at once, that they may assist my son in his work for the empire. It is a long journey. The sooner they leave, the sooner they can reach.'

Noor smiled. 'The only place they are going to are the slave houses. Their treasonous act of taking arms against the empire has cost them everything, their military commissions, their houses, their property, the safety of their families, their name and their honour. They and their families will be broken and retrained and sold as slaves for the mines or the pits, wherever the requirement is greatest. Think about them as you go to the dungeons, Shubhadrangi. It was your leading them that resulted in those men and women losing everything. You are responsible for their fates.'

'No!' Shubhadrangi cried out. 'You cannot do this! You cannot punish those soldiers for simply following me to the city outskirts. They have done nothing wrong. Nor have their families.'

'They are traitors who followed a traitor. The penalty for treason is forfeit of life, property and all rights.'

'This is unjust and cruel. It is monstrous. You cannot take such steps without even giving me a chance to explain my case.

We have laws in Mauryavansh. That is what separates us from the barbarians. I demand a court hearing and an opportunity to face my accusers, whoever they may be,' Shubhadrangi glared up at Noor pointedly, 'and speak my part.' She turned to a nearby palace sentry. 'Guard, go inform the Emperor that Rani Shubhadrangi wishes an audience at once. It is a matter of the greatest urgency.'

The sentry, a Khorasani of course, neither acknowledged Shubhadrangi's order, nor glanced at her.

'It is no use flapping about desperately like a beached fish,' Noor said. 'You have sealed your own fate. Guards, take her to the dungeons. And send for the Torturers. We will learn everything this traitor has to say about the conspiracy and the others involved.'

The Kh'uars were receiving a small bag of coin from one of Noor's servants. They smiled and sala'amed Noor as they turned their horses and trotted out, grinning and winking shamelessly up at the queens and even at the princes and princesses as they went.

Noor's own inner palace guard came forward, all but pulling Shubhadrangi down from her horse, grasping her arms and pinning them with an iron rod and shackles, then chaining her feet as well. Shubhadrangi looked dazed, unable to comprehend what was happening. In the gallery, the queens and royal offspring displayed a range of reactions, varying from shocked, disgusted, or revolted to amused, entertained, delighted. Shubhadrangi, like Tissyanka and a few of the Eastern queens, were considered too sophisticated and snobbish by the rest of the tribes, and few would have any complaints about how Shubhadrangi was treated. Some might actually find it entertaining.

'Where is Bindu? I demand to see my husband,' Shubhadrangi cried out, her voice cracking as she struggled to move with the heavy chains and impediments. The royal guard hustled her along, almost shoving her across the courtyard to the small doorway on the far side, which led to the kitchens, pantry, and from there, to the dungeons below the palace. 'You cannot do this, Noor. He will find out and when he does, there will be hell to pay—'

Noor laughed. 'You poor fool. Do you think I speak only on my own? I speak for the Emperor himself. He has entrusted me to act in his stead during his absence.'

Shubhadrangi was at the door now. The guards attempted to make her go through but she resisted and turned back, her hair dishevelled and face distraught. 'I don't understand. Absence? Where is he?'

'On a spiritual retreat,' Noor said, 'At his guru's ashram. He will be back in a few weeks.'

'Weeks! But by then it will be too late. The situation in Takshashila—'

'Forget Takshashila, Shubhadrangi. From now on, the only place that will matter to you, the whole and sole of your existence, is the dungeon. More specifically, the torture hall. Take her away now and if she speaks again, you have my permission to strike her and use whatever force is necessary to silence and subdue her. Tell the torturers, they are to show no mercy. She is a traitor and an enemy of Mauryavansh and must be treated as one.'

Shubhadrangi uttered one final howl of anguish as she was shoved through the dark doorway that led to the dungeons. It was cut off abruptly.

On the viewing gallery, Rani Noor Khorasan turned to leave, queens, princes and princesses scattering like wheat chaff before a gale. Her gaze met that of Rani Tissyanka who was weeping openly. Noor smiled happily and strode out. It was time for her afternoon bath and change of attire.

13

In the time it took Shubhadrangi to descend from the courtyard level to the dungeons, she felt her entire life sink from light into darkness. The surreal journey from a queen to a traitor condemned to the dungeons dislodged something in her mind. Her chains and shackles were extremely heavy and the edges chaffed and cut into her skin, drawing blood instantly. She could barely walk in them. The Khorasani soldiers escorting her didn't care. They took perverse pleasure in her pain and discomfort, jabbing her in the sides and back and stomach and breasts with the blunt ends of their spears, shoving her from one side to the other. They would cause her to stumble but then catch her before she went tumbling down the stairs. The stone-cut stairway was uneven, damp and stank of a variety of odours, including food, vomit, feces and urine. She too felt like upheaving the contents of her belly but there was nothing to lose except bile. She twisted her ankle, banged her head, slammed her elbow, was struck in the ribs so hard she thought one might have cracked, on the head hard enough to make her see white flashes and stars, but her escort kept moving her downwards, ever downwards. She thought the descent itself would last a lifetime; she must have climbed down hundreds of steps. The lower she went the more pervasive the stench, the wetter and slimier the steps under her bare feet, the colder the air. All her energy was focused on simply staying upright and not slipping or giving her captors reason to pummel and prod her again. She didn't realize when she was at the foot of the steps.

'Move!' Another unnecessary prod in her back, striking her lower spine hard enough that her legs spasmed. Laughter and abuses in Khorasani with the occasional Sanskrit word thrown in that she caught. They kept pushing and prodding her on through a succession of wet, cold, slimy dark hallways where the walls seemed to weep green ichor and the most pervasive odour was that of an oceanic rawness, like a cave washed by the sea during high tide. She knew there was no ocean anywhere near Patliputra, it was literally in the middle of the subcontinent, so couldn't understand why the smell was so oceanic. She was still trying to make sense of that when the narrow hallway abruptly widened into a large high-ceilinged chamber.

'Here you are, Rani Shubhadrangi,' said one of the Khorasanis. 'Welcome to your new palace!'

They all laughed at that.

Shubhadrangi had had enough.

She turned on them, picking up her chains like she was girding her skirts, drawing herself up to her full height, ignoring her aches and pains and injuries, and faced her escort with all the fierce pride she could summon.

'There will be an accounting,' she said. 'Every one of you will pay for your actions and words against me. Starting with your queen and her family. Nobody will be spared. My son Ashoka will see to every last one of you. As the Goddesses Durga and Kali are my witnesses, this I vow.'

Utter silence.

They stared at her.

Shubhadrangi pointed at one of them, the one most fond of prodding. 'I see you,' she said in a clear piercing voice that echoed through the dungeons. She turned and pointed at the next, then the next, to every last one, in turn. 'My goddess sees you. And you. And you. All of you will pay when the time of reckoning comes.'

They glanced at each other, faces devoid of all expression. No fear there yet, for they were not fools. But a kind of superstitious dread. Khorasani could face any physical threat, even certain death, and not back down. But they feared the supernatural, particularly the Vedic gods and goddesses whom they did not fully understand.

Shubhadrangi's threats had struck that chord, touching upon their superstitious dread.

Then one by one they broke the gaze, looking away.

As one woman, they began to back away from her.

'Let's go,' one said. 'Our task is done.'

'Leave her to the torturers,' another said.

The one who had been prodding and tormenting her the most looked at her one last time, a peculiar mixture of emotions on her face. Then she too turned away and followed her fellow soldiers. The sound of their bootheels echoed and faded down the damp hallways.

Shubhadrangi turned, her chains clanking and clattering, and looked around at her new 'palace'.

Her breath caught in her throat.

Suddenly, all her bravado, the dignity she had been able to summon up to harangue the soldiers, her fierce pride, was all gone. The strength went out of her body, and her legs already battered from the descent and aching under the weight of the heavy chains and shackles, failed her.

She almost collapsed in a heap on the slimy wet stone floor but managed somehow to retain her balance.

She let the chains and shackles drop as she saw the horrors that awaited her. They fell around her with a loud metal clanging that echoed and reverberated through the large chamber.

'Mother Goddess,' she prayed, 'Protect and save us.'

14

Ashoka opened his eyes and saw the familiar weathered face of War Marshall Jezza Khorasan. He knew then that this was not just another coup or rebellion, it was the end of everything. He was a fool and had been played for one. He assessed his situation even though he knew it was hopeless. They were on a rocky mountain top, further North West, judging from the angle of the sun and the lack of tree cover. As far as he could spy, there were only the same barren-rock mountain ranges stretching in every direction. The horses were lathered and drooping, and the day was almost at an end, which meant a longish ride, probably about fifty miles or more. That meant they had brought him beyond Gandahari borders, into No-Man's Land. Another fifty miles beyond this was Seleucid territory, which was certain death for him or any Mauryavanshi. East of here would be the Himalayas, West were a number of kingdoms, all enemies of Mauryavansh. The only safe direction was South and that was now in the hands of enemies too, even though Jezza Khorasan was supposedly the protector of the Mauryavansh Empire.

'Awake, boy?' she said, matter-of-factly. 'Good. I wish to get back to Takshashila before nightfall.'

'The Pashtun rebellion was a good touch,' he said, ignoring the throbbing in his skull from the blow. 'But next time, pick someone with some fight in him.'

Dwadesh, standing behind the War Marshal, shook his head. 'Who asked you to go fight them? Fool. All we had to do was accompany Sushim and he would negotiated a deal. We would have had Takshashila back without any bloodshed. You had to go and get us into a brawl. We lost good men because of you—not counting the brahmins that got caught in the middle.'

Jezza Khorasan turned and dealt Dwadesh a backhanded blow that knocked him off his feet. 'Shut your meat-hole. You've done your part. It doesn't include talking.'

Dwadesh rose to his feet glaring at the War Marshal, his hand on the hilt of his sword. 'Who do you think delivered Ashoka to—?'

Jezza drew her sword and pierced the point through Dwadesh's throat before he could draw his own sword. The point of her sword passed through Dwadesh's Adam's apple and emerged, spewing blood. She put out a hand to brace the man's chest, and jerked her sword free, tearing out his throat. Blood and bile spilled down Dwadesh's chest as he clutched at his ruined gullet, eyes bulging. He pitched face forward and thrashed about on the rocky ground, dying noisily.

Jezza resheathed her sword without a second glance at him and looked back at Ashoka. 'You surprised me with the Pashtun, boy. I knew you had some fight in you, but not that much.' She nodded her head curtly. 'Nicely done. Saves me paying them the coin I promised. But it still leaves me with the problem of Takshashila. You see, the plan was to negotiate a deal, as your idiot of a former lieutenant was pointing out just now, and have Sushim take the credit for restoring order and peace to the anarchist North West.'

Ashoka's throat was parched but he would not ask for water. 'And I was supposed to be martyred while protecting my brother, who would then become the hero of Takshashila.'

'Something like that. But the bigger problem was what you did after you took Takshashila back from the rebels. You actually restored peace and order to the Afghanas. Gandahar heard of your efforts and were unwilling to deal with us for the rebellion we were planning there. They got it into their stupid Afghani heads that you were actually a good man and a just satrap and they wanted to take their chances working with you rather than joining our program.'

'And what is your program, exactly?'

She smiled. 'To take over the Empire of course. And for that we needed to foment war with the fucking Greeks.' She jerked her head northwards. 'Which is where the Pashtuns came in. They were to pretend to deal with the Mauryavansh while brokering a deal with the Greeks at the same time. Double dipping. They would convince the Greeks that they had control of the region from Gandahar to Takshashila, and were willing to provide the Greek armies a corridor to use to invade Mauryavansh. Seleucus Nicator would finally be able to strike at the heart of the empire that had defeated him so humiliatingly, and finally achieve his master Alexander's dream. The whole known world would be his to rule.'

'Except for a tiny pocket he would leave to the Pashtun,' Ashoka suggested.

Jezza snorted. 'The Pashtun would be crushed like ripe fruit once Nicator got Patliputra. Those Greeks don't care about deals and treaties.'

Ashoka jerked his chin at the body of Dwadesh lying behind the War Marshal's feet. It had fallen still now, the pool of blood soaking rapidly into the white rocks. 'And the Khorasani do?'

'I don't expect you to understand, boy. What we people went through when the Greeks tore through our land...we will do whatever it takes to have our vengeance on those sons of whoremothers.'

'How does letting the entire Greek army invade Jambudwipa and take over Mauryavansh count as vengeance?'

'Who says the Greeks would make it to Patliputra? Once they came into our territory, that would be the last battle they ever fought. And with Seleucus Nicator dead and the Greeks eliminated, not only Jambudwipa, this entire empire would be ours.' She swept her free arm to encompass the West, North and East.

'Including Khorasan again,' Ashoka said, finally understanding. 'And I presume that your former homeland would then be the capital of the new empire? The Khorasan Empire? All you would have to do is kill off my father and siblings as well, eliminating the entire Mauryavansh dynasty. After which your daughter would be free to finally find herself another mate and bear heirs. Heirs to a Khorasani Empire, not a Mauryavanshi one. That is the real reason why she has never allowed my father to sire children upon her, is it not?'

Jezza looked at him intently for a long moment. 'I told Noor, this is a smart one. A fighter too. Take him for a mate and you will have good daughters and sons. But you being your father's son complicates things. Can't have Mauryavanshi mingling with our line. Which is why your journey ends here.'

Ashoka did not say anything to that.

He watched Jezza's hand tighten on her sword hilt and waited for the quick slash that would end his life. He had always known it would end with a blade through his flesh. Whether a Khorasani one or some other, what did it matter? Steel spoke, and flesh listened.

But the slash never came. Instead, Jezza Khorasan strode back to her horse and leaped on, taking the reins and turning the mount's head, facing back towards Takshashila. The Khorasanis with her mounted up as well. Only the mercenaries remained.

'You leave me here?' Ashoka asked.

Jezza smiled down at him. 'You are too good a fighter to leave standing, boy. I would kill you and be done with it. But you are also a valuable piece in the game of empire. The first-born son of Emperor Bindusara of Mauryavansh, rightful claimant to the Lion Throne. The Greek whoreson asked for proof of our intentions. What better than the heir to Mauryavansh.'

'I am no heir,' Ashoka said. 'I renounced my claim—'

'Shut up, boy. Your renouncing means nothing. If you come back to Patliputra tomorrow and stake your claim, there are a hundred chiefs who will support you, because that is how politics works. You're too dangerous to be left alive, and too valuable to be killed. Which leaves me with only this option.'

Khorasan gestured to the mercenaries who moved forward slowly, leisurely, as if gathering for a social function.

'Break every bone in his body,' she said to them, with no change of tone or emotion, 'but make sure you leave him alive. Seleucus Nicator wants him alive, he shall have him alive. Crippled in every limb, but alive, yes!' She laughed, throwing her head back. Her Khorasani soldiers laughed with her.

Ashoka watched the mercenaries approach. They were all hulking brutes, almost twice his size. He tested his bonds, assessing how long it would take him to slip free and get to Dwadesh's fallen sword by his feet.

'One more thing,' she said.

He jerked his head up. He had already stopped thinking about Jezza Khorasan. His entire focus was on the mercenaries and on surviving. She grinned down at him. 'We have your mother. In the dungeons. If you resist, if you fight, if you try to survive this and attempt to come back to Patliputra and stake your claim, she will suffer such pain as no one has experienced before.'

Then with a grin that was both mocking and regretful, 'Fare well, Lion of Maurya.'

The mercenaries moved in and took hold of him, a pair of muscular hands on every part of his body. They began to do their job, efficiently and with a minimum of effort and emotion. They broke his body into pieces, then each piece into smaller pieces. The pain was excruciating, the sense of utter helplessness and desolation indescribable. They broke him and went on breaking him until he could feel nothing anymore—until the next breaking when the agony attained a new level that he had not thought possible.

They broke him.

And he let them.

15

Tissa was going to hell and he was terrified out of his wits, but somehow he found the strength to keep his feet moving forward. He walked through endless corridors so narrow that sometimes he had to turn sideways and slide slowly along to get by, despite his thin frame, like a mouse between the walls of the palace. His mother had sent him through this secret passageway between walls, kissing him repeatedly and blessing him with the protection of the gods. He knew how vital his mission was because it was the first time his mother had ever asked him to put himself in harm's way. It made him feel important and manly. But it also terrified him. Still, he kept moving, trying not to think about what lay ahead.

He had heard of hell from his brother princes and sister princesses but had never truly believed such a place actually existed.

His mother had never told him anything about it, and every time he had asked her, she had tousled his hair lovingly and said, 'Time enough to learn about the terrors of life when you grow up to manhood. Enjoy the innocence of youth while it lasts, my sweet.' Even when, by Mauryavansh standards, he would be considered a grown man, all of twelve and old enough to hold a sword and take up soldiering, she would still refuse to talk about such things. Instead, she continued telling him the same fables and tales she had been narrating since he could remember.

He knew she was only trying to protect him because she thought he was too fragile. Everyone thought he was too delicate and sensitive. He had been bullied and made fun of mercilessly since he was an infant because of it. Only Ashoka's friendship and protection had prevented his siblings from actually hurting him—or worse. The princes and princesses of Mauryavansh all knew the order of succession—it was at the centre of their entire existence, and their mother queens' existence—and there was always the unspoken understanding that if something 'happened' to any one of the princes, not outright murder for that would be assassination and treason, but simply an 'accident' that was the natural result of tomfoolery or 'princes being princes', then it would not fetch any severe penalty, and incidentally, would reduce the long queue by one. Tissa knew of at least three brothers who had been eliminated in this 'accidental' manner, and while there had been some shouting and recrimination, especially by the queens whose sons were killed each time, nothing serious had come of it. So he had no doubt that if not for Ashoka he would not have survived to be twelve, leave alone be left alone.

The turmoil in the palace since Rani Shubhadrangi's arrest and the news of Ashoka's own alleged treason in Takshashila had shattered the daily equilibrium of the palace routine. All the queens had forgotten their own bickering and palace politics to talk excitedly, but in hushed whispers, about what these events would mean for them.

Each of the five hundred queens of Emperor Bindusara were chosen from one of the five hundred tribes that made up the uneasy coalition formed by Acharya Kautilya almost three quarters of a century ago, in effect uniting all the warring tribes of the subcontinent into a single subcontinental empire for the first time in the history of Jambudwipa. There always had to be at least one queen from one of each of the five hundred tribes, and one chief of each tribe present at the sabha, the parliament that legislated and administered the vast empire. But whether or not each queen (and hence, each tribe) produced a child, or even an heir, depended entirely on the gods of fornication and fertility. Word had it that Kautilya had unofficially advised Chandragupta never to produce more than a hundred sons, nor much less than that number. This would ensure that sufficient tribes felt optimistic about their queen and prince someday taking over the reins of empire, while creating sufficient competitiveness that no one tribe would ever become too arrogant. And so it was almost curious that despite crib deaths and accidental deaths, the number of sons always hovered around the one hundred mark.

Tissa had long since stopped counting or caring what position he occupied in the order of succession. As far as he was concerned, he was content with simply being a prince of Mauryavansh. But he had always hoped that Ashoka would ascend the Lion Throne after their father, Bindusara's passing. That this could never come to pass, he understood. Ashoka's mother had faced a terrible struggle being accepted by the other queens because she did not belong to any of the five hundred tribes, and Ashoka had sworn the vow surrendering his claim and swearing allegiance to protect the next eligible heir, Sushim, in order to ensure she and he could both live their lives peacefully.

Now, Tissa wished Ashoka had never sworn that vow nor surrendered his claim. What had it gotten him? Betrayal by his own father and family? Unfounded accusations of treason and treachery? Tissa knew Ashoka. He knew Ashoka was not guilty of any of the things of which they were accusing him. But he still blamed Ashoka for having compromised with them and given up his rightful inheritance, even if it was for good reason. Look at how they had repaid him? Especially father? Bindusara had picked a very convenient time to go on his spiritual retreat with his guru. Right when his eldest son and queen were being charged with treason and relegated to the most ignominious fates possible under Mauryavansh law! What sort of emperor did that?

What sort of husband and father did that?

Tissa was sensitive, not stupid. He had seen enough of life to know what was and what wasn't. He was a prince of Mauryavansh.

He knew the politics of empire. He understood now that his step-mother Khorasan was making a play that had been planned a long time ago. All that was happening now, in Takshashila and in Patliputra, was a carefully orchestrated series of events designed to shift the balance of power. Just as he understood why his mother, despite her heart being near bursting at the sight of her friend and sister queen Shubhadrangi being put in chains and marched off to the dungeons, had not protested aloud on the gallery. Had she done so, she would have been packed off to the dungeons as well. Tissa's heart lurched at the thought of his mother being sent below. But he knew that so long as her family wielded power, wealth and military might, had valuable alliances with many other powerful and wealthy tribes, and were players in the larger game of empire, Rani Tissyanka and he, Prince Tissa, would not be harmed.

Shubhadrangi was different. A queen without a kingdom or dowry of her own, no military force, no wealth, she was a soft target. So long as the Emperor had protected her, she had been safe. Now, for whatever reason, Bindusara had removed that umbrella of sanctity, and Shubhadrangi was fair game, as was her only child, Ashoka. But the House of Tissan was not one to be trifled with. That was why, even though it was a Tissan military escort that had been apprehended leaving the city with Rani Shubhadrangi, the blame was still being put squarely on Shubhadrangi's shoulders. The Tissan soldiers, despite being Rani Tissyanka's private guard, were assumed to have been corrupted by the traitorous queen, and sold into slavery. Tissa felt tears gather in his eyes at the thought of those brave men and women and their families—many of whom he knew well and loved—being made to suffer for simply doing their duty, but he also knew that this was the way the game of empire was played. Were Rani Tissyanka to protest or intervene she would be sharing the blame in the 'conspiracy'. So she had no choice but to stand silently and allow her brave soldiers to be subjected to unspeakable suffering and slavery. Few would survive and they would not be the lucky ones.

Tissa had reached his destination. The passageway between the walls had been broadening and descending at an increasingly sharper downward angle for a while now. He felt like he had been walking for miles, which was probably true. In order for the secret passageway to remain undetected it would have to take the most circumspect route, going around in circles to get to its destination. And Patliputra Palace was not small by any means. He had smelled horses and even elephants on the long walk and suspected that the passage traversed the grounds of the palace, which would indeed mean a walk of several miles. Yet the knowledge of where he was going and what he was likely to see made him forget his weary legs and scraped elbows and knees.

He emerged from an alcove cleverly hidden in the shadows where three hallways intersected. He stood in the open intersection, breathing the dank fetid odours of the palace dungeons, and looked back at the egress. It was hidden in a curve of the wall where the hallways intersected. Even though he had just stepped from it, he couldn't see it now from any angle. He hoped he would be able to find it again when the time came. The thought of being trapped here in the bowels of hell made him shudder. Or perhaps it was the cold and damp.

He heard and saw no one despite the wide hallways. The sounds of water dripping at irregular intervals, the faint sense that things furry and sharp-toothed were alive and scurrying along the corners, the stench of human offal, every sensation added to the growing horror of what he might see. He had heard stories of Naraka and Patal, the Vedic levels of hell described in the great Sanskrit epic poems Mahabharata and Ramayana. But those were mythological tales, surely. Fables. Legends at best. There were no asuras, no rakshasas in the real world. Only mortals. And mortals, however cruel and malevolent, could not have created places dedicated to such epic suffering as was described in the epics.

Then he turned one final corner and came face to face with a scene straight out of the epics themselves.

It was a vast chamber. So vast that he could not see the ends of it. It stretched for hundreds of yards, perhaps even miles for all he could tell, in every direction. He was standing at one end of it, looking inward. The ceilings were high, perhaps a hundred yards high or more, it was hard to tell because most of the space was unevenly lit. What light there was came from oil lamps hung from ropes at irregular intervals and torches placed along the walls, also at irregular gaps. The entire space was built with no geometric pattern or design in mind. It was just a vast space filled with its contents, which too were spaced out at random intervals. The walls were stone turned slimy with growths from the incessant dampness that oozed down from above, the floor was a swampy pool that resembled a bog. And the whole place stank and echoed incessantly. It was the most foul-smelling, wretched-looking place he had ever seen in his short life and the very place itself made him want to turn and flee back to the safety of his mother's apartments and her soft, embroidered gowns into which he could sink his head and find solace.

He forced himself to stay.

It was not the chamber itself that turned his stomach, parched his mouth and made his body prickle with horror.

It was the contents of the room.

There were hundreds, no, thousands, perhaps even tens of thousands for all he could make out in the dim expanse, filling the space. People of course. Though it was impossible to call them people anymore. Subjects, then. Thousands of subjects tied down, roped up, chained to, hanging from, dangling from, stretched out on, and otherwise placed in an infinite variety of angles and positions to devices, contraptions, seats, rope-and-pulley systems, and an endless range of rigs and setups, all along the length and breadth of the dungeon. Most were just dimly glimpsed blobs in the distance. The ones closest to him were more recognizable human in their shape and form. But that was where their resemblance to humanity ended.

Tissa gagged and felt the familiar bilious heat of his own stomach acids rising. It would not matter if he puked here. He suspected that many already had. That bog-like pool of scummy fluid that covered the dungeon floor was not merely water, he suspected, it was bodily fluids from these thousands of subjects, collected over years, perhaps decades, forming a knee-deep pool of blood, vomit, shit, piss and body parts. He could see skeletal remains in the filth, skulls grinning mindlessly, random bones and joints sticking out, long since separated from their owners. From the state of the subjects on some of the contraptions, it was very likely that the owners of those bones and joints were still alive, somehow sustained through the ingenious methods of the torturers and dungeon-masters, so they could enjoy further atrocities and inhumanities over time.

He saw bodies in conditions and states of suffering that he could not have imagined had he spent a lifetime trying. No human mind could have imagined such torture, such evil methods and devices of inflicting pain and agony on fellow mortals. Only a demon could have conceived of such horrors. Only a devil could have created such a place as this.

Tissa had just discovered hell. It was real. It existed right below the very palace in which he had lived since his birth, spent his happiest hours and days and years, eating, playing, bathing, sleeping, blissfully unaware of the terrors that lay beneath his feet.

Those feet wanted nothing more than to turn his body around

and run back to the secret passageway, all the way up those many winding miles, to the safety and warmth and comfort of his familiar home.

It took every ounce of self-will to force his feet to move again. He still had to complete his given task. He had to find Rani Shubhadrangi and deliver the message his mother had entrusted to him.

He stepped down into the horrid pool of human waste and began wading through it, searching the endless rows of suffering souls for the former queen of Mauryavansh.

Hours later, he was weeping helplessly, barely able to lift one foot before the other. The thick bog of human remains and fluids felt like molasses to his tired feet. The stench of human suffering was so pervasive he had already vomited thrice till not even bile was left to come out, and still his stomach clenched and unclenched like a fist. The endless displays of depravity, the varieties of human agony being suffered by the subjects on the various rigs and devices and contraptions, the cries of those still alive and semi-conscious as they saw him and called out in desperation, the dull-eyed gaze of those too far gone in their own anguish to even want to be saved anymore, the dead stares of those who had either died or lost their minds completely, all merged to make his journey through the torture chambers seem a nightmarish fever dream. Hell. Narak. Patal. That was where he was. Trapped forever. He would spend the rest of his life trudging through this pool of human filth, until his life above ground would seem like the dream, an impossible fantastic dream of a world that could not possibly exist when such suffering existed.

'Tissa.'

The voice was weak but familiar.

Tissa stopped, the disgusting goop swirling around his feet. He was filthy, sticky, coated from head to foot with unspeakable filth, mostly splashed up onto himself, some of it dripped from the subjects hanging overhead, under which he was forced to pass. He felt as if he could never be clean again, as if even a million baths in sacred Ganga water could not wash the sin and suffering from his skin.

'You have your father's face.'

He turned around slowly, forcing himself to look at each of the faces in turn carefully. Straining his eyes against the dim light and flickering shadows. Some of them were no longer recognizably human. They were so deformed and misshapen by years of torture, the mind instinctively compared them to animal faces...

He stopped, then went back three bodies.

There.

Was that...?

It couldn't be.

It was.

Yes.

'Acharya?' he said, hearing the incredulity in his own hoarse voice.

The man who had once been Kautilya, the greatest guru of all time, preceptor of the Mauryavansh dynasty, maker of kings and emperors, master of Patliputra, looked down on him with gaunt haggard features beneath a hairless pink skull. Tissa forced himself not to look at the rest of the body. There were things there... He kept his gaze firmly fixed on the Acharya's eyes. The eyes were what he recognized. They were the closest to the guru he had once known.

'Prince Tissa. The most sensitive and spiritual of Bindusara's sons. It must be agony to you, to be here. To see such human suffering.'

Tissa tried to answer but no words would come out. His throat was choked with emotion. He felt fresh tears break free of his filth-encrusted eyes and drip down his cheeks. 'Guru...why are you here?'

Kautilya's face flickered with the ghastly imitation of a smile. 'Why do we all come back to this mortal realm? To suffer for our past sins.'

Tissa tried to regain clarity. His mind was filled with a fog that would not clear. Strange monstrous shapes lurked in the fog, threatening to overwhelm and overpower him. He wanted to run, to hide, to seek shelter in soft embroidered garments, but he was unable to remember who wore the garments. It was someone dearly beloved to him.

'Acharya, I am seeking Rani Shubhadrangi. I have a message for her from...from...' He could not remember who the message was from.

The Acharya's face lost whatever little animation it possessed and lapsed into a deathlike mask. It was a look Tissa had seen on hundreds of other faces here. He understood that it meant that the subject had suffered too much for too long, and had passed beyond the borders of human comprehension. Emotions, expressions, language, nothing meant anything anymore. There was only the torture chamber, the stench and the pain.

'Guru,' Tissa said again after a long moment. 'Please, I must find her. I must deliver my message.'

But the Acharya's mind had wandered into some other realm. His eyes remained open but Tissa thought that perhaps the Guru had fallen asleep with his eyes open. Either that or he had...

'Tissa?' the voice was feeble and hesitant.

It came from the person right in front of Acharya Kautilya's station. The two faced each other across a span of barely five yards. Close enough to see every detail of every suffering the other endured.

'Rani Maa?' Tissa said, staring up at the woman who had

always been kind and affectionate to him, almost as close and caring as his own mother. 'What have they done to you, Rani Maa!' He heard his voice rise above the moaning and crying of the tortured, heard the echoes rise and fall through the chamber, but didn't care. He averted his eyes from the horrors that had been inflicted upon Ashoka's mother. He had thought he had reached the limit of what he could see and still endure, but he had been wrong. This was it. This was the limit.

'Ashoka…?' she said, her voice cracking.

He understood that she was asking if Ashoka was back. 'Not yet, Rani Maa. But my mother has sent word back home to House Tissan. They are speaking with the other Houses to bring a petition against the unfair treatment meted out to you. We will not rest until you are taken out of here. I come to swear this to you on my mother's life. We will do whatever is necessary to free you.'

She was silent for a while. He heard her breathing, hoarse and rattling in her chest. He had heard a dog wheezing and rattling like that before it died of a lung sickness. Rani Shubhadrangi sounded far worse than that wretched dog. He continued to cry.

'Ashoka…' she said again.

'I will bring you news of him as soon as we get word,' he said. 'I promise you, Rani Maa.'

'Ashoka…' she repeated.

He realized she was trying to say something. He waited. Somewhere in the bowels of the torture chamber, an animal howled with anguish. Except it was no animal. It was a man.

'Ashoka will come,' she said finally. 'When he does, tell him to kill them all. Every last one of the whoresons. Tell him…no mercy.'

Tissa was shocked by her language and by the intensity of her hatred, despite her extreme weakness and the hoarse almost man-like voice with the unnatural rattling. He understood that, like Acharya Kautilya, the part of Rani Shubhadrangi's mind that he had known was either gone, destroyed completely by the suffering she had endured, or lost for a while. But the hatred was real. She meant what she said.

'I will...tell him,' he said weakly, not sure what else to say.

She coughed pitiably, spitting bloody chunks of phlegm that spattered into the filth, then lost consciousness.

Tissa waited, not sure what to do or say.

'I shall return soon, Rani Maa,' he said at last. He repeated the message his mother had entrusted him to bring. 'We shall not rest until you are free. Stay strong and survive.'

He turned to go.

'Tissan.'

He saw that Acharya Kautilya was awake again. Or aware. If there was a difference.

'Guru?' he said nervously.

'Ashoka will come. I have foreseen it. The Vyag will protect him. He wears their mark. The Vyag chose his grandfather and they chose him as well. They have marked him as their own and will protect him.'

'Yes, Acharya,' Tissa said, unsure what to make of this bizarre speech. Vyag protecting Ashoka? Clearly, the guru had lost his mind.

'He will return and when he does a terrible reckoning will come upon this family. He will wash the land clean with blood.'

Tissa stared at the Acharya, dumbstruck. There was something convincing about the Acharya's pronouncement. Despite the old tortured man's state, Tissa still felt his hackles rise.

'Mark my words, young Prince Tissa,' Kautilya said. 'When that day comes, you must be ready. You stand beside Ashoka. You and a handful of others. Everyone else will be swept up and washed away by the tide of vengeance. A river of blood!'

Tissa shut his eyes, unable to process anymore. He felt as if he would collapse from exhaustion right where he stood. It was only the filth he stood in that made him control himself. He did not want to fall into the bog.

He looked up at the Acharya. Kautilya was staring down at him with clear almost eerily normal eyes.

'Guru,' Tissa said, 'how did all this come about? Who allowed them to build this place, this torture chamber? Who sanctioned the creation of this hell? Was it a monster, an asura or a rakshasa?'

Kautilya stared down at him. Suddenly, a sound escaped the Acharya's throat. Tissa thought it was a cough at first. He stepped back, not wanting to be struck by any fluids.

He realized it was laughter, of a sort. The only laughter the old guru was capable of producing.

Kautilya was laughing.

'That is the sublime irony, Prince Tissa. There are no asuras or rakshasas, no demons. Only us humans behaving inhumanely. We built this place. We sanctioned the torturers. We created the torture dungeons. Why...I ordered the place to be built myself, fifty years ago. It was I who was responsible for the building of the very torture chamber in which I myself am incarcerated today. I myself!'

Tissa stared up at his former guru with pity and disgust.

He turned and began trudging back the way he had come. He had a long, horrible way to go, all the way back to the secret passageway and then miles more to climb through endless narrow corridors until he reached the safety and sanctity of the palace again. If he was not caught himself.

The Acharya's manic laughter echoed and reverberated around the torture chamber, following him as he went. It would haunt his nights for the rest of his life.

Book Three

1

The lone kshatriya took up a fighting stance on the river bank.

Behind him, the holy city of Ujjain straddled the river Shipra, its temples covered by a light shawl of morning mist. The brow of the horizon was smeared with ash tinted with vermilion as red as the sindhoor on a newlywed bride. Nestled in the vast plains of madhya desh, the middle country in the heart of the subcontinent of Jambudwipa, Ujjain was a monument to worship. The city's tallest structures were the iconic stone piles of her temples. Even her richest residents would never presume to build their mansions higher than the neighbourhood place of worship; their ostentatiousness was reserved for the interiors of their grand residences.

Outwardly, all buildings wore the same plain facade, whitewashed with limestone tinged by the ever-present ash from the many holy yagnas conducted across Ujjain Nagari. The ash represented the hopes, dreams, aspirations of its tens of thousands of devouts.

Many came to Ujjain seeking god. They stayed because they found gold; there was wealth to be earned from worship here and everyone partook of the munificence. Pilgrims passed through by the thousands, leaving behind bestowments, donations, hopes, and prayers. They took with them solace and fulfilment, as much of it as could be had from the shedding of wealth.

Those who resided here permanently were all associated in some way with the business of religion: if not part of the substantial brahmin community which dominated the population and the economy of the region, then vaishyas, merchants who worked with the brahmins to do all the things that they did not—the bargaining, handling, collating, dispensation, accumulation and multiplication of wealth in all forms.

Unlike in most metropolitan cities, Ujjain Nagari's cleaning, sweeping, sewage, and other menial forms of work were not undertaken by lower castes. There were brahmacharyas enough to serve the city's needs, and acolytes could be seen everywhere at all times, doing whatever was needed. Many of these were not young boys as might be expected but older men, pilgrims who came to worship but stayed to serve. Ujjain was a haven for brahmins and devout from all across the vast central plains and forested areas of Jambudwipa.

These men of god and the vaishya merchants who profited enormously from the business of worship made up the entirety of the city's population. There were no kshatriyas here nor likely to be any in future. There was no place for warriors in the city of god. None came, even though both the Uttarapada and Dakshinapada, the great Northern and Southern highways, passed through Ujjain, linking the great nations of the high North to the lush kingdoms of the deep South. Warriors knew well enough to bypass the city, even the region, and lower castes travelled by underground highways, preferring to remain invisible in a region where so many brahmins resided.

On this cold winter's morning in Ujjain, the solitary kshatriya in the city stood on the west bank of the Shipra, looking northwards, and worked his way through his morning niuddham, a series of practice manoeuvres with a shastra—a weapon—that were second nature to any warrior.

His shastra of choice this morning was a sword, a beautifully balanced piece of craftsmanship that glinted in the gloam of first light, its jewelled hilt catching and flinging back sparkling highlights from the river.

He worked his way through the various asanas, bare-bodied and wearing only a langot. His young body was covered with a light sheen of sweat from his exertion, but his breathing was calm, his eyes clear, his concentration absolute. The tone and strength of his movements suggested a lifetime of practice and experience with these moves, but there were moments when a certain action, or pose, or turn, would bring a grimace to his young face, or cause a twinge in a muscle, or evoke a grunt of obvious pain.

Oddly enough, there were few evident scars or obvious injuries to indicate the cause of this discomfort. He had a few scars and signs of old battle injuries, but these were not what troubled him. His pain came from within the muscles and bones themselves. It was a deep, lasting pain and though his grievous injuries had healed, the body still remembered the unspeakable agony it had endured. As he pushed his body through the rigorous manoeuvres, his mind recalled the teachings of his guru: '*Such is the burden of existence: we carry what we experience to the end of our days. The weight of the burden itself is not ours to control; all we can do is make ourselves stronger to bear the weight.*'

The young kshatriya had worked very, very hard to strengthen himself, for his burden was heavier than most. He carried the weight of an empire on his slender shoulders. In a world where violence was omnipresent and life commonly cheap, most young men his age would have been crushed by the growing burden and succumbed long before now. He, on the other hand, grew stronger with each increase in weight, gaining power from adversity, stamina from enduring, strength from suffering. It was his gift; it was his curse.

The young warrior was the rarest of the rare. A protégé of none other than the legendary maha-guru Kautilya, better known to the common man as Chanakya.

This young acolyte had been taught by his master to feed on the meat of pain and suffering, derive nourishment from it, and grow stronger and more powerful with every new adversity he was forced to endure. Like a sword that grew more resilient each time its metal was heated, melted, beaten and folded over itself, he had become a more resilient fighting machine, a perfect weapon.

As he worked his way through the asanas, his mind's eye flashed on images from the recent past.

The face of Jezza Khorasan, War Marshall of the Mauryavansh Empire.

The face of Noor Khorasan, First Queen of Mauryavansh, and one of his many stepmothers.

His father, Emperor Bindusara.

His elder brother, First Prince Sushim.

His younger brother, Tissa. His friend and advisor, Radhagupta.

His guru and mentor, Acharya Kautilya.

His mother, Queen Shubhadrangi.

There were many more, others who had played a minor or fleeting role in his young life. Lovers, friends, siblings, relatives, enemies, hostiles. But they all merged into an insignificant blur. The ones that mattered were the only faces he remembered as vividly as if they stood this very instant in front of him, on this same bank of the Shipra, watching him as he practiced his asanas.

His sword slashed through the forms of Khorasan, mother and daughter. Stabbed his father Bindusara. Hacked at his brother Sushim. As his mother, guru, brother and advisor watched.

Shubhadrangi, Kautilya, Tissa and Radhagupta said nothing, but their faces showed no disapproval of his actions. They watched impassively, as if understanding his pain, his fury, his thirst for vengeance. He had been wronged, they had all been wronged, he and his loved ones, and those three people were chiefly to blame: the Khorasans and his father. Even his brother Sushim was only a passive aggressive pawn in the larger game. It was the Khorasans who were directly responsible, and his father who had aided and abetted their crimes against him and against those for whom he cared.

He spun, dancing, flying, somersaulting, rolling and turning, twisting and striking at unseen opponents. His movements grew faster, seemingly more frenzied, but despite the fiery emotions that drove him he was ice cold, in control of every motion of every muscle. Even the stabs and spears of pain that shot from deep within his bones and joints were overruled by his mind.

The rigour of his training, his years of schooling by the master teacher of this era—perhaps of *any* era—and his own relentless pursuit of perfection served him in good stead, carried him through actions that were literally impossible only two years ago, when he had lain broken and bleeding, every bone in his body cracked, his body immobile, his limbs a spiderweb of the worst agony imaginable.

They had broken him and left him for dead, in the hills above Takshashila, War Marshall Khorasan and her minions, playing out a deadly game conceived by her ruthless daughter Noor Khorasan. They had thought they had killed him in the worst manner possible for a warrior, broken and defenceless, without even putting up a fight.

Yet, even in that ultimate failure, he was the master of his fate.

It was he who had permitted them to do it.

He had let them break him.

Because of his mother. That was the bargain, and he had traded his strength for her life without a second thought. Recovering from such brutality had seemed nigh impossible. Yet he had done it. He had survived, recovered, healed, and now, after two full years of painful agonizing rehabilitation and struggle, he had finally regained his strength and his ability to fight as before. And he had done it because he owed them a debt. He had to face the Khorasans and give them back what they had given him, but worse. Much, much worse.

'*True strength comes from suffering, true mastery from failure. You can never truly understand what it means to succeed, until you have failed, and failed again and yet again. The repast that comes at the end of a long, bitter fast is the sweetest you will ever taste. Endure, that you may conquer. Suffer that you may savour. Fall, fall, and fall again, that you may rise when your enemies no longer expect it. A thousand times fail, succeed one thousand and one.*'

The voice of Acharya Kautilya echoed in his mind.

Ashoka slowed his movements, bringing the cycle of asanas to a gradual halt. The final movement done, he bowed, giving thanks to the gods and to his guru, to his ancestors and to his mother. The vandana called for him to thank his father as well and he did so, without allowing his emotions to cloud his recitation. Whatever his father had done to him in life, the fact remained he was his father. Ashoka thanked him for that gift of life. When the time came, he would thank his father for the gift of pain and betrayal as well. That would be a different recitation, one spelled out with steel and blood, not Sanskrit mantras.

'You train as if about to go into battle, Ashoka,' said a voice behind him.

Sword in hand, he turned to greet the person.

2

War Marshall Jezza Khorasan raised her sword and her voice. One was stained red with the blood of the score of rebels she had slain that morning, while the other was cracked and hoarse from shouting orders to her lieutenants. Still, when she opened her mouth to speak, the words carried well enough on the cool mountain air to be heard over the clash and clatter of weapons and men.

'Rebels!' she shouted. 'Behold your leader!'

She jerked her head to the soldiers standing behind her. They dragged a bearded man with a great mane of wild hair to where she stood. He struggled even now, despite his many wounds and the broken bones, his leonine head twisting, teeth bared between bloody lips, as he tried to break free. For a moment, she thought he might actually be strong enough to do it, and her sword angled itself in anticipation. It wouldn't do for him to take her by surprise, perhaps try to throw her off his mound. As the Commander-in-Chief of the Magadhan Empire's vast military forces, she was a feared and hated legend across the length and breadth of Jambudwipa. For her to be knocked down, even for a moment, by an unwashed mountain rebel, would not do. It would not do at all.

One of her lieutenants backhanded the rebel leader with the hilt of his own sword, opening a new gash in his forehead and mashing his already broken nose. The blow stunned the man just enough for the soldiers to regain their grip on his limbs. Another blow knocked out the man's feet from beneath him, forcing him to fall to his knees on the stony ground. A third and fourth hammered down on his neck and clavicle reminding him of his powerlessness and the eternal reality of that pain.

'Here he kneels before me,' she called out. 'Broken and pathetic!'

The fighting below did not cease entirely, but it did slow down. Though the wild-haired mountain rebels continued to exchange weapon blows with her soldiers, their attention was divided now. More than one face looked up between parries and thrusts, to see if this was just another Magadhan ploy or if their fierce leader had actually been captured. Just one look was enough to confirm the latter. There was no mistaking this giant-sized brute even at a glance from a hundred yards away.

She saw that the reserve cavalry she had held back by the treeline was awaiting her order to attack. She shook her head, indicating to her lieutenants that they were to wait. This was more important than simply slaughtering the enemy. An enemy that had been massacred would often grow stronger in death, leaving behind a sense of outrage that could fuel even non-warriors to take up arms and join their cause. There was nothing as romantic as a lost cause, although she had never understood why. People should know when they were conquered, after all. But people could be stupid when it came to causes and war.

They needed to be shown proof.

She was about to supply that very proof.

'What was it he said in his missive to Patliputra?' she said aloud. 'That he would sooner gouge out his own eyes than gaze upon the flag of Mauryavansh flying over your mountain fortress? Rip out his own throat rather than swear an oath to obey and serve Patliputra? Slice off his own cock and balls rather than father children who would grow up as servants of the Magadhan Empire? Well, I think it's time he lived up to his promise!'

She instructed her soldiers to stretch out the rebel leader, akimbo on the ground. He struggled fiercely but his efforts were futile. In moments, he was splayed in the dirt, his muscled limbs stretched out in four directions. He grinned as his eyes stared up at her defiantly. She had seen men and women smile like that often before; the smile always disappeared once the pain began.

'Strip him,' she ordered. The rags that hung on the man hardly deserved to be called garments. They used their daggers to cut them away, leaving the man naked.

Still, he glared at her, defiant to the last.

Her gaze lingered on his manhood, proudly, inappropriately tumescent despite his dire circumstances. Then again, perhaps it was appropriate; after all, this would be his last erection.

Jezza Khorasan took up her curved sword. She sharpened it herself every morning, regardless of whether or not she was about to go into battle. Freshly sharpened, the blade was sharp-edged enough to rip a silk scarf thrown upon it.

She wielded it once, twice, thrice, then a time or two more.

The rebel leader's screams came despite his powerful will. Everyone screamed in the end. Even the strongest substance had its breaking point.

She ordered him raised to his feet. Her soldiers complied, their grip slipping more than once on the now-bloodied limbs. The once-handsome, once-virile rebel leader was now awash in his own gore. He thrashed in agony, all defiance lost with the use of his sight and manhood.

She turned to call out to the clashing hordes below.

'Behold your great leader. Eyeless. Cockless. Ball-less. And to fulfil the last of his own promises...'

She flicked her blade in a single deft motion, ripping out the man's throat.

The screams died, replaced by a wet gurgle and the splashing of heart's blood on the ground.

She made her soldiers keep him upright till he died.

Then she bade them toss him over the edge.

The ruined corpse tumbled in a mass of crimson limbs like something fresh off a butcher's block. It came to a rest only yards from the edge of the fighting.

The rebels roared with fury, renewing their attack, hacking at the Magadhan army with anger born of righteous outrage. But even in their mad, final rally, there was the stench of desperation, a wild-eyed awareness that the end was nigh. Their rebellion was done, and they knew it. Their heart died with their leader.

It was over only an hour or two later.

The surviving rebels surrendered, a snarling but pitiful mass of ragged, unwashed rabble.

Jezza ordered them executed on the spot and strode away to her tent.

It was time for afternoon prayer, and then lunch. She was famished.

She had just finished lunching on a raan of roasted meat when one of her lieutenants came to her tent. Behind him, she could see more soldiers guarding a rebel bound hand and foot.

'War Marshall,' said the lieutenant. 'I think you should hear what this one has to say.'

Jezza looked up at her officer. She was one of her favourites, a veteran of several battles and a former lover. If Jezza no longer welcomed her into her tent at night, it was only because she preferred her lovers of a certain age and this one had grown a little too long in the tooth for her liking. Besides, once she promoted someone to a commanding position, it was best not to maintain intimate relations: it led to jealousies and in-fighting among her officers. Yet she could see in the woman's eyes, battle-hardened as she was, that the lieutenant still had hopes of being taken back into her warm bed at night. That was all right: no harm in keeping hope alive. Hope was the folly that empires were built on.

'What does he have to offer?'

The lieutenant glanced back over her shoulder. 'You should hear it with your own ears,' she said quietly, dropping her voice to a near-whisper.

Jezza looked at her for a moment, reading her eyes. Then she nodded.

'Bring him in.'

The man was trembling as he was led in. There were bruises and cuts on his face and arms and the way he favoured one side of his torso suggested he had been wounded lightly. He was in chains, cuffed and manacled and hobbled to anticipate any chance of an assassination attempt. A hundred different powerful factions across the subcontinent—and beyond—would pay dearly to have the notorious War Marshall of Magadha eliminated.

But this was no assassin, she saw at once. This was a man accustomed to an occupation other than fighting, judging from his soft hands and softer eyes. A merchant perhaps, or a priest, forced into action due to the rebellion's dwindling numbers in the face of imminent defeat.

Whatever his background, he was terrified for his life now, and ready to talk. The only thing she would have to be wary of was whether the information he gave her was true or a carefully manufactured lie. It wouldn't be the first time the enemy used misinformation to try to lead them on a merry dance—or into an ambush.

She regarded him stonily, saying nothing.

He joined his palms before her, both arms trembling so badly, he could barely keep his hands together. Tears brimmed in his eyes.

The lieutenant cuffed him on the back of his head. 'Stop wasting the War Marshall's time. Speak!'

'Great one,' said the rebel. 'I have valuable information for you. Please, I beg you, spare my life.'

Jezza waited. When nothing further seemed forthcoming, she inclined her head. The lieutenant hammered the rebel on his shoulderbone, hard. The man cried out and sank even lower, all but grovelling. He began babbling freely, needing no more prompting.

'We are only a small part of the resistance. Our deployment was strategically designed to draw you away from the main centres. The main rebellion is fomenting elsewhere, growing stronger by the day. Soon, there will be an uprising the likes of which have never been seen before. Our group is but a drop in the immense ocean that is aligned against you. When the wave comes, it will be as a tsunami. Your grand Magadhan army will be obliterated. You will be brought to your knees, as I am on my knees today, and will answer for your war crimes. As will your daughter and the rest of your family and co-conspirators against the land the people. The time of oppression is at an end. The time of the people is about to dawn.'

Jezza frowned at the man's choice of words and phrasing. Even though it was all delivered helter-skelter, in one mad verbal vomit, there was something *composed* about the language. As if the man had memorized it and was only repeating it now. Either that, or he was a bard with a literary flourish. She examined the man intently, seeking out subterfuge and deceit, sniffing out any hint of a performance. All she saw was a snivelling, grovelling coward who was trying desperately to bargain for his life in the face of certain death.

'Is that all?' she asked.

He raised his eyes but kept his brow lowered, in a posture of defeat. 'I can give you names, places, details. I cannot be sure if they would still be there. My information is weeks old. Since you cut off our supply chain, it has been difficult to pass messages. Our couriers—'

'Who are you?' she asked, interrupting him.

His eyes flickered uncomprehendingly.

'What is it you *do* in the rebellion?' she clarified impatiently. 'You're no fighter, that's for sure.'

Her lieutenant snorted in agreement.

The man replied with downcast face, 'I am a scribe. A brahmacharya.'

So. She was right. He was a priest and a bard, in a manner of speaking. A brahmin acolyte training to be a priest which mostly meant scribing for a mentor and cooking and cleaning. That explained the cowardice. Still, she had to be sure he hadn't been planted to feed her disinformation. There was only one way to be sure of that.

'Take him away,' she ordered the lieutenant. 'Find out everything he knows. Confirm what you can with our spies. If it's worthwhile, report back to me.'

The lieutenant nodded, saluted smartly, then jerked her head at her soldiers. They began dragging the turncoat backwards on his knees. He realized what was happening and jerked his head up.

'Great one!' he cried. 'I beg of you! Spare my life. I will be invaluable to you. I know a great deal. Let me serve you, please!'

Jezza raised her hand. The soldiers stopped.

'Tell us everything you know,' she said to the man. 'You will be suitably rewarded.'

They resumed dragging him away, out of her sight.

She sat back, thinking. Her people would torture him until he gave up everything he had that was of value, even things he didn't want to give up. That was the only way to be sure, to break him down below the veneer of any possible subterfuge. If he had been planted to mislead them, he would give that up as well.

And when he had told them all he had to tell, he would be rewarded.

The reward was death.

3

'Greetings, father,' Ashoka said, sheathing his sword. He joined his hands in a namaskara to greet his father-in-law.

Vedsagiri greeted his son-in-law with a slight bow, his hands occupied by a small copper vessel. The merchant was clad in his usual white garb, his forehead marked with the ash and raw rice indicative of a morning pooja. 'Your form is masterful. It is difficult to believe that the same body that we found broken on the rocks of Takshashila is now strong enough to break rocks in gentle Ujjain.'

'It is not rocks that need fear me,' Ashoka said. 'And I have nothing but gratitude and grace in my heart for gentle Ujjain. Will you pardon me if I wash off the salt of my exertions, father?'

'By all means go ahead. I would not bring you back home bathed in sweat! Your mother-in-law would throw us both out of the house and tell us to go bathe with the buffalos!'

Ashoka waded into the shallows of the Shipra. The current was strong but he kept his footing easily, moving in a wide stance, keeping his body sideways to the flow. As he washed himself, he continued talking, raising his voice to be heard above the rushing water. 'I must speak with you later, father. There is something I need to discuss.'

The older man nodded. He was a well-fed man, like most merchants who were wealthy enough to spend more time counting their growing wealth than earning it. Well past middle age, he was older than Ashoka's own father, a consequence of his daughter being the youngest of her several siblings. He enjoyed his meals and his sweets too, and did not apologize for either pleasure, but he was no glutton. He was a man of some intelligence, well versed in the scriptures and with a keen, sharp mind. 'I have some notion of what it is you wish to discuss. I have been expecting this talk for some time now.'

'Then you know what I wish to say.'

'You wish to return to Patliputra.' Vedsagiri made the statement in a matter-of-fact tone, giving it neither a positive nor a negative inflection.

Ashoka dipped his head into the rushing water and raised it

to look at his father-in-law, water dripping from his long hair. 'You knew?'

'It was only natural. I told Devi just this morning after you left that sooner or later you would want to go home. It was only a matter of time.'

'What did she say to that?'

Vedsagiri sighed. 'What could she say? Which wife would want to part from her husband? She has had three years with you. They have been good years. You two are very good together. But all good things must end. Even Rama and Sita were separated through circumstances.'

'We are not separating. We are husband and wife, our lives are intertwined forever. I love your daughter dearly.'

'I know you do. But I also know the reality of our world. The brahmins like to say that varna was created by the Manus to better enable the division of labour. It is their way of appeasing us less privileged castes, by making us believe that it was all ordained by the gods and demi-gods to serve all mortalkind. But the truth is that it is a man-made institution, and like all man-made institutions, it was created by those who controlled more resources to ensure they would continue to control those resources without having to work too hard for the privilege.'

Ashoka emerged dripping from the water, pushing back his long lustrous hair from his face. The rising sun behind his back suffused his wet skin with a golden sheen, delineating every muscle and tendon. He wrung out the excess water from his hair. 'I know the reality too, Vedsagiri. I am a kshatriya born of a brahmin mother and a kshatriya father. I have seen the prejudice faced by my mother in her husband's kshatriya household. All my life I have been treated as inferior because of my partial brahmin parentage. I have no illusions about varna being an equitable division of labour. If it were genuinely for the betterment of society then the best suited to each task would be given that task. You and I both know that there are brahmins who belong in sewers and kshatriyas who don't even deserve to be beating leather hides, but the sun is more likely to rise in the west than such things come to pass.'

Vedsagiri chuckled at Ashoka's turn of phrase. 'True, very true. So then you understand why taking home a vaishya wife to Patliputra is impossible for the Second Prince of the Mauryavansh Empire. If your mother was treated with such indignity, imagine how my daughter might get treated. Vaishya wife to a half-brahmin. I can already hear them gossiping in the hallways of the high palace.'

'There is a difference, Vedsagiri. I am not my father. I will not tolerate such bigotry.'

'How will you stop it?' The merchant indicated Ashoka's sword, a personal gift he had given him on his wedding day. 'Will you lop off the tongue of every gossiping aristocrat? Or cut out the eyes of every insolent fool who looks down on Devi? Accept it, Ashoka. This is the way the world is. Caste bias, skin colour bias, racial prejudice, class superiority, male over female, North versus South, these are all a part of the way we are as people.'

Ashoka untied his langot and wrung it out thoroughly, squeezing every last drop out till the corded muscles in his arm stood out like strings beneath a full skein.

'I don't accept these things. I don't accept injustice and social inequality. Or any inequality. It must change.'

'Who will change it?' Vedsagiri asked. 'You, Ashoka?'

Ashoka paused as he retied his langot, then wrapped his dhoti around himself. 'If no one else will, then yes. I am willing to try.'

The merchant regarded his son-in-law. 'Ever since we found you upon that rock in Takshashila, in a condition which no man should expect to survive, and watched you fight your way back to life, I knew that you were an extraordinary young man. Anyone who had been following Mauryavansh political developments knew of your exploits, your adventures, your achievements. But as I watched you these past three years, regaining your strength and your vigour, marrying my daughter and making her happier than she has ever been in her life, bringing your revolutionary thinking and outlook into our dusty part of the world, I knew you were destined for great acts.'

Ashoka shrugged. 'I don't know anything about great acts. I only care about just acts.'

'Spoken like a Mahavira or a Buddha,' Vedsagiri muttered. He sighed and passed a hand across his face. 'I am just an aging merchant, I know little about the devious plots of palace politics or the cunning schemes of conspirators and assassins. But as a Buddhist, I know grace when I see it. You are touched by grace, Ashoka. The grace of the greatest force on Earth. Love. You embody love in its purest, most heroic form. Your thirst for justice, your abhorrence of inequality, your fiery determination to overcome prejudice and end exploitation...these are not ambitions of any young warrior. Or even a prince. They are something much greater.' He leaned forward, touching the gold-tinged shoulder. 'You have the heart of a Lion, and the mind of an Emperor.'

Ashoka laughed. It was a mirthless laugh. He had not had occasion to smile or laugh aloud these past three years even once. His laugh now was not an expression of joy, but a response of denial. 'I am no emperor. I have no ambition to be emperor. Let my brother Sushim fall into that bottomless pit.'

'That is one of the very qualities that proves you will make a good emperor! Your refusal to take the throne that is yours for the having. It is why I was asked to speak with you.'

'You were asked?' Ashoka looked at his father-in-law. 'By whom?'

Vedsagiri glanced at the risen sun. 'Let us return home first.

Our wives will both be wondering why we have not come to partake of their morning feast. We will speak on this later today. I have a proposal for you, Ashoka. And all I ask is that you hear me out. Come now, let us go home before my daughter comes running barefoot to twist our ears and fetch us home!'

4

War Marshall Jezza Khorasan strode angrily through the vaulting corridor of the Imperial Palace. She was not happy. For one thing, protocol—the protocol she herself had laid down years ago—dictated that the Khorasani Imperial Guards were to be stationed every three yards. Yet, the long corridor was virtually empty. Except for the occasional sentry loitering in an alcove, either with a cup of wine in their hand, or a naked body part cupped in their hand, or one of each in both hands, the guards were all but absent. Shameful!

True, no intruder had ever attempted to breach the inner sanctum but that was no excuse for such flagrant violation of their duties. It had been too long, she realized, since she had last performed a surprise inspection. That, and the fact that she had been away so long this time that none of the sentries looked familiar to her. She made a mental note to reprimand the captain of the Guards for being too lax; but that would happen only after Jezza finished with her business in the palace. Something had to be done here and now to correct this unforgivable lapse. Discipline, she had learned through bitter experience, was like a barrel of Kashmiri apples: ignore one spoiled apple and the rot soon spread to the entire barrel. Besides, she had a reputation to uphold. She couldn't have her enemies or her subordinates thinking old IronCunt Jezza Khorasan had gone soft in her middle age.

She stopped before an alcove where, in the shadow of one of the great pillars that lined either side of the corridor, two of Khorasan's finest were having their way with one of the Empress's concubines. Correction, she saw as she looked closer: one Guard was having his way with a male consort, while the other Guard was being pleasured orally by a concubine.

All four bodies were so closely entwined that at a glance they merged into a single beast with four heads. The Guard fucking the consort was approaching his climax, grunting and groaning in that tone peculiar to men while the receiver of his attention, leaning against the pillar, was having his cock hand-fucked by the concubine. The solitary woman in the foursome was somehow able to keep this feverish rhythm going while swallowing the entirety of the other Guard's substantial length. For his part, the consort being ass-fucked was fisting her while giving her cunt an energetic tongue-lashing. It was quite the harem orgy scene, except that two of the foursome were men oathsworn to stay alert at all times and be prepared to sacrifice their lives to protect their imperial lieges.

The physical positioning that was involved in keeping this intertwined foursome going was nothing less than acrobatic. Jezza was well aware of the legendary skills of the Empress's staff. All consorts and concubines went through a rigorous training and even more rigorous testing before they earned the privilege of serving in the Imperial zenana. Jezza had first-hand experience of how accomplished they could be: she had enjoyed the skills of many trainees as well as accomplished veterans of the harem more times than she could recall. Quite likely, she had enjoyed the talents of this very harlot in her own bedchamber: there was something familiar about those rose-tipped nipples and mango-shaped breasts. But whatever Jezza had done was in her hard-earned hours of leisure, in the privacy of her chambers. Not during her hours of duty! And certainly not by deserting her post and violating her oath to serve her Empress and Emperor! This display of sexual gymnastics was wholly unacceptable dereliction and could not be tolerated.

Jezza drew her curved sword and slashed the air with it.

The head of the Guard who was buggering the consort detached itself from his body and flew through the air. It struck the marbled pillar, leaving a splatter of blood, and fell onto the back of the consort, who was on the verge of his orgasm. Both the stunned consort and the decapitated Guard reached their climax at the same time, cocks spurting even as one man tumbled to the floor in a bloody, headless heap, and the other screamed with terror as he slipped on a floor now slick with the other's blood. He raised his hands protectively at the sight of Jezza's raised sword, though he had nothing to fear. The concubine and the consort, though involved in the transgression, were not to be blamed since it was literally their job to provide pleasure on demand, to whomsoever demanded it at any time. Meanwhile, the concubine had not fully absorbed what had just happened when the War Marshall's sword, still moving, stabbed its point into the throat of the second Guard. Blood fountained from the ruined throat, drenching the concubine. In her shock, she bit down reflexively on the cock impaling her throat, giving the man his second mortal wound. Gushing blood from both ends, the Guard fell to the polished floor, thrashing about wildly as he gurgled wordlessly. Khorasan finished him off with another quick jab.

She then raised her voice and dripping sword so she could be heard all the way down the corridor: 'Anyone else not at their posts can expect the same!' she roared. 'You are Warriors of Khorasan! Act like it!'

The concubine held her flimsy garment before her nakedness in a pathetic gesture of shame. 'My Lady, forgive my lapse! I only live to serve my Empress!'

Jezza snatched the diaphanous robe and used it to wipe her blade clean before sheathing it. She glared at the young woman, barely a girl even by Khorasani standards. 'Next time a soldier on duty tries to have their way with you, remind them that the penalty for dereliction is death.'

She tossed the bloody garment aside and strode off.

The corridor, seemingly deserted only moments earlier, was now bristling with Khorasani Guards of both genders, arms at the ready for presentation as was customary in the presence of the War Marshall. Several of them wore their uniforms haphazardly or in disarray, but not a single one of the men, she observed as she passed by in a flurry, had anything resembling an erection. Fear had a way of shrivelling the hardest cock.

5

Her anger had not dissipated by the time she arrived at the Empress's private apartments. She ignored the bowing servants but was pleased to note that the Empress's private sentries—the all-female cadre that she personally hand-picked, trained and assigned to this post—were all in perfect order, appearances immaculate, eyes alert and bodies oiled and ready for combat. At least the rot had not spread here then. Still, this was not enough to appease her.

The Empress was reclining on her usual diwan in her private court, enjoying what appeared to be a recitation of poetry. No, not poetry. A narration accompanied by music. The musicians sat on white mattresses, playing softly so as not to overpower the lyrical narration of the storyteller. The story being narrated was familiar. From the snatch or two of verse underway, Jezza recognized it as an ancient legend about a heroic warrior who encountered numerous natural and supernatural challengers on his long, entertaining adventures. It was a tale handed down orally since well before Jezza's own birth, and had many versions in different regions. She had heard it recited by itinerant storytellers at her grandmother's campfire when only a girl.

If Empress Noor Khorasan had noticed the entrance of her War Marshall, she did not indicate it in any way. The servants who had ushered Jezza into the innermost chambers stood by silently rather than announce her arrival as was the usual custom. This too was new.

Jezza frowned. Had so much changed during the period she had been away? There had been a time when Jezza had only to disembark from her chariot or horse before word of her arrival would reach the Empress. Every guard, servant, consort and concubine on her route would then be waiting, ready to salaam her with the respect due to the foremost warrior and protector of the Khorasan Nation and the Magadhan Empire. She was War Marshall Khorasan, Commander of the Imperial Armies. Now, she was expected to wait until her Empress deigned to acknowledge her presence? This was ridiculous!

She stepped forward, about to raise her voice again and address the Empress—her own daughter—directly. Before she could utter a syllable, Noor Khorasan raised her head and directed her sleepy-eyed gaze at her mother.

'The War Marshall has returned,' said the Empress. 'I will have audience with her. Leave us.'

The chamber emptied with astonishing speed, leaving the two women almost entirely alone within seconds. Only two Khorasani Guards remained at the doorway, facing outwards, and a single concubine inside the chamber. This one Jezza knew not only by sight but by name.

'Orzala,' said Jezza, casting a critical eye over the young woman. 'I see you still have your mistress's favour.'

'By Your Grace,' Orzala said coyly, bending her knee to sala'am in that seductive way that only the finest courtesans had.

On the contrary, Jezza thought, eyeing the much younger woman's physical attributes with open appreciation, *if it were up to me, you would have been serving me years ago, travelling by my side on all my campaigns, keeping me warmed in my tent on all those cold, endless, thankless campaigns.* She wondered briefly if Noor had deliberately denied her Orzala precisely because she knew how much she desired her. It would be so like Noor to deny someone something they craved just to give her the upper hand in a negotiation. And with Noor, everything was always a negotiation.

'How was your trip?' Noor asked pleasantly as Orzala offered Jezza refreshments and wine, both of which she declined.

'The report can wait until later,' Jezza said brusquely. 'I have some unexpected news. Send them away.'

The lone serving girl disappeared without being told but Orzala remained.

Jezza looked at her daughter.

Noor smiled at her indifferently. 'Orzala is my trusted confidante.'

Sure, Jezza though cynically, *and your most trusted spy. You use her and her underlings to seduce the Emperor and his inner circle so they can bring you word of the things they let slip while under the influence of wine or passion. And while I rely on spies myself, I don't trust them as intimately and unreservedly as you do.*

'Tell her to leave,' Jezza said curtly, keeping her eyes on her daughter, while secretly watching the concubine. She would be damned if she shared this particular piece of news with a spy-for-hire.

Noor's eyes lost their satiated, sultry look. It was replaced by a cold, dark serpentine stare. But she moved her chin, and Orzala left without a word or backward glance. As she went past Jezza, the War Marshal sensed a hint of a smirk playing on the concubine's perfectly formed mouth. *That one bears watching,* she thought to herself, then put the thought away with the ten thousand other cautions, doubts and suspicions that occupied space in her constantly calculating mind.

'Does this mean your campaign of consolidation in the southwest did not go as planned?' Noor asked with more than a touch of spite in her tone.

Even as a child, she had never liked her wishes being countermanded. In a sense, she was still that child, only now she wore a grown woman's body. An Empress's body, Jezza reminded herself. It was hard at times to decide where her duties as a mother and a War Marshall ended, and her service to her Empress began. It was a perennial tightrope walk, with a bed of knives awaiting her if she should fall.

Jezza said brusquely, 'The campaign goes extremely well. So much so, that I left the last part of the tour to my second in command to see through. I returned post haste to Magadha.'

Noor stretched her supine body languorously, resulting in a lazy yawn. 'Why the hurry? Couldn't wait to return to your lover? Or perhaps, seek out a new one?'

That was meant as a taunt. Jezza's favourite partner in bed, a dark-skinned slave she had renamed Lash for the diagonal scar mark across the woman's face and upper body, had been murdered by unknown assailants. Jezza had a suspicion that her daughter had orchestrated the assassination, using a series of go-betweens as cut-outs that made it impossible to trace the order back to her. Even if she had been able to trace it back to Noor Khorasan, there was nothing she could have done. Even the War Marshall could hardly accuse her Empress, let alone retaliate. The assassination had been a reminder to Jezza that she worked for Noor, and that her status as mother did not give her control over her daughter's actions. Like all political assassinations, it was a power play. Jezza was being punished for questioning her Empress's orders on more than one occasion.

Jezza ignored the taunt. 'I learned something from a captive we were questioning. A Kalingan.'

Noor sat on a privy and relieved herself loudly. She showed Jezza a mocking smile as she pissed, once again asserting her dominance and showing the older woman who was the master here.

'When he finally broke, he had some interesting things to say.'

'Regional politics bores me to death,' said the Empress, daubing between her thighs with a priceless silk scarf. She dropped the scarf into the privy as she rose, naked, and walked over to the diwan.

'There is a movement afoot,' Jezza went on, undeterred by Noor's familiar tactics, 'an unofficial aligning of forces with a common cause.'

Noor reclined on the diwan, leaning back to sit with her knees raised and her sex revealed. She sipped a rich crimson drink with pomegranate buds floating on top, feigning indifference to Jezza's presence.

'The common cause being their aim to overthrow the Magadhan Empire,' Jezza said, seating herself on a bolster and leaning forward to stare directly at her daughter. 'Now, this in itself is nothing new. The Empire has many thorns in its side. That was the point of my campaign of consolidation: to quell any remaining pockets of rebellion and mete harsh punishment to any who oppose Magadha in any way whatsoever. The collection of tithes and tax being, of course, a natural corollary of that military action. Those who dared to raise a finger against us paid for that trespass; those who raised a fist, lost the entire hand and paid a heavier price; and those who raised a weapon, lost their lives and had all their assets confiscated. But what this Kalingan spoke of was no mere uprising or rebellion. He seemed to believe it was nothing less than a full-blown challenge to the Empire.'

Noor began pleasuring herself slowly, carelessly, almost as an afterthought. Her eyes drifted away into the distance, lost in some erotic imagining—or more likely, knowing Noor, a sadistic erotic fantasy.

Jezza ignored this as well and went on relentlessly.

'This too is not new in itself, though it's to be taken more seriously. Any challenge that dares to organize against the Empire is a conspiracy, and conspiracies tend to be better funded than spontaneous uprisings. They also tend to find some support within our own walls. The All-Merciful god knows that Bindusara has his share of enemies within the Council of Chiefs. Most notably the fathers whose daughters are not Queens, or whose constituencies have been neglected politically. A conspiracy means war and war is always a serious business.'

Noor Khorasan's manicured and henna-painted fingernails flashed reddish-orange in the musky dampness of her groin as they flicked in a faster rhythm. Her eyes were closed now, mouth open in a moue of rising pleasure, and naked body limned with a thin patina of sweat.

Jezza continued: 'The Kalingan said that the conspiracy was organized around a prospective rival to the throne, one who had a legitimate claim based on blood, and that sentiment was strong in his favour.'

The Empress was approaching her climax. Her body undulated, loosening into a limbless state of relaxation, pressing her head and back into the cushions as she worked her way to the highest plateau. She threw her head back, exposing her long, graceful neck and engorged nipples, pricking up on her pert, full breasts. Her legs had parted wider but now she drew them in closer as she approached the peak, seeking to prolong and enhance the moment of culmination. There was no sign that she was even listening to Jezza anymore, but the War Marshall was undaunted.

'Ashoka,' she said. 'That is the claimant the Kalingan named. The conspiracy is organized around the drive to place Ashoka upon the throne of Magadha, toppling Bindusara.'

Noor gasped. Her thighs clenched tightly together, immobile fingers clutching at her sex. Her other hand, flung out, now grasped hard at the nearest thing within reach—a silk cushion. She crushed it in her grip as she thrashed her head from side to side, gasping out her ecstasy. Not for Noor the typical aristocratic woman's tendency to cover her mouth or stifle her cries of pleasure: she expressed her orgasm with full-throated energy, holding back nothing. Her body shuddered. Then finally grew still.

She lay motionless for a long moment, until even Jezza began to wonder if she had drifted off to sleep. She had done that once while Jezza was delivering a report: fallen asleep and began snoring loudly midway through a recitation of new holdings and expansions.

But that was not the case this time.

She opened her eyes and stared directly at her mother. Clear, focused, and sharp as a Khorasani dagger. She raised a finger to her lips and licked it.

'So,' said Empress Noor Khorasan. 'Ashoka lives.'

6

'Your father wants me to make a bid for emperor.'

Devi continued doing what she was doing: lighting the oil lanterns in their bedchamber. She finished lighting the last one and doused the taper. Ashoka admired her graceful movements, watching her as she changed from her daytime attire to night-time comfort wear. 'These things,' she grumbled, unwrapping the saree, 'yards and yards! I feel like I've been wrapped in a bundle rather than dressed in a garment. And on a hot day, all those layers...so stifling! Who decided that imitating the Greek toga would make a good garment for us to wear in Jambudwipa?'

'My step-grandmother.'

Devi turned her head to look back at him over her shoulder, frowning down at him. Ashoka lay on the bedding, stretched out and with his hands behind his back. He had already washed and changed after the evening meal. 'Your grandmother?'

'Step-grandmother. Apama. The story goes, my grandfather Chandragupta Maurya saw her in a toga and was so besotted, he asked her to always wear one. She loved our silks and weaving patterns. Over time, she adapted it to suit our local conditions and climate, using our silks and patterns.'

Devi continued frowning down at him while she unfastened her upper garment and removed it. Ashoka swallowed as she turned to face him, exposing her breasts. 'Utter nonsense. You talk such rubbish sometimes, Ashoka Maurya! Complete fiction!'

She removed her lower garment as well, then proceeded to fold the layers of cloth neatly, either not aware of the effect her naked form was having on him or not caring. 'Everyone knows that the saree developed right here in Jambudwipa. Though the old weavers say that there were similar garments worn in the great land of the Nile and in the desert kingdoms of the bedouin.'

She held up a strip of cloth to her waist, briefly obscuring her naked lower body, while letting her breasts dangle freely. 'This is a kachcha, what you men call a dhoti when you wear it. It's been used by our people since the days of the Vedas, and long before that too. At some point during the Harappa-Dholavira civilization, probably around the reign of Raja Sudas, they began to weave it in cotton, and we began calling it a neevi.'

She dropped the kachcha, exposing her triangle of pubic hair, the curve of her very shapely hips and her slender waist, around which she still wore a gold chain. She picked up another piece of cloth and held it against her breasts, causing them to jiggle in a way that made Ashoka's heart stop and groin respond. 'This is a patta, a simple strip of cloth, which women never actually wore back then but which more *civilized* and *decent* women are expected to wear nowadays in the name of modesty. Though I can't for the life of me see why you men are so afraid of something as harmless as a woman's breasts!'

She picked up another length of cloth, a much longer one. 'And this is yet another layer that was added for fashion's sake, probably so the rich could show off their ability to afford so many yards of expensive woven and coloured fabric. Put all three together and you get our saree. Not a Greek Toga or your step-grandmother's invention, just a variation on our very own local fashion staple, the kachcha-patta.'

She was naked again, hands on hips. 'What were you saying about my father earlier?'

He held out a hand and gestured with his fingers. 'Come here a moment.'

She frowned, looking coquettish and coy. 'What for?'

'Just come here.'

'First tell me why.'

'Come here and I'll show you why.'

'At least let me finish dressing in my night garments.'

'To naraka with your night garments. Get here, before I come there and get you.'

She cocked an eyebrow. 'Oho! You're going to get me? You know I can run faster than you.'

'But when I catch you, I'm stronger so I can hold you down.'

'Big man! Able to hold down a woman. What were you saying about my father? Tell me that first.'

Ashoka reached out and grabbed Devi's leg. She tried to dodge him and he grappled with her a moment. She squealed and he grunted, and there was a scuffle but in the end he got hold of her and pulled her to the bedding and made her lie down on top of himself. There was very little talking for some time after that and the oil in the lanterns had burned low by the time they found their voices again. The hour was later and the house and neighbourhood were silent.

They lay together in bed, bodies naked and slick with sweat from their exertions. Devi traced the lines of his limbs gently. 'I still remember the day we found you,' she said softly. 'It makes me want to cry. How could any human being do such cruel things to another living being?'

'They do far worse every day. What I endured...' he shut his eyes briefly, then opened them slowly and continued, 'terrible as it was, was nothing worse than what goes on every day all across the world.'

'I know this, my mind knows this, my heart knows it, but when I saw you that day, I could not believe my eyes. I thought you were dead. I begged my father to help you because I thought it would ease your suffering. It was when he saw you chewing the leaves that he said perhaps there was a chance you might survive.'

'Tell me again about the leaves.' They had had this talk many times before but it was only now, as time separated him from the fresh pain of the experience, that Ashoka was able to discuss it in greater detail. 'You said that you saw I had been sustaining myself by eating leaves. I don't remember anything. Only lying there in agony, unable to move, to do anything, barely able to breathe.'

Devi took a moment to wipe a tear from her eye. 'I could not bear to look closely at you that first day. After we came upon you lying there, I was so overwhelmed, I could barely speak. All I could manage to say was, "Father, help him." My father got down from the wagon and went to you with Svobodha, our oldest servant. It was Svobodha who examined you more closely. He was a warrior himself once. He has seen many men and women in the battlefield, with horrific injuries. He studied you and told my father that you ought not to be alive, but somehow, you were. It was beyond human endurance, what you had suffered, but yet you endured.'

'Tell me about the Vyag.'

'Svobodha said that you had been kept alive by the Vyag.'

'He said that exactly? That the Vyag had kept me alive? He didn't mean the Cubs? Because that was what I called my regiment, Ashoka's Cubs.'

'No, Ashoka. He wasn't speaking of people. He meant Vyag literally. Lions, to be specific. He said that he saw the pugmarks of a young female lion near you, as well as others, older Vyag of different species, including one very large, very old Vyag.'

'How could he tell all this just from pugmarks?' Ashoka scoffed though he had known men and women who could read tracks and spoor as well as brahmins read scripture.

'You don't know Svobodha. He is a gifted man, he remembers his past lifetimes. He once walked by the side of our Lord Gautama himself. He knew those Vyag as well as I know the difference between a toga and a saree.'

'Was there anything unusual about the pugmarks?'

'What do you mean?'

'I mean, the young female lion he mentioned. Did he notice anything unusual about her tracks?'

Devi raised herself to an elbow, wrinkling her forehead as she remembered. 'He did, as a matter of fact. He called her Tridevi.'

Ashoka smiled. 'Like the holy trinity of goddesses?'

'Yes. And when I asked him what he meant, he said she walked on three legs, but was sent by the goddesses to guard over you. He said she had been watching over you since your attack, and had ensured no other predators or scavengers attacked or harmed you. She also called for the other Vyag and on their instructions, fetched healing herbs and fed them to you with her own mouth, chewing, and mixing them with her saliva to make a special healing blend. He said that was why you were still alive, and why your bones were already beginning to show signs of healing.'

Ashoka stared up at the lime-washed white ceiling. 'Trishul.'

She frowned. 'The trident of Lord Shiva?'

'It's the name I gave her. Because she has only three legs.'

Devi looked at him. 'Who are we talking about here? And don't tell me it's one of your former sweethearts!'

Ashoka smiled. 'She was a sweetheart. I barely got to spend a few months with her then we were parted by fate.' He glanced at Devi and saw the look on her face. 'You think I'm talking about a former lover, don't you?'

She punched his shoulder gently. 'Don't tease me about other girls! I know how you princes of Patliputra live. You treat all womenkind as a garden of flowers to be plucked at your whim. I know you must have had your share of lovers before I met you, but I don't want to hear about them.'

Ashoka laughed. 'I'm talking about a Vyag cub! A lion cub. I rescued her from the jungle after all her brothers and sisters were killed by wolves.'

'Oh,' Devi said, 'that's different.' She frowned. 'Why were you in the jungle rescuing lion cubs?'

'I killed her mother because she attacked my brother Sushim.' Ashoka lost his smile and looked away. 'It was not something I wanted to do but circumstances left me no choice.'

'All life is precious. Our Lord Gautama taught us that unless we respect other lives, we can never appreciate our own. This gift of life is the most precious thing we have. If we violate its sanctity by resorting to violence against others, we are setting into motion a chain of karma that always comes back to us. We are, in effect, doing violence to ourselves, and to our own loved ones.'

Ashoka sighed heavily. 'Those are wise words. I love every creature that walks this earth or flies, or swims, or creeps or crawls. There is such beauty in nature, Devi, I sometimes think that we humans are the only evil in this world.' He shook his head. 'But enough of philosophy. I was referring to Trishul, the three-legged cub. She was my companion from Patliputra to Takshashila. The pugmarks Svobodha saw must have belonged to her. She must have come to me when I was lying there, broken and dying, and somehow had sense enough to bring me nourishment.'

'She did more than that, she saved your life, Svobodha says. He is very wise in these matters. He says that you are unique, that your soul is destined to accomplish great things in your lifetime. You will be the light that leads the way to enlightenment for millions of people in this dark age.'

Ashoka shook his head. 'I don't see myself as a leader or a guiding light. I'm just a man trying to live in peace, but life doesn't seem to leave me alone. Violence keeps seeking me out no matter where I go and what I do.'

Devi stroked his brow, trying to smooth out the wrinkles that furrowed it. She placed her cheek against his. 'Then end the cycle of violence. Stay here with me for the rest of our natural days. We shall raise a family together and build a stupa and a vihara to our Lord Gautama. We can spread his wisdom and bring enlightenment to many people who are in need of spiritual sustenance.'

He kissed her gently. 'That sounds wonderful. I would be content to lie here in your arms forever. And your Lord's wisdom is great indeed. I am constantly learning new insights every time I hear more of his teachings from you or Svobodha.'

She turned to him, her eyes flashing.

'Ashoka, my love, I don't say this because of blind faith. There are many who believe that we Buddhists only want to attack and criticize brahmins. But they are wrong. Our struggle is not against brahminism itself, but against the corruption of the varnas. Brahmins as priests and keepers of knowledge are commendable. But brahmins who rule through puppet emperors and kings and use their power to oppress others less fortunate than them? Unacceptable. My people only want justice for all. We are all inhabitants of the world, we all deserve equally to share in the bounty and rewards of nature. But too many brahmins use their power and influence to dominate and oppress. They retain the right to knowledge only for themselves, and pass it only to their chosen pupils. It is forbidden for any non-brahmin to even hear the scriptures recited—the penalty is to have boiling oil poured into our ears! By controlling the flow of knowledge through violence and oppression, they control the flow of wealth and power. They are not keepers of knowledge, they are users and exploiters of knowledge for their own personal ends. That must stop. Knowledge should be free, it belongs to all of us. Our Lord Gautama teaches us that all are created equal, without any need for varnas or prejudice. Equal rights, equal voices, equal opportunities. No more nepotism which keeps brahmins in charge of key functions and empowers only other brahmins. It is time to break these shackles and live free as equals. You are in a position to help our people achieve these goals.'

'Me? What can I do? I am only an outcast of Patliputra, a nobody.' He touched her bare breast. 'I can love with you and live with you to the end of my life. I can help spread your Lord's word, once I assimilate it fully myself. But beyond that? You give me too much credit, my love.'

'You give yourself too little credit. You are Satrap of Ujjain, official representative of Mauryavansh. That means something!'

Ashoka rose from the bed naked, standing before the open window to let the night breeze cool his body. The scent of flowers wafted in from the garden outside. The rose bushes outside the window were so tall now that they concealed almost all the view, leaving only a glimpse of sky and the half moon. When he had come to Ujjain three years ago, those rose bushes had barely reached the bottom of the large windows. 'That position is not one I asked for or willingly accepted. It is Mauryavansh's title, not mine.'

'You *are* Mauryavansh, here in Ujjain. You are the second eldest son of Samrat Bindusara, second in line of succession to the throne of the world's greatest empire. You cannot deny your family, your heritage, your blood.'

Ashoka raised his hands, indicating the veins in his muscled forearms. 'I would drain my body of every last drop of this blood if I could. Perhaps I already have. Svobodha himself said he had never seen anyone lose as much blood as I had and yet live. My Mauryavansh blood was drained there on that rock in Takshashila. I paid my debt to my family, my heritage, my bloodline. This life I have now is my own. I am no prince of Patliputra. I am just Ashoka, husband of Devi.'

'Father to be of Mahendra or Sanghamitra.'

He started to say something else then stopped. He turned and looked at her. 'What did you say?'

She smiled, touching her bare belly and looking down shyly. 'It was confirmed today. I consulted the wet nurses.'

He came to her, reaching out slowly, touching her belly with a look of awe on his face. 'You mean...'

She looked at him, a tenderness in her eyes. 'If it is a boy, I will name him Mahendra. If a girl, Sanghamitra.'

He stared at her. He laughed. 'You may name him Sanghamitra and her Mahendra if you wish! I do not care about names. But is it true? We are to be father and mother to our child soon?'

'Not too soon. Not for another seven months at least. But yes, we will bring a new life into this world. Another small light to brighten this age of darkness.'

Ashoka laughed and shook his head, still keeping his hand pressed to her belly. He stared at her body, disbelief and awe on his face. 'I cannot believe it, Devi. I am to be a father? I hope I will be a better one than my own father was to me!'

'You are Ashoka, not Bindusara. You will be a wonderful father. Now come here and kiss me, and show me again how we achieved this miracle of love.'

He grinned at her. 'Now that, my lady, is something I will gladly do.'

He climbed into bed with her again and they spoke no more the rest of the night.

7

Emperor Bindusara sat upon the Lion Throne of Patliputra, the seat of the Magadha Empire. Before him in the vast assembly hall were the chiefs that represented the five hundred major tribes of Jambudwipa. Despite their rivalries, enmities and feuds, this unlikely alliance of formerly warring chieftains and warlords had held together for longer than anyone had deemed possible. The first empire in this part of the world. It was a historic achievement that had amazed the civilized world.

His father, Chandragupta, had been the first Emperor of Magadha, the one to build that alliance, but it was Kautilya who had been its architect. Under Chandragupta's rule, the alliance had become an empire. Now, Bindusara's job was to hold that empire together.

Right now, as he listened to dozens of angry chieftains

shouting at the top of their voices, he felt more like the owner of a fish market than an emperor. There were even cats present, as there always were at a fish market: the serving girls who kept their masters' wine cups full and their beds warm while they were in the capital city. They flitted through the sabha hall, their svelte bodies on display beneath their seductively designed robes, serving and fetching for the chieftains. A few were even administering sexual favours right there while the sabha was in session: either on their knees or using their hands, a bold few even sitting on their master's laps and riding their cocks as wantonly as if they were merely out for a ride in the countryside. Those chieftains who weren't having their priapic needs serviced, were sozzled blind, half-asleep in their chairs, or engaged in shouting matches with their neighbours and rivals. More than a few would come to actual blows, and there would be bandaged heads and limbs on display come the morrow. Yes, a fish market described it nicely except that fishmongers didn't bicker and brawl this baldly; they were more interested in selling their wares before they rotted. This band of merry fools, on the other hand, were already wealthy and powerful enough to not want for anything, and were more interested in pursuing petty feuds and differences, rather than actually engaging in the business of empire.

And as always, it was up to Bindusara, as Emperor, to restore order and attempt to maintain some semblance of décorum. Easier said than done.

He summoned one of his aides, and told him what he needed announced.

Moments later, the official crier announced in a resonant voice that managed to rise above the gruff shouts of the squabbling chieftains that all those out of order on the sabha floor would be fined a tithe of their annual tax. That got their attention at once. The uproar subsided and the brawling chiefs returned to their chairs, with only a few bruises. No blood had been spilled—a fact aided by the prohibition against the bringing of weapons to sabha, another of Kautilya's brilliant rules—and as such things went, it was a fairly 'peaceful' session compared to some of the most boisterous ones this season.

The august gathering then proceeded with the next order of business, a dispute over grazing rights in a disputed border territory. It was one of several such mundane yet necessary matters that the sabha routinely dealt with during session.

As Bindusara listened to the parties state their cases and grievances, his mind wandered. He was distracted by one particular serving girl, a slender figure with surprisingly muscular legs. He watched as she bent over to serve her chief some savouries on a copper plate, admiring her rear view. Something about the way the muscles in her bum moved beneath the flimsy garment aroused him. That in itself was unusual. It had been a while since he had been attracted to a mere serving girl. His Empress Noor's boudoir arrangements were so devilishly exotic that he couldn't recall the last time he had found just the bum of a young woman sufficient to arouse him. These days, it took far more than mere physical beauty to raise his interest. But for some reason, he was aroused now.

The girl finished serving her master and, without straightening her body, turned her head to look over her shoulder—directly at Bindusara. Their eyes met and he saw a knowing gleam of mischief in her light eyes. She was aware of his attention and was deliberately displaying herself for his viewing pleasure!

That aroused him even more and he felt himself grow tumescent. That too was a rare occurrence. Not that he didn't partake of pleasure during session: in his first years as emperor, he had participated with full gusto in the orgiastic feasts that regularly punctuated the sabha sessions back then. But as he had matured, as an emperor as well as a man, he had found himself less easily aroused and much less easily satisfied. That too was the doing of Noor Khorasan; she had introduced him to such unimaginable indulgences in bed that a mere tumble in the hay was no longer enough to please him. He had come to depend on her constantly innovating sexual offerings, until he had reached a point where he could no longer find arousal or achieve climax without the help of her devilish machinations.

Yet here he was, responding physically and erotically to a mere serving girl bending over.

He watched the girl as she walked away, her rear bouncing rhythmically from side to side as her powerful thigh muscles worked. There was nothing exceptional about the girl's looks; in fact, she was not particularly attractive. Her face, hands and feet were larger than most, her muscularity almost...masculine in its definition. Only her backside and the graceful way she moved and gestured was recognizably feminine. Yet somehow, that very combination of male and female attributes was what made her seem so erotically charged to his senses.

Bindusara rose from his throne, gesturing to his aides. He strode out of the hall even before the crier had finished announcing that the Emperor was retiring from session. The ministers would continue to hear the pleas and weigh in on the issues; in any case, it was they, not he, who made most of the decisions in sabha. He depended on them to navigate the complex webwork of truths, lies, history, politics and manoeuvring that were essential to understanding the context and reason for any plaint, and only put his official seal, or voice, to the judgements they recommended. There were times he arrived at his own conclusions and issued his own judgements, against their advice, but those were usually for cases that were argued before him and whose issues he was able to make sense of himself. These were rare exceptions, few and far between, and the only reason he ignored his advisors and spoke his own mind at these times was because he wanted to remind them that while their advice was often as good as a judgement, he and he alone was the Emperor, and the Emperor had his own mind and made his own decisions.

He wondered what it had been like for his father Chandragupta, who had overseen his sabha with only one advisor by his side to offer guidance: Kautilya. Had that made it easier or harder? How much of Chandragupta's bold, brilliant empire-building had really been Kautilya's work? How dependent had the first Emperor of Magadha been on his guru? Was it true, as some still believed, that it was Kautilya who was the brains of the Emperor, with Chandragupta a mere physical body that carried out the brahmin's plans and schemes?

Perhaps, Bindusara thought as he walked back to his own palace apartments, if he had let Kautilya live, the old priest might have enlightened him. No doubt, he would have tried to pass off everything as the product of his own genius, but there would be some element of truth in those claims as well. Kautilya was always one to give credit where it was due.

But the point was moot. He had sent Kautilya to the Torture Palace where the old brahmin had succumbed to his wounds, breathing his last in the arms of the old twin hags, Pain and Suffering. And Bindusara trusted no guru, no brahmin, no advisor with his innermost thoughts, plans and schemes. He was his own man, and made up his own mind, and would always do so.

He had pointed out the serving girl on his way out of the sabha hall, ordering his aides to have her brought to his chambers. After all, she was the cause of his arousal which had occasioned him leaving sabha in mid-session; it was only fitting that he repay her for that distraction.

He settled into a rose-petal-filled bath as he awaited her arrival.

Basking naked in the large warm pool, his limbs washed and cleaned sensuously by equally naked maids—or perhaps they were queens or concubines, he could no longer tell the difference, given the sheer number of his partners—he dreamed of a time when he would be free of the petty encumbrances of sabha sessions, negotiations, and the constant politicking that made up most of an emperor's life.

Would it not be a fine thing to simply indulge himself, travel, visit exotic new locales and experience new hedonistic experiences, without having to interrupt his days with bickerings over river rights or border disputes? Either that or a good war. It had been far too long since the Empire had embarked on a major campaign. That was mainly because Magadha had expanded to the maximum extent possible in Jambudwipa. Certainly, there were still vast swathes of the subcontinent that were not under Magadha's sway, but by now, he knew that those territories were either too remote to govern from afar, or simply not profitable enough to overcome.

Yes, the Magadhan Empire as it now stood was as large as it was feasible. He had expanded it considerably since his illustrious father's time. True, he had also lost some ground in the process, but he would not dwell on that aspect right now. He had achieved a great deal in his lifetime, an enviable historic achievement with no parallel in this part of the world, or perhaps not in the entire civilized world. Surely he deserved to be able to enjoy the spoils? To simply take some time off from politicking and governance and all the boring, mundane, brain-sucking routine of running a great empire? To be his own man, do what he desired for a change, instead of always having to think about what was best for the empire? What good was such enormous power if he could not enjoy it?

He drifted into a doze at some point in his day-dreaming. A familiar voice roused him.

'My magnificent stallion.'

Bindusara smiled even before he opened his eyes. 'My wild mare,' he said in response.

It was a familiar exchange. His Empress and he said the same words to one another every time they met. Even though—and Bindusara felt no remorse at this awareness—neither felt anything remotely resembling emotion when speaking the words. They were empty praises, and yet, empty praises and promises were all they had left. Noor and Bindusara had run their course a long time ago. What kept them wedded to each other was simple power politics. They needed each other to maintain what they had, and to attain what they still desired. If not for that fact, either one would have sent the other to the Torture Palace without a second thought.

But they did need each other for the moment, and so it was with a smile on his lips that Bindusara greeted his Empress.

'Sabha is still in session,' she said, walking around the pool slowly. She towered over him, looking down at his naked body without the slightest attraction, just as she might look down at an object that she possessed but had no remaining love for. 'I wasn't expecting you back for hours yet.'

Bindusara picked up a sponge and squeezed soapy water on the back of his neck. The maids were nowhere to be seen: he assumed they had left when he dozed off, having completed their ministrations, or perhaps Noor had ordered them out. She always preferred their trysts to be private. Noor trusted nobody, not even the oldest, most loyal servant, unless they were Khorasani, and even then only partially.

'I am tired of running the fish market,' he said. 'I came to wash the stench out of my skin.'

She tilted her head, considering his choice of words. 'That stench can't be removed with soap and water. It is the stench of power. That only leaves you when you die. And yet,' she said, moving her open hand across his crotch lightly, 'it is such an invigorating perfume.'

'To me, it's a stink. I want to be rid of it, for a while at least. Perhaps a change of scenery. I have always wanted to travel the world. See the many wonders I have heard about only from emissaries and ambassadors until now. What good is power if one does not use it?'

She frowned now, completing a full circle of the bath pool. 'You wish to expand the empire?'

He considered his next words carefully. While he did speak his mind to Noor in private, he knew it would be unwise to reveal his inner thoughts entirely. To bare naked his mind as he was baring his body right now, would be a mistake.

Noor was no loving mistress or eager-to-serve concubine. She was a Khorasani, and an Empress. In many ways, this was her Empire as much as his. Without her mother, her Khorasani legions, and their brutal, rapacious methods, he would not be in a position to enjoy the luxury of a noonday bath. He would have been out on a dusty battlefield, watching his forces fight to suppress one challenger after another. Perpetual war, perpetual unrest. The Khorasans had ended that constant conflict by resorting to actions and methods so vicious, so unimaginable, that even the most virulent enemies had been stunned into reconsidering their options. They were the reasons for the uneasy, forced but stable period of peace the Empire was going through.

Sure, there were still rebellions and pockets of unrest. This was an empire, after all, and empires were built on foundations of violence. But they were the exception rather than the rule. It would not do to speak of peaceful travel, of touring for experience alone, to Noor Khorasan. She would see such foolish dreams as a sign of weakness.

And if there was one thing that Khorasani hated, it was

weakness. She herself had personally drowned or choked to death any infant born of his seed in the royal harem that displayed anything less than total perfection. He had not seen it himself but he had been told that she often bore a look of delight on her face as she murdered the newborn infants. This was a woman who took pleasure from causing pain, suffering or violent death to other living beings.

'It's a thought,' he said neutrally.

She looked at him with a curious expression, as if reappraising him. 'Now, that is the way I like to hear my husband talk. Conquest! Invasion! Expanding the empire. These are the thoughts that should occupy an emperor's mind.'

She considered this, continuing to pace slowly around his pool. *Like a panther circling her prey,* he thought. Her beautiful features were fixed on some intense thought.

'There is an opportunity I was going to speak to you about,' she said at last. 'Perhaps our minds are in sync for once.'

He ignored the jibe. He had learned to do that over the years. There was never any point to calling her out over the subtle insults and put-downs she voiced. It would only make her angry, and if calm Noor Khorasan was a formidable person, then angry Noor Khorasan was a frightful one.

She spoke at length, as he listened, not wanting to have this discussion at all, but unable to find a way to interrupt her without arousing her wrath or, worse, arousing her suspicions. He listened without comment. If she knew that the way he felt was the exact opposite of what she had just presumed—that, far from wanting to go out on another exhausting, soul-sucking campaign of conquest, he was in fact sick and tired of the business of empire, was in fact entertaining thoughts of simply going on an extended vacation tour around the world and to hell with politics and power plays—that would make her more than just angry. It would be like poking a queen cobra with one's finger. Or a panther.

'So,' he said at last, when she paused to allow him a chance to speak. 'Seleucus Nicator has withdrawn his forces from the northwestern frontier? Sending most of them westward to deal with the threat from other Greek nations?'

'He has,' she said with rare enthusiasm. 'That's exactly what all those troop movements and withdrawals means. I'm pleased to see you grasped it so quickly this time. I thought you might need it explained more than once before you understood. Geographical power politics has never been your strong suit.'

That stung. He was an Emperor, the son of the founder of the first Empire in this part of the world. Yet she still treated him like a schoolboy out of his depth. He ignored it. It suited his purpose to have Noor think he was deficient in certain ways. When playing chaupat opposite a deadly enemy, it was always best not to reveal the full extent of your knowledge of the game until the final move. Someday, it would be time for that final move and when the time came, he would take pleasure in seeing the shock on Noor's face, perhaps the first shocked look on her face in her entire life.

'So our northern and northwestern borders are porous now?' he said instead.

'More than a leaking sieve,' she said. 'You could send an army through the passes and they would face no more than the weakest resistance imaginable.'

He mulled on that. 'And that is what you think I should do? Send an army through the passes? To expand our interests northwards and westwards?'

Her angular face was lit by a feline smile. 'Yes. But more than that, my stallion, I believe you should lead that army yourself. You did say you are eager to go to war again, as men always crave after a period of idleness. This way, you could satisfy your itch for bloodlust, as well as achieve what everyone believed impossible until now. Even your father's great guru said it could never be done. You can do it, Bindu. You can expand the Empire beyond the northwest frontier and the Himalayas. That would put you on the doorstep of the great northwestern continent, the one that stretches to the icy north, the land of white people and golden hair. The world would be yours for the taking, my tiger. Isn't that exciting?'

That's suicidal, he thought. *And maybe that's why you want me to do it, maybe this is your clever scheme to eliminate me without having to get your own hands bloody. I go off on a madcap quest from which I would never return and you would be free to install my replacement upon the Lion Throne and rule by proxy. It would be the closest you could come to being emperor yourself. And that is what you really want. The ultimate power.*

But instead of voicing these thoughts, he smiled.

And said, 'You are a genius, my mare. Whatever would I do without you?'

8

Ashoka was greeted warmly by the merchants of New Market, the high street of Ujjaini Nagiri's shopping district. The wares on display here were not as rich and varied as the high streets of Patliputra but then again, this was not Patliputra. He was impressed by the sheer volume and variety of product here, as well as by the amounts of money that changed hands daily. Many of the traders who made the biggest purchases and came back to buy more at regular intervals, carted the goods to Patliputra where they resold them at marked-up prices twice or even thrice the original cost.

A grama train had come in only three days ago and the wagons were being loaded up even now as he rode by on his roan horse.

It was strange to think that in a few weeks, all these colourful garments, toys, cooking utensils, leather wear, footwear and almost every other conceivable object he could spy, would be stacked on the shelves of his home city's stores.

The Patliputra traders saw him as he rode past and word spread among them. Several of them tried to catch his eye or called out obsequious greetings. Some used 'Satrap', others 'Yuvraj' and a few sycophants managed to use both in a single greeting. He barely acknowledged them. He had successfully avoided all visitors from Patliputra for these past three years: he had no intention of changing that practice now. Once in a while, someone would exert every ounce of influence and effort to gain a personal audience with him. All had failed. Ashoka had left Patliputra and even though Patliputra would not leave him alone, he would continue to resist her efforts.

'Ashoka!' Gupta, a merchant who was affiliated with Ashoka's father-in-law, raised a meaty arm in greeting as he rode past the store's large display of wooden implements. 'I have new stock from up North. Come take a look!'

'Perhaps later, Guptaji,' he called back. 'I am expected somewhere.'

'Anytime. My shop is always open to you, night and day.'

He had similar brief exchanges with a few other businessmen. Then the town children caught sight of him and he was surrounded by a flurry of young boys and girls all looking up adoringly, waving, shouting his name, asking him to come play with them, show them how to fight, tell them the story of how he killed a thousand assassins in a single day, and other assorted requests. He laughed and called out greetings and promised to stop by later that day and spend some time showing them a few more sword tricks but for now he was already late to an important appointment.

Leaving the children still yelling and shouting his name as they ran back through the marketplace, he found himself wondering at the news Devi had shared with him. He tried to imagine himself as a father, a young son and daughter of his own running beside him, riding on his horse (one in front, one behind him on the saddle), two little beings, perfect and wonderful, created by him and Devi from their love.

It was overwhelming. It filled him with emotions he could not describe, that he had never felt before. There were strange feelings in there too. Odd sensations, doubts, anxieties, fears, even some anger and sadness—not directed at his future progeny, but at his own father, whose absence coloured his own early childhood. Bindusara's absence, Shubhadrangi's solitary existence, raising a son alone in a remote forest hermitage, waiting years for her husband to return and take her to his house as promised, a promise that was never kept, then finally being persuaded by Acharya Kautilya to go to the palace and work there as a maid—a maid in her own husband's palace, when in fact she was a queen!

He recalled his own childhood, watching his mother waiting each day, watching the path that Bindusara had left by before Ashoka was even born, resenting this absent father who had promised his mother so much and delivered nothing at all, resenting also the absence in his own boyhood, the lack of a father when he was needed to show and lead and guide a growing boy.

He remembered the anger, the hurt, pain and confusion he had felt. The nights he had spent listening to his mother cry herself to sleep, that he had tried to comfort her. The anger that had grown into a cold fury as he grew from an uncomprehending infant into a boy who understood and yet could not understand how any husband and father could be so heartless. Then the journey to Patliputra, the pretence and humiliation of having to work as a maidservant and a maidservant's son in the palace of his own father. Of enduring daily abuse and humiliation at the hands of the cruel, entitled, spoiled young queens, concubines and assorted dross that clung to the Emperor's vastra like fleas on a shaggy dog's fur. The fear of knowing that at any time a single wrong word or minor misstep could end with the worst penalties imaginable, even a fatal beating, and that people lived their entire lives like this, beaten down and exploited, treated inhumanely for no reason other than the fact that they were not born into the right house, family, caste or gotra.

He remembered watching his other brothers and sisters living their childhoods in an endless display of lavish indulgence, while he spent every waking minute either working or studying under his guru's tutelage, determined to learn as much as he could learn, so he would not become one of *them*.

As he turned away from the High Market and into the quieter, almost deserted locality where the merchant's warehouses were located, he could not reconcile the memories of his cold, distant, brutally indifferent father with the man his mother had spoken of.

He believed his mother; knew she must be telling the truth. So what had happened in the years after Bindusara had met, loved and married his mother in the forest, and when he went back to Patliputra? How could a man change so much? Did all the love and tenderness his mother described simply leave him one day like a fever that broke and passed? Or did some infection of power change him into a different person altogether?

Ashoka had never been able to reconcile the Bindusara his mother had described to him during those years in the forest with the cold distant silhouette he had glimpsed within curtained chambers in the palace. Even when he was in his teen years and his mother and he were finally presented as Bindusara's legitimate wife and son, and given their rightful place in the imperial family—a feat which took all of Acharya Kautilya's dwindling influence and brahmin caucus politics to achieve—Bindusara had become no warmer, no more accessible to either Ashoka or his mother.

As far as he could tell, his mother and father had never again enjoyed life as man and wife, but she was included in all official events and given her place in the seating order, and shown due respect by all, no matter how much they resented this 'maid' and 'wood nymph' being given such an exalted promotion. Shubhadrangi had justified his father's remoteness with the perennial reason: imperial politics. What she couldn't explain away as easily was his dalliances with the other queens, concubines and even the assorted maid who caught his fancy over the years. And when he had finally settled into an evidently passion-filled relationship with First Queen Noor Khorasan, his mother had finally given up speaking of him altogether. Ashoka had taken her silence to mean defeat and his childhood resentment and anger had grown to monstrous proportions, driving him to rage fantasies in which he confronted his father and demanded to know whether he was a man or a statue made of stone.

Now, as he turned his horse into the courtyard of the brick building that served as one of his father-in-law's many warehouses, he reminded himself that by becoming a father, he would also be making Bindusara a grandfather. What does that even mean? Can a man who never showed any love for his own son have anything to offer his grandchildren?

He exhaled and dismounted. He had arrived at his destination. Enough thinking about what it would mean to be a father when his own father had been, let's face it, a cold-hearted absentee parent who had never once shown his son any real affection, generosity or warmth. Not even a hug and an 'I love you, my son'. Time to be himself—Ashoka.

There were many more people assembled in the large room than he had expected. When Vedsagiri had said some of Ujjain's most prominent merchants wanted to meet with him, he had thought three or four, at most a half dozen. But the large room was almost full. He saw almost two dozen familiar faces, many of them showing the fleshy signs of prosperity. Everyone who mattered in Ujjain was here! This was much more than a conversation. This was a national convention!

'Greetings, father,' he said, 'greetings to all of you.'

Everyone greeted him enthusiastically, offering the customary blessings and benedictions. Merchants and traders all, but they were Ujjaini merchants and traders, and the holy city demanded showing gratitude to the gods at every occasion. What was the saying Devi had told him? 'In Ujjain, even thieves and drunkards pray to their gods before doing anything.'

The ritual formalities dispensed with, Ashoka took the seat proffered to him and looked around at the expectant faces. His father-in-law spoke.

'Owing to our relationship, I have been asked to speak on behalf of all.'

'Of course, father. Please, speak your mind.'

'Ashoka, we shall speak directly and plainly. We are not Greek orators or Sabha Chiefs of Patliputra. We are simple, pious merchants and traders of Ujjain Nagiri, the holy nation. We are accustomed to speaking our minds. Please don't mind it.'

'I welcome your directness, father. It is one of the things that endears Ujjain to me. I grew up around the complicated subterfuges and tongue-twisting doublespeak of Patliputra politics and I can assure you, I do not miss them in the least!'

Many balding, greying heads nodded approvingly.

'We thank you for that leave of license. I shall come straight to the point then. We are here to petition you to build an army.'

Of all the things Ashoka had been expecting, this was not one. 'Did you say, an army?'

'Indeed. Ujjain Nagiri is a peaceful nation of devout people, mainly brahmin, vaishya and some lower castes. We have almost no kshatriyas and none feel inclined to come here due to a lack of opportunities. We have among the lowest rates of crime and violence anywhere in the Empire.'

Ashoka nodded. This was another thing that had endeared Ujjain to him. It was a place he would like to bring up his children. A safer place by far than Patliputra, leave alone Takshashila.

'We also contribute the highest taxes to Mauryavansh. Almost double that of the next highest, and several multiples more than some of the less generous regions—even though some of those are far greater in size and population than our little satrapy.'

'I am aware of this fact,' Ashoka said. 'But what does that have to do with wanting to raise an army?'

'These are dangerous times, son. The Empire is facing many internal uprisings as well as foreign threats. There is unrest in more kingdoms than there is peace. You have witnessed the cauldron of violence that is Takshashila first-hand. The Southern kingdoms are in no better condition. Their uprising against the Empire was crushed but they remain restless, resentful of Patliputra's yoke. Many of the five hundred kingdoms are openly defiant of the Empire's policies and laws. Mauryavansh is on the verge of breaking apart, and when that day comes, the fragmentation of Empire will leave a hundred, nay a thousand hungry chieftains each wanting to call himself or herself Emperor of the World. When that day comes, Ujjain as the richest contributor to the Empire's coffers, will become the biggest target. And undefended target.'

Ashoka sighed. 'And you believe that raising an army will protect you?'

One of the older merchants spoke up. 'Only a sword can stop a sword. Our survival depends on us being able to fight to protect our wealth and our families.'

'Already, there are more incidents of thievery and murder involving Ujjaini merchants on the Dakshinapatha and Uttarapada,' said another younger, relatively less bulky trader Ashoka knew to be the largest dealer in metal goods in Ujjain Nagiri, even in the whole Empire, some said.

'Two months ago, the daughters and wife of Manas Uday were abducted at knifepoint while returning home from Patliputra and held for ransom. He had to pay ten lakhs in imperial gold to get them back, and all had been brutally violated.' This from another long-whiskered merchant whose name Ashoka didn't recall but whom he had seen visiting his father-in-law often.

'If the incident occurred in Imperial territory, Mauryavansh will deliver justice,' Ashoka pointed out.

'Mauryavansh? Mauryavansh does not care about us!' cried a merchant with a high-pitched voice. 'When Manas Uday took his case to Patliputra, he was told that nothing could be done as he had already paid the gold. He was advised that in future he should call upon Patliputra before paying any ransom and let the Empire handle the matter.'

'If he had done that,' said another Ujjaini, 'he would only have recovered his wife and daughters in little pieces.'

Several other incidents were narrated, each with its own ensuing corollary of how the Empire had failed to assist the victims and hadn't shown even the slightest twinge of concern.

'All they care about is getting our taxes, not protecting us. If we are to take care of our safety in the dark days ahead, we have to take our own measures.'

Everyone nodded and 'ayed' in agreement. Several cross-conversations had broken out as the Ujjainis added further details to each of the narratives and contributed their own comments. It was obvious that this discontent had been simmering for some time.

Ashoka held up his hand to ask for silence. The crosstalk died down as they all gave him their attention.

'It is not that simple. One does not simply raise an army from nothing. In most nations, the kshatriya varna itself forms the heart of the armed force or militia. Without any kshatriyas, it would be impossible to start an army here. I wouldn't know where or how to begin. Nobody would!'

'Patliputra's imperial guard is not home-grown,' someone pointed out. 'It's Khorasani! They're all outsiders who serve the capital city. And before that, it was the Chandikas, who were a special Order who were created to protect and serve the imperial family. Why can't we do something similar?'

'Create an Order to protect and serve Ujjain by hiring warriors from outside?' Ashoka shrugged. 'It is possible, theoretically. But it would not be easy. And if the Empire crumbles, then you will be surrounded by armed mercenaries with no loyalty to you other than the salary you pay them. What if they decide to kill you and your families and simply take all your wealth, instead of working for you? How will you stop them?'

'That could happen to the Emperor too. It happened with the Chandikas.'

'*No*,' Ashoka said it louder than intended. 'No,' he repeated. 'The Chandikas were loyal to their last drop of blood. They were betrayed. They were the most loyal warriors I have ever known in my life, or heard of. My guru, Acharya Kautilya himself supervised the creation of the Order. No one understood politics and economics better than he did. He anticipated every possible outcome and set in place safeguards that would ensure that the Order remained true to their task no matter what the political circumstances. The Chandikas would have died performing their duty even if they were not paid a single coin. They lived to serve. And they died serving. Do not ever speak another word against them in my presence.'

There was a brief silence after that as the gathering observed and noted Ashoka's emotion.

'Then form a new Order of Chandikas,' Vedsagiri said.

Ashoka looked at his father-in-law. 'That is impossible. The last of the Chandikas died three years ago, executed for the false charge of treason. There are no necromancy mantras that can resurrect them! The Chandikas are all dead and gone, buried to boot rather than cremated, so their souls cannot be reborn and find moksha from the cycle of karma. My father would not even allow them that much.'

'But if there were still Chandikas, then it is possible?' Vedsagiri asked gently. 'An Order with such fierce loyalty and devotion to duty could serve Ujjain in its time of crisis?'

Ashoka didn't know how to respond to his father-in-law. He settled for spreading his hands, and saying, 'If the Chandikas could be resurrected, then yes, perhaps it could be done.'

'You would consent to train and lead this force for Ujjain's defence?'

Ashoka frowned. 'To what end? I have put down my sword. I am no longer a fighting man. I retired from that life three years ago. I am a man of peace the same as all of you here.'

'But you are still a kshatriya. A great warrior at that. A yoddha among warriors. Trained in warcraft by the great Acharya Kautilya himself.'

Ashoka exhaled. 'This is pointless. I am not your man. This task is beyond me.'

'No, Ashoka, you are the only man. You are the man Ujjain needs and deserves. We knew that your being found by us that day in Takshashila was for a reason. It served some cosmic purpose. We believe that the purpose was for you to come here to Ujjain and help us in our hour of need. As we helped you in your hour of need.'

Ashoka shifted uncomfortably. 'Father, I owe you my life and that is a debt I can never repay. But this is something beyond my abilities. You are asking me to do something that is impossible. Even if I agree now to do as you ask, where would I find soldiers as loyal, as fierce, as dharmic as the Chandikas? I would have to scour the world like Alexander the Greek, and even he never found the Paradise he was seeking in the end.'

Vedsagiri smiled. 'No, my son, that is where you are wrong. You need do nothing except play your part. Fate has already brought the army to us. All we ask is that you lead it.'

Ashoka frowned. 'Father?'

Vedsagiri stood. 'Forgive the theatricality. We wanted to be sure you would agree before we summoned them. That is why I told them to wait in hiding outside Ujjain until we called for them. They have been so eager to see you again, they can hardly wait.'

'I don't understand. Who are you speaking of?'

Vedsagiri clapped his hands. People began to stream into the warehouse from the far entrance, several of them, all wearing the familiar dark garb that he had not seen for years. For an instant, he thought that somehow, by some miracle, the Chandikas had indeed been revived from death. Then he saw that these were men as well as women. He saw familiar faces, some more familiar than others. One most familiar of all.

Tissa came forward, grinning. Beside him was Uttam, one of his Cubs, and after Uttam came the only white-clad person in the group, Radhagupta.

9

Shubhadrangi was watering her plants when she heard the tinkle of jewelled feet in the corridor outside. She paid no attention at first, assuming they would continue past her door. But they were followed by the sound of the bolt and latches being unlocked and the creak of the door being opened. It creaked because it was so rarely opened. The tinkle resumed, entering her room and stopped. Shubhadrangi detected a perfume she had not smelled for a long time. She continued pouring water over the tulsi plant without turning around, but despite her apparent preoccupation, her hands were trembling now. She had dreaded this day for a long time and had rehearsed it in her mind over and over, preparing herself. Now that it was finally here, all her preparations felt inadequate, her rehearsals pointless. Still, she willed the tremble in her thin arms to subside, breathing in and out in the calming pattern that always soothed her in times of crisis.

'I see you have new additions to your décor,' said the voice of Noor Khorasan.

The watering can—really just a small earthen pot, the same lota Shubhadrangi used for her own toilet as well as for a drinking cup—was empty at last. She set it down on the ground, taking care not to drop it. The last time the pot had developed a crack, the guards did not replace it for days. As it is, they only refilled it for her twice a day when they brought her meagre meals.

Shubhadrangi mustered all the remaining dignity she possessed and turned around to face her nemesis.

'Sister Noor,' she said. 'I was not expecting you.'

Noor Khorasan's rich, husky laughter filled the small room. '*Sister* Noor! Now that is rich indeed. If I didn't know you so well, I might be tempted to think you were being sarcastic. But sarcasm is not in your vocabulary, so I have to assume that was meant sincerely.'

Shubhadrangi fought to control the twitch that was threatening to erupt in her cheek as she stared at the other woman. 'It is the proper honorific with which all queens of Patliputra are expected to address one another.'

'So you were just being polite then. I like that you were just being polite. It's not sarcasm but it's better than the half-dead stupor you were in the last time I visited.'

The last time she had visited was well over a year ago. Shubhadrangi knew because she had counted the days off carefully, knowing that it was important to keep one's mind busy when in solitary captivity. Back then, she was still recovering from the trauma of the Torture Palace, and barely able to tolerate Noor Khorasan's presence without breaking down completely out of fear and anxiety. Even now, she felt terror lurking just out of sight, threatening to rear its head and strike her down at any minute. She kept breathing slowly, willing herself to maintain her dignity. It was all she had left.

Her visitor strolled over to the spot where Shubhadrangi had placed the two plants. The handful of soil in which they each grew was contained in broken parts of Shubhadrangi's earlier clay pot. In the afternoons, the sun came in through the high slitted window and fell on this spot briefly for an hour or two before moving on. It was the only sunlight the room received. The tulsi plant was the larger of the two, almost six inches high now. Had it been seeded in a healthier portion of earth and received more sunlight and water, it would have blossomed long since. As it was, it was barely surviving but alive.

'They actually appear to be growing,' said the Empress. 'Quite impressive. I always admire how you poor-born folk manage with so little. Then again, if you weren't so thrifty, there would be less wealth for us in the world! So I'll say, well done, *sister* Shubhadrangi.'

Shubhadrangi said nothing. She focused her limited strength on keeping herself upright without trembling.

Empress Khorasan walked to one end of the room—the end with the pit in the floor and the hole which her captive was compelled to use as a toilet—then to the other end, which contained the door. Between these two extremes was the pallet on the ground where Shubhadrangi slept, sat, said her prayers, and spent most of her time. The room contained nothing else. Only the little slit in one wall, up near the twelve-feet high ceiling, broke the monotony of walls and floor. It was a sad little prison cell of a room, and Shubhadrangi knew it well, but after the horrors of the Torture Palace, it had seemed a blessed and merciful place. Now, for the first time in over a year, she saw it through Noor Khorasan's eyes, saw how pathetic and miserable a hole it was, and what a humiliation it was for her, a titled queen, rightfully the true Empress of the vast and powerful Magadhan Empire, to be reduced to this fourteen-feet-by-ten-feet space.

Noor finished her little walk-around and turned smartly on her heel to look directly at Shubhadrangi, who now saw that that had been her rival's express intention. Noor wanted to remind Shubhadrangi of her plight, to rub it in. The gleeful smile on the younger woman's pretty face only underlined that fact.

'So I trust you are keeping well?' Noor asked, deliberately posing the question in the tone and manner of any titled royal inquiring after her fellow royal's health, as if they were both having this conversation in Shubhadrangi's former palace chambers rather than this prison well. The Khorasani had not changed, Shubhadrangi thought, even in her presently impoverished and pitiful state Noor still treated her like a rival rather than the long-suffering wretch she had been reduced to. Did the woman have no shame or empathy? Of course not. That would make her human. And whatever species Noor Khorasan belonged to, it was certainly not humanity.

She is a rakshas, she told herself. A monstress in the guise of a mortal woman. Whatever she says or does now, remember that.

Noor continued as if Shubhadrangi had already answered her

absurdly formal query. 'Good to see you doing well. I thought I might come by and share some news with you. Perhaps you've already heard by now, but I said it would be nice to come by and have a chat about it anyway.'

You know very well I will have heard nothing, Shubhadrangi thought. *Because your Khorasani guards at my door ensure that I am never allowed to leave this room or be visited by anyone. Even in those months when I was recovering slowly, painfully, from the injuries inflicted on me in your house of horrors, not even a royal vaid was permitted to tend to my wounds and broken bones. No concessions were made to my health, no herbs or ointments, or bandages provided, just that hard pallet on the cold stony ground, and this mud pot in my hand. Even the food given to me is put on a leaf, dry millet cake, or stale bread crusts, and watery daal, sometimes a little vegetable, and rarely, a piece of fruit. You can see the result on my bony body, I see it in your eyes when you look at me—or rather, avoid looking at me. I have no source of news or conversation. Apart from my silent, indifferent guards, you are the only other living soul I have seen in over a year. So, go on and mock me some more. Why not? After all, you are a demoness who takes pleasure in other people's suffering.*

Despite her determination not to let anything Noor said rattle her, the next words shocked Shubhadrangi.

'There is news of your son.'

Shubhadrangi felt a powerful surge of emotion. It was a mixture of joy, hope, elation...and also dread. She said nothing in response, controlling her urge to ask a dozen questions. Any reaction from her would only please her tormentor and encourage Noor to torture her mentally.

'Well?' Noor asked. 'Wouldn't you like to know the news?'

When she received no answer, the Empress made a sound as if to show incredulity at Shubhadrangi's lack of reaction. She was trying to provoke Shubhadrangi. 'Surprising that a mother would not want to know about her son, after so many years apart. But then again, what kind of son abandons his mother without a word? Like mother, like son, I suppose.'

Don't react, Shubhadrangi told herself. *That's just what she wants: to provoke you into an outburst, to hear you outrage and vent your frustration. Remain impassive and she will say whatever she intends to say anyway. She came here, after all; she must have a reason for this visit. She wants something from you, even if it's just to see you shout, or cry, or rant and rave. Don't give her the satisfaction.*

'In any case,' Noor said after another prolonged silence, 'I will share the news with you out of the goodness of my heart. It's only right that a mother should be informed of her son's demise.'

Shubhadrangi felt an arrow pierce her heart, more painful than any instrument of torture that had been used on her during her time of incarceration. She felt her heart's blood spilling on her tumultuous emotions, and it was all she could do not to turn to face Noor Khorasan and cry out. *Ashoka dead? No, it could not be! Don't believe anything this witch says. She is only trying to torture you again.*

'But then, you are an indifferent mother,' Noor went on, 'during these past years, you've never once inquired after his well-being or whereabouts, never sent for him or even spoken of him. It's almost as if you don't care about him anymore. I suppose that's in keeping with your character. After all, if you had cared for Ashoka, you would never have sent him away on such perilous missions in the first place.'

Ignore her, ignore her. She's only trying to make you angry with her lies and false accusations. Ashoka is my heart and soul, he is the only reason I am still alive. It's because of him that I was able to survive these unspeakable times; why I continue to live despite all this woman has done to try to destroy me. I believe in him, and I know he needs me as I need him. Focus on that. Focus on love. I love Ashoka and I know he loves me and will find a way to return to me. If she is speaking of him, that means he is either on his way or working to come here to Patliputra. Read between the lines. Listen not to her actual words but to the political motives behind her speaking these particular words. She would not bring up Ashoka in this manner, with this unusual visit, unless there was a political angle to it. She only does things for political reasons.

Noor continued in this vein for a while, constantly casting aspersions on Shubhadrangi's character, while she endured it silently and patiently. Curiously enough, her hands were no longer trembling. It was as if the mere mention of Ashoka's name had instilled new hope and courage in her. She was not distraught over the suggestion of his 'demise', because she knew Noor well enough to understand that she had a larger agenda. The longer Noor babbled, the stronger Shubhadrangi felt. If Ashoka had indeed been dead, Noor would have harped on that over and over, torturing her with the details of his demise, his gruesome wounds, his suffering, the indignities and torture visited upon him in his last moments. Instead, she was ranting about the northwest, about Greek troop movements and Seleucus Nicator and the importance of imperial expansion. Behind the veil of words was a sense of something bigger at stake here, and Shubhadrangi waited patiently until she could glimpse the shadow behind the veil.

Finally, Noor stopped speaking. Either the Empress realized that something had changed in the balance between them or she had decided to change tack.

'He will never make it to Patliputra,' Noor said.

With those seven words, Shubhadrangi felt life, hope, joy and courage all flood back into her being. It was as if she had been given a new lease of life. Ashoka was coming back to Patliputra! That was clear. Noor had said it in so many words. And she had said it with hatred and pique and even, if she was reading her right, a tinge of anger. Anger came from fear. If Noor was affronted by the thought that Ashoka would even dare attempt to return home, that meant she was afraid he might succeed. Where there was fear in her enemy's heart, there was hope in her own.

'He will be killed before he gets here,' Noor said confidently. 'And when he dies, I will have his body dragged behind a chariot and brought here to string up and display for all to see. The Traitor of the Empire. The Wayward Son. The Treacherous Turncoat. He will be an example for everyone to see as they pass his corpse on the high street. An example of the unassailable power of the Magadhan Empire.'

Shubhadrangi said nothing. She had heard all she needed to hear. She had learned that Ashoka was coming.

She wanted to tell Noor Khorasan that when her son came, he would avenge her, he would pay Noor and her cohorts back for their betrayal. For they were the turncoats, the traitors, the treacherous ones, who needed to be made an example of, and her son would set that example. It would be their bodies put on public display, to prove to the world that even the highest and mightiest could fall if they turned against their own, that Patliputra was still a city ruled by dharma. That good would always triumph over evil. Ashoka would show them.

But she said nothing. She had no need to speak the words. She had heard it in Noor Khorasan's voice already: she feared the slim, remote chance of Ashoka succeeding. And that fear was enough.

Noor grew impatient at the end of the visit. 'Your indifference and cruelty towards your own flesh and blood is only to be expected, *sister* Shubhadrangi. But you will yield yet. Once your son is dead, your own death will follow immediately after. Mother and son, separated in life, will be united in death. You will die in shame and humiliation, without dignity or rank, your names stricken from the official records and your memory lost in the annals of history. Years from now, centuries, millennia even, no one will even know the names of Shubhadrangi and her son Ashoka. They will only know Empress Noor Khorasan, ruler of the great Magadhan Empire, the architect of the greatest empire the world has ever seen.'

Shubhadrangi frowned and turned for the first time to face her fellow queen. She saw a flicker of surprise briefly flash across the other woman's face.

'You?' asked Shubhadrangi. 'Surely you mean Emperor Bindusara? He is still Emperor, is he not?'

Noor recovered quickly from her surprise. A sly look crossed her pretty face. 'For now,' she said. 'But who knows what tomorrow might bring? He is preparing even now to embark on a great campaign of expansion. He leaves soon for the northwest frontier and beyond, to expand our great holdings beyond the mighty Himalayas.'

'Seleucus Nicator's territory?' Shubhadrangi asked.

Again, that sly smile. Yes, this was the heart of Noor's devilish plan. That much was writ plain on that beautiful face. 'Not for long,' said the Empress. 'The Greeks are retreating to Greece to deal with unrest in their homeland. Their satrapies in the northwest will be left unguarded for the most part. It is a rare opportunity.'

'What of Queen Mother Apama?' Shubhadrangi said, her mind whirling as she began to glimpse what really lay behind the veil of words that Noor had been spinning all this while. 'She will not let Bindusara leave on such a campaign. She would not let him go to war with her own people. His people too, in a manner of speaking, since he is half-Greek.'

Noor Khorasan beamed, her fair features flushed with the pink of a woman thrilled. 'But Shubhadrangi, surely you remember?'

Shubhadrangi frowned. 'Remember what?'

Noor Khorasan removed an object wrapped in a cloth from her robes, unwrapped it and tossed it onto Shubhadrangi's pallet.

Shubhadrangi looked down at it.

It was a dagger.

A long, curved dagger, covered with blood.

Freshly spilled blood, not yet congealed.

'That is why I came here,' Noor Khorasan said, smiling sweetly, 'to ascertain the truth for myself. When I heard the news, I could scarcely believe it. Yet I cannot deny my own eyes. There is the dagger, on your bedding.'

'You put it there,' Shubhadrangi said.

Noor clicked her tongue, admonishing Shubhadrangi. 'Now, now, *sister*. Don't lie. I found the dagger there, still wet with the blood of your victim. Somehow, you were able to escape your guards long enough to slip into the Queen Mother's chambers and murder her. You killed Apama, your own mother-in-law. Don't even try to deny it. I have witnesses, I have proof.'

On cue, the two guards entered the room, went straight to the pallet and picked up the bloody knife. They took it and left without even a sideward glance at Shubhadrangi.

Noor Khorasan smiled. She had accomplished what she had sought. She had made Shubhadrangi's life worse than she found it, only a half hour earlier.

'Now, I will leave you alone to contemplate the error of your ways,' she said, as she exited the room. 'Murderess!'

10

'Tissa!'

Ashoka embraced his brother with a hug tight enough that he could feel Tissa's bones creak.

'As skinny as ever!' he said, releasing the slender young man.

Tissa laughed. 'What I lack in meat, Sushim makes up for by the hundredweight. You should see him, Ashoka.'

Ashoka made a face at the mention of their eldest brother. 'Don't talk to me about that idiot. Tell me about yourself, how are you?'

'Like a boat on a choppy sea, buffeted on all sides.'

Ashoka heard the gravity beneath the outward veneer of good humour. He knew better than to probe further. 'We shall speak at length shortly.'

He turned to the others. 'Uttam! Well met, fellow Cub!'

Uttam hugged him with an embrace that was as strong as Tissa's was gentle. He touched Ashoka's face and shoulders with an awed look. 'You truly are a lion, my Lord. A Vyag in human form.'

Ashoka laughed. 'Come now. Do I have a mane and four paws? A tail? Do I creep through tall grass and hunt antelopes? I am just a man, Uttam. And your friend. You have seen me fight, you have seen me shit and you have seen me bleed. You know how mortal I am.'

Uttam's face did not lose its expression. 'Nay, Ashoka. You can make light of it, but to us, it is a legend years in the making. Everyone knows how you were nursed and nourished by the Vyag till the Ujjainis found you. They say the Vyag fed you the herb Sanjeevani itself that revived you and knit your broken bones together.' Uttam squeezed Ashoka's bicep, feeling the muscle and trying to feel the bone beneath. 'It is a miracle wrought by the gods themselves.'

Ashoka laughed uneasily, glancing around at the serious faces of the other men. Nobody was smiling or treating this lightly. They really believed he had been saved by some supernatural force. 'Don't be absurd, Uttam. It's true that Trishul might have fetched me some herbs while I was laying on the rock in Takshashila. But that's all.'

'No ordinary herbs, Ashoka,' Radhagupta spoke up. 'And there were many other pugmarks besides those made by your three-legged companion. Including the oldest Vyag known to be still alive. Acharya believes she is the Queen and Procreator of the species itself. She was watching over you and guaranteeing your safety and recovery. That is why you survived while anyone else would surely have perished.'

Ashoka didn't know what to say. 'Acharya himself said that?' He shook his head. 'All I know is that I felt a will to live that was so strong, it carried me through the pain, the rage, everything.'

Radhagupta looked at him in a way Ashoka never recalled Radhagupta looking at him before. As if Ashoka were some kind of otherworldly being now. 'Do not underestimate the power of karma, Ashoka. You have lived many lives before. Your past actions have brought you much pain in this lifetime, but they will also bring you great glory. Victory is writ on your face in big bold letters.'

Ashoka rubbed at his forehead uneasily. 'I will have to remember to wash my face more thoroughly then. You make too much of me, Radhagupta. But I am pleased to see you. You look older, and you sound wiser.'

'Adversity brings out the best and the worst in us,' said the young brahmin. 'Times like these push us all to the brink of actualization. Those who are evil reveal themselves. Those who are good stand up and are seen for what they are.'

'Hear, hear,' Uttam said solemnly. The others nodded their heads in agreement.

Ashoka looked around. 'I seem to be the only one here who doesn't know what we are talking about.'

'We are talking about you, Ashoka,' Radhagupta said. 'It is time for you to return home, and to reclaim your rightful place.'

Ashoka shook his head. 'My place is here now. In this beautiful, peaceful holy city. I have a wife, a family,' he nodded at his father-in-law who was standing and listening with folded arms, 'And last night I learned that I have a young one on the way.'

'Congratulations!' Tissa said, 'I am to be an uncle! That is such wonderful news, brother!'

'Thank you, Tissa. Thank you, thank you,' Ashoka acknowledged the congratulatory gestures and greetings of the others. 'So, as I was saying, I have no intention of leaving anytime. This is home now. My place is here.'

'You cannot deny who you truly are, Ashoka. You have a destiny. Your place is on the Imperial Throne of Patliputra. It has been so ever since you were born. That is why Acharya took it upon himself to visit your mother and you in the forest, to bring you both to Patliputra, to risk his own life and career to ensure that you found your place in the Mauryavansh dynasty. He saw in a dream that you were the Lion of Maurya reborn. Chandragupta himself, returning two generations later, to restore his Empire to its original glory and lead Jambudwipa into a new age of peace and harmony. The presence of the Vyag in Takshashila and his recent dreams only confirm this fact. You are chosen and protected by forces far greater than any of us can ever understand. There is no point resisting your fate.'

'Guru Kautilya's dream?' Ashoka said, incredulous. 'You speak of him as if he is still alive, Radhagupta.'

Radhagupta looked at him levelly. The brahmin had grown

taller and more broad-shouldered since Ashoka had seen him last but his face remained as smooth and beatific as ever. If anything, he had gained an aura of calm gravitas that was unlike his younger self. He had always been knowledgeable and wise beyond his years, but there was something about him now that suggested a deeper wisdom. As if he had lived through and seen a lifetime's worth in a few short years. Ashoka could relate to that. He wondered if he had a similar look on his face. What was it Acharya Kautilya had called it? *Touched by Shiva.*

'Acharya Kautilya is alive, Ashoka,' Radhagupta said. 'It was necessary to keep his existence secret until now, for his own safety. His enemies are many and his friends few now, and it was vital he survive long enough to guide the Empire he designed and built through this final transition. It was by his own wishes that we kept his survival a secret.'

Ashoka was stunned. 'I...I thought he died in the Torture Palace. Along with...' he gestured, unable to complete the sentence.

Behind Radhagupta, he saw Tissa and Uttam exchange a look of deep sorrow.

Radhagupta reached out and took hold of Ashoka's arm gently. 'Your mother is alive too. Both she and the Acharya survived the Torture Palace.'

Ashoka stared at him in utter disbelief. If the news of Acharya Kautilya being alive had stunned him, this revelation struck him with the force of a herd of elephants. He felt all the blood drain from his head and every sound suddenly faded to a keening echo. He turned away, no longer hearing anything else anyone said, though he knew their lips were still moving and they were still speaking.

He took a moment to regain his senses. When he recovered, he turned back to Radhagupta, gripping him by the shoulders harder than he meant to. The brahmin had grown in width and height, but he was as skinny as ever, even skinnier than Tissa, and Ashoka felt the round balls of Radhagupta's shoulder joints under the palms of his hands. He felt as if he could crush them to dust if he squeezed hard enough. The ringing in his ears still continued but he could hear voices and sounds over the ringing now. The blood that had left his head roared through his heart now, like the Ganga in spate in spring.

'Where is she? Take me to her now!'

Uttam and Tissa both stepped forward, extricating Ashoka's hands from Radhagupta's shoulders. 'Easy, old Cub,' Uttam said with a soldier's firm tone. 'We are only the messengers. There is much more you need to know.'

'I don't care about anything else,' Ashoka heard himself say, too loudly, too brusquely. 'Take me to my mother this instant. I want to see her. I have a horse outside, we shall ride to Patliputra together.'

There was a moment of dead silence as everyone shifted uncomfortably, avoiding looking at him directly. Ashoka looked around, reading the silence, reading their expressions or lack of expressions.

'What is it?' he asked. 'Tell me!'

Tissa came forward. 'She is alive and in Patliputra, Ashoka. My mother and our allies succeeded in exerting political influence to save her and Acharya Kautilya. They were released from the Torture Palace but...' Tissa looked as if he were searching for the right words. His eyes glistened with sudden emotion.

'But what?' Ashoka cried. 'Tell me!'

Radhagupta made a reassuring gesture. 'Shantam, Ashoka. Shantam. Calm yourself. Haste and anger will not serve you at this time. These events we speak of took place years ago. There is nothing you could have done to have prevented them back then, there is nothing you can do now to undo them. They happened, and they are in the past now.'

'Not to me,' Ashoka said bitterly. 'To me, it is happening now. Why did I not hear of this before? Why was I not told? Why hide this from me all these years? My mother? Alive? Why did you not tell me, Radhagupta? Or you, Tissa? Uttam?' He turned to seek out his father-in-law's face in the group. Vedsagiri was looking down sadly. 'Did you know about this, father? Did you keep it from me as well? All those times that I grieved and cried for my mother—were you lying to me when you comforted me and quoted scriptures of your Lord Gautama on the loss of one's mother?'

'Ashoka,' Radhagupta said gently, 'Try to understand. We could not tell you until now. Acharya Kautilya himself forbade it. We had to honour his wishes.'

'And what about me? What about me, thinking my mother was dead? While all the while she was alive in Patliputra? Enough of this talk now. Take me to her. I wish to see her for myself.'

'You cannot do that just yet,' Uttam said. 'That is why we are here, Ashoka. The time has come for you to return to Patliputra. But not as a son returning to visit his mother.'

Radhagupta nodded slowly. 'Yes. You will return to Patliputra, Ashoka. But not as the son of Shubhadrangi alone. You will return as the son of Bindusara, and as the grandson of Chandragupta. You will be the saviour of Patliputra, and the new emperor of the Mauryavansh Empire.'

Ashoka stared at his old friend and spiritual guide. He looked around at the room filled with sombre faces.

'I cannot do this. I have no wish, no desire, no ambition to be your saviour, or your champion, leave alone your emperor!' He laughed bitterly at the word. 'That title alone represents everything I resent. To be lord and master of millions, to rule over a dominion so vast that a person cannot travel across it in a single day, or even in a single masa—it takes months to travel the length of the Mauryavansh Empire! That is madness. To conquer and rule over so many lands, so many nations, so many people. It is not something I desire to do. People were not meant to rule and be ruled over. They should live free. Like the beast of the forest, air and sea, we are born free. We should live freely, as equals, not as emperor and subjects.' He shook his head. 'Nay, I love and respect all of you and I know you have just cause but I am not your man. I am no emperor, or even a prince. I am merely Ashoka, husband of Devi, son-in-law of Vedsagiri, son of Shubhadrangi whom I long believed dead but who, I am grateful to learn, still lives. I shall be a father soon and an uncle someday,' he gestured at Tissa, 'and a grandfather in time, gods willing. But not an emperor.'

'You have no choice,' Radhagupta said. 'This is not your decision to make. It is what the Empire asks of you. The people, the era, that destiny itself asks of you.'

'Then you ask too much of me. I have given all I could to serve Mauryavansh. I sacrificed much. So did my mother. I have no more left to give.'

'Then would you have all those sacrifices be in vain?' Uttam asked. 'All those comrades in arms who died fighting alongside you?'

'The suffering you and your mother endured? That she endures even now?' Tissa said. 'What did you think, brother? That she was dead and now she is alive? She is alive, yes, but she is a prisoner of Queen mother Khorasan. She lives like a prisoner in her own palace, imprisoned in her quarters, reduced to a bag of bones in a hovel, no better than being incarcerated in the Torture Palace. She lives in misery, eking out a life in measures of pain and humiliation. Is that how you desire she stays till the end of her days?'

Ashoka felt hot tears spill from his eyes, rolling down his cheeks. 'I will free her from her suffering. I will break her free from her incarceration in Patliputra. I will ride today itself and go to fetch her. I will bring her here to Ujjain to live with me and my wife, to be grandmother to our children, to be safe and well and happy for the rest of her natural life.'

'She will not go with you,' Radhagupta said flatly. 'She has sworn an oath, sealing it with her own blood, sworn it before her patron goddess, Durga. She has sworn that you will come and undo all the evil wrought by those monsters—mother and daughter Khorasan—and their equally monstrous pawn, your father Bindusara. She has sworn an oath to the memory of all those who died serving those unjust masters—from the Chandikas to the hundreds of thousands of others who have been systematically tortured, impoverished, oppressed, and slaughtered by the unjust rule. She has promised all of Patliputra and all of Mauryavansh that you will come one day and end this cruel, oppressive, unjust regime, and restore Mauryavansh to the greatness that your grandfather sought to achieve. She has become a symbol of hope for Mauryavansh's future, of the future that can be, and there are so many people who would gladly give their lives to ensure that her oath is fulfilled. Many already have.'

Uttam nodded. 'We were only a few handfuls back in Takshashila, but we still took back the province. Now we are twenty thousand strong, Ashoka.'

'Twenty thousand? The Cubs?'

'We call ourselves the Chandashokas now, in your honour.'

Chandashokas—the terrible ones without remorse. The name was apt. He wiped the tears from his cheeks with the backs of his hands.

'And there are more,' Radhagupta said. 'We have allies. Allies that your mother and Queen Tissyanka secured just before Shubhadrangi's incarceration and the attack on you at Takshashila. That alliance has grown stronger with every passing year as dissatisfaction against the present regime has grown with every new oppression. We have a mix of seasoned troops and royal guards, numbering close to fifty thousand.'

'That is an army,' Ashoka said, marvelling at these numbers. 'Fifty and twenty thousand...seventy thousand in all.'

'And the chiefs are with us,' Radhagupta said. 'The Sabha chiefs have assured us of their unilateral support. If you lead the coup, they will stand behind us. Over four hundred are on our side.'

'Four hundred out of more than five hundred,' Ashoka said. 'What of the remaining one hundred?'

Radhagupta did not answer. 'I think you can guess.'

After a moment, it came to Ashoka. 'Of course. The hundred queens. Their nations will stand behind my father because they have a vested interest in his continuance as Emperor.'

Tissa nodded. 'They support him because their sons and daughters are in the line of succession. All except for my mother and our nation. We stand with you, Ashoka.'

Ashoka tried to absorb the full import of these revelations. 'A fighting army of seventy thousand. Four hundred chiefs...the four hundred chiefs alone could raise a much larger army. You have enough fighting men. Why do you need me?'

'The four hundred chiefs support us only if you lead the coup and are successful in taking back Patliputra and...' Radhagupta looked at Ashoka levelly, 'ending the current regime and extinguishing all traces of its claim to the throne.' Ashoka understood what that meant without needing it to be spelled out: *Killing my father, stepmothers and siblings.* 'Once you have taken back the palace and city, and call the Sabha to session, they will stand up and officially support you in a vote. Protocol must be followed. You have to take the initiative. Till the time that you stand before them in the Sabha and officially assume office as the new emperor, they cannot ratify you or be seen supporting you. That is the law of Mauryavansh, as written by our Acharya himself.'

'And what of my mother?' Ashoka asked. 'She is a prisoner of the Khorasans. What happens when I storm the palace and confront them?'

Everyone was silent.

Ashoka nodded. He knew what they could not say. 'That is why she is alive, isn't it? As a hostage. Noor Khorasan let her live when she heard that I had survived in Takshashila. She needed a safeguard against the unlikely event of my return to Patliputra. She kept my mother alive in case I come back. And when I do re-enter the city, she will use my mother's life as a bargaining piece against me. What am I to do then?'

Radhagupta, Tissa, Uttam, none of them met his gaze.

Vedsagiri stepped forward, the other merchants of Ujjain moving to let him pass.

'Son, I have not spoken until now because everything that had to be said was being said by others better qualified than I. But in this matter, there is something I wish to contribute. I am a father and I lost my wife, Devi's mother, many years ago, when Devi was still a young child. Were she alive today, she would be so happy and proud to see you and Devi together, happy, and about to start your own family. But what good is to start a family if you do not ensure the future of your own children?'

'Father, you know I will do everything to make sure our children have the best life we can give them. That is why I wish to see them grow up here in peaceful Ujjain. Not in the bloodthirsty streets of Patliputra or the Imperial Palace where nobody is safe night or day and everyone schemes to kill or harm everyone else to get ahead.'

'Yes, Ashoka, but you speak of Ujjain and Patliputra as if they were on two different planets. They are only a few hundred miles apart. They are connected. Everything is connected. What happens in Patliputra echoes in Ujjain. If there is an evil regime in the capital, it affects us all here as well. It is already affecting us. We called you here to speak of the security of Ujjain. You must now think that was only a ruse to get you here, so your friends could present their case for your return. But Ujjain still needs to be secured. We still need you to help build an army to protect our interests, not as an aggressive or invasive force, but for our defence and security. The two causes are one and the same. By fulfilling your mother's oath, going to Patliputra, leading this coup, ending the oppressive regime and taking back the Empire to the path it should be on, you are helping ensure your own children's future. You are doing your duty not only as a son but also as a father to be. If not for yourself, Ashoka, do this for those who need you to do it. Do it for your unborn children. Give them a world worth living in. That is all I wish to say to you.'

11

Devi was trying hard not to cry, but Ashoka could see the effort she was making. He finished tying his sword and rig to the saddle and patted his horse gently. Tissa, Uttam, Radhagupta and the others were waiting a respectful distance away, giving him space and time to say his farewells.

He looked at the house, so simple, clean, unostentatious. It was one of the things he liked about Vedsagiri. The man never felt the need to display his wealth, power, and influence. The house was large, airy, well lit, and comfortable enough to house a clan, not merely the small family and staff that currently resided there. But there were no vulgar displays of wealth or kitsch, as Ashoka had seen in other houses.

He thought once again of how fortuitous he had been when Vedsagiri and Devi had happened to take that particular remote mountain pathway on their way back from a trade trip north of Takshashila. What circumstances had conspired to make them pass that way that very day, what balance of nature and happenstance had shifted so that they would find Ashoka lying on that rock, broken, bleeding, near death but still alive. Why had someone else not found him? Someone who might not have given a damn about him and simply passed on by without a second thought. Or someone who would have laughed and taken pleasure from his suffering and maybe thought to put him out of his misery.

No, it had to have been this kind, generous merchant from Ujjain and his daughter, because Ashoka had to meet and fall in love with her. Svobodha had to have been the servant who could read the pugmarks around the rock and know the herbs that he had been chewing in his dazed, delirious, feverish state. Everything had turned out exactly as it should have. As it was turning out now. There was a powerful sense of predestination about it all, and he felt himself being swept up by it, a ship on a wave, a bird on a current, a snowflake in a blizzard.

He was only one part of a great storm, he was not vain enough to think of himself as the storm itself, but he played his part, and it was an essential part. Just as it took every snowflake to make a blizzard, every bird to make a flock, every drop to make an ocean, so also he had his role in this great drama.

And this part of his story was coming to an end. He felt it and he knew Devi felt it too, and that was what they both feared most. That their time together was ending and there would be no more Ashoka and Devi hereafter. He felt it as keenly as he felt the salt of his own tears stinging his eyes.

He went to his wife, standing proud and straight before her father's house. Vedsagiri stood two yards behind her, but kept his distance, allowing his son-in-law and daughter to have their moment.

'Devi,' he said.

'Ashoka?' she said, and came to him, into his arms, into the embrace that had united them through hundreds of nights, leading to the creation of the new life that now grew within her womb.

He embraced her tightly, holding her as if he would never let her go till the end of time itself.

He felt her shuddering, and knew she was fighting back her tears with every ounce of strength. He knew she was too proud and brave to allow herself to break down and spend their last moments together weeping and howling. She was not that kind of woman.

'You are a warrior,' he whispered, stroking her head and her back.

She pulled away at last and looked at him. They were the same height: she was tall for a woman, he was short for a man. It was just one of the many ways in which they were equals, perfectly matched to each other.

'You are an emperor,' she said. 'Not a merchant. This is your destiny. This is the path that leads to your future.'

He felt his heart tighten like a fist clad in a leather glove was squeezing it. 'I shall return.' He did not say that it would be soon, because that would be a lie. He did not say that he would send for her because that would be a lie too. All he could say was that someday, he would come back, whether for a day, or a lifetime, that only time would tell. It was the truth and the truth hurt like a knife in the heart.

She released him and he turned. He went to his horse and rode away. He joined the others and they began riding too, cantering away from the house, from his beloved Devi, from his new home Ujjain. And he carried with him the weight of all his and Devi's unshed tears.

12

They rode in silence until they had left Ujjain Nagiri. They did not take the Uttarapada but used smaller paths unlikely to be travelled by anyone en route to Patliputra. All of them had covered their heads and faces for the road as was normal to keep themselves free of the dust of the road on any long journey, and Radhagupta had covered his whites with a nondescript cloak that made him blend in with the others.

These were all usual precautions but in addition they had riders tracking their journey ahead and behind, ensuring that they were neither followed nor awaited at any place. Patliputra's reputation as the capital of Spydom, as some wag had termed it, was well-deserved. Ever since the peak of the Empire, when Acharya Kautilya had formed the first League of Spasas—the vast network of spies that kept the steady stream of information flowing that enabled the Emperor to keep his finger on the pulse of the Empire—the use of spies had proliferated. Every nation had its own network, loyal to their own cause, though Ashoka had long suspected that many of these spies were merely the same Mauryavansh spies playing double duty by spying on Patliputra for their own nation and vice versa, thereby keeping both sides well informed and themselves well paid.

But the past few years had been particularly eventful. A complex system of double, triple and counter-spies had sprung up, until nobody was certain of anyone's loyalty anymore. A string of incorrect reports, leading to reprisals where there had been no attacks to begin with, and attacks without reprisals because the spies had spread misinformation about those behind the attacks, and similarly tangled situations had led to chaos in the intelligence world. Most of the original Mauryavansh spies had vanished completely. The official word from Patliputra was that they had been eliminated by the enemies of the Empire, but Radhagupta revealed to Ashoka now that they were in fact instructed by him, following Acharya Kautilya's directions, to cease reporting to Patliputra and report only to him directly.

Acharya Kautilya's political importance may have ended decades ago, but his foresight and canny planning had anticipated all eventualities. He had designed the spasa network with a special 'backdoor' system. In the event that the forces controlling Patliputra were acting antithetically to Mauryavansh's interests, Kautilya would issue a prearranged coded message to all his spasas. On receiving the coded message, every Mauryavansh spy would immediately go into hiding, and instead of reporting to Patliputra, they would be reporting about Patliputra—to Kautilya himself. How the Acharya received the information from these spies and where he was currently located was unknown to everyone. Even Radhagupta claimed not to know where the great guru was at present. Ashoka wasn't sure whether to believe him, but it hardly mattered. All that counted was that Radhagupta had a way to communicate with Kautilya, wherever he might be, and by using the spasa network, they could now use the Empire's own considerable resources to spy on the Empire itself!

They changed direction constantly, riding in a complex series of moves that made it virtually impossible for anyone to determine where they were actually headed or to be able to plan how to ambush them or head them off. Besides these elaborate precautions, they also made deliberate stops at certain inns and ashrams two or three times a day, giving false names and itineraries, thereby laying down a stream of overlapping and confusing information for any spies unfortunate enough to be reporting to Patliputra.

A few days after leaving Ujjain, they arrived at their first destination.

The trees of Girvan loomed out of the horizon, and Ashoka felt a strange pang of regret and sadness for so much that had been, could have been, and would not be again. He said nothing as he rode into the woods with the others, but his heart was full and his head full of memories.

Many of the crucial events of his life had taken place in this forest. His birth, his early childhood, then his frequent visits to Acharya Kautilya's ashram, and of course, those last eventful days with Sushim. He thought of the Mother Lion he had had to kill to save his brother and found himself thinking that if he had that to do over again, he might not be so quick to save his brother this time, knowing what he did about the years to come. Then again, if he had not killed the Mother Lion, he would not have saved the three-legged cub, and if he had not saved the cub, how would Trishul have fed him herbs and kept him alive on that rock in Takshashila till Vedsagiri and Devi found him?

It was a chain of cause and effect, and though the scriptures said Karma was the process by which one's deeds were judged in later lives, Ashoka thought that perhaps there was such a thing as Karma in the same life too: Do unto others as you would have them do unto you. The world would be a better place for it.

They rode into the woods for several hours, Uttam leading the way. Finally, he called a halt, rose in his saddle, cupped both hands to his mouth and issued a series of ululating bird cries. After repeating the calls for several minutes, Uttam sat back in his saddle and settled down. They waited. After an interval, an answering call came from deep within the forest. After another interval, another call came from another deeper part of the forest. This continued, the calls getting farther and farther away, deeper into the woods.

Finally, several hours later, the forest began to come alive. Men and women appeared, all clad in the dark garb favoured by the Chandikas. It had been years since Ashoka had seen anyone dressed in those colours. The sight stirred strange memories in his being. A girl with unmistakably feminine hips evoked a powerful memory of Chaand. He remembered the way the knife had slid into her chest and the soft gasp she had released at the end, the scent of her sweat during sex, the sound of her ecstasy... He pushed the memories out of his head. Chaand was gone. The Chandikas were gone. These were different warriors, different times.

And I'm a different man. Not the same Ashoka.

'Chandashokas,' Uttam said, gesturing at the warriors surrounding them.

Ashoka looked around, turning his horse in a full circle. They were impressively silent, standing still, a part of the forest. He saw their faces and lean, taut bodies and knew they were not the same ragtag group of orphaned bastards he had met years ago. That original core of a few dozen had grown into this army. He could see only a few hundred, perhaps a thousand or so, but knew the rest were there, surrounding him, twenty thousand of the fiercest warriors all awaiting his leadership, his command.

They made camp in the woods that night. He learned from Uttam that the Chandashokas kept no permanent camp. They had done so once, years ago when they were first banded, but betrayal by spies had led to a raid by Patliputra, and they had learned their lesson. Now, they stayed nowhere for more than three nights in a row, constantly moving, always moving, owning and keeping nothing that would slow them down. *The clothes on our backs and the weapons in our hands*, their chant went.

But the weight in their hearts remained. They carried it everywhere with them and as Ashoka sat by the fire those first nights, listening to their stories, getting to know them one by one, he heard an unending litany of horrors. Much had changed in Patliputra since he had left for Takshashila years ago. Mauryavansh was no longer a symbol of hope and prosperity. It represented only the richest of the rich, the strongest of the strong, the highest of the high. And how did the richest get rich? The same way a merchant became a millionaire, as his father-in-law would say: by taking one coin apiece from a million people. While the merchants and traders of Ujjain offered their wares for sale and people chose to buy them, Patliputra sold things that nobody wanted to buy but which they had no option but to buy. There was now a security tax, under the guise of paying for the policing of highways and trade routes, this was nothing more than a tax to ensure one's security from being persecuted by Patliputra itself. He learned how bands of thieves and brigands operated with impunity in certain regions, looting, killing, raping, stealing, and how despite the Empire's best efforts, were never caught or punished. How was this possible? Because the thieves themselves paid an official 'tax' to the Empire's representatives, sharing half of their spoils to guarantee their right to profit by any means possible.

This was the new Mauryavansh, the Empire of Greed and Dread. He felt his cheeks burning as he heard one story after another of unrelenting terror and mayhem. How could his father permit such things to continue in his reign? His first thought that his father was not even aware of these things because he was being fed false information by the Khorasans, was proven false when he began hearing stories where Bindusara himself was personally involved or aware of atrocities, genocides, abuses of power, profiteering from terror and violence, until finally, when he had heard perhaps the hundredth or was it the thousandth story, he had had enough. He rose from the campfire and walked into the forest, unable to speak or express the anguish in his breast.

He could not believe that such things could be allowed to happen, that such a world could exist. Yes, he was naïve to think this way, to expect any better of people like the Khorasans, or even his own father for that matter. But the truth was, these past years had changed him. He had been broken and he had let them break him. And he had been reborn in a sense, and the Ashoka that had awoken again in Ujjain, who had grown to love Devi and appreciate the simple quiet pleasures of a peaceful domestic life, was not the Ashoka he had been before. He had changed from deep within, turning away from violence, turning towards a new way of thinking, a way more in step with Devi's Lord Gautama, that gentle lovely mind that had seen so deeply into the human condition and arrived at such powerful insights into the causes of suffering. Ashoka had been on the verge of embracing the Buddha's way of life.

He had not said as much to Devi or anyone else as yet but he had felt himself powerfully attracted to that philosophy and outlook. In a world so violent, so blood-crazed, so insane, only peace and love could be the cure. He had needed to heal and Gautama's philosophy had helped him heal. It had been a season of rest for his battered soul. He had slept long and deep in a garden of peaceful delights these past years.

But while he had slept, the world had continued to go from bad to worse. The madness had intensified, the insanity had spread like a malaise. Now it seemed it would overwhelm all Jambudwipa, wash the entire subcontinent in a flood of crimson. Every nation seemed to be ready to go to war with everyone else. There was talk of war brewing in every direction. The Lichchavi Confederacy was long gone, crushed into dust by the boot heel of Mauryavansh hegemony, but a dozen others had risen.

Most of all, the spectre of Greek empire. Seleucus Nicator had been growing stronger by the year, increasing his satrapies north and west of Jambudwipa, and word was that he had made certain regions his satrapy in all but name. Kalinga was mentioned with great conviction. Other places as well with less conviction. Ashoka didn't know what to think of all this information. Some of it was too much information for him at this moment. He could only make sense of some of it. The rest would take a mind as vast and prodigious as Acharya Kautilya's to process and analyze.

He put aside all the larger problems, the complexity of international empires and the threats of foreign invasion. For now, he had to focus on the immediate challenge. Taking back Patliputra.

He heard a rustling in the woods and his hand went to his sword at once. He turned, expecting to see Uttam or one of the other Chandashokas. But it was Tissa, gentle Tissa.

'Do you need to be alone?' his brother asked. 'Say the word, and I will leave you.'

'No,' Ashoka said. 'We have been apart too long. Come, walk with me.'

They walked through a grove of fruit-bearing trees of different kinds. The air was rife with the scent of ripening fruit but when Tissa plucked a mango and nibbled at it with his front teeth, like a rabbit, his reaction left no doubt that it was not ripe enough to eat. He offered the green mango to Ashoka, who declined it. He did not care for kairi, though his mother loved sour raw mangoes. He still remembered seeking out and finding them for her and taking great pleasure in watching her relishing eating it with her food, like a pickle.

'It is worse than I thought,' he told Tissa. 'I never thought that things could deteriorate this badly.'

'It is worse in Patliputra,' Tissa said. 'And much worse for some than for others.'

Ashoka sensed something in Tissa's tone. 'You are speaking of my mother.'

'She is not well kept, I cannot deny that. But I meant those of us who do not conform to the norm. Who are not the ideal model of what people are expected to be.'

Ashoka was lost. 'What are you talking about? What ideal model?'

Tissa glanced at him. 'You know that I prefer men.'

Ashoka nodded. 'It was so from the time we were boys. You used to say even if you became emperor, you would never have any queens, only kings by your side!'

Tissa smiled wistfully, reminded of his childhood naïvete. 'I was a kid then. But I'm not now. I enjoy the company of men, not women. There are others who enjoy the company of their own sex. And those that enjoy both, like Noor Khorasan herself. But in her regime, such things are forbidden.'

'Forbidden? How can anyone forbid love? Everyone is free to love whomever he or she pleases.'

'You know that, and I know that, but our father passed a law that forbids persons of the same sex to find companionship with one another, or enter into spousal relations. Transgression is punishable by torture and imprisonment.'

Ashoka shook his head. 'Surely that cannot fly in the High City? Most of those High Houses are same-sex lovers.'

'The High Houses conduct their affairs in private, behind closed doors guarded by private guards. The ones who suffer these laws are the common citizenry, even those whom the High Houses patronize.' Tissa looked away for a moment. 'I lost my lover, a man who was very dear to me, in one of the raids last year. They tortured him for weeks in the Torture Palace, keeping him alive and sending me parts of his body as "gifts". That was Noor Khorasan's way of getting back at me. That was when I finally knew I had to do something to stop them.'

'Such madness,' Ashoka said. 'As if the Empire doesn't have more pressing concerns than to victimize its own citizens.' He looked at his brother. 'I am so sorry that you had to endure such a loss.'

Tissa smiled back at him. 'You speak as if you haven't suffered worse.'

'The suffering must end for all of us,' Ashoka promised. 'We will end it together, you and I. And when it is done, you must come back to Ujjain with me and hear the word of our Lord Gautama.'

'I have heard of him. But all religious teachings are also forbidden by law now. All religions other than our own, of course.'

'Of course,' Ashoka said. 'Guru Kautilya taught me that one of the first signs of a tyrant is intolerance. Our father has become one. And as his sons, we must end his tyranny.'

13

Jezza Khorasan was going over last-minute details with her lieutenants when her sentries announced the arrival of the Empress. She frowned as she dismissed everyone. Noor Khorasan swept into the tent accompanied by the perpetually present Orzala. Both were dressed somewhat more appropriately than the last time Jezza had seen them, although Noor's ostentatious garb appeared less imperial and more harlot to her gaze. She kept her opinion to herself.

'What is it?' she asked brusquely.

Noor cocked an eyebrow. 'On edge, are we? You were always tense before a battle, mother. Relax. That ragtag band of rebels is no match for the sheer size of the Imperial Army.'

'I'm not interested in discussing military strategy and odds with you,' Jezza said sharply. 'And now is neither the time nor the place to have any other discussion. Whatever you wish to talk about, I suggest you table it until I return to Patliputra.'

Orzala leaned close and whispered something into Noor's

ear. Noor looked at her, eyes dancing, and both women burst out laughing, glancing at Jezza as they did.

Jezza crossed her arms across her chest, not an easy thing to do with her tightly braced armour. She felt her biceps bulge. She was resisting the urge to give both these women two tight slaps.

'Is there something amusing about this?' she asked through tight jaws. 'Or is the prospect of the largest rebellion ever faced by the Empire not daunting enough for you two ladies?'

'Oh, be at ease, mother,' Noor said carelessly. 'I'm in a good mood tonight. Don't spoil it with your usual gloom and doom.'

Jezza shook her head and exhaled as she uncrossed her arms. 'You are a far cry from the Khorasani girl I brought to Patliputra once upon a time, Noor. Back then, you would have fought me if I forbade me from riding into battle with me. Now, look at you. You have turned into a self-absorbed hedonistic pleasure-seeker who has lost touch with present reality.'

Noor laughed as if Jezza had said something uproariously funny. Orzala, on the other hand, sensed the down-shift in Jezza's mood and only smiled to keep her mistress company; her eyes took in Jezza's tight jaw and bunched muscles and lowered her own level of girlish playfulness. Jezza had to give the woman credit: she played the part of a doe-eyed courtesan and playmate exceedingly well but under that disguise, she was a shrewd, intelligent woman with as much political acumen as Noor herself. She knew better than to push Jezza Khorasan when her blood was up as it was now. Then again, she had shared Jezza's bed and body more than once, and had been born into servitude. Noor, on the other hand, had known nothing but power and pleasure for all her adult life.

'Oh mother, really, you can be so adorable when you're mad. That's what Orzala here was just saying. Except, she meant it in a sexually attractive sense. Please stop your fussing. I need to talk to you about a few things before you leave to deal with that pesky problem.'

Jezza knew well enough to be suspicious of her daughter. She wasn't fooled by Noor's playful mood and sweet talk. The Empress was like the wind, capable of being gentle and soothing one minute, tempestuous and stormy the next. Noor wouldn't be here on the eve before a major battle unless she had an agenda. And she would use whatever tactics she felt would achieve her agenda, including being nice. Still, Jezza had no choice but to listen. For all she knew, Noor might have information that could make a difference in tomorrow's battle. Jezza's spy network was excellent, but Noor had her own network, and methods that were spoken of in fearful whispers throughout the Empire, and she always somehow found ways to extract information that even Jezza did not possess at the crucial time.

'Speak then,' Jezza said cautiously. 'Keep it brief. I have a long day tomorrow.'

Noor smiled sweetly, almost reminding her mother of the young girl who had ridden with her to Patliputra all those years ago. Almost. The knowing gleam in her eyes belied that innocent smile.

'Once you have crushed the uprising, I want you to bring Ashoka to Patliputra to be executed if he is still alive. If he's killed on the field, then fetch his body.'

Jezza would have done that anyway. 'You came all the way here at this hour just to tell me that?'

Noor held her smile, meeting Jezza's eyes. 'Queen Mother Apama is dead. Murdered by Shubhadrangi.'

'I see,' Jezza said slowly, not seeing at all. Shubhadrangi was a skeletal wretch, barely able to feed and clean herself, incarcerated in a tiny room at the far end of the palace complex. She was in no condition to undertake such an assassination, not to mention the fact that in order to do so, she would have to overpower the two strapping Khorasani guards constantly at her door, make her way through a busy palace complex, past several hundred armed guards, sentries, palace servants, concubines, other queens, princes and princesses, every single one of whom knew her and would react at the very sight of her, then make her way into the heavily guarded main palace itself—the security of which Jezza had beefed up considerably just recently—fight her way through a few dozen of Patliputra's fiercest and Jezza's own hand-picked warriors, into the Queen Mother's private chambers, then overcome and murder a Greek woman who, though older, was in far better health and almost twice her size and strength, while any number of people watched passively.

It wasn't just impossible, it was so out of the realm of possibility that it would have been more logical had Noor said that the Queen Mother had been struck by a bolt of lightning.

Noor held her gaze, communicating the awareness of these things through her dancing eyes. 'She will be put on trial, of course, found guilty, and summarily executed. I wish her son to witness her execution, to be followed by his own. In the sabha hall, in full view of all the chiefs.'

Jezza stared at Noor.

'I heard that the Emperor is planning a campaign to the northwest,' she said at last, not quite changing the topic, but steering it into an area that aligned with the torrent of thoughts rushing through her mind. 'Since Seleucus Nicator appears to have withdrawn the bulk of his troops in that region to go to the aid of his home state back in Greece.'

Noor's head bobbed. 'The time of the Greeks in this part of the world is at an end. The time has come for the rise of a great empire, the greatest the world has ever seen, and will ever see. Magadha will be more powerful than anyone has ever dreamed. Someday, I will be more powerful than the Greek states too. Then, they will know what it is like to be invaded and conquered.'

Jezza raised her eyebrows. '*You* will be more powerful? You mean the Emperor, do you not?'

Noor tossed her hair carelessly. 'Emperor. Empress. What's the difference? Besides, Bindu is tired. He is weary of politics and bickering. Perhaps he is tired of life itself. He is aging after all, and has lost his virility and his drive. He is not the same man he once was.'

What did you expect, with your debauchery? No wonder Bindusara is tired and old before his time. You played a major part in that.

'And the northwest is a treacherous region,' Jezza said aloud, 'anything might happen on a long campaign. Who knows. Bindusara might not come back home alive at all.'

Noor sighed dramatically. 'He would have sacrificed himself for the greater cause of empire.'

She mimed scribing in the air with an invisible quill in her hand: *'He died building the greatest empire.'*

'Leaving you to be an Empress without an Emperor. Ruler of the great Magadhan Empire.'

Noor's eyes flashed. 'Ruler of the *world!* Can't you just see it, mother? With your military brilliance, and my political genius, we would be unstoppable! The world will be our oyster.'

Jezza felt sick to her stomach. She had known for a long time that this woman was no longer the young, fiercely ambitious but still honourable Khorasani wildcat she had brought with her to Patliputra all those years ago. Now, she saw that the girl had become not a woman, but a monstress. She knew that the path Noor was on would lead ultimately to self-destruction. It was the way such things went. In time, when even Jezza's presence became...inconvenient, Jezza would find a blade thrust into her throat while she slept in her tent of night. Quite likely put there by that sly-eyed vixen, Orzala. She would have bet any sum that it had been Orzala who killed Apama. Other queens, even princes, princesses, some no more than a year or two old, had been snuffed out simply because they, or their tribe, fell out of favour with Noor Khorasan. As brilliant a lover as she was, Orzala was a far more brilliant assassin.

She saw Orzala watching her with the cold, unblinking stare of a snake. *I should take my sword and run it through her right now,* she thought. *Through both of them. This is as good a chance as any.*

But as corrupt as she herself was, she was not yet her daughter. She could never be Noor. In her breast, a mother's heart still beat. And she could never dishonour herself and her line by murdering her own daughter.

And that weakness will be your downfall, she thought sadly.

Aloud, she showed nothing of these emotions.

She only said, 'You are a genius, daughter. I shall do as you say. I shall bring Ashoka to you, dead or alive, hopefully alive. And we shall finish this masquerade once and for all.'

Noor laughed and clapped her hands, delighted. Jezza saw that she had been expecting an argument, an outburst, perhaps even anger and outright disagreement. Perhaps Orzala had a dagger concealed in her robes even now, just in case. After all, legendary though she was as a commander, she was replaceable. All military commanders were. A structure as vast and storied as the Magadhan army could survive the loss of a Jezza Khorasan. It was crucial to Noor's plan that whomever commanded the army was aligned with her political agenda, and that was what she had come to make sure of tonight. She did not want any disagreement or surprises when the time came to execute Ashoka and his mother on trumped-up charges. She needed Jezza to side with her unwaveringly. And if Jezza had shown any resistance tonight, well, an orphan Empress was still an Empress.

'How wonderful,' Noor said, rising to leave. 'I will leave you to your preparations then. And wish you good blooding on the morrow. Would you like Orzala to stay and keep you company awhile? She is wonderful at helping take one's mind off the cares of tomorrow.'

Jezza forced a smile. 'Not tonight, thank you. I have no cares. I am prepared and ready to do what's needed to ensure the supremacy of the great Magadhan Empire. Good night, daughter.'

They left as dervishes in the night, leaving her tent opening flapping briefly, and the lingering fragrance of their attar perfumes.

To Jezza Khorasan, it smelled like death and corruption.

14

They met up with the main force about fifty miles from Patliputra. As they emerged from the shelter of the forest, Ashoka looked back over his shoulder and viewed the entirety of the Chandashokas for the first time. Twenty thousand strong, all dressed in the sombre black of the parent Order from which they had risen—they made a formidable sight. He felt a strange surge of pride for these revolutionary outcasts. The seed of outrage at the injustice meted out to the Chandikas had grown into this mighty oak. But it was more than just that: from all the stories he had heard these past weeks on the road, he knew that the revolution had attracted people who had suffered injustice in all walks of life. There were lower castes, outcasts, abused women, servants and even former soldiers in this small force. The one thing all these disparate groups and individuals had in common was that they had all suffered injustice at the hands of the Mauryavansh Empire in these past years. Come to think of it, he was one of them too, because he too had suffered injustice at the hands of his own Empire.

Someone ahead shouted out to the leaders: Ashoka, Uttam,

and Tissa were the three to whom everyone looked for leadership at present. Though Uttam had said they would meet the other leaders of the Chandashokas here. The shouts were to alert them that someone was coming, fast!

Ashoka scanned the horizon and saw riders approaching at a full gallop.

Ashoka and the other leaders reined in their mounts and waited for the riders.

They arrived with horses frothing at the mouth, and their faces darkened by the dust of the road.

'Mauryavansh is on the march!' said the first rider. 'Their armies are to the North and East of the capital city!'

The other riders brought similar tidings with different locations. Mauryavansh armies were being sighted on the move, heading away from the city in several directions.

'What are they up to?' Tissa wondered. 'Are they going to quell a rebellion somewhere?'

Uttam shrugged. 'What does it matter? There is unrest everywhere. This is good news for us! The more Mauryavansh regiments leaving the city unguarded, the better it is for us! Our path to the capital is clear now. Let us ride straight for Patliputra and take it. We can be there within the week!'

Both he and Uttam looked at Ashoka. He shook his head. 'This is not good news. The movements are not for our benefit. They are not leaving the capital city unguarded. They are taking up positions to keep us at bay.'

Ashoka dismounted from his horse and used a stick to draw a large circle.

'Patliputra,' he said. He pointed with the stick at the forward scouts. 'Call out the locations where you sighted Mauryavansh regiments on the move, and their direction.'

As the scouts called out the information, Ashoka drew rough

arrows indicating the troop positions and directions. When he was done, the large circle was surrounded by arrows heading in a definite pattern.

Uttam cursed. 'You are right. They are forming a protective chakra around the city.'

'All they have to do is keep rotating fresh troops to whichever direction we are attacking from and they can keep us at bay forever.'

As Ashoka reviewed numbers aloud, the situation began to seem even more bleak.

Mauryavansh had its own standing army of some 150,000 footsoldiers, 20,000 cavalry, 12,000 chariots, and 8,000 elephants. These were all garrisoned in and around the capital city itself. Apart from these forces, the Imperial Army conscripted resources from all the five hundred tribes and nations that made up the republic of states that was the Mauryavansh Empire. Every tribe or nation was required by law to dedicate two-thirds of its fighting resources to the Empire: this served as a deterrent against rebellion as well as gave Mauryavansh a military advantage that was unmatched by any other army in the known world. According to their intelligence, the Imperial Army currently counted 900,000 footsoldiers, 180,000 cavalry, 94,000 chariots and 26,000 elephants. These were apart from the capital's own garrison.

New riders kept arriving, bringing further updates.

The good news was that the majority of the Empire's armies were garrisoned in far flung locations, mostly occupied with quelling dissent and unrest in troubled areas, or maintaining borders. This took up the majority of the resources. But from the accounts coming in from their scouts, anywhere between 80,000 to 100,000 foot-troops, at least 50,000 cavalry, some 40,000 chariots, and 9,000 elephants were being moved back in the vicinity of Patliputra.

It took several days before the entire picture emerged. They set up camp and established a Command Centre as they added new incoming information and added the numbers. The final tally was staggering.

'Two hundred and sixty-five thousand foot soldiers, seventy-five thousand cavalry, fifty-four thousand chariots, seventeen thousand elephants,' Uttam reeled off. He looked at Ashoka. 'Their cavalry alone equals our total numbers.'

'Tell me again,' Ashoka said, 'what is our final strength?'

'Seventy thousand in all. Forty thousand on foot, thirty mounted.'

'No chariot or elephants?'

Uttam shrugged. 'Maybe two thousand chariots, five or six hundred elephants, but they hardly count.'

'Everything counts in a war.' Ashoka made a note of the numbers.

'Ashoka, this is impossible. We cannot face such large numbers.'

'The numbers were the same when you came to me. Nothing has changed.'

'Everything has changed! When we came to you in Ujjain, we were not expecting Patliputra to know we were attacking. The Imperial Troops were deployed elsewhere. Now, they have all been pulled back to defend the capital city. It's an unbreakable wall.'

'We always knew they outnumbered us.'

'This is not being outnumbered. This is being massacred. Look at those numbers, Ashoka. How can we fight such forces?'

'What would you like to do then? Give up and continue living a life as an outlaw, making small strikes against the Empire for the rest of your life?'

'What choice do we have? How do we face such a formidable force?'

Ashoka looked down at the maps and the scrolls covered with numbers. 'The way all wars are fought, with strategy and determination.'

Tissa set down the stringed instrument he had been toying with all day. 'Ashoka is right. The Imperial Army is not going to get any smaller over time. It will only keep growing. The longer we wait, the more we have to lose.'

'Our numbers will also grow,' Uttam said. 'We are gaining new recruits every day, they come in from every corner of the Empire, people who want to join our cause, who believe in what you represent, Ashoka. A new Empire, a new hope. In a few years, we could be twice as strong in numbers.'

'And Mauryavansh will double the forces against us. Do you think they are going to sit still? You know the first law of empire. Acharya Kautilya calls it the cornerstone of empire building.'

'An Empire is a tree, either it grows, or it withers and dies.' Tissa recited. 'What Ashoka means is that if we double our numbers, Mauryavansh will also grow in territory and annexations, and its Imperial conscripts will be another hundred thousand, perhaps two hundred thousand more by then.'

'And they are still only sending barely two in ten of their total number against us now. In a few years, if we survive and continue to be a threat, they could throw four hundred thousand against us. Or half a million. Even if we number two hundred thousand by then, how would we fight five hundred thousand? The odds will not improve in our favour, Uttam.'

A new voice spoke from the tent entrance: 'The only time is now, the only way forward is through.'

They looked around.

Ashoka saw a young woman, accompanied by two women of varying ages, and a younger man, barely a boy.

'That was also said by your guru, Acharya Kautilya, was it not?'

Ashoka inclined his head. 'It was. He was speaking of the moment in a battle when things seem their worst. He was referring to the fact that sometimes, despite the odds being against you and the tide of battle seeming to oppose you, you could still turn an impending defeat into victory provided—'

'Provided your desire to win was greater than that of your enemy.' The woman who had spoken went over to a table where refreshments had been laid out. She picked up a clay bowl and sipped from it, made a face, put it down, and picked up another one. 'That is why we are all here, is it not? Because we want to defeat the monster that is Mauryavansh?'

Uttam gestured towards her. 'Meet Kaurwaki of Kalinga.' He gestured towards the other two women and the solitary man. 'Sharda of the Gujjars. Namonamah of Myanmar. And Kaurwa, also of Kalinga, Kaurwaki's brother.'

Ashoka and Tissa both greeted the new arrivals. Tissa too was meeting them for the first time, as his role until recently had mainly involved assisting the revolution from within the imperial family.

'Well met,' Ashoka said to the woman who had first spoken. She was still picking up and tasting different bowls, tasting various fruits and breads. He noticed that she did not touch any of the meats. 'How is it that you know of the Acharya's teachings even in distant Kalinga?'

She looked at him over the rim of a bowl, sipping it slowly. 'People in distant Athens know Kautilya's teachings. So do our brothers and sisters in the great Cathay kingdom. He is a philosopher ranked alongside the greatest minds of all time. In Cathay, they called him the Sun Tzu of Jambudwipa, but I told them they were wrong.' She took another sip from the bowl and considered it with a sceptical expression. 'I told them that it was Sun Tzu who was the Kautilya of Cathay!'

Ashoka smiled. 'Well said.'

He picked up a bowl and offered it to her. 'Sample this one.'

She tasted of it and shook her head, making a face. 'No, that will not do at all. I have been on the road for weeks. I need nourishment, not intoxication.'

'Honey mead from Vrindavan is both,' Ashoka said.

She snorted. 'Everyone does not have the palate of you princes of Patliputra, Samrat Ashoka. We ordinary mortals prefer something more down to earth.' She raised the only bowl she had sampled more than once. 'I will stick with this, thank you.'

'You call me a prince of Patliputra, and emperor in the same sentence. I am neither.'

She dipped a heel of bread in the bowl and bit off a big bite. Crumbs dribbled into the bowl. 'You are one by birth, and the other you will claim by force.'

'Only if it is what the people want.'

She laughed, spraying bread and broth. 'The people? What do you know of the people? You lived your early years in the forest with your mother, then spent your youth in the Imperial Palace and now you have come out of Ujjain where you lived as the son-in-law to the wealthiest merchant. A silver spoon has never been far from your lips, son of Bindusara. You know nothing of the people or of their wants and needs.'

Ashoka dusted off the crumbs she had deposited on his vastra. 'I do not deny my birth or the facts of my life. But if you know that much about me, then you also know that all was not roses and wine for me. I have experienced my share of injustice as much as anyone else in the Empire.'

She ate ravenously, seemingly more interested in her nourishment than in the conversation. 'Oh, I know all about your suffering. So what? Do you think that makes you special? Are you the only one who has suffered in all of Mauryavansh?'

'No, but—'

'You have a title, a claim to wealth, privilege, power, opportunity that millions live and die without ever having. Do you know how hard it is to be born without anything, to have to eke out a survival as a nobody, a mere cipher in the uncounted unwashed populace of the Empire? To be the lowest of the low castes, the one who gets treated worse than even the dogs of the whorehouse? To be born differently abled, or to have anything different about yourself, like not being good-looking or pretty, or to be fatter or odd shaped, or have a preference for your own sex, or to have a mind or body that works differently than most "normal" people? Do you know what it means not to be perfect, beautiful, strong, rich and powerful?'

Ashoka found a brief moment when she paused to swallow. 'I can't claim to be all of those things or none of those things. But in case you haven't noticed, I am not the handsomest of men. Beautiful is not a word anyone would use when describing me.'

'Oh, I feel so sorry for you!' she exclaimed with venomous irony. She tore off a piece of a roasted yam and attacked it with the same intensity as she was attacking the argument. 'You poor little rich prince of Patliputra, sleeping with anyone you choose, going incognito to the Lower City to see how the other half lives, fighting in the pits to hone your skills. You had such a hard, horrible life.'

'Kaurwaki,' Uttam said from behind her. He shook his head at Ashoka, making a face and gesturing an apology. 'He is one of us...'

Kaurwaki turned on Uttam, her dark brown eyes flashing. 'He will never be one of us! Don't you understand? If we succeed, he will be Emperor and sit high above us all for the rest of his life. He will be ruler of the greatest empire in the world! And if we fail, he can go back to Ujjain and live out his life as a rich merchant's son-in-law. He has nothing to lose in this fight. He is and will always be a Prince of Mauryavansh, no matter what he says or does. That is what privilege and entitlement mean. You are either born with it or not. You can deny it and abuse it, that doesn't change anything. He has something which elevates him above everyone else and whether or not he realizes it, that sets him apart from the rest of us ordinary people. He is not one of us. He is nothing like us.'

Everyone was silent. The other new arrivals were eating as well, listening quietly to the argument. Kaurwaki's brother was grinning openly, clearly pleased by his sister's outburst. From his expression, Ashoka guessed he had witnessed her doing this before.

He spread his hands, tilting his head. 'You are right.'

Kaurwaki looked at him, still chewing.

'You are right, Kaurwaki of Kalinga. I am privileged, a prince, an heir to an empire, I am all of the things you say about me. I have never denied that. But there are other princes of Mauryavansh. My elder brother Sushim is one. He is crown prince of Patliputra now. Heir to the Empire. He is privileged, entitled, all the things I am, as well as many more—he is handsome, enjoys all the privileges of his position to the hilt, treats everyone around him as inferior, abuses and tortures those weaker than he, and is a tyrant in everything he does. Do you see no difference between him and me?'

Kaurwaki chewed her food thoughtfully. 'I did not say you were like Sushim.'

'But you did. When you made such sweeping statements about me, you put me in the same league as him and my other brothers and sisters. Are you saying we are not all the same?'

She tilted her head, still eating. 'You are not Sushim. He is a monster.'

'And I am not?'

'Perhaps not.'

'Then you admit that all those who are privileged are not the same.'

'Of course. But they are unlike the rest of us who live in the real world. And so you can never truly know what it means to be the likes of us.'

'I have never claimed that. Each one of us is born within his or her own skin. We only know what we live through ourselves. But that does not mean we do not have empathy. I am not a Vyag or a dog, yet I find them both beautiful lovable animals.'

'You love Vyag?' she asked, raising her eyebrow.

'I love all animals. I find them more fit to live on this earth than we mortals. I do not have to possess four paws or a tail to feel as I do for them. It is possible to be one thing and yet have empathy for those who are unlike us.'

She nodded. 'Perhaps.'

'Then consider this. I may not have suffered as others have. But I *have* suffered. I am no Sushim who simply experienced power and privilege and knew nothing else since his first waking moment. I have known pain, sorrow, suffering, torture, anguish, grief, loss, betrayal, treachery, misery... I have known and seen things that are not meant to be known and seen by princes of Patliputra. I did not go into the Lower City and fight in the pits because I was bored or sought adventure. I went because I consider all people to be one, because I wanted to know what those not like me felt, experienced, lived through and suffered. I wanted to experience life as a person, not a prince. I am still doing that. My father-in-law's wealth is not my wealth. I had no say in the matter of his choosing to help me that day in Takshashila. I fell in love with his daughter because our hearts met and we found true love. Have I known happiness in my life? Privilege? Power? Wealth? Royalty? Yes. I did not ask for it, nor did I misuse it, as Sushim does. I discarded it, turned my back on it. That is why I am here today. Not to regain my position in the dynasty, or to unseat my father and brother and move up in the line of succession. I am here because I want all people to have a better life, myself included. Not just princes and princesses, rich and beautiful, but you, Kaurwaki, and everyone else. I believe all beings are equal, and have equal right to the resources of our world. And the only way to do that is fighting this fight and winning this war. I am not here to lead you or order you because I am superior. I am here to fight alongside you and bleed and struggle with you.'

Kaurwaki finished eating and set down the bowl, dusting off her tunic and wiping her mouth with the back of her sleeve. She looked around and caught Uttam's eye. 'He'll do.'

She turned back to Ashoka and winked. 'You've come a long way from Takshashila, lion of Maurya. You weren't ready to take on this challenge then. I think you're ready to do this now.'

15

The Business of War. That's what it all comes down to in the end.

Ashoka looked across the field at the lines of black-clad Chandashokas, twenty-two thousand strong and still growing by the day. He felt proud to be leading them. The past days had been rigorous and gruelling, preparing for the coming battle. But ultimately, preparations could only achieve so much. At some point, every army went to war, and only war itself proved if they were ready. He felt confident the Chandashokas were ready. And so were the rest of the revolutionary army.

Queen Tissyanka and Tissa stood at the head of the main army, fifty-five thousand strong and also growing each day as new recruits turned up demanding to join their cause. The Tissar regiments formed the core of the main army, with other allied forces sympathetic to Tissar joining in, but the bulk of the revolutionary army consisted of people from assorted tribes and nations across Jambudwipa. Ashoka swept his gaze across their ranks and, as in the case of the Chandashokas, he saw a diversity of features, skin colours, eye shapes and races as varied as that of the subcontinent itself. Three hundred different languages, religions, cultures and sets of traditions, but here on this field, they were all one force, fighting for one cause. Freedom from the tyranny of the Mauryavansh Empire as it was today.

He could see movement amidst the lines at the far end of the field as new arrivals kept rushing to join. Uttam was at that end, along with his lieutenants, managing the inflow. At the current rate, over a thousand new arrivals were joining their ranks. If only they could wait a few more months, even a year, they would have a formidable army. But that assumed too many things: that the rate of new inflow would remain the same. That Mauryavansh would remain static. And that all else would remain the same.

Nothing was static in life. Everything changed all the time. Either one grew or one withered, like a tree. A year from now, the revolutionary army could be four hundred strong—and the Mauryavansh army could be two million strong. They had received word that Patliputra was conscripting recruits at thrice the rate they were: by offering war wages. War wages? Ashoka and his allies could hardly manage to feed and clothe their forces, leave alone pay them. Over the course of a year, how would they survive? Elephants and horses need feeding, saddles and shoes needed repairing, chariots needed refurbishing, weapons needed forging, stomachs needed filling... Ashoka knew—as did his friends—that they could not sustain even a single winter like this. Mauryavansh could sustain—and grow. They had access to granaries in every nation, dedicated legions of hunters, butchers, cooks, blacksmiths, furriers, shoemakers, carpenters, woodcutters, every conceivable kind of craftsman, and a war chest of virtually unlimited depth. A war tax had been levied on all the five hundred kingdoms, and even at a conservative estimate, the fortune amassed by this tax alone could sustain the Mauryavansh army for a year. Patliputra would not even need to touch their own treasury or reserves for this war. While Ashoka's people were living hand-to-mouth, barely able to sustain themselves day by day.

The Business of War.

It was a dirty business. One that reduced lives to coin. But if they wanted to defeat an Empire, they had to fight both battles: the war on the field and the war of the spirit. And the war of the field was an expensive enterprise. Which was why they had to engage the enemy sooner rather than later.

Mauryavansh could afford to wait them out, to grow fatter and richer and stronger over time. While they grew poorer and weaker and thinner.

They had to fight while they still could, while the weather was still endurable, their weapons still sharp, their bodies still strong.

But that did not mean they had to fight the Empire on its own terms.

Or on its own ground.

That was what their strategy was based on.

The Business of War.

Ashoka gave the signal to Tissa and to Kaurwaki.

Tissa passed the word to his mother. Queen Tissyanka called her troops to order and announced their marching orders.

Kaurwaki did the same with her lieutenants. The Chandashokas uttered their trademark 'Ho' in a belligerent tone, slamming their feet down on the ground. Ashoka felt the ground shudder beneath his horse's hooves. Both regiments were eager to march out. Weeks of preparation and training and drilling were all well and good, but they were itching to fight Maurya troops, to avenge their past injustices and right wrongs. And to do that they needed to go to battle. They would get their chance.

He watched as the long lines of black clad troops rolled out proudly. The lines of elephant and chariot and cavalry were smaller than that of any Maurya contingent he had seen, but he felt a surge of pride as they marched past.

We may be few but we fight for the right reasons.

Uttam came riding up to him as the last of the legions were going by.

'Ashoka, we have sightings of Mauryavansh forces ten miles north east. They are standing on the plains, just waiting.'

'How many?'

'At least one hundred thousand footsoldiers strong, I am awaiting detailed breakdowns of akshohini, but it's safe to say that there will be at least forty thousand cavalry, thirty thousand chariots and ten thousand elephants.'

Ashoka nodded. This confirmed the reports of troop movements they had been receiving the past few weeks.

'And there's more.'

Ashoka waited.

'Another thirty thousand foot are coming up on our west flank, and about the same number on our east flank. Those are mostly cavalry and elephants.'

Ashoka nodded. It was as they had expected. 'They are looking to box us in. Surround us on three sides and crush our vanguard, then push us back the way we came. Once we turn to retreat, they will chase us and hunt us down.'

Uttam nodded. 'Aye, just as we anticipated.'

Both men looked at each other.

Then both men grinned.

Ashoka raised his hand. Uttam slapped his open palm and clasped Ashoka's forearm.

'Our spies did their jobs,' Ashoka said. 'They passed on the news that we were planning to march on Patliputra today and launch a direct assault on the capital.'

'And Patliputra responded by sending their main force to meet us halfway. Seeking to stop us before we could get too close.'

Uttam continued grinning. 'They think we will meet them in the open field, in a head-to-head battle, and with their superior numbers, they will easily crush us and trample us into the ground.'

'They're right,' Ashoka said. 'If we face them head on in the field, they *will* crush and trample us into the ground. It would be over for us in less than a day.'

They grinned at each other.

'But we will do it anyway!' Ashoka said.

'Yes we will!'

'Because we are revolutionaries.'

'We are fighting for freedom.'

'For justice.'

'For equality.'

'For a new hope.'

'An Empire that serves the people, not oppresses them.'

They laughed aloud.

'Shall we go about it, then, brother?'

'Yes, brother, let's go to war!'

And with the same mad grins on their faces, they rode after their marching army, all the way to the heads of the long lines, where the leaders of their forces rode.

Kaurwaki took one look at their faces and said: 'Idiots.'

Tissa and his mother had ridden up to join them.

'What are you two grinning about?' Queen Tissyanka asked. 'You look like two cats who have eaten the dog!'

'Not yet, my Queen, but soon we shall, soon we shall,' Uttam said, riding off to issue instructions to the lieutenants of the Chandashokas. Ashoka remained with the other leaders.

'Queen Mother,' he said to Tissyanka. 'We are not marching to Patliputra.'

'We are *not*?' she asked, astonished. Tissa looked just as surprised.

'No,' Ashoka replied. 'We had no intention of ever marching directly on Patliputra at all. It would be madness. We do not have the numbers for a direct assault.'

'Then what do you intend to do?' she asked. 'Mauryavansh's forces are only a few miles away now. We will reach them within two days at most. They will not simply let us retreat now. They mean to crush us outright.'

'We are counting on that,' he replied. 'Our entire plan revolves on their coming all this way to meet us. That is what we were waiting for before we could make our move.'

'I don't understand,' Tissa said. 'Where will we go now? What will we do?'

Ashoka gestured at the hills to the far right, on the horizon now, but barely thirty-five or forty miles away. 'There is a pass through the hills, it is the only way across the range. Mauryavansh's forces will not use the pass because they will fear it could be a trap. They will come around it from the west.'

'Yes?' Tissyanka said. 'And then?'

'We will go through the pass.'

'Through it?' she said. 'But that pass does not lead anywhere except...'

Ashoka watched her frown as she recalled the geography of the region.

'It does not lead anywhere except to Kalinga,' he offered.

She frowned. 'I don't understand.'

Tissa grinned. 'I do.'

She looked at her son. 'What?'

Tissa pointed at the hills. 'He means to take us through to

Kalinga. Mauryavansh will converge from all three sides on where they expect us to be, while we slip through the pass and race towards Kalinga. They will have no choice but to follow us there.'

'But what will that achieve?' Tissyanka asked, looking confused. 'Kalinga is no ally of Mauryavansh. Nor is it party to our revolutionary cause. It remains suspicious of all of us. Their enmity with our people is old and deep. They are not likely to welcome us with open arms.'

Ashoka nodded. 'They won't. But someone else will.'

'Who?'

Ashoka smiled enigmatically. 'We will meet them soon enough. You will see for yourself. I will say no more at this stage, except to ask you to divert your forces to the pass. For now, that is all our soldiers need to know. The rest will become clear very soon.'

'But Ashoka—'

He smiled at Tissyanka. 'There will be fighting, and it will not be easy. Blood will be shed and we will have to fight hard for our cause. But if this goes as planned, we have a fighting chance of coming out of it alive. That is more than the odds we had if we were to march directly on Patliputra.'

'I still don't understand.'

'It doesn't matter, Queen Mother. We are all fighting the same war. The rest is strategy. And the business of war itself.'

He waved goodbye and rode away from them.

Kaurwaki rode with him, easily keeping pace.

'That was typically cryptic.'

'We agreed that only the three of us would know the final strategy.'

'Yes,' she agreed. 'We did.'

'And that we would not reveal these manoeuvres until it was too late for Mauryavansh to counter them.'

'True.'

'Then we are doing what we agreed.'

'Agreed. But do you have to be so damn smug about it?'

He grinned, showing her his teeth.

She reached across to slap him, but he rode away, dodging the slap.

She shook her head, smiling too, despite herself. 'This had better work, Prince of Patliputra. A lot of lives are depending on us now.'

16

They came through the pass without incident.

Ashoka had stopped grinning days ago. The initial euphoria he had felt at having tricked his father into sending the army to stop him had passed. It was a very minor success and it only meant something if the next stage succeeded as well. If they were wrong and the Mauryavansh armies came through the pass, it would be a slaughter. They would have been boxed in on all sides in a narrow pass, with nowhere to go, overwhelmed by vastly superior numbers. Ashoka had suffered nightmares worrying about this very moment. But when he saw the clear open fields ahead and the ground began to dip again, he knew they were through and out.

He pulled his horse over to the side and waited as the long lines passed by. The other leaders saw him and also turned their mounts aside, joining him. Tissa, Tissyanka, Uttam, Kaurwaki, Kaurwa, Sharda and Namonamah. When they were all beside him, and the bulk of their forces had exited the pass, he turned in his seat to address them.

'We have only a short time before Mauryavansh realizes what we have done, so I will make this brief,' he said. 'By now you have all realized that we are not heading directly for Patliputra.'

'We guessed as much,' said Sharda in the dry caustic way she had.

'I am sorry that I could not reveal more to you before now, but it was imperative that we let the spies believe that we were marching to Patliputra. That was the only way we could force the Emperor to counter us by sending the bulk of his forces to block us off.'

'What if he had not done that?' Namonamah asked.

'He had no choice,' Uttam explained.

'Why is that?'

'Because we intercepted and stole the soldiers' pay wagons last month. If he kept the army at the capital city, they would demand to be paid. He sent them after us with the goal of getting back the pay wagons we stole.'

'Where are these pay wagons?' Tissyanka asked.

Ashoka gestured to Kaurwa. The young boy grinned. 'They were stripped off all the gold meant for the soldiers pay and refilled with boxes of rocks.'

'Rocks?' Tissa asked. 'But what does that achieve?'

'The Mauryavansh armies will continue to chase us because they believe we have their pay. We are counting on that. To maintain that illusion, we needed the wagons to appear as heavy as if they were carrying coin. That's why we used rocks.'

'And the actual coin?'

'It will be passed around to our soldiers, as their first pay. Compliments of the Empire,' Uttam said proudly.

'What does all this have to do with this detour?' Sharda asked. 'Why are you leading us out of the killing trap and into the serpent's lair? No offence, Kaurwaki, Kaurwa. Everyone knows that while you two are revolutionaries, your nation doesn't support the revolution itself politically.'

'They still don't,' Kaurwaki said. 'Kalinga neither wishes to join the Mauryavansh Empire nor to support our revolution. I am here in my capacity as an individual, as is my brother. We have past grievances with Patliputra. They killed our parents and my elder brother. I want to see Bindusara dethroned and in an ideal world, I would like to see the Empire dismantled and thrown into the cesspool where all Empires belong. But until that day, I would settle for a less rapacious emperor than Bindusara, someone who is still from the privileged class, but not as much a bastard as his father and brothers.'

'We all know why you agreed to support Ashoka's bid to replace his father. But that still doesn't explain this manoeuvre. Why lead our forces into your sovereign territory when you know that will bring the Mauryavansh army in our wake? When Bindusara learns that Kalinga has allowed the revolutionary army to enter its territory, he may not care for the fine distinctions you have about supporting us as individuals or as a nation.'

Kaurwaki looked pointedly at Ashoka. 'This is the extent of my agreement with Ashoka. He asked me to permit us to enter Kalinga territory up to a point. We cannot go closer than a hundred miles from the capital city. This is only a military tactic, he said. To know more, you will have to ask him yourself. That is the extent of my knowledge.'

Everyone turned to look at Ashoka expectantly. 'I apologize for the secrecy but I ask you all to bear with me a little longer. All I can say right now is that we will be turning around and taking a stand soon. Mauryavansh will realize that we slipped through the pass and they will come after us soon enough.'

'Especially since they want their salaries!' Uttam added.

Sharda made a sound of disbelief. 'And you expect us to fare better then? Is there some sorcery in the soil of Kalinga that you expect will double or triple our numbers overnight? We will still be outnumbered and outmatched, and still no closer to Patliputra than we are now. In fact, we will be farther away!'

Ashoka nodded. 'I know it seems insane. We are counting on Mauryavansh thinking the same thing. We want them to believe we lost our nerve when we saw their numbers and tried to escape into Kalinga out of sheer desperation. The pay wagons will draw them in and when they see us, they will rush at us trying to destroy us in a single clash. Our plan depends on this happening.'

'And how is this a plan at all? Unless you intend to get us all killed!' Tissyanka asked. 'Surely that is not your intention?'

Ashoka smiled grimly. 'All I can say is that we have reached out to allies who we hope will come to our aid in our time of need. All we need to do is hold out until they arrive and outflank the Mauryavansh forces. When that happens, we will push forward and hopefully crush Mauryavansh on the field.'

'Crush Mauryavansh on the field! He makes it sound like we are grinding grain in a corn mill!' Sharda laughed caustically. 'I know you are not talking of Kalinga helping you. That will never happen. So who are these mysterious allies?'

Ashoka smiled enigmatically but did not answer the Gujjar's question.

He gestured at the last of the lines going past. 'Time now to rejoin our ranks. We need to move fast and take up defensive positions on the plains below. Uttam, Kaurwaki, Kaurwa and I will explain the positions we have scouted out and selected for our stand. Word would have reached Mauryavansh already about our little detour. We had best be making haste. There is much to do and little time in which to do it. And on the morrow, perhaps two days at most, we will have a battle to fight.'

17

They watched as the clouds of dust on the horizon resolved into the frontlines of the Mauryavansh army. Chariots and cavalry rode out first in alternate regiments, spreading far and wide to cover a front of several miles. Even spread out as they were, they made a formidable sight. Tens upon tens of thousands of wheels rumbling, hooves pounding and armour and helmets gleaming in the early morning sun. They kept coming and coming in seemingly endless rows, until the entire horizon was covered from end to end with a sea of glittering metal.

Behind them would come the infantry, with the elephants dispersed among them. The chariots would act as the battering ram, breaking the face of the enemy army. Next came the cavalry, riding through fast and furious, cutting down those still reeling from the crushing chariot wheels. And if you survived the wheel and the horse, the elephants would pound you down, with the footsoldiers following to finish the job. It had served the Empire well in a thousand battles and a hundred wars and there was no reason why it should not work here as well. The revolutionary force was less than a third of the Empire's army and with barely any wheel or elephant to speak of. There would be no need for elaborate tactics or finesse to this battle. One battering charge was all it would take.

Ashoka was counting on that. Everything he had planned up to this point depended on that charge.

'Ready for range,' he said to Uttam. Uttam nodded and gave the signal. It was passed on through their lines.

Ashoka watched the approaching cloud of dust. He could distinguish the chariots from the horses now, and the cavalry behind them as well. The chariots were finding the going relatively easy so far but he could see the patch of stony ground a few hundred yards ahead of them. He was waiting for the chariots to reach that stony ground and be forced to slow down.

Beyond them on the rise, he saw the footsoldiers of Mauryavansh appear, as numerous as a swarm of ants on the carcass of a dead buffalo. So that was what a hundred thousand men looked like in battle. Like a swarm of ants and a cloud of dust. Except that every one of those ants was armed with a sword and a spear and even if Ashoka cut him down, he would be replaced by a hundred more, or a thousand.

'Ready for firing,' he said. Uttam passed it on.

Ashoka watched the approaching frontline of chariots. They were still a good mile away from his position, but the instructions he was giving were being conveyed to a regiment much closer to those onrushing wheels.

He watched as the order reached that regiment and they rose as one man from the rocks behind which they had been waiting all morning. Archers. Each with a longbow and a quiver of arrows with metal tips designed to fly three hundred yards and punch through armour, skin, flesh and organs. There were only three thousand of them, against thirty-five thousand chariots, but he had high hopes for them.

He watched as the first of the chariots reached the stony patch and slowed. Ashoka had gone over that ground twice before, once when he had scouted out this site a month earlier, and yesterday, when he had gone over the final tactics for today's battle. The stones were loose and far between, which would force the charioteers to go slow enough to avoid damaging a wheel or breaking the leg of a horse. He waited until the bulk of the chariots were in the stony patch before he gave the next order.

'Prepare for first volley,' he said.

The order went down the line and he saw the archers on the

rocks below raising their bows skywards, gauging the angle and distance to the approaching chariots.

It was time.

'Loose!' Ashoka cried.

He watched as the first volley of arrows rose, sliced the upturned blue bowl of the sky, and turned earthwards again. He heard the shouts and yells of the charioteers as they saw the incoming volley. The hail of arrows fell on the chariots with a sound like rain on a tin roof, clattering tunelessly.

He saw charioteers struck by the arrows, falling from their chariot wells, pitching forward onto the ground, under the hooves of their own horse teams, or falling where they stood.

'Again!' he shouted.

Again the arcing rays of death defied the earth and rose, again the earth called them back and they returned to her. More charioteers fell. Those that survived tried to push on faster through the stony patch, breaking wheels, horses' legs, and some even overturned as chariot teams who had lost their charioteers turned head and collided with other chariots and horses.

'Again!' and yet again, over and over, till the quivers of the bowmen were empty and the stony patch was a crazy quilt of fallen men, panicked horses and overturned chariots.

He saw Uttam frowning as he tried to assess the fallen chariot and waited for the numbers.

'One in seven down!' Uttam cried out. 'Maybe even one in six!'

'Replenish the bowmen! Prepare for the next volley!' Ashoka ordered. He took a moment to gauge the first attack.

Those were good numbers. Any battle which took one in ten of enemy numbers was a decimation. They had taken down one in six or seven of enemy chariots in their first assault itself. And without losing a single one of their own men.

But this was not the time to gloat or celebrate. The battle was only an hour old and there were hundreds of thousands of the enemy still on the field.

The first chariots were across the stony patch now. Ashoka watched as shouts rang out and then the chariots began to turn, racing towards a new target: the rocks where his bowmen stood. The charioteers all had their shortbows ready and as he watched grimly, they began firing. Their first arrows fell short or went wide, but as they drew closer, they found the right range and he saw bowmen struck, falling, toppling from the rocks. The fresh quivers were being passed up to them, and the archers began to fire back at the approaching charioteers, but this time the charioteers had the advantage. More and more of their arrows found their mark, and more and more bowmen fell, sprouting arrows with the distinctive fletching of Mauryavansh.

'Bowmen, retreat!' Ashoka called, and watched as the signal was passed on. The surviving bowmen scrabbled to get into cover, disappearing into the gaps between the large rocks. The charioteers continued to loose arrows but when they saw their quarry had disappeared, they turned the heads of their horses and resumed their original charge—heading directly towards the main body of Ashoka's forces.

'Bowmen to loose from cover!' he called out.

He waited till the order was conveyed, giving the bowmen time to estimate the trajectory and angle required to loose from *behind* the rocks which gave them shelter. Their bows were aimed almost straight up at the sky, angled just enough to carry their missiles over the first wave of charioteers who were already across the stony patch. It was no use continuing to harangue those chariots, they were already past the line of the rocks so that would mean firing backwards towards the revolutionary lines—never a good idea.

As the chariot regiments struggled across the stony patch, stopping to help downed comrades, manoeuvring around overturned vehicles or stopping to put screaming horses out of their misery, Ashoka saw a new threat rising.

'Ashoka!' Uttam called out to him. 'Do you see?'

He saw. The Mauryavansh cavalry had watched the progress of their chariot regiments and the fate they had suffered on the stony patch. The same stony patch would play hell on the legs of their burdened horses and so would the archers. They had decided on a new manoeuvre.

He watched as lines of horse regiments peeled off from their current position, pouring around the stony patch in a wide arcing crescent, the points of the crescent intended to rejoin across the stony patch. Damn. That was troubling. He had placed his archers in the rocks to give them cover as well as position them perfectly to loose at the stony patch. The trajectory chosen by the enemy cavalry now would take them almost out of bowshot range.

He had two options: Move his archers into the open where they would be vulnerable. Or keep them where they were and order them to fire backwards, towards his own lines, once the enemy rode past them. Neither option was appealing but he had no choice.

'Bowmen, prepare to loose!'

Uttam signalled back that the bowmen were ready.

'Volley!'

He watched as the volley rose and fell—some arrows striking chariots, others falling uselessly short of the cavalry lines. The casualty count was almost nil.

Time to change tactics.

'Forward elephants!'

Uttam glanced back at him, checking that he had given the order he intended. Ashoka nodded sharply. Uttam passed down the order.

They had only a few elephants compared to the enemy. Barely two thousand. But he had put them in a position which he hoped would leverage their numbers to make them as effective as an elephant akshohini ten times that size.

The ground sloped downwards from where he stood, rolling all the way down to the rocks and the open ground to either side. The enemy cavalry was riding around the rocks and stony patch, curving around from either side, then turning inwards again. Their intention was to form a solid unbroken line for a full charge. Their strength was in numbers. If they threw that massive weight of cavalry at his army, tens of thousands of laden horses, even his uphill vantage would not make much difference. Against such numbers and those pounding hooves, his force stood no chance. His only hope was to break the back of their advance before it broke his front.

He smelled the elephants before they came into view.

A long line of dark grey giants trundled up the hill behind him. They were each pulling a cart behind themselves. As they reached the top of the hill, their handlers and infantry platoons rushed to unhitch the carts from the animals, then to unload the carts of their loads and position them on the rise, in front of the elephants.

While this was happening, he watched the enemy chariots and cavalry. The first wave of chariots had slowed and were approaching the rocks. They were still firing arrows into the rocks blindly. That was a smart move. Their nonstop volleys were designed to keep his archers dodging arrows, thereby ensuring they were too busy to be able to fire on their cavalry when it passed by. It was an effective move: His bowmen were all hiding in the rocks. When any of them attempted to come out, the charioteers used him for target practice. The first wave of chariots continued to circle the rocks. Clearly, they had been assigned the task of containing the revolutionary bowmen, and they were doing it well.

His archers had been effectively taken out of the battle, for the time being at least.

In the meantime, the enemy had plenty more chariots to spare. While several hundred chariots and horse teams lay broken or arrow-struck in the stony patch, thousands more were pouring across. These continued around the rocks, converging on Ashoka's side, at the far bottom of the sloping rise that led to his present position, barely half a mile away.

They queued up smartly and efficiently, gathering strength until in another hour, they were several dozen rows deep, and over half a mile wide on an unbroken front. The sight of that massed akshohini of chariots gleaming in the sunlight was intimidating. He could feel the tension among his ranks. If those chariots managed to make it up to where he stood now, they would be like a wave of metal rage washing across the revolutionary forces. He had seen enemy armies incapacitated by Mauryavansh chariots before. It was a brutal sight. Neither infantry nor cavalry could withstand a direct charge by chariots in such large numbers.

The only chance he had was to stave off a direct charge, for as long as possible.

'Elephants, ready!' Uttam called.

Ashoka watched the chariots below. The slope was a gradual one, a genial thirty degrees or less. Just high enough to make the chariots upward progress slow, but not enough to pose a major impediment. And once they picked up speed and reached the top, their speed wouldn't matter because Ashoka's army was behind him, on the other side of the hill, and that slope was steep, almost forty-five degrees. This immense wall of chariots now pushing up towards him would roll downhill to strike his army like a stone wall falling on an infant. Also, so long as the chariots were climbing upwards, arrows were useless, as the well of the chariot protected the charioteers from both angles, below and up. Even if his bowmen were not penned in by the first wave of charioteers, who were still encircling the rocks where they were concealed, they would still be mostly ineffective firing arrows upwards at the chariots at that angle.

The wall of chariots were rising steadily towards him, now about seven hundred yards away, and closing. The tension on the hill around him was thick, everyone watching the approach of those golden wells with trepidation. He breathed in and out slowly, forcing himself to remain calm. *A warrior fights with his shastra, a king fights with his akshohini.* His guru's words rang in his head, reminding him that he was no longer fighting with a sword, but with the men and animals under his command. There were costs and consequences to be paid for every decision he took. And, if he did his job right, rewards too.

'Elephants, loose!' he called. He was pleased to hear that his voice sounded steady, confident. His army deserved that. They were all inexperienced with combat at this level. Most had never experienced the sheer scale and tactics of a battle of this magnitude. *They depend on you to do the right thing, Ashoka. Their lives are in your hands. Don't let them down.*

The long line of elephants on either side of Ashoka grumbled and grunted as they pushed forward. Their infantry platoons had positioned boulders before them. The elephants now used their trunks to manoeuvre and their forelegs to shove the boulders to the lip of the rise—and then push them over.

Slowly, the boulders began to roll down the slope. For a moment, Ashoka's heart caught in his throat. It looked like the slope was too gradual for the boulders to roll down. But then they began to pick up speed, gaining momentum. To his left and right, boulders were leaving the ridge and rolling downhill, for half a mile on each side. It made quite a sight. Two thousand elephants rolling two thousand boulders, ranging from twice the size of a man's head to five or six times as large. The elephants trumpeted their relief at their tasks accomplished, their lowing filling the air.

He saw the charioteers looking uphill.

He imagined what they must see: Two thousand boulders of varying sizes, rolling downhill towards them, gaining speed.

The sound of the boulders rose steadily, growing louder. The elephants continued calling, stamping their feet. The rumbling of the boulders grew and grew, until it sounded like an avalanche Ashoka had heard once in the northern mountains. It was an avalanche, a man-made one. Hundreds of tons of stone rolling downhill for five hundred yards, picking up speed and force all the while.

Some of the smaller boulders were bouncing now, skipping and hopping yards, as if eager to reach their quarry.

The frontline charioteers were yelling now, calling to those behind them. It would do no good. They were packed too closely together, the military precision of their rows and columns lining them up perfectly in the path of the oncoming onslaught.

The larger boulders were bouncing too now, racing downhill at great speed. Ashoka estimated that the boulders were rolling now at thirty or forty miles per hour, a speed which would triple or quadruple the impact of their weight. The charioteers were screaming now, seeing certain death racing toward them. Their horses were screaming too, poor creatures. They were the innocents trapped in the middle between the weapons of men and the men themselves. Ashoka prayed their forgiveness, hating to have to harm those beautiful innocent creatures who had spent their lives in service of their human masters, and would now die in that service. He regretted the things one had to do to make war. But one had to do them all the same? He had never found a satisfactory answer to that question.

He knew what would come next, but forced himself to watch

regardless. He had struck the blow, he ought to be able to endure the sight of his opponent's pain and anguish.

The sound of two thousand boulders striking forty thousand chariots is like nothing else on earth. A giant gnashed his teeth, and blood spurted everywhere.

Ashoka watched as horses were thrown up into the air, flailing and screaming. Chariots shattered like children's toys. Men and women were flung helter-skelter, tumbling like tiny dolls to break their bodies on the chariots behind them. The boulders bounced and leaped over the chariots, striking those five or ten or even twenty chariots behind, bouncing again, and again, leaving swathes of death and destruction in their wake. Thousands of chariots and horses and charioteers were destroyed in that first assault itself. Each boulder wreaked destruction out of all proportion to its size. The boulders themselves were only tools—it was gravity that was the real weapon. Ashoka had known that the genial slope of the rise was perfect for this manoeuvre and he had been right. He was now witnessing the brutal results of that tactical choice.

'Again!' he called, even as his watching army roared and cheered the destruction caused by the first round of boulders.

Another two thousand boulders, another landslide rolling towards the already devastated chariot lines.

Another wave of death and agony below.

'Again!' he called. He had made his infantry spend all of one full day finding and loading boulders onto the carts, as many as the carts could bear and the elephants could pull. All that tonnage was now being sent rolling downhill to greet the chariots of Mauryavansh.

The rear lines of the chariot regiments were retreating now, seeking to distance themselves from the relentless waves of stony death raining down on them. But the smaller boulders were finding their way all the way to the end, obstructing the retreat, creating more chaos. The scene below was chaotic in the extreme: there were so many tangled horses and bodies and chariot wells turned every which way that it was hard to tell the survivors apart from the victims. It was nearly impossible to get an accurate count of the toll but looking at it right now, it was safe to say that the chariots of Mauryavansh would not be attempting any direct charge today or perhaps even for the rest of this battle.

'Elephants, out!' Uttam called. The signal to inform him that they were out of boulders.

Ashoka glanced to the western horizon and was shocked to see the sun already slipping behind the mountains. When had the day passed by?

Time flies when you're in the killing zone.

'Withdraw!' he called.

His army roared their approval. All around him, revolutionaries were smiling, laughing, slapping each other, happy to be alive, to have survived the first day of battle.

There was still work to be done, but the fighting was over for today at least. The sun reached the horizon and he sighed a small private sigh. It was a sigh of relief at having got his people through their first day of battle successfully, but also a sigh for all the lives he had taken today, both human and animal.

18

The second day of battle dawned dull and cloudy. It smelled like rain, and by the time Ashoka had resumed his position at the top of the slope, the first drops were falling. It was cold and wet, the late autumn showers that fell in this part of the subcontinent, and he could smell the wet earth and grass, and fresh animal dung. The rain felt cool and refreshing on his face. He had not had time to bathe or even wash his face for days, and he enjoyed the feeling of the dust being sluiced off his skin. He assumed his position and examined the field of battle.

That the army of Mauryavansh had paid a heavy toll the day before was no longer in doubt. The hillside below was carpeted with the debris of yesterday's assault. Thousands of broken upturned chariots and corpses of horses and humans lay strewn like wheatgrains on a chaffing floor. Uttam had brought him the approximate count earlier that morning, excited: 'More than half destroyed, as many as two-thirds incapacitated.' Those were staggering numbers, unbelievable numbers. *All without losing a single one of our own soldiers!*

He was old enough and seasoned enough to know that such luck could not last.

Mauryavansh had been arrogant the first day, made bold by their vastly superior numbers and military strength. They had underestimated the revolutionary army—and had paid the price. Now, they intended to correct that mistake and balance the odds.

He stared at the scene before him with awe and respect.

It was a complex sight.

Even with two-thirds of their chariots gone, Mauryavansh still had over thirty thousand chariots left, almost twice as many as Ashoka. Those chariots had been deployed in a formation he had never seen before. In single columns of some one hundred chariots long, arrayed front to end. The chariots were lined at the extreme corners of the field now, barely visible from his position—his runners brought the news of their exact locations to him through the morning.

Their cavalry formation was even stranger. They had deployed their horses into curious rectangular formations, each perhaps ten thousand strong, in groups spread out across the field.

Between these were the infantry, waves upon waves of infantry, more than the eye could absorb at a glance. One hundred and fifty thousand soldiers made for a huge force and that force was mostly visible to Ashoka as he looked down now.

In front were the elephants, all twenty thousand of them, outnumbering his own animals ten to one. They had taken the place of the chariots but spread wider now, and in columns ten deep. They had built their own wall, a dense dark grey wall of solid tonnage, a juggernaut by any standard. The elephants would have some difficulty climbing this slope in this rain, but eventually they would make the climb and when they did, they would make an avalanche of hard muscle and bone—a landslide crashing down on Ashoka's forces on their side of the hill.

The way the Mauryavansh army was deployed and arrayed made it clear that this time, Patliputra was not looking to simply attack the revolutionary forces. They were looking to destroy them.

'They have put in every last man, woman, animal and weapon they have,' Uttam said. 'They mean to roll across us and wipe us from the face of the earth.'

'It is a simple but effective choice,' Ashoka admitted. 'Instead of following the usual protocol as they would against an equally matched force, they mean to simply attack us and keep us on the defensive until they crush us with the sheer weight of their numbers.'

Uttam was silent, considering what this meant. 'We cannot withstand such an attack. If they throw all that at us, we will crumple like a thatched roof under an avalanche.'

Ashoka nodded. 'That is why we will not wait for them to attack.'

Uttam blinked, wiping the rain from his face. 'What?'

'We will attack them first. Throwing every last soldier and animal into the fray.'

'Everything?' Uttam looked shocked.

'Everything and everyone, all at once.' Ashoka pointed beyond the Mauryavansh army. 'Our goal is to attack, engage, and then continue.'

'Continue?' Uttam repeated. 'But—'

Ashoka slapped his friend's shoulder, water splattering. 'It is time.'

Uttam stared at him with his mouth open, collecting water. He closed his mouth, hawked and spat, nodding in understanding at last. 'It is time.'

'Remember. Once we go in, there is no turning back. All the way.'

'All the way!' Uttam said, perking up. 'Yes, I understand. Of course. It is time!'

'It is time,' Ashoka agreed. 'We will pay the price, but we will go through, no matter what.'

'Yes,' Uttam said. 'I will pass on the message to Tissa, Tissyanka and the others.'

'Do that. We move within the hour.'

Uttam snapped off a salute and rode away, hooves splashing water and mud.

Less than an hour later, Ashoka found himself at the head of the mounted regiment of the Chandashokas. The rain was still pelting down without respite. The ground had turned to muck and there were streams of water rolling downhill towards the Mauryavansh lines. The rocks where his bowmen had been stationed the previous day were pooling with water now. The bowmen had been extracted and were with their regiment again, ready like the rest of the revolutionary army for the day ahead.

'Chandashokas,' Ashoka cried, 'Ride with me!'

They roared as one being, a beast with twenty thousand heads. The roar was echoed and repeated by the rest of the revolutionary army, almost eighty thousand voices roaring above the rain. Their horses and elephants neighed and trumpeted as well, echoing their riders. The sound rose, seeming to still the rain in the sky for a moment.

Ashoka raised his sword high and rode his horse over the rise, starting the long descent.

His army came with him.

His horse whinnied, complaining about the slushy slope. The ground underfoot was soggy but threaded with rock and stones which helped keep it solid. In a hundred yards, she found her footing and proceeded more confidently. He kept her at a steady canter, banking her energy. The wall of elephants was less than five hundred yards now and approaching fast. He didn't bother aiming himself and his regiment at any particular spot, it was all the same. The enemy had been careful not to leave any gaps in the wall, keeping the line tight and the formation unbroken. He knew they were watching his forces charging and were probably thinking he was insane. How could he possibly hope to charge and defeat an enemy thrice his numbers, and double his strength—if you counted the advantage in elephants and chariots and horses—on an open field? It was unthinkable. He was expecting them to think that he was insane, and to be pleased at his taking the initiative. *Let him come and dash his brains out, they were probably saying. We shall welcome him with open swords.*

But he knew something they did not.

Three hundred yards now.

Two hundred.

One hundred.

The final fifty yards.

The wall of elephants loomed like a cliff of grey rock. The rain sluicing down the lowered heads and trunks of the animals made the wall of elephants resemble a waterfall. A wide grey waterfall.

He reached the waterfall and struck out with his sword.

The elephant trumpeted and raised his trunk, eyes rolling with fear and fury as it eyed the human daring to charge at it. It raised its foot to stamp him. Ashoka wrenched the head of his horse, pulling her aside at the last instant. The heel of the elephant crashed down just behind his mare's haunches, the impact reverberating in his spine. He felt and heard the cries and thuds of thousands of other elephants attacking his revolutionaries, heard the whinnying of their horses, the screams of the soldiers and horses who were not as fortunate as he, the terrible sound of living bone and flesh being trampled.

The mahout of the elephant he had managed to dodge threw a spear at him—it grazed his back, tearing his skin and leaving a streak of fire. He struck upwards with his sword, missed, and continued riding. Behind the elephant was another elephant—and yet another, stretching around him in all directions like the trees of Girvan's densest sections. He knew that if he was caught in this forest of grey giants, he would end up a pulpy mass of flesh and gristle. He had to get through and out as quickly as possible.

He dodged spears, arrows and elephant legs and trunks, sustaining some more cuts and scratches but somehow escaping any major injuries. He was forced to strike out with his sword at the belly of an elephant that turned and almost knocked him and his horse down. The sword-tip tore open the poor animal's belly and its stinking entrails burst down on him like a hot flood. The elephant squealed in agony and went berserk. Other elephants were going crazy as well, rampaging to get away from the wounds inflicted by his Chandashokas. He forced himself to ignore the suffering of the elephants and do what had to be done. If this was animal abuse—and it was—then it was only part of the larger crime of human abuse they were inflicting on one another. The field was madness and elephants and rain. Ashoka was hard pressed just to stay on his horse and survive. He saw an elephant flailing, throwing her mahout, smashing the back of a Chandashoka and her horse, then crashing into another elephant, hitting it sideways hard enough to knock it down. The elephant fell onto two other Chandashokas, killing both instantly, and its kicking legs maimed several Mauryavansh infantry as well.

People and animals were dying everywhere.

He saw a squad of infantry racing at him, swords raised. From his left, several mahouts were throwing spears. He felt his unfortunate mare take one spear in her haunch, then another in her neck and the poor beast collapsed, grunting and gasping for breath around the spear choking her throat. He could not even spare the time to put her out of her misery: the soldiers were upon him.

He rolled free of his horse and slashed off the legs of two or perhaps three soldiers, their swords passing just above his head. As they fell, he leaped up, slashing two other oncoming soldiers, rolling, tumbling, stabbing an elephant in the foot and forcing it to rear up in terror, falling back and knocking another elephant over as well. He ran then, through the muck and elephant shit and human body parts, stopping only to cut, kill, slash, defend.

At some point, he found a riderless horse and leaped on its back. It was panicked but unharmed and after a moment of struggle, he succeeded in bringing its head around and forcing it to ride. He galloped through the forest of grey giants, and was surprised when he broke free only moments later, finding himself faced with the unexpected sight of a formation of chariots.

The charioteers were even more surprised than he, but they were ready. Their short bows were out and they loosed as one man.

Ashoka ducked, letting his poor horse take the brunt of the volley. He felt the beast shudder as several missiles struck, one passing through his own thigh. He pulled out the arrow, stood up on the back of the horse and flung himself at the nearest chariot.

The charioteer was stringing another arrow to the bow when he saw Ashoka leaping at him.

Ashoka pinned the man to the floor of his chariot with his sword, the blade passing through the man's chest and striking the metal of the chariot floor with a clanging impact.

Ashoka looked around and saw the man's bow. He picked it up and fixed the same arrow to it. Rising up, he fired the arrow at the nearest chariot. The arrow took the surprised charioteer in his throat. The woman cried out and fell, her own arrow going wild, clanging off the side of another chariot.

Ashoka saw other Chandashokas emerging from the wall of elephants, breaking out, some wounded, others whole. They were greeted by volleys of arrows from the chariots, and lines of cavalry ready to welcome them to the afterworld. Fighting was breaking out all across the field as his forces pushed their way past the elephant lines and into the main body of the enemy army.

For the next several hours, everything was a blur of rain, blood, steel and screaming. Ashoka drove the Mauryavansh chariot straight at a formation of infantry that was sticking a dozen or more spears into a single revolutionary elephant that had somehow managed to make it this far—at least, he assumed it was one of his elephants because a revolutionary soldier was mounted on its back. The chariot struck the infantry with a bone-smashing force, sending weapons and helmets and the severed head of one soldier flying. He felt the horses and the wheels shake violently as they passed over the bodies of the fallen Mauryavansh soldiers. Above him, the elephant was making a sound unlike anything he had ever heard before, its dark hide pierced and bleeding from more than a dozen spears, its bowels voiding with a foul stench.

He rode through the next few hours, crashed the chariot, went on foot for a while, was almost killed by a regiment of enemy cavalry, saved in the nick of time by his own cavalry riding in, found himself another horse, lost that one as well, then found yet another. He lost count of how many enemies and animals he killed or was responsible for killing—not that he was keeping count to begin with. The rain stopped and the sun came out and there was a strange hallucinogenic interval when a rainbow rose in the sky, and the light was beautiful, grand, inspiring, but he was covered in blood and shit and guts and vomiting up the bile in his empty stomach. He drove a dagger into a woman's belly and saw the look in her eyes as she died, and later he fell from a horse and saw another horse lying on the ground, dying in great pain, and the look in the horse's eyes was exactly like the look in the enemy soldier's eyes, and he was struck by the insight that all living creatures were exactly alike at birth and death, the first shock of arrival and the last disappointment of departure: or was it relief at being freed at long last?

He had no accurate sense of how the battle was proceeding. From a single man's point of view, it was only death everywhere. It was impossible to make any assessment of success or failure, victory or defeat, because everything was reduced to individual survival, of killing that enemy soldier before he killed you, of getting out of that elephant's or chariot's or horse's way, of avoiding that spear or dodging that arrow, or countering that sword. The day melted into blood and madness. He killed and was wounded and killed again and kept killing. He survived, he lived, he did what he had to do to endure, and there were bodies and pain and blood everywhere he looked. The colour of the day was red. The rainbow in the sky failed to inspired. The colour of the sky was blue but false: it should have been red. How could it not be red? The sky was a lie created by gods to delude mortals. Reality was red.

He didn't know when it happened, but at some point in the

late afternoon, when the sun had dipped low in the western sky and the rainbow had faded, he heard it. The unmistakable sound of brass trumpets rising above the cacophony and screams of battle.

He saw a flurry of movement far at the edges of the field, to the west. He turned and saw another flurry to the east. And then all around. As if some new wave was sweeping into the field of battle from both flanks.

He saw enemy riders racing across the field, yelling to their regiments and lieutenants. He saw the reactions from their own soldiers, turning to stare in shocked disbelief then breaking off their encounters with his revolutionaries and turning and riding, racing, running *away*. Heading one way, then turning back and going another way, confused, scared, angry.

One of his own soldiers came riding up, calling out his name. He was surprised she could even recognize him with all the blood and offal on his person. He himself felt unrecognizable, as if he was no longer himself, not Ashoka.

'Uttam said to tell you when they came. They have come. They are here.'

Ashoka wiped something from his face and eyes. It felt like blood but could have been something else entirely. He could no longer identify anything by smell alone. His nostrils were clogged with his own blood after a blow from the sword hilt of a Mauryavansh rider and his nose felt broken and swollen.

'Tell Uttam to meet me on the west flank.'

The soldier paused, looking at him oddly.

Ashoka looked at her, not recognizing her at all, but knowing that she must be one of Uttam's closest lieutenants if he had trusted her with the information she had just brought him. Uttam himself had been told of this part only this morning by Ashoka. Was that just this morning? It felt like a hundred years ago.

'Uttam is dead,' she said. 'He died in the first clash, trampled by an elephant. He passed on his last orders as he was dying.'

Ashoka looked at the sky. He didn't say anything further to the Chandashoka. He asked no more questions about Uttam. There was nothing more to be said. There were no more questions. Death was the final answer.

He got onto the horse he was currently riding, either the sixth or the seventh, he was no longer sure of numbers. He saw bizarre sights and heard terrible sounds as he rode through the battlefield. The fighting had all but stopped, reduced to a few half-hearted skirmishes and some methodical slaughter of the wounded and maimed.

He ignored the cries and howls for help, unable to tell whether they were his own soldiers calling out or the enemy. They probably didn't know either. All they knew now was pain and fear and all they wanted were their mothers. All men and women cried out for their mothers when they lay dying on the battlefield. It was a universal truth as old as life itself.

He reached the western flank as the sun was approaching the horizon.

Burnished armour reflected the setting sun, flinging gold spears into Ashoka's face. He shielded his eyes with a raised hand and looked into the face of the most powerful Greek emperor since Alexander.

'Congratulations, Lion of Maurya,' Seleucus Nicator said, 'The field is yours.'

19

Jezza Khorasan felt no anger. She ought to have, she knew. The enemy had been outnumbered, outmatched, outmanoeuvred. And yet, they had overcome. The Greek forces joining in at the crucial moment had helped their cause tremendously, that was true, but even before that, their tactics and strategy had been superb. It had been the most brilliant display of military acumen she had witnessed in her career. It was obvious that it was all the work of one man. No other commander she had ever faced had displayed such ingenuity, inventiveness, such resourceful use of the landscape itself, turning the theatre of war into a vast charnel house instead of the victory field she had envisaged.

She admired him.

As she rode her horse back towards Patliputra, the dregs of the surviving legions following in her wake, she could not help but appreciate the vast achievement of that one young upstart.

It was hard to believe that this was the same young man whom she had broken on a mountain in far Takshashila. Whom she had taken to the edge of mortality, made witness the precipice of eternity, and left as food for vultures and wolves. That he had survived was impressive; that he had recovered his strength and vigour was the work of youth and good caring; but to see him today, on that field, leading a force of decidedly mixed groups, turning them into an army capable of standing up to, battling, and then defeating the great host of Magadha? That was incredible. It was history in the making. She felt honoured to have been present on that field today, to see such genius at work.

No, she was not angry. She was relieved in a way.

Ashoka had won the battle. He would be coming to Patliputra soon. She could have stayed and tried to stop him. She could have laid ambushes and blocked the imperial highway, done all kinds of things to try to delay and slow him. But she had decided not to do any of that.

He had won. And he had had the support of the Greeks to boot. That meant that the power and might of Seleucus Nicator was behind him.

That changed things.

Not just, militarily, but politically.

And politics was not Jezza's area of expertise.

She needed to speak with Noor at once.

The gates of the city were shut, she saw. A precaution she herself had insisted on. More than one invading force had tried to use the time-tested ruse of meeting the defenders on the field, while simultaneously sending a smaller incursion force into the capital to take it by stealth. Nothing like that would happen on Jezza's watch.

The gates remained shut even though the gatewatch could clearly see her colours flying by now, even see Jezza herself. That too was good. It was as she had ordered.

Still, she waited impatiently as her last surviving lieutenant exchanged the secret passcodes that would authorize the opening of the gates.

The vaulting doors had barely parted when she pushed her way through, spurring her exhausted mount into one final spurt of speed.

She dismounted and went into the palace, ignoring the salutes en route. From the faces of the guards and servants, she knew that word of the Imperial Army's defeat had reached the capital already. That was to be expected.

'Noor,' she said, striding into the Empress's private chambers. She stopped short.

The woman who stood ready to meet her was not Noor.

'Orzala,' Jezza said. 'Where is your mistress? I need to speak with her urgently.'

Orzala stared coldly. 'She is otherwise occupied, War Marshall. She gave instructions not to be disturbed.'

Jezza heard herself scoff. 'Is that so? Well, too bad. She's an Empress. An Empress doesn't get to have private time when she feels like it. This is an imperial emergency.'

She started forward towards the inner chambers. Orzala blocked her way, one hand holding something concealed inside the folds of her robes.

'You may not pass unless the Empress wills it,' said the woman who had shared Jezza's bed more than once.

Jezza didn't hesitate. She drew her sword and had the edge of the curved blade to Orzala's throat before the woman could even draw the dagger from her robes. Tired as she was, she was still ten times the warrior this chit of a young woman would ever be. That was the difference between learning from battlefield experience, and learning by stealthy assassinations and covert murders. On the field of battle, one did not think and plot and scheme; one simply killed and moved on to the next kill.

'Move,' said Jezza.

Orzala looked into her eyes and saw her death.

She moved aside.

Jezza hacked aside the diaphanous curtain that obstructed her way as she strode into the bedchamber.

'Noor,' she said.

Her daughter glared at her from the enormous, luxuriously appointed bed. 'You failed! How could you let me down this way? I should have you whipped.'

Jezza laughed at the absurdity. 'No, Noor, I should have whipped you myself, years ago. That would have kept you from getting so out-of-hand, so full of your own megalomania that you lost sight of everyday realities. War is unpredictable. While we can do everything possible to ensure victory, the unexpected is always at hand, ready to move in at any time. Today, a very brilliant young man routed the great imperial army of Magadha. True, he had some help, perhaps even a lot of help. But ultimately, it was his superior military strategy and leadership that won the day. He won. We lost. It happens. Get over it.'

Noor screamed. It was an ear-splitting scream, the kind a spoilt little girl would emit when her desire was not fulfilled at once. She picked up whatever she had at hand and began to throw it across the large chamber in Jezza's general direction. Since this happened to be no more than a few throw pillows and cushions, the War Marshall ignored them. She had expected no less than this petulant childish response.

Jezza used her sword to bat aside a cushion or two as she approached the bed. Noor's screams heightened in pitch and volume, and as she neared, the Empress threw herself at her mother, long painted nails reaching for her face, her eyes.

Jezza struck Noor on the side of her head with the flat of her sword.

The scream broke off. Noor tumbled back on the bed, stunned, eyes shut.

Jezza put the point of the sword to her daughter's throat.

Noor's eyes opened and widened as she saw the blade looming in her vision. Yet her first reaction was not fear but rage.

'YOU DARE!' she cried shrilly.

Jezza poked the point of the sword into the soft hollow at the base of Noor's jaw.

Noor held deathly still. Her eyes shot daggers into her mother.

Jezza raised her head to glance behind her. She scanned her surroundings in her peripheral vision. She needed to be sure nobody, especially not Orzala, was coming up behind her to stab a blade in her back.

Satisfied there was nobody there, she said quietly, 'Ashoka is coming to Patliputra. Get a hold of yourself. You can turn this around even now. He cannot simply execute you without proof, and knowing how shrewdly you plan all your schemes, I am sure he will find none. You are still his father's wife, his stepmother, and the Empress. He is obligated to treat you with respect due your position.'

Noor spat the words: 'What makes you think he will!'

'Because he is honourable.' *Unlike you,* she wanted to add, but didn't. 'He will uphold the laws and traditions and formally approach the sabha to clear his name of past accusations. I suspect he will succeed.'

Noor glared a question at her which Jezza answered.

'He has sympathizers in the sabha. More than you might expect, more than you might ever know. Many chiefs play both sides, to hedge their bets. Now that Ashoka has triumphed on the field, that gives him a great advantage. This is still a male-dominated land. Military prowess count for more than anything else. A prince who proves himself so decisively upon the field cannot simply be ignored or shunted aside. Like it or not, he is a major player now. He has won the right through victory. You must deal with him on equal ground, sticking to the rules and laws. I know this will be hard for you, but you must do it anyway. Anything else would be political suicide. You know this better than I do, but I am reminding you of these basic facts because I know you are angry, and when you are angry, you lose your reason. Accept Ashoka, acknowledge him, welcome him back. Play the role of the proud Queen Mother, make a show of convincing Bindusara to forgive Ashoka and put bygones behind them. Act the part of the peacemaker, make the world believe that you are the one who reunited father and son, repairing the family's differences. Play this right, and you can still come out of it smelling of roses.'

Noor's eyes were still filled with murderous rage, frustration and disappointment. But there was a scheming look in them as well, a sly, shrewd glint that told Jezza that she had calculated the odds and accepted good reason. What Jezza said made sense. It was the only play left now. Politics involved more unlikely compromises than this one; royal families schemed and plotted against each other, but ultimately found compromise and stayed together. The politics of power and public image demanded it. Noor would fall into line. She was too smart to throw away all that they had worked for.

The Empress moved forward, as if to sit up. The sword blocked her way.

Jezza hesitated, then removed the blade. She sheathed it in the battered, stained scabbard. 'I'm glad to see you're listening to reason for once. Plans change. We have to change with the tide.'

Noor sat up slowly, massaging her throat. There was not so much as a pinprick of blood. Jezza had applied just enough force for the point of the sword to be felt without actually breaking the skin.

'And you think if we do all this, he will simply forgive and forget? All that we did to him, his mother, his guru, his friends and allies within the palace and the city?'

Jezza shrugged, walking over to a side table where a jug of water stood. She had a mighty thirst after fighting all day. She couldn't recall the last time she had taken so much as a sip. She poured herself a goblet full of water and raised it to her parched lips.

'He will do what is politically expedient,' she said. 'After all, he is—'

A piercing pain tore through her spine and chest, ripping her lungs and forcing the air from them. Instead of water in her throat, she tasted hot blood. Her own blood. It poured out of her mouth and onto the polished floor, spattering into the goblet. She let the water fall and tried to turn, reaching for her sword. The agony in her back and chest was beyond description. She had been wounded before, more than once, but had never felt such pain. She had never suffered such a wound before.

As she turned, Noor stabbed her again, this time in the throat.

Once, twice, and a third time. Blood spurted from Jezza, filling her vision, arcing out into the air.

She lost her balance and fell, trying to reach for the table and striking the water jug instead. It fell with her, shattering to the floor, and sending shards of painted clay and water everywhere. Her jaw struck the floor with a solid thud, breaking on impact. The pain was nothing compared to the fire roaring in her chest and throat.

'You traitor!' Noor Khorasan cried. 'You dare tell me what to do? I am Noor Khorasan, Empress of the World! Nobody will take what is mine from me.'

Jezza sputtered and coughed, trying to see through her diminished crimson-stained vision. She wanted to tell her daughter that she was being a fool, that there was a time to be victorious and a time to compromise. She wanted to tell her that Ashoka was not an enemy to take lightly. He had proven that today. He was going to be Emperor, it was only a matter of time now. Their best chance was to align with him, to make him believe they would cooperate and not plot against him anymore. That they regretted their past trespasses against him. If they did not, then he would kill them. Even Jezza could not protect Noor if Ashoka came after her.

Then she remembered that she had been mortally wounded. That she could not protect Noor at all. She could not protect herself either. She was finished.

And if she was finished, Noor didn't stand a chance.

Veteran of a thousand battles, she forced herself to rise from the cold marble floor of her daughter's bedchamber. She had been as good as murdered by her own but that did not mean she was done yet. It would take more than just one mortal wound to bring down Jezza Khorasan, she thought fiercely as she made her way towards the main hallway.

20

Patliputra was burning.

He could see the smoke from miles away as he rode down the Uttarapada. Great gouts of smoke billowed up into the sky, rising up to form a small cloud. The darker monsoon clouds looming overhead dwarfed the smoke but on the rooftops of the Upper City, the tongues of flame licking hungrily were unmistakable. He guessed that most of the fires would be in the Upper City. The city had been rioting the past several days, since word reached them of the revolution clashing with the Imperial Army. The ages old conflicts of class, caste and aristocracy versus citizens provided easy excuses for violence. But the real conflict was between the Upper City and Lower City. *Good,* he thought, watching the burning rooftops grow closer as he rode, *let it burn down to the ground. From the ashes, we will build a new Patliputra, one Patliputra. No Upper or Lower, just one city, one people.*

Before he could do that, he first had to take the city.

The battle had been won, but the throne was still in the hands of his enemies.

As they reached the city gates, the Chandashokas roared behind him. There were less than seven thousand left alive and able enough to follow him, a sad reflection of the unequal odds they had faced on the battlefield yesterday. Their overall losses had numbered almost a third of the total force: twenty-seven thousand dead, sixteen thousand wounded or disabled, and thirty-seven thousand with minor injuries but able to ride, walk and fight, including himself. They were all coming with him to Patliputra but he had elected to ride ahead with only the Chandashokas to secure the city. *Secure it, or die trying. No point squandering the lives of the rest.* If they faced the full might of Patliputra's defensive forces, seven thousand would stand no chance at all, or even thirty-seven thousand for that matter. But he was counting on help from the inside to enable this final stage of the takeover. Just as he had depended on the Greeks to win the day on the battlefield in Kalinga.

They met no resistance at the gates. The gates were open in fact. He rode right through, noting the dozens of corpses, all Khorasani, strewn around the gates, the entrance, the bridge... all defences were down, all posts unmanned. The stench and noise in the city itself hit him like an open hand across his face. He coughed and retched. Even after the stenches of the battlefield, this was overwhelming. The smells of a hundred thousand people and as many animals crowded together in a large walled space, now filled with death, butchery and fires, produced a head-spinning odour. There were food smells, offal, animal smells.... He lost track of them all, his nostrils still unclear after the dried blood from the blow yesterday. Even his skin felt unclean, despite washing himself for an hour and wearing fresh clothes.

The scenes that he passed in the streets, in the open houses, many of them burning or half-destroyed in the fighting, were sickening, gut-wrenching. He had seen worse in the field, and yet somehow these hurt deeper. Because those had been soldiers and war animals, conscripted to battle. While these were ordinary people, living their lives—fathers, mothers, sons, daughters, infants, wet nurses, traders, shopkeepers, cooks, scribes. He forced himself to keep his focus on what lay ahead, not around. The real challenge was not this but what lay ahead. In the palace.

There was fighting still in progress in the Upper City. Khorasani forces versus militia, citizens who had allied with his cause and taken up arms of their own accord. He had sent word to them to stand down and let him and his revolutionaries do the fighting. Clearly, they hadn't heeded him. He didn't blame them. These people had suffered enough under the cruel regime of the Khorasani queen to miss this opportunity. He saw many un-uniformed bodies lying about but for every three such corpses, there was at least one Khorasani corpse, either a bearded Khorasani man or a long-haired Khorasani woman. The militia had paid dearly but they had bought their dignity back with blood. He admired that.

They met their first real resistance in the palace complex. Jezza Khorasan herself stood at the head of the steps that led up to the main hallway, surrounded by what seemed like an army of Khorasanis. More likely, it was twelve or fifteen thousand strong: his spies had been unable to pin it down closer because many Khorasani servants, maids and wet nurses were also fighters, ready to drop their serving spoons and pick up their daggers at a moment's notice. From the bloodstain still spreading freely, he could see she had been grievously wounded; yet she still stood upright and met his gaze with the strength of a fighting fit warrior. He could hardly help but admire her resilience.

'Lion of Maurya,' she said, her tone mocking and scornful. 'We have been awaiting you. Welcome home to Patliputra.'

He didn't waste time bantering with her. Instead, he drew a throwing spear from the clutch on his saddle and threw one straight at Jezza. She was forced to duck down low, almost losing her footing, and the spear struck one of her close lieutenants standing right behind her. As the woman fell, clutching the pole sticking out of her chest, the War Marshall rose, her voice shrill and angry now. 'Kill them!' she shrieked. 'Kill them all! Mauryavansh scum!'

The fighting that followed was fierce and brutal. He had expected nothing less.

It lasted all morning and part of the afternoon, and when it was over, he had lost another three thousand Chandashokas.

But the Khorasanis had lost twice that number. And by that time the rest of his forces had arrived, marching at double speed to reach him in time. Now he had thirty-four thousand against the surviving seven or eight thousand Khorasani. The tables had turned.

'Surrender!' he called out to Jezza Khorasan. She was already badly wounded, a sword cut on her side that he had inflicted bleeding profusely, but she snarled and spat in his direction. '— you!' she shouted. He didn't understand enough Khorasani but phrases like that rarely needed translation.

'Kill them,' he told his revolutionaries. 'Kill them all.'

By sundown, the palace was taken, the Khorasanis all dead. To be certain that there would be no daggers struck from behind when least expected, he had given the order to 'show mercy'. This bitter euphemism meant the exact opposite of what it suggested. The only way to show mercy to an unrepentant enemy was to kill them. He himself cut the throats of the last spitting and cursing Khorasanis on the marbled floor of the queens' palace.

Then he rose and went in search of his mother.

'Ashoka.'

Noor Khorasan was standing in his way, wearing a diaphanous robe with nothing underneath. She stood imperiously, smiling at him with half-closed eyes. 'I have been expecting you.'

He looked down at her. 'Do you expect to seduce me?'

She laughed. 'No longer a boy then. Good. I like that. I don't have to pretend passion the way I did with your father. You look like a man who knows what he wants and takes it.'

'I just killed every last one of your countrypeople and kin.'

She shrugged. 'I am Empress of Magadha. I have infinite armies and resources at my disposal. Khorasan is only one of five hundred kingdoms that serve me.'

He studied her. She had the light of madness in her eyes.

There was blood on her robes and on her forearms. This was not the Noor Khorasan he had expected. This was a mad woman who had fallen prey to the insanity of power.

She arched a shoulder. 'I have your mother in my custody. If you want her safe and sound, you would do well to make peace with me.'

He clutched his sword tighter. 'I want nothing to do with you that doesn't involve a sharp blade.'

'If you want to play it that way, I can arrange that too. Khorasani women will do rash things in the heat of passion. I can even provide for your...more savage tastes, if you favour such things.'

'Stop playing games with me. Where is my mother?'

She smiled coyly and clapped her hands once.

A curtain parted and an old woman emerged. A young Khorasani woman held a knife to the old woman's throat. Ashoka realized with a shock that the old woman was his mother.

'Maa,' he whispered, 'what have they done to you?'

She looked at him through watery eyes that could barely focus. She could barely stand of her own accord and he could see that every movement caused her pain. The Khorasani woman behind her gripped her shoulder roughly, twisting her around to keep the blade at her throat. A thin trickle of blood dripped from the razor-sharp edge.

'Ashoka,' she said in a voice he barely recognized. 'Don't... trust...'

The Khorasani woman struck her with the side of her fist on the temple. Shubhadrangi staggered but the woman caught her with the knife hand and forced her to stay upright.

Ashoka gritted his teeth. 'Release her.'

Noor Khorasan smiled, her eyes cold. 'We can bargain.'

Ashoka looked at her. 'Never.'

He drew out the dagger and threw it in a single fluid motion. The Khorasani woman holding Shubhadrangi upright was not expecting such a move, but even if she had, she could do nothing to counter it—except use her hostage as a block. But Ashoka had anticipated that. He had aimed not at the woman but at something behind her. The woman twisted Shubhadrangi around, using her body to protect herself from the flung dagger. She grunted in surprise as the dagger passed above and behind her, missing both her and her hostage by several inches. It struck the vase above her as it was intended and the vase shattered into smithereens. As the pieces fell on the Khorasani's head, she instinctively put up the only free hand she had, the one with the knife, to guard herself from the falling fragments. In that instant, her hostage was free of the blade at her throat, and Ashoka had his moment.

He threw his second dagger, this time aiming it at the Khorasani's face. The point struck the woman in the eye and the dagger embedded itself deep in her skull. She fell back, releasing Shubhadrangi and shuddered, beating out a death tattoo on the floor. Ashoka's mother exhaled and collapsed on the floor next to her, exhausted but unharmed.

Noor Khorasan's eyes blazed. 'Orzala,' she said, regretfully. Then shrugged. 'There are more where she came from. There are always more.'

Ashoka was on her throat before she could finish the sentence. 'Not for you,' he said, and cut her throat, almost decapitating her.

She fell back on her couch with a shocked expression, clutching at her throat. She fell back in a pool of her own spreading blood. She stared up at him, trying to say something. The words never came out. Only blood flowed. Noor Khorasan had given her last command. He watched the light go out of her eyes, then kicked her body aside.

Ashoka dropped his sword and picked up his mother in both

arms. He was shocked at how light she was, how like a broken bird she felt, frail and fragile. He carried her to another apartment, found a clean bed and set her down. His Chandashokas crowded around the doorway, concerned.

'Watch her,' he said. 'Don't leave her side, no matter what. If anything happens to her...'

'It won't,' they assured him.

He went in search of his father.

There was a crowd outside the Emperor's chambers. He slowed, remembering his sword. But when they saw him, they looked relieved not hostile. He recognized several of them, they were his father's Council of Ministers, the sixteen highest ranking chiefs of sabha. Together, they represented the most powerful of the five hundred kingdoms. Only one other group was as powerful. The brahmin caucus.

He saw the white-clad brahmins standing apart from the chiefs. Amongst them was one face older and even more lined than the other old, lined faces.

'Acharya!' Ashoka said, genuflecting to greet his guru.

'Ayushmaanbhava,' Kautilya said. He smiled at Ashoka and wiped a smear of blood off his cheek. 'You have done your Karma. Your forces have taken back the city. Now it is time to take back the Mauryavansh Empire.'

Ashoka inclined his head.

Kautilya motioned him forward and led the way into the Emperor's chambers. The sabha chiefs followed, as did the brahmins. It was a considerable crowd that filed into the large bedchamber. Ashoka smelled the distinctive odour of sickness as soon as he entered.

His father lay on his bed, ghastly pale and sweating profusely.

Ashoka looked at Kautilya.

The Acharya sighed. 'Your father is in his last moments. You arrived just in time to ask his blessings. Go, Ashoka. Go, pay your last respects.'

Ashoka went forward slowly. His father's face had become even more gaunt, stretched, skeletal. The mark of death was clearly visible on his features. But at the sight of Ashoka, his features twisted. He stared intensely at his second eldest son.

'Father,' Ashoka said, 'I come to seek your blessing.'

Bindusara turned his head away, staring at the wall.

Kautilya shuffled forward. 'Bindusara. Your time is at an end. Ashoka has the support of the sabha and of the gurus. Grant him your blessings that he may rule as the next Emperor of Mauryavansh. He will take the Empire of your father forward into great realms.'

Bindusara turned his face back, ignoring Ashoka, and stared at Kautilya. 'Send for my son, Sushim.'

Kautilya was silent.

Ashoka looked around. Nobody else said a word or moved an inch, though he knew everyone had heard the Emperor.

Kautilya came a little closer. 'Bindusara, give Ashoka your blessing.'

Bindusara looked at him again, his eyes boring into Kautilya. 'Sushim. I want Sushim.'

Again, nobody moved or spoke.

Kautilya acted as if Bindusara had said nothing. 'Ashoka is your son. Give him your blessing to rule. Pass on the sceptre as your father passed it to you in my presence.'

Bindusara continued to stare at him. Ashoka could see his father's skull clearly delineated beneath his skin, the fever sweat limning his features with a sheen that reflected the yellow light of the oil lamps. 'My son Sushim...' Bindusara said, but this time his voice was feeble and fading.

Kautilya took Ashoka's hand and pressed it into Bindusara's

hand. Ashoka was surprised at how cold his father's hand was, he had expected it to be burning.

Bindusara pulled his hand away with an effort, and turned his face away. He stared at the light of the oil lamp. He said nothing else.

They waited.

After several moments, Kautilya leaned forward. He turned and beckoned to his fellow brahmins. Several of them hurried forward, and at Kautilya's indication, checked Bindusara's vital signs. They looked up and shook their heads.

Kautilya sighed and turned away, still gripping Ashoka's hands. Ashoka was surprised at the strength in his guru's bony wrist. How old was he? Ninety-five? Ninety-six? Where did his strength come from?

Kautilya raised Ashoka's hand high, displaying him to the assembled sabha chiefs.

'The Emperor is dead. All hail the new Emperor of Mauryavansh. Ashoka. Lion of Maurya.'

The chiefs kneeled on the marble floor and bowed their heads.

And so it begins.